HEGEL'S LOGIC

Northwestern University
Studies in Phenomenology
and
Existential Philosophy

HEGEL'S LOGIC

Between Dialectic and History

Clark Butler

Northwestern University Press
Evanston, Illinois

Northwestern University Press
www.nupress.northwestern.edu

Copyright © 1996 by Northwestern University Press
All rights reserved
Printed in the United States of America

10 9 8 7 6 5 4 3 2 1

ISBN 978-0-8101-2806-4

The Library of Congress has cataloged the original, hardcover edition as follows:

Butler, Clark, 1944–
    Hegel's logic : between dialectic and history / Clark Butler.
        p.   cm. — (Northwestern University studies in phenomenology
    and existential philosophy)
    Contents: Includes bibliographical references and index.
    ISBN 0-8101-1426-7 (cloth: alk. paper)
    1. Hegel, Georg Wilhelm Friedrich, 1770–1831. Wissenschaft der
Logik. 2. Logic.   I. Title.   II. Series: Northwestern University
studies in phenomenology & existential philosophy.
B2942.Z7B88 1998
160—dc20   96-35414
                                                                 CIP

♾ The paper used in this publication meets the minimum requirements of the
American National Standard for Information Sciences—Permanence of Paper for
Printed Library Materials, ANSI Z39.48-1992.

Universal History exhibits the gradation in the development of that principle whose substantial purport is the consciousness of Freedom. The analysis of the successive grades, in their abstract form, belongs to Logic; in their concrete aspect to the Philosophy of Spirit. Here it is sufficient to state that the first step in the process presents that immersion of Spirit in Nature which has already been referred to; the second shows it as advancing to the consciousness of freedom. But this initial separation from Nature is imperfect and partial, since it is derived immediately from the merely natural state, is consequently related to it, and is still encumbered with it as an essentially connected element.

—*G. W. F. Hegel*, Lectures on the Philosophy of History, *trans. J. Sibree, 56*

A study of Hegel's Logic—and there have been many such—which regards it as the "thought of God," and hence as an "end in itself" far above any "finite," merely human purposes, is not merely worthless, it is actively pernicious.

—*H. S. Harris*, Hegel's Development: Night Thoughts, *342–43*

Contents

Acknowledgments

This book began as class notes for a yearlong course I taught on Hegel's logic in 1987–88 at the University of Strasbourg. I am most indebted to the special receptiveness to Hegel shown by students in the Rhine Valley. The book has been completed in its present form thanks to a 1994–95 sabbatical from Purdue University. None of the chapters, apart from the brief final chapter, has been previously published. This final chapter was presented as a paper in the session sponsored by the Hegel Society of America at the 1993 World Congress of Philosophy in Moscow. It is published here in slightly expanded form from the version that appeared in the Society's journal, *Owl of Minerva* 26, no. 1, 29–34. Among the many persons who might well be singled out for appreciation, Kenneth Long, my former student and current Purdue University colleague at the Indiana-Purdue Fort Wayne Campus, stands out as a valued discussion partner of well over two decades. Nor can my wife, Rose-Aimée, who recently gave me our living room for my research, yet escape my appreciation.

Introduction

1. Aims of This Book

The present volume is a rewriting of Hegel's *Logic* in which I set four tasks. *First*, I intend to interpret the *Science of Logic* as the immanent, self-moving rational reconstruction of an actual science of logic, which is at once, contrary to many contemporary interpreters, essentially a theology or theo-logic. Unlike John Burbidge, for example, I do not "ignore Hegel's suggestion that the logic is a metaphysics."[1] (Readers less interested in rational theology may still be able to view my interpretation of the science of logic as a topography and development of purely conceptual determinations in actual use.) I also intend to show that Hegel's reputedly most difficult work can be made intelligible without mysterious initiation to some nonanalytic mode of thought.

This book seeks to clarify the overall project of the *Logic* as well as its different sections. Hegel views the concept of the *Logic* and its project as presupposed by the *Logic.* Thus he does not claim presuppositionlessness in every sense. The work is presuppositionless in that no one definition of the absolute is presupposed as true. "Thus the beginning . . . *may not presuppose anything*, must not be mediated by anything nor have a ground; rather it is to be itself the ground of the entire science."[2] Yet the project of defining the absolute—a single all-encompassing entity, no species of entities as in ordinary definition—is certainly presupposed. The Introduction to the *Logic* indeed denies that the full concept of metaphysical logic is presupposed at the start, since a purpose of the *Logic* is to articulate this concept.[3] The full concept of dialectical logic is no more presupposed in its method than in its eventual result; indeed, the method and the idea are, we shall see, identical, though under different descriptions. One must, like Hegel himself, begin by abstracting oneself from contemporary knowledge of both the enterprise of dialectical metaphysics and the nature of the absolute as spirit.

1

Yet Hegel does claim that both the abstract concept of absolute knowledge and its transcendence of reflective consciousness in its opposition to an object are presupposed as having been derived in the *Phenomenology of Spirit*. "The Notion of pure science and its deduction is therefore presupposed in the present work in so far as the *Phenomenology of Spirit* is nothing other than the deduction of it. . . . Thus pure science presupposes liberation from the opposition of consciousness."[4] Absolute knowledge is the thinking subject's speculative self-recognition in the cosmic object or "substance,"[5] and it is derived in the *Phenomenology* by a gradual transcendence of the opposition of reflective consciousness to the world, to the infinite object natural to us in the modern world. The *Phenomenology*, we may say, is the formal or textual "presupposition" of the concept of absolute knowledge in the *Logic*. In a quite different sense we may also speak of the historical "presupposition" of the *Logic*. As a construction of absolute knowledge in its developed form, the *Logic* logically presupposes the undeveloped concept of such knowledge. But as the hermeneutic reconstruction of the historical tradition in which the original construction of absolute knowledge is embedded, it empirically presupposes that tradition and knowledge.

The concept of absolute knowledge constructed in the *Phenomenology* is the undeveloped concept of speculative philosophy at the start of the history of philosophy, in the Pythagorean understanding of the soul in relation to the cosmos to which it is assimilated.[6] To those who say it is absolutely impossible to understand the *Logic* without understanding the *Phenomenology*, I reply that what is necessary to understand the *Logic* is transcendence of the opposition of reflective thinking or consciousness, and that such transcendence transpired in the Presocratic (e.g. Pythagorean) history of philosophy long before publication of the *Phenomenology*. Consciousness of the postreflective speculative position accompanies us in the background even as modern reflection, so characteristic of Fichte, occupies the foreground of our consciousness. The *Phenomenology* is not an original construction, but is the reconstruction of our speculative tradition. That tradition accompanies us independently of the *Phenomenology*, and is at least nonsystematically known independently of it. Though we refer to the *Phenomenology*, we will proceed without systematic reference to the earlier work.

Second, I seek in this book to confirm the Hegelian authenticity of my immanent reconstruction by references to the letter of the *Logic*, which in general was the original inspiration of this reconstruction. This does not mean that I seek a restorative reconstruction of the text which would exactly correspond to my ideal rational reconstruction. Errol Harris's excellent book on the *Logic* is closer to a textual reconstruction that "follows the course of the exposition"[7] than the present one. There is room for different approaches. I seek, under the guidance of Hegel, to rethink the science of logic, to provide a reconstruction that plausibly states what Hegel really intended, and in places even should have written to overcome ambiguity, indeterminateness, inconsistency, or distracting factual error in the context of current belief. Instead of tracing all the byways of the *Logic*, I have sought to throw into relief and insistently underscore the main outline of a certain science of logic that has forced itself on my attention in reading and rereading precisely Hegel's texts on the logic.

Third, I shall show that transitions in the logic from one definition of the absolute to the next occur by a version of indirect proof,[8] hence by deductive logic. The argument for deducibility, contrary to usual Hegel interpretations, is central. It is informally given in each chapter. We are forced to proceed in the face of John Burbidge's caution on this matter, too: "To evaluate Hegel's logic against the conventional standards of formal logic begs the question. For Hegel is asking about the grounds of all logical validity."[9] I propose that the *Logic* is about definitions of the absolute by pure thought, not about grounding validity, and that Hegel uses formal logic from the very beginning in the self-testing of such definitions.

The general pattern of such indirect proof is indicated provisionally here in figure 1. The fuller explanation is given in the chapters that follow. The self-refuting indirect proof assumption occurs in step 3 in the figure. The recognition of contradiction occurs in step 6, while the scope of the indirect proof assumption is dropped in step 7. The entire derivation of the *Logic* embraces numerous such indirect proof cycles. Apparently coherent categories in the logic of being are characterized by fixations on step 3, while explicitly contradictory categories in the logic of essence stem from fixations on on step 6.

Figure 1. Dialectic Schematized as Indirect Proof

1. Abstraction of x under predicate F.

2. Absolutization of term x apart from any related term, or absolutization of its true predicate F apart from any other such predicate of x.

3. Theological absolutization of absolutized term x under absolutized predicate F. Example: "The all-encompassing absolute x exists apart from any other term y under the absolutized predicate F, apart from any other predicate."

4. Abstraction of a second term y, or of x under a second predicate G. Example: "There is some y apart from the absolute x" or "There is some predicate G apart from the absolutized predicate F."

5. Negation of *y* or *G* recognized as incompatible with the absolutization of *x* or *G*. Example: "No *y* apart from the absolutized *x* exists" or "No predicate *G* apart from *x*'s absolutized predicate *F* exists."

6. Self-negation of absolutized *x*, or of *x* under absolutized predicate *F*. Example: "The absolute *x* to the exclusion of any *y*, or to the exclusion of any predicate other than *F*, contradictorily is what it is through some *y* other than *x*, or some *G* other than *F*."

7. Negation of the negation: negation of the alleged absolute *x* absolutized as a term negating any term *y* other than *x*, or as negating any predicate other than *F*. Example: "The absolute *x* negating any other term, *y*, or any predicate *G* other than *F*, is negated as a definition of the absolute."

8. Negation of theological absolutization "3" . . .

From a purely logical point of view, the deduction of a conclusion such as *Fa·Gb* can of course dispense with indirect proof. If we grant on trust the premises that *Fa*, and that to be *F* is to be *G*, it follows directly that *Fa·Ga*. The expansion of this simple argument into a more elaborate indirect proof—by the addition of the assumption that *a* is merely *F*, and by the self-negation according to which *a* is not merely *F* since it is also *G*—may seem gratuitous. But this expansion, however unnecessary logically, is justified by the self-propelling rationality of its motivation. Indirect proof is rational, nonauthoritarian deduction, since the deduction is internally self-motivated by the need to escape contradiction, not externally by trust in the interest of the conclusion on the authority of the argument's source. It includes an internally motivated fall into contradiction due to the fact that no other predicate *G* is yet discovered, followed by an internally motivated escape from contradiction. Error-correcting dialectical rationality eludes direct deduction externally motivated by a premise and line of deduction laid down on the authority of the argument's author.

2. The History of Philosophy and the Limit of This Book

A *fourth* task that I shall undertake cannot be fully accomplished in this book. This task is to argue that the *Science of Logic* I reconstruct is itself a reconstruction of history. Following Hegel's own lead,[10] I shall build an empirical case that the text that I rationally (and correctively) reconstruct itself contains a rational reconstruction of the empirical history of speculative theology. My last chapter seeks to account for discrepancies between the empirical and rational order in the history of philosophy. Not limiting myself to interpreting the *Science of Logic* through understanding the science of logic, I raise the question as to whether the logic may help us understand the history of philosophy that finds its concrete context in the philosophy of spirit. Although Hegel's chosen exposition of the system begins with pure logical thought and ends with concepts of spirit, paragraph 86 of this very exposition points to an alternative exposition,[11] in which the logic presupposes spirit, including the history of philosophy. The *Logic* is even included in the history of philosophy (and hence in spirit) by constituting one of its culminating contributions. I have thus made a choice which again separates me from the following choice by Burbidge:

> Although Hegel makes reference to philosophies and philosophers of the past . . . such material is used simply to illustrate the structure of pure thought. For reasoning, which has been used to justify their philosophical claims and to show their limitations, need not be historically contingent but may be objective and universal. By appealing simply to the history of philosophy, Hegel could not justify his claim to science . . . Hence we shall not pause to discuss Hegel's remarks on possible applications of his discussion either to the history of philosophy, or to nature and world history. Hegel's lectures on these topics can be appropriated on their own. By proposing a purely logical exposition, we will face the more fundamental difficulties in Hegel's philosophy, which are conceptual.[12]

Though the science of logic is conceptual, it is contributes to a culminating conceptual grasp of spirit and nature. Taking an opposite approach from Burbidge, I follow a path closer to that pursued by André Doz:

> Speculation, metaphysics, ontology, categories, dialectic: these terms show that the logic of Hegel attaches itself in its very constitution to what for it is the past of philosophy. We may expect the content of his work to confirm this connection. In fact Hegel himself affirmed that the succession of systems of philosophy in the course of history is the same as that of the conceptual determinations of the Idea. . . . But for one who seeks to understand Hegel, and through Hegel "the thing itself" by taking some distance from Hegel and by maintaining inquiry open, it is not enough to rest content with what Hegel himself said. . . . The manner in which he understands the general principle of correspondences can be questioned; the active presence of the past may extend beyond what he indicates, even beyond that of which he is conscious.[13]

It is evident that the difference between Burbidge and myself (with Doz) is mainly one of intention. Are we chiefly trying to understand Hegel and his text the *Logic*, or are we trying to understand something of what Hegel called spirit, especially absolute spirit and the history of philosophy, with the aid of the *Logic*? In this book I settle on the larger goal (and hence compromise) of seeking to do both things. I find this a more highly motivating, less arid approach to Hegel. The *Logic* is not by itself the inner sanctum; it is the key.

This fourth task implies an overall interpretation of Hegel that I have explained elsewhere.[14] We first put aside J. N. Findlay's Neoplatonic interpretation of the Hegelian system as the endless, asymptotic approach to the absolute as a transcendent one which can only be intuited.[15] Briefly, I maintain (contrary to the panlogism that Schelling's descendants attacked as essentialism) that the system as exposited in the texts is not the absolute. There is more to the absolute than the system of categories strictly understood. The system is the self-comprehension of the absolute in and through us. This system is panlogistic in that self-knowing absolute spirit—philosophy and all that it presupposes, not merely the absolute idea at the end of the *Logic*'s pure imageless thought—can be derived from the science of logic through the philosophy of nature as the only true definition of the absolute. Yet, in another sense the absolute is not "panlogistic," because the reality of sentience and feeling are irreducible to abstract thought objects, whether categories or concepts. Because the history of philosophy is dialectically integral to philosophy itself and hence to spirit, to view the science of logic as a reconstruction of the history of philosophy is to encompass this science in the philosophy of spirit.

Yet a text which to its author, Hegel, was a rational reconstruction of empirical history creates a new deposit of further such history, open to renewed rational reconstruction. Reason remaking rational history—*la raison qui se refait*—becomes a historical deposit which we must remake for ourselves. Some may see in this book an impossibly nostalgic ambition to return to Hegel. We will be reminded that we can never go home, or return to the past, refusing openness to the arrival of the future.[16] The present constitutes itself only by differentiating itself from the past. Yet to differentiate oneself from the past is also to develop the past. If the past is a living, developing tradition, the choice between continuing the past and differing from it is a false one. Behind the apparent ruptures perceived by actors in the great events of history is, in theoretical restrospect, a development of those events. In opposing the past, revolutionaries are not well placed to see their continuity with it. This book contains a reparticularization of a general Hegelian position. Since a central insight in the Hegelian logic is that to be in general is to be in particular, that the universal survives only through self-particularization, to return to the logic and make it live is to open ourselves to its self-particularization beyond Hegel's general position.

The task of showing the history of philosophy in the *Logic* is not secondary in itself. But the effort devoted to it in a book on the *Science of Logic* (rather than, say, his *Lectures on the History of Philosophy*) remains secondary to clarification of the logic. This is the limit of the present volume. This fourth task will nonetheless be taken up and pursued at least allusively in each chapter. Clearly, a program for further research becomes possible here. The extent to which this program is worth pursuing will depend on the importance of the *Logic* itself to us, as an epic on the level of pure thought reconstructing our identity in the world-historical story of freedom. The present book evidences of the *Logic*'s importance in this respect as already recognized by Hegel.[17]

One problem posed by any construal of the science of logic as a reconstruction of the history of "speculative theology" is determining who is a speculative theologian, and determining how post-Hegelian philosophers are to be comprehended within the science of logic, assuming that this science (in the panlogistically extended sense including the whole system) is, as it claims to be, somehow complete. Hegel believes that everyone has a definition of the absolute, but that does not mean that all individuals consciously dedicate themselves to speculative theology. Speculative theology in the tradition of Pythagoras, Aristotle, Spinoza, and Leibniz is no doubt less widely recognized today. Indeed, the most influential thinkers—Marx, Nietzsche, Freud, Heidegger, Wittgenstein, Derrida, Rorty, Lyotard, and Habermas—are known for critiques or deconstructions of the classical speculative tradition.

Yet, for Hegel, Hume had an empiricist definition of the absolute even if he was a skeptical critic of the classical metaphysical tradition. The absolute is a collection of sense impressions. If we treat the just mentioned post-Hegelian philosophers on analogy with this treatment of Hume, we would expect even the most skeptical to have some definition of the absolute. If the Hegelian science is complete, Habermas and Derrida, for example, would at least partially be illuminated by positions they hold within it.

Certainly Russell had no desire to be sucked into Hegel's system. Yet consider his logical atomism. It equates that apart from which there is nothing with the class of simple stubborn facts, of their indefinable constituents, and of the propositions asserting and denying those facts.[18] Containing propositions as well as facts, logical atomism belongs to Hegel's subjective logic. "The judgment *in its immediacy* is in the first instance an *abstract individual* which *simply is*, and the predicate [corresponds to] an *immediate determinateness* of property of the subject."[19] In this definition of a true (correct) proposition, proposition and fact match perfectly. Yet if the fact that the grass is green is the instantiation of greenness by the grass, facts are abstractions from concrete things and events. I have argued elsewhere that Hegel himself is an event ontologist.[20]

I hold that there is a place for anti-Hegelians in the science of logic, and that they can acknowledge this without becoming Hegelians. Part of the strategy for winning has always been to know how one would be interpreted by one's opponent. (As for myself, I confess I have yielded to a Hegelian science of logic, at least for heuristic reasons. Having tried to rid myself of it and failed, I now gladly hand the task over to others.)

Hegel's *Logic* can easily be developed to accommodate post-Hegelian positions viewed as specifications of pre-Hegelian positions. Hegel wrote that philosophy was the present comprehended in thought. The *Logic* is the history of philosophy up to Hegel's own time comprehended in pure thought. Much philosophizing has occurred since Hegel's time. The question I ask is whether any of it has superseded rather than fallen behind the modernist quest to institutionalize self-knowingly human rights, which is grounded in the concluding position of the *Logic* on the absolute (practical + cognitive) idea.

The present book does not pretend to be a comprehensive treatise of contemporary philosophy from the standpoint of the science of logic. It is only a treatment of that science. Yet by way of illustration I shall indicate how I suspect three contemporaries, Heidegger, Derrida, and Habermas could be grasped as offering, at least incidentally, definitions of the absolute within the Hegelian system.

Heidegger thought of himself as a post-Hegelian thinker. Yet, under the influence of the Schellingian tradition, he misunderstood Hegel as an essentialist driven by a will to power, reducing mittances of being to objective things-which-are. Heidegger's own position in the science of logic is in the objective logic, in particular the category of power. He does not attribute authentic power to human beings, but to Being. "*Physis* is being itself, by virtue of which essents [things that are] become and remain observable. . . . Physis means the power that emerges and the enduring realm under its sway."[21] Our role in relation to Being is to let it be, to open a clearing in which it can manifest itself to us. The absolute is not simply power, but (like other definitions of the absolute in the objective logic) it implies correlation. Being must manifest itself to someone—to there-being. There-being is a subservient power whose vocation is to elicit the self-manifestation of Being. If this brief analysis is correct, Hegel would disagree with Heidegger. The absolute as an inner essential power which is irreducible to finite objects, and which must manifest itself if it is not to lose its power, is contradictory if it does not equally empower there-being. But for Heidegger supremacy and lordship are maintained by Being and its sovereign initiatives. Heidegger, in short, is pre-Hegelian, with little grasp of the absolute Kantian idea of "personality" at work since the American and French Revolutions.

Derrida is essentially a post-Hegelian thinker who has studied Hegel deeply. Remaining sovereign precisely by his criticism of Hegel, he holds that the absolute whole, contrary to Hegel's alleged intentions, escapes total presence to Hegel himself. There is something in this whole that is forever absent from his system of philosophy. Yet Hegel admits as much. Only in the first book of the *Logic*, the logic of being, does thought even intend full, intuitively given presence. Hegel still asserts the crucial importance of a concept of the absolute as the absolute's own individualized self-knowing. Hegel asserts the primacy of speech—for Derrida the promise of mastering a total context by the speaking subject—over writing, over the loss of mastery of the context of interpretation, over self-negation. Derrida asserts the primacy of writing (producing enduring signs, traces whose trail is lost in otherness) over speech. Derrida does not take the system seriously as the self-definition of the absolute. He mocks Hegelian pretension. Where Hegel stresses the heroic assertion that every dialectical problem (self-negation) has a solution (negation of the negation), Derrida makes the complementary and self-effacing assertion that every dialectical solution gives rise to a new problem, further differentiation, displacement of established limits, difference, a ceaseless deferral of closure. But Derrida knows that self-negation, the understanding's voice of skeptical protest against absolutization of what is abstract, is an ever recurrent voice of negative reason internal to concrete rationality itself. Since self-negation in Derrida negates any falsely totalizing negation of the negation, and since negation of the negation overcomes self-negation, Derrida and Hegel cannot be separated from each other except by false abstraction.[22]

Hegel, as we shall see, agrees with Derrida about the self-deception of claiming total presence. To be in general is to be endlessly self-particularizing. It is hard not to conclude that Derrida views Hegel as an essentialist in the Schellingian tradition of Hegel criticism. Despite the strength of some Derridean insights on speech and writing, Hegel did not pursue lordship or mastery in general, or by assigning primacy to speech in particular. He was not fixated on a closed definition of the absolute. The system coincides with the absolute only by contemplation of an ideal system at the conclusion of a never to be realized endless dialectical progression—a bad infinite. Despite the gravity and negative fixation of the old Hegel before the menace of the 1831 revolution, the *Phenomenology* was most playful with the stubborn fixations of the understanding.

Can a declared radical critic of Hegel have a place in the sequence of definitions of the absolute in the *Logic*? Being a declared critic of Hegel is a risk only for chronological post-Hegelians. Yet Plato, Hume, and other pre-Hegelians can qualify as implicit critics of Hegel. Though no philosopher can be reduced to a certain niche in the Hegelian system, this does not prevent everyone—and hence every philosopher—from having a logical category defining the absolute.[23] If the science of logic is complete, it is still abstract relative to spirit, and its concrete realization in the history of philosophy remains open. Derrida is not *für sich* a speculative theologian. Yet he implicitly defines the absolute as an endless process of differentiation, distancing, or self-negation—which is simply the ever resurgent other side of the coin from Hegel's endless process of self-recuperation. He theologically absolutizes negative reason. His originality is to absolutize the skeptical negation of Hegel's alleged definition of the absolute, viewing the absolute as limited by endless differentiations left over from discourse fallen silent. This means that, within the Hegelian logic, Derrida formally holds to a second-order definition of the absolute as no particular absolutized term, but as the open-ended process of negating all absolutized terms (including Hegel's). I introduce only one brief string of quotations from Derrida:

> To be indifferent to the comedy of the *Aufhebung*, as Hegel was, is to blind oneself to the experience of the sacred, to the [Nietzschean] heedless sacrifice of presence and meaning. . . . The *continuum* [Georges Bataille] is the privileged experience of a sovereign operation transgressing the limit of discursive difference. . . . Pushing itself toward the nonbasis of negativity and expenditure, the experience of the *continuum* is also the experience of absolute difference, of a difference which would no longer be the one that Hegel had conceived more profoundly than anyone else: the difference in the service of presence, at work for (the) history of (meaning). . . . Sovereignty transgresses the entirety of the history of meaning and the entirety of the meaning of history. . . . Unknowledge is, then, suprahistorical, but only because it takes [assumes] its responsibilities from [given] the completion of history and for [given] the closure of absolute knowledge, having first taken them seriously and having then betrayed them by exceeding them or by simulating them in play.[24]

Yet for Hegel, too, presence is in the service of absence as much as the other way around:

Just as philosophy pushes the sciences [to compensate] for their conceptual deficiency, so they [ceaselessly!] drive philosophy to give up the lack of realization [*Erfühlung*] stemming from its [insurmountable residue of] abstraction. . . . The *content* of such a philosophy [as Hegel's] . . . *immediately leads by itself to the positive sciences* [which pursue but never exhaust endless differences manifest it in concrete form,] in its further development and application.[25]

In the final analysis an ambiguity developed in Hegel's position, due to the increasing rigidity of his thinking with advancing age.[26] Yet the system, the finite construction of the *Encyclopaedia* which underwent expansion through successive editions, must forever be further developed, is never closed. The absolute itself develops:

You [Hegel] yourself . . . intimated orally to me one day that you were entirely convinced of the necessity of new progress and new forms of the universal Spirit even beyond the form of science achieved by you, without, however, being able to give me any more precise account of these forms. . . . With you, however, this conviction finds itself in flat contradiction with your systematic teachings, which far from demanding such a progress of the world spirit, on the contrary definitely exclude it.[27]

My suspicion is that the Hegel against whom Derrida rebels is a Hegel who had become a comic parody of his own self. There was once a more Derridean, and indeed more Hegelian Hegel who asserted that the truth is a "Bacchanalian revel"[28] disowning the "dogmatism" of a "fixed result"[29]; "the pure certainty of self abstracts from itself—not by leaving itself out, or setting itself aside, but by giving up the fixity."[30]

Unofficially, Derrida advances the story of freedom consistent with the absolutization of personality at the end of the logic. His work defending philosophy in the cause of emancipation is known.[31] But since Deborah Chaffin is right to remind us that Hegel does not evince a will to mastery over the finite,[32] Derrida's definition of the absolute, though a legitimate skeptical metadefinition within the science of logic, fails to target Hegel himself. Only a will to sovereign laughter breaks the spell of the science of logic over us.[33]

Habermas, like Heidegger and Derrida, is under the spell of the panlogistic view of Hegel as expressing a "totalizing viewpoint."[34] He carries forward the interest in freedom or emancipation, but from the standpoint of his own antireligious "postmetaphysical thought."[35] Yet placed within the science of logic, a framework he calls into question because of its "messianic" content,[36] Habermas develops a new version of the Kantian standpoint of the emancipatory "practical idea"[37] divorced from any "theoretical idea" which would reconstruct it theologically. He implicitly defines the absolute as an endless historical activity of emancipation encountering various material obstacles, surmounting them only in part.

> Reason's interest in emancipation, which is invested in the self-formative process of the species and permeates the movement of reflection . . . assumes the restricted form of the practical [hermeneutic] and the technical cognitive [natural scientific] interests. . . . Orientations toward technical control, toward mutual understanding in the conduct of life and [ultimately for critical theory] toward emancipation from seemingly "natural" constraint establish the specific viewpoints from which we can apprehend reality in any way whatsoever.[38]

The above comments on Russell, Heidegger, Derrida, and Habermas point allusively to another possible book on the science of logic in relation to contemporary philosophy. In this book, devoted to the science of logic, such comments, without being demonstrative, simply serve to show that interest in the *Logic* is not antiquarian.

3. Formalism

Our procedure in reconstructing the science of logic deviates from Hegel's in the *Logic* in that our reconstruction of the logic presupposes the above formal model of the dialectical pattern present in the *Logic.* This pattern was nowhere so explicitly stated by Hegel. We proceed with a general model of dialectical development, and with a proposed translation into ordinary deductive logic by the rule of indirect proof.

The danger for Hegel was one of "formalism."[39] It lay in the temptation to take an abstract model of dialectic as evident, and then impose it mechanically on history. We might call this approach, which Hegel attributed to Schelling and rejected for himself, "dialectical foundationalism."

Despite initial appearance, the present volume is distant from such an approach. The above abstract model of dialectic is not self-validating. It is abstracted from Hegel's own dialectical practice, and is to be used as a guide in interpreting the most difficult of his transitions. The procedure may seem circular, but it is not vicious. Our model of dialectic is a general interpretive hypothesis to be tested and fine-tuned through repeated encounters with the texts.

4. Noun Capitalization and the Prepositional Style

The present treatment of the logic is linguistically faithful to Hegel in preserving his prepositional style of expression. Proliferation of prepositional expressions such as the "in-itself," "for-another," "for-itself," "outside-itself,"[40] and "in-and-for-itself" have been largely abandoned by many English-speaking scholars.[41] They disclaim any desire to revive Hegel's most distinctive language in recalling what is distinctive in his thought. This prepositional idiom derives from Kant's distinction between the thing-in-itself and the phenomenal thing-for-us. But Hegel attributes it to Jacobi, and approves prepositional expressions as abbreviations.[42]

Although the prepositional style is currently out of favor with some scholars, it was not completely dropped after Hegel. Marx toyed with it, and Sartre employed a version of it systematically. Though I retain the idiom, like Hegel I assign no ultimate explanatory value to it. As a means of abbreviation, it is in principle dispensable.

Like Hegel, I unpack the prepositional terminology in a neo-Aristotelian rather than Kantian way. Being-in-itself is potential being in contrast to achieved being-in-act, and being-for-itself is the higher form of being-in-act which comes from reflection on what is achieved prereflectively. This is neo-Aristotelian rather than simply Aristotelian only because being-in-itself is conceived as actualizing itself in its being-for-self, not as being externally actualized by what is already in act. G. R. G. Mure wrote: "Hegel . . . accepted the general Aristotelian principle of development. He strove to close the chasm between the absolutely real [eternal being-for-self, thought thinking itself] and the relatively potential by recasting and absorbing within the absolutely real the whole succession of stages which in the Aristotelian system had led up to but failed to reach it."[43] I differ from Mure's rather Neoplatonic reading in that I am unable to interpret the highest level of being-for-self as eternally actualized independently of genuine developmental stages which it "absorbs." Yet I pass without much scruple back and forth between Aristotelian and Hegelian language, retaining the Hegelian terminology both for abbreviation and as a reminder that the relation between Hegel and Aristotle is one of distance as well as proximity.

One matter of English style on which I have deviated from most Hegel scholars is the capitalization of common nouns. Today writers, reflecting that all nouns are capitalized in German but not English, have ceased to capitalize nouns used to refer to the Hegelian categories. They prefer "being" to "Being," "becoming" to "Becoming." It is time to go further by speaking of "the absolute" instead of "the Absolute." "*Das Absolut*" is a metaphysical term, not a religious term like "God." Though "God" and the absolute have the same reference, metaphysical language avoids the pious reverence of religious language.

5. The Texts

My method applies the procedure used in understanding any text. When we first encounter a text, we respond with a conjecture as to what it means. We then reread it with our conjecture in mind, not to read the conjecture into the text, but to test it.

I carry out my project by continual reference to Hegel's mature texts on the logic: *Science of Logic*, written in Nuremberg between 1808 and 1816, when Hegel was rector of the city's classical gymnasium. The first book on the logic of being was published in 1812, and rewritten and republished shortly before Hegel's death (1831). The second book on the logic of essence was written in 1813, and the third book on the logic of the concept in 1816, the year of Hegel's transfer to a professorship at the University of Heidelberg. Between 1808 and 1811, while preparing to publish the *Science of Logic*, he also prepared simplified versions of the logic for the gymnasium students.[44] But one should not use these outlines as a major basis for understanding the *Science of Logic* anymore than a necessarily aborted acorn should be used to understand an oak tree. It remains to be seen to what extent his last lectures on the logic, those of 1831, may confirm or disconfirm an account of the science of logic, since at this point they have not been edited and published even in German.

Hegel did not manage to rewrite either the second or third book prior to his death in 1831. The rewrite of the first book is longer and often different in detail, but I do not find it shows philosophically fundamental revisions. Labarrière and Jarczyk, in their translation from the 1970s, have even preferred to use the 1812 version of book 1 over the 1831 version.[45] I shall cite both editions.

When I quote texts, I shall either translate myself or, more usually, give recognized English translations with original German terms occasionally in brackets, with sources both for the English and German. The A. V. Miller translation of the *Science of Logic* will be used, and the translation by Theodore Geraets, W. A. Suchting, and H. S. Harris, designated as the *Encyclopaedia Logic* (1991), will be used wherever the text borrows translations from part 1 of the *Encyclopaedia.*

We shall thus also refer to the *Encyclopaedia of Philosophical Sciences* (1817, 1827, 1830). The account of the logic in the first part of the *Encyclopaedia* often moves too fast, but is also often clearer than the *Logic.* Yet it is written without the intensity of the original voyage of discovery. We will also use von Henning's Additions to Hegel's numbered paragraphs and the attached Remarks by Hegel. Though they are based on student notes not authored by Hegel, their clarity has won them lasting influence.

Hegel made a strategic decision to devote himself in Berlin to teaching a circle of adepts rather than to the authorship of further books. As long as notes coming out of the inner circle are clearly marked as such, they have some authority in the contextual interpretation of Hegel's texts.

I shall refer only incidentally to the Jena lectures on the logic,[46] which preceded the *Phenomenology.* To a certain extent I also shall cite commentaries on the *Logic* by other Hegel scholars. Yet a dominant systematic concern with our main text's prehistory and posthistory would take us beyond the manageable proportions of a reconstruction of the *Logic.* The best recent attempt to meet such a concern is by Giacomo Rinaldi.[47] Yet the reader deserves some indication of where my interpretation lies on the map of other Hegel interpretations.

In the case of both the *Logic* and the *Phenomenology* Hegel complained in letters of hurried and harried conditions of authorship. In Nuremberg his career was stalled. He clearly wished to write a sequel to the *Phenomenology* which would earn him a university professorship. He apologized for the unevenness of the exposition and clarity.[48] Today such a manuscript would probably not be published without revision, but in Hegel's time the romantic cult of individual genius helped overcome such reservations.

Ultimately in Hegel's favor was the fact that his immense profundity was recognizable. A distinction then existed between an individual's philosophy and his text—in this case between the science of logic as science and the *Science of Logic.* Based on a romantic divorce between the inner and outer, some readers were willing to grant that Hegel had a perfected science or system which could be detected in his lectures and texts, even if not perfectly expressed.[49] This distinction worked in Hegel's favor though he himself opposed it, insisting in the *Logic* itself that there is nothing more (or less) in the essence of a thing than what actually appears.[50] "Everyone knows how to judge what is finished, but from what is unfinished it is impossible to tell whether it contains a seed capable of producing something."[51]

6. Interpretive Method

Contemporary interpretations of the *Science of Logic* illustrate the full range of current hermeneutic strategies. These strategies may be distinguished as intratextual, textual, contextual, pretextual, and post-textual. We shall see that objections to these strategies largely arise from viewing them as mutually exclusive, but that they can also be viewed as complementary within a comprehensive hermeneutic strategy.

Intratextual interpretation construes the whole text from the privileged perspective of only one among different voices in the text. So-called Christocentric interpretations of the Bible are illustrative. Interpretations of the *Logic* which privilege the logic of the concept as the key to understanding the whole text fall into this hermeneutic category. Thus Philip Grier has written that "Hegel's use of the terms 'abstract' and 'concrete' [throughout the *Science of Logic*] is so interwoven with his doctrine of the Concept that any attempt to make sense of all the occurrences of those two terms in the text without [drawing on the logic of the concept] . . . is bound to collapse in a heap of paradoxes."[52] According to this approach, the first two books of the *Science of Logic* cannot be understood except in light of the logic of the concept in the third book.

Textual interpretation, known as formalism or new criticism in literary criticism, interprets the text grammatically and lexically. But grammar distinguishes first, second, and third persons, singular and plural subjects, personal and impersonal pronouns. Personal pronouns, whether individual or collective, refer to voices which speak, are spoken to, or spoken about. Textual interpretation construes the text as the possible world of all intratextual voices, at least in juxtaposition if not in dialogue.

Voices present in the *Logic* prominently include particular voices, each espousing a successive definition of the absolute. They also include: (1) a more general voice of optimism about the abstract definability of the absolute by what Hegel calls the "understanding"; (2) a voice of skeptical criticism directed at all such one-sided definitions by the understanding; and (3) the voice of "speculative reason," which reconstructs the entire succession of definitions, and which periodically speaks up in "external reflection" in the Remarks on the succession also contained in the text.

A textualist approach to a sacred book, legal constitution, or novel refuses to privilege any one intratextual voice as the voice of the text unless the text itself so designates that voice. Whether the Bible so designates the voice of Christ depends in part on equivocal Old Testament prophecies. Since the *Logic* culminates in the absolute idea which merges with the method (including the skeptical voice of "negative reason"), arguably the voice expressing the absolute idea is the voice of the text as a whole.

A strict textualist approach forbids conjecture as to whether a voice expressed in the text is anyone in the text's real-world context. The authors of *Introduction à la lecture de la Science de la logique de Hegel* espouse such a pure textualism, in which reference to anything outside the text is excluded: "Hegel's speculative discourse establishes itself by discounting every ontology. . . . The philosophical discourse thus has no [external] referent if one means by this term something external to which language should relate."[53] According to strict textualism, voices in the *Logic* are purely possible voices as far as the actual world goes. They are considered real only in the text, not in the context.

Strict formalism, abstracted from and absolutized apart from all contextual interpretation, comes close to the fallacy of quoting out of context. It can avoid this fallacy only if the text invokes no standpoint in the context. A more moderate textualism allows the interpreter to refer to the context so long as the text itself at least implicitly makes such reference. The *Logic* at least obscurely refers to historical philosophers, Hegel's contemporaries, and Hegel himself.

Moderate textualism does not exclude the possibility that the voice behind certain Remarks in the *Logic* is that of Hegel himself. And the voices of particular definitions, each with only one opportunity or section in which to speak, may be those of historical philosophers, depending upon historical allusions in the text itself.

By the contextual method of interpretation I mean interpretation by a context *not* definitely referred to (singled out) in the text. The context includes individuals indefinitely referred to within the text. Thus a novel may contain concealed bits of autobiography which refer indefinitely to the life of the novelist. These fragments are discovered to be autobiographical, not by the text itself, but by exploring its context. By contrast, the historical author of a self-professed autobiography, who is definitely referred to in the text, is known to be in the text's context from the text itself, without any independent exploration of the context. Likewise with Parmenides, insofar as the *Logic* says explicitly that Parmenides defined the absolute as pure being.

The extratextual context includes authors' intentions expressed in the text but not definitely referred to in it. Ever broader contexts are introduced to clarify the author's intentions. These contexts include the author's biography embracing past and projected works, the polemical context of strategy and tactics against predecessors, the literary context of the text's genre, the artistic context of art forms other than literature, the social context of current history, the ecological context or natural environment of this history, and the absolute context defined by the cosmos—all are introduced to clarify the author's intentions. The author's intentions, moreover, may have unconscious dimensions.

The author's lingering reaction to criticism of past works, his or her polemical targets, the operative literary models, the author's choice of a particular art form and of art itself within a social setting, ecological fortunes of sand or snow, the truth or falsehood of materialism—all this can cast new light on the author's intentions, allowing the interpreter to understand the author better than the author understood him- or herself.

"In the following sections we encounter an interweaving of philosophy, polemics, pedagogy, critical response, and biography in the year of Hegel's most intense preoccupation with the *Logic*."[54] Using his letters to fill out further this fragment of contextual interpretation, we could show that Hegel sought to establish absolute idealism in the *Logic* by writing a logic text for secondary schools, by replying to the criticisms of a secondary school colleague, by polemicizing against the superficiality of substituting intuition for conceptual grasp in Friedrich Jacobi's school, and by drawing on a professed new determination to communicate coinciding with his marriage. But from a Hegelian perspective he also wrote the *Logic* by serving as the agency by which the absolute cosmic context raised itself to systematic self-knowledge.

The line between things in the context referred to in the text and things not referred to is not always clear. This is because something in the context may be referred to in the text, but only indefinitely. In such a case only the contextual method, only independent study of the context, makes the textual reference definite. *Animal Farm* does not definitely refer to twentieth-century totalitarianism, but our knowledge of the historical context makes this reference quite definite.

To interpret a text is in part to trace the contextual references of referring expressions in the text where those references are not clearly singled out in the text. It is to know, among other things, what the text is about, even where the author did not know or at least did not say. Little is added to our understanding of the *Logic* by learning that Hegel undertook to write it under the pretext of writing a logic text for secondary schools. But considerably more is added if we learn that materialism is the true theory of the cosmos to which Hegel's text, like virtually all texts, refers. Hegel's use of "spirit" then either completely fails to refer, or refers to something quite other than spirit under a false description. The author's intention to refer under a correct description becomes at least in part a failed intention, which is surely to understand something about the intention which the author did not understand.

The pretextual method of interpretation, a subtype of contextual interpretation, is the historical method. The context which the text brings with it includes the past. Such interpretation insists that understanding by the author's voice behind the text is incomplete unless one also understands various voices from the real historical context prior to the author. Pretextual understanding is a further completion of contextual understanding by the author's intentions. If the author and his intentions are a prolongation of pretextual history, that history illuminates the text by illuminating influences on the author beyond contemporary polemical influences. Thus pretextual interpretation of the United States Constitution typically invokes the voices of Locke and Montesquieu.

Stanley Rosen defends pretextual interpretation of the *Logic* as a necessary complement to textual and contemporary contextual understanding by the author's intentions: "Hegel cannot be properly understood without careful analysis of his relation to Greek philosophy."[55]

Posttextual interpretation may be tradition-bound interpretation in light of the historical tradition of the text's subsequent reception (e.g., *Wirkungsgeschichte* in the school of Gadamer). Or it may be creative interpretation by means of the reader's idiosyncratic resolution of the presumed indeterminacy of the text's meaning (e.g., Derrida).

The first type of posttextual interpretation is not generally considered to be applicable to the *Logic*. A first apologetic tradition of interpreting the *Logic* was cut off by the decline of the Hegelian school in the last century. A second Marxist tradition continues through Lenin to the recent past, as likewise a third English idealist interpretive tradition. A recently founded interpretive tradition centering around the Hegel-Archiv in Germany is directed at recovering Hegel's intentions by interpreting the text only in the light of prior meticulous text criticism. As two representatives of this fourth tradition write regarding work inspired by the Hegel-Archiv: "Only the reception Hegel has had in the last twenty years has at last given to *Science of Logic* the status which belongs to it according to Hegel's own self-understanding."[56]

The second type of post-textual interpretation has arisen even in the midst of recent German text criticism. The labors of such criticism have suggested to some that Hegel had no coherent self-understanding in the *Logic*. Thus Gabrielle Baptist writes: "The great merit of contemporary Hegel-research is that it has taught us to recognize in Hegel's thought the tireless search of a work in progress. Hegel's thought is not a monolithic whole whose compactness is to be defended at all costs, even through modifications. . . . There is a problematic side to it which calls for further questioning on our part."[57]

Different methods of interpretation may be applicable to different texts. Interpretation by the author's intentions, in the context of the world as it really is, is more applicable when the text is a straightforward and clear expository textbook. Biographical interpretation in terms of the author's idiosyncrasies is more applicable to texts that impress us as puzzles or simply erroneous.

If interpretive methods have varying conditions of justified application, what about the *Science of Logic*? The following chapters attempt to show that it can be interpreted in part intratextually through its partial voices, in part textually through its whole voice, in part contextually through a cosmically situated voice of the author, in part pretextually through the voice of the author's predecessors, and in part post-textually through our own creative resolution of the text's hesitations and indeterminacy of meaning.

The main error to be rejected lies in choosing one of these interpretive methods to the exclusion of the others. Baptist is mistaken to suppose the *Logic* is *either* a "monolithic whole" intended by Hegel (and his school) *or* the expression of a "tireless search of a work in progress." Hegel's primary intention was to express holistic coherent meaning, though at once modifiable and open to further development, not stonelike or "monolithic." Recognizing that he succeeded only incompletely, his secondary intention was to search tirelessly for further completion of his initial aim; in modern language, to establish an ongoing research program.

But this does not mean that the *Logic* is only a work in progress. It is both determinate in meaning and determinable through further determination. Our task as interpreters is to continue that search creatively. Yet it is also to do so with respect for the determinate though still determinable meaning which the text through its author conveys.

There is no fully established determinate sense to the text, which becomes clear by "modifying" parts of the text as written. And our own creative efforts will never result in a closure of its meaning. But this does not prevent the existence in the *Logic* of a viable self-correcting theoretical intention and enterprise. It was Hegel's personal intention to give space to this intention of the text.

I believe his success was sufficient for contextual interpretation in terms of misguided author intentions to take second place to interpretation through the author's intention to state something true about the the absolute context. The intention to construct a perpetual motion machine is misguided and erroneous once we learn that the cosmos is so constituted so that a machine of this description is impossible. The statement "I have built a perpetual motion machine" is surely understood better once we realize that it is not really about such a machine. It is about the author's misunderstandings.

In this sense, the common claim that we must first understand the meaning of a statement before beginning to assess its truth must be qualified. If to understand the meaning of a statement is to know what it is about, and if we can know what it is about only by correctly redescribing what the statement falsely describes, we must know the statement is false before understanding what it means.

On the other hand, if we know a statement correctly describes its referent, we know that the text's intention to state the truth is successful—which allows us to understand something further about the intention. If what we know of the absolute licenses us to say that it can progressively define itself by pure imageless thought, Hegel's intention to abandon himself to the text's intention of pursuing such self-definition may be successful viewed in an absolute or cosmic context.

His own successive formulations in the *Encyclopaedia* and in his lectures already established a tradition of seeking to realize and understand the intention of the *Logic*. We may take up this intention again. The intention of the text is not so unclear as to leave us without clues as to how to carry on, or where to pass over certain of Hegel's digressions in relative silence. To understand the *Logic* is to develop and more closely realize that intention by recognizing its authority as sometimes superior to even that of Hegel and his words.

Lying between mere textual interpretation determined merely by the grammar and vocabulary of the printed page and purely creative interpretation ranging free of the text, the present book is an essay in rational interpretation. "Rational" here may be understood in a Hegelian sense: renouncing the artificial separations of the "understanding," it integrates methods ranging from intratextual and textual interpretation to cosmically contextual interpretation in a total strategy. It is an ideal reconstruction of the textual intention designed to give it still greater realization in light of what we claim to know of the absolute and its contents. It aims at a clear view of the science of logic which Hegel in the *Science of Logic* conveys sometimes clearly and sometimes less so.

The meaning of the text should first be sought in what the author intended to say, restated as clearly as we ourselves can restate it in light of our knowledge of our total contemporary context. This is the standard by which we should first seek to resolve "hesitations and impasses" in the text grammatically interpreted. Only a failure of serious effort to restate the author's theoretical intentions can warrant a more creative resolution of hesitations and impasses independently of the author's constructive theoretical intentions.

Purely grammatical interpretation leaves meaning indeterminate, leading to seemingly endless deliberation of alternative interpretations of the dominant intention of the text. When neither the text nor the context excludes it, such deliberation should be resolved in favor the interpretation one finds the most plausibly true and enlightening. This is not to say that Hegel (or Aristotle or Plato) is interpreted incorrectly unless he is interpreted as stating profound truth. Great philosophers can make mistakes, even great ones as Nietzsche saw. Rather, equivocations in his language should be resolved by a rule of hermeneutic charity favoring the interpretation which is the most intelligent even if not true. Among the alternative meanings grammatically allowed, the one to be retained is the most enlightening.

Allowing the benefit of the doubt in this way applies to all interpretation. There is already enough error in the world, and little reason to multiply it if we are not under any grammatical/lexical compulsion to do so. The rule of hermeneutic charity does not apply with any extra force to a Hegel or Aristotle. Great philosophers are not as such the founders of churches. But it does apply.

Reconstruction of a house as of a text may attempt historical restoration, but it may also attempt a correction of the original historical construction. In rational interpretation we have forsaken any attempt to faithfully restore the text Hegel wrote. For we attempt to correct that text in places. However, only what is good can be improved. The *Logic* inspires the thought that it contains something important (if not true) that in places can be said more clearly.

Rational interpretation is interpretation in the context of all we claim to know of the world. Its assumption is that the author intended to state some truth. The interpreter may claim to grasp this purported truth more clearly and cogently. The interpretation, informed by knowledge of the context which may go beyond the author's own knowledge, purports to refer, under a more coherent and accurate description, to a set of facts to which the author referred under a description which was in part implausible, ambiguous, or less clear.

Rational interpretation in scholarly form is not applied to just any text. Its use presupposes first that the text is difficult enough to require methodical interpretation. Second, the text must be authoritative enough, or intrinsically great enough, to require an intellectually arresting if not true interpretation. Though there is no church in which Hegel's or Plato's texts are authoritative, they are great works from which one comes away transformed, enlightened by new perceptions of oneself and the world. Rational interpretation seeks to account for this encounter by a theoretical account of such perceptions.

A rational interpretation in some cases diverges from the plain meaning of certain passages of the text, and from the author's conscious intentions. This is also true of classics from the history of sciences. Thus it is usual to abstract from Kepler's number mysticism in interpreting his texts.

It is less usual to practice rational interpretation with philosophical texts. This is perhaps because it is less common to suppose that there is an objective truth which philosophical texts attempt more or less successfully to state. Hermeneutic charity is less respected in the interpretation of philosophical texts than in natural science. Thus we are left to interpret them merely according to the psychology of the author, the requirements of the language, the *Wirkungsgeschichte*, or the interpreter's own creative reading. In practicing rational interpretation on selected philosophers such as Aristotle, Spinoza, Kant, or Hegel, we pay them a rare compliment.

Corrective reconstruction of a text differs from restorative reconstruction by not seeking to follow all the odd twists and turns of the author's language and intentions. Yet this does not mean that corrective interpretation can be pursued completely apart from restorative interpretation. Since it attempts to rethink and rewrite the text, it must be sensitive to the text which is rethought, especially where it is rethought. Corrective interpretation presupposes a restorative interpretation's recognition of certain ambiguities, inconsistencies, and obscurities to disambiguate or correct.

Hegel's treatment of noncontradiction in the *Logic* may be taken as a classical illustration of the sort of ambiguity or even incoherence which rational reconstruction tries to resolve. At one point Hegel, reflecting the general disrepute into which formal logic had fallen in his time, rejects the formal law of noncontradiction.[58] Scholars such as Sarlemijn[59] and Stanley Rosen[60] practice restorative interpretation of this particular textual letter. They hold that there are for Hegel ontological contradictions which formal logic cannot grasp, which can only be grasped by contradictory statements.

This book practices corrective rational interpretation of Hegel's statements against the law of noncontradiction. It does so partly in the textual context of the role the law plays in the *Logic* as a whole. Recognition of the law is the motor of dialectical progress. "Contradiction is the very moving principle of the world; and it is ridiculous to say that contradiction is unthinkable. . . . The only thing correct in that statement is that contradiction is not the end of the matter, but cancels itself."[61] In this statement Hegel corrects his own denial of the law of noncontradiction. We take this statement to be the correction and not the error because it is operative throughout the logic.

But we have also opted for it because it is consistent with the intrinsic rationality of the law of noncontradiction as a law of the world independent of Hegel's text. To understand Hegel is to understand what he intends to say restated as clearly and plausibly as we can restate it in the context of all we hold true—both what he knew and what he did not know. If the author had consistently denied the law of noncontradiction, even the greatest hermeneutic charity would not allow us to say that he affirmed it. But since his text is ambiguous if not strictly inconsistent, the context of the actual world as known guides us to a charitable resolution of the ambiguity.

The rational interpreter must avoid the pitfall of reverently identifying with the text's author while twisting the text into saying what the interpreter and not the author is subjectively impelled to say. Even worse is the pitfall of external criticism, in which the text is interpreted from the interpreter's own point of view, which is assumed to express objective truth.

In the first case the text is distorted into saying what the author does not even unconsciously aim at saying. In the second case it is left undistorted, but is attacked for not agreeing with what the interpreter believed even before taking up the text. But we may interpret the text in the light of contextual facts neither affirmed nor denied by the author. For, in the absence of any clear expression of the author's intention to the contrary, we may assume that the author intends truth. What Bultmann called "demythologization" is not contrary to the author's intention if that intention is to make a controversial case while not otherwise putting at risk the truth of his text.

Where the interpreter disagrees with clearly false statements intended by the author due to contextual knowledge the author did not have, external criticism can be avoided only if the critical standpoint does not precede an interpretive encounter with the text. The critical standpoint must arise only by a genuine encounter with the text and the possible kernel of truth it contains. The test of a rational interpretation's success is in part the intrinsic merit and truth of the interpretation as a theoretical construction. But in part it lies in its merit as an interpretation of this text. By this I mean its merit as a plausible internal correction clearly analyzing the author's polemical intentions "remythologized" in the context of belief current in the interpreter's own present.

DISINTEGRATION OF THE EASTERN LOGIC OF PANTHEISM IN WESTERN ANTIQUITY

1

Defining the Absolute in the Parmenidean Orbit

1. Pure Being

Let the voyage to which Hegel invites us begin. We first surrender our own contemporary perspectives to the most primitive and abstract definition of the absolute. We find ourselves defining the absolute by the sole property of pure indeterminate being—being to the exclusion of all determinate properties that would make one being distinct from another. Hegel designates such being as both "pure" and "indeterminate."[1] Pure being is being unadulterated by any other, co-instantiated property; being is absolutized as the only property of what is. Indeterminate being is being without any determinate property that would distinguish such being from another. Clearly, the indeterminateness of being is implicit in its purity. If what is has no other property than its being, it can have none which distinguishes it as *this* thing which is or *that*.

Pure being, mere being, being without any distinguishing determination, can have no property logically independent of this mere being. Thus, if (as Parmenideans held) it is immobile, this immobility must be logically dependent on mere indeterminate being. And so it is. For if being moved, it would have a determinate time and place.

Being as "indeterminate" (i.e., "nondeterminate")—contrary to being as "pure"—is explicitly (not just implicitly) negative. Yet the determinate being that indeterminate being explicitly negates has not yet been explicitly constructed in the dialectic of the *Logic*. We remain more faithful to Hegel's studied practice of hermeneutic self-alienation—alienation from the familiar ground of our own conceptual system—by speaking of "pure" being.

Yet it seems Hegel himself is not wholly faithful to this method. He himself refers in the first section of the *Logic*, by anticipation of the next section, to "pure being" as "indeterminate." He does this in the main text, not just in Remarks.

We, too, in reconstructing the logic invoke concepts for immediate use that are derived only later. Reference is made early not only to the "indeterminate" and "determinate" but also to the "universal" and "particular," which Hegel constructs only in book 3 of the *Logic*. The objection that Hegel illegitimately presupposes later categories in explaining earlier ones was made already in 1812 by Hegel's Nuremberg colleague, mathematics Professor J. W. A. Pfaff. Hegel, in replying, admitted use of such categories to facilitate exposition of the deduction. Yet he denied that the deduction was vitiated by such logically dispensable expository helps.[2]

It is thus one thing to use the distinction between the determinate and the indeterminate, and another to explicitly deduce it. The distinction is part of our contemporary conceptual baggage. We use it in characterizing the historical Parmenidean position on pure being,[3] even if Parmenides did not. In our examination of Parmenides we are explicitly aware of what, since Parmenides, has gone on beyond his horizon. Parmenides's being is objectively nonmediate for us, even if not for Parmenides.

It follows that hermeneutic self-alienation into a transcended definition of the absolute does not require that we abstract from all we know. It requires only that we project ourselves out of our own definition (or nondefinition) of the absolute into Parmenides's, and that we allow that definition to analyze and critique itself. The method cannot restrict us, in reconstructing that self-critique, to a conceptual scheme as simple as Parmenides's own if his position itself moves beyond such naïveté.

Hermeneutic self-alienation into one's own individual or cultural past is in any case a tactical illusion. For it initiates the deductive reconstruction of one's own contemporary position and identity. Yet long before our contemporary position is reconstructed, the distinctions it contains may be used in negatively determining prior positions, so long as the deduction proceeds without depending on this expository clarification.

To illustrate, it is fair to comment before the deduction of determinate being that pure being is not determinate, before the deduction of quantity that quality is not quantity, and before the deduction of essence that being in general is not essence. Yet, precisely for this reason, the fact that pure indeterminate being *becomes* determinate, that quality becomes quantity, or that being in general becomes essence comes as a dialectical surprise.

Universal being as a property of everything that is must not be confused with pure indeterminate being, i.e., with mere being. Universal being is plausibly equated with exemplification; and though exemplification in one sense is general, in another sense it is determinate. It is determinate as the exemplification of some one determinate property and not another. In the language of the theory of types, exemplification is a second-level property. It is the second-level property of having some distinguishing first-level property of the same type. Universal being is the indeterminate property of having some first-level determinate property or other. Particular being is the determinate property of having a single determinate property and none other.

In the terminology of Gustav Bergman, exemplification is a tie and not a relation, since the other term to which that-which-is refers, and refers simply by its universal being, is of a higher type.

Relations between entities of the same type and ties between entities of successively higher types share something in common, and may be conveniently classed together as nonintentional references. The autobiographer refers to himself, smoke refers to fire, and entities refer to determinate properties. Further, all references have terms in a generalized sense.

The limiting case of a term is a term that refers to no other term. The important point is this: the Parmenidean absolutization of solely one term of a monadic tie of being (which thus fails to include exemplification of any level-one property) implies absolutization of the property of such being into the only property of what is. This property is the level-two property of not exemplifying any determinate level-one property. Exemplification of this level-two property is consistent with the nonexemplification of any distinguishing level-one property.

Things which are in fact have some property other than the property of being. For they have being as a dyadic tie, the property of exemplifying some determinate property beyond this being. Parmenidean being, by contrast, is both pure and indeterminate. The impure indeterminate being of an entity ties it as an instance to some determinate property or other in general, but to none in particular. Yet what has pure (mere) indeterminate being, excluding reference to any instantiated determinate property, can have no other property than that very second-level property of indeterminate being. If it had another property, pure indeterminate being would not be pure; it would presuppose the determinate exemplification of whatever that other determinate property turned out to be. It would not be the indeterminate exemplification of nothing, not the collapse of exemplification, at the limit, into nonexemplification.

Speaking of "reality" in the sense of "pure being," the *Logic* says that God is "the pure reality in all realities."[4] The absolute is that which merely is in all that is. The statement that God, the absolute, is pure being and nothing more goes beyond the absolutizations of a term as monadic and of a property as exclusive we have just evoked. It amounts to apotheosis, i.e., theological absolutization: the absolute is (merely pure) being.

Parmenides expresses this theological absolutization in the statement "Only being is; non-being cannot be."[5] Only that which merely is, which is without further determination, is. The description of merely being without further determination, as exhausting the description of that outside which there is nothing, defines the absolute.

Ontology is the universal science of that which is. Speculative theology is the science of one thing that is—the one apart from which nothing else is. Ontology seeks a set of categories necessary to describe and explain all that is. Speculative theology seeks no set of categories in this Aristotelian or Kantian manner. Rather, it seeks the one and only category with which to define that outside which nothing is.

The Aristotelian/Kantian treatment of categories does not compete with the Hegelian treatment, but complements it. The theological category gives a wholesale definition of that apart from which nothing is. At the "retail" level the definition must be manifested ontologically in all things that are. Theology receives its cash value in ontological categories.

The distinctions between absolutization of a term, absolutization of a property, and theological absolutization are not external to Hegel's text. They are found in the *Encyclopaedia* (par. 86). First, the predicate "being" in the initial definition of the absolute is monadic: Parmenidean being refers to no property beyond itself. Further, what is as an absolutized term refers to no other term. Absolutization of what is as the term of a monadic predicate means that pure being is "the undetermined, simple immediate."[6]

The pure being by which the absolute is defined is its only property. As pure being the absolute can neither hide under any external appearance nor ever reveal itself anew. It is intuited under but a single description, revealing itself immediately and all at once.

What is present to intuition, insofar as it is mere pure being, is nothing. Hegel himself speaks of intuition: "There is *nothing* intuited in it [pure being], if one can speak here of intuiting."[7] To intuit nothing at all is not to intuit at all. Or, as Hegel suggests, it is an intuitive act without an object.

Yet this is to anticipate. We have not yet arrived at nothing. While we remain with pure being, intuition ostensibly has in pure being an object.

False absolutization of a term under a given predicate leads to false negation of its different particularizations. For example, a giver conceived as bearing no gift falls under no further description of giving this gift or that. Similarly, what merely has pure being is not independently redescribable as this determinate thing or that. Yet by referring *generally* to some determinate property, a determinate property that it does not imply *in particular;* being indeterminate being is no longer completely pure. It is no longer the monadic property of an absolute term. The property of being becomes true of something falling under a second, logically nondeducible determinate description.

The simplicity and indetermination of what is merely as pure being means that such being lacks internal and external differentiation: "It has no differentiation either within itself or relative to anything external."[8] Its lack of external differentiation refers to the absolutization of what is as a term. Its lack of internal differentiation means that the absolute defined as mere pure being is not the product of dialectical construction out of the collapse of a more abstract definition of the absolute.

That the absolute is mere pure being, however, does mean that it is all that is entailed merely by such being. If the absolute's oneness, eternity, or indivisibility can be deduced merely from its being, the absolute merely as pure being is one, eternal, and indivisible.

Such deduced properties are not internal "differentiations" of pure being beyond mere pure being. To exemplify mere pure being is to exhibit all that pure being logically implies. Pure indeterminate being remains the sole independent property. The sense of the above quotation on internal differentiation becomes clear when we consider the logic of the concept, the third book of the *Logic.* One can partly understand the beginning of the *Logic* without reading the whole, but after reading the whole one surely understands the beginning better.[9]

Internal differentiation in the logic of the concept specifies the general property without that specification in particular being deducible from the general property. To think of one's death is to conceive oneself as dying at some time and in some way, though the time and manner are not deducible from the general concept of one's mortality.

Absolutization of the property F belonging to b means that b has F and no other property of the same level as F. Absolutization of the term b that has this F implies that F is not a polyadic property requiring more than one term. Abstraction, absolutization of a term, and absolutization of a property prepare the way, in a dialectical deduction, for theological absolutization. This is the absolutization that defines the absolute in the *Logic.* The absolute is the object x such that it has merely the property of pure being without reference to any further term.

The predicate B, standing for "being," construes being as a property. The decision in these chapters not to restrict being to existential quantification permits construction of a theory of "being," not just use of the concept of being in constructing theories of other predicates.

2. Nothing

The first definition of the absolute passes into a view upheld shortly after Parmenides by Gorgias (487–380 B.C.). According to the new view, the absolute is nothing in particular, thus nothing at all. It is, by contrast to being, nonbeing. The followers of Gorgias argue thus: "Nothing exists [nothing is being insofar as it is indeterminate in the Parmenidean manner]; if being existed it would not be thought [since what is thought is something in particular]; and if it were thought it would escape the grasp of language [which singles out referents by contrast to determinate other referents]."

Gorgias is mentioned by Hegel in the lectures on the philosophy of history but not in the *Logic.* Instead—in an addition to the 1831 edition—Hegel cites nirvana as the theological absolutization of nothing.[10] Yet the original tradition of Buddhism does not interpret nirvana theologically; it is an atheistic theology. Without leaving the Parmenidean orbit, Greek philosophy itself embodies the claim that the absolute is nothing in Gorgias's denial of the Parmenidean absolute, as contained in his claim that only nothing is.[11]

If only nothing is, the absolute is nothing. It is nothing on Parmenides's assumption that it is merely pure being. For to be indeterminately is to be determinately or in particular. Taken as absolute, pure being proves contradictory and self-nullifying.

Gorgias's definition of the absolute is a subassumption under the main Parmenidean assumption. We are forced to conclude from the subassumption that in defining the absolute there is nothing to define. "If Being is, it is contradictory to predicate a quality of it, and if we do this [as we must if Being is not nothing at all], we express something merely negative about it."[12] If the absolute is merely pure being without differentiation, and if it nonetheless must have a differentiating quality, it is contradictorily not pure and without differentiation. Yet what is contradictory cannot be; it is nothing, nonbeing.

The absolution of a term implies that is bears no reference to any other term. Yet an absolutized term may refer, we may allow, to a higher level entity if not one of the same level. Suppose that an individual has the property of having some virtues of a saint. This is a second-level property referring at least indeterminately to some first level property, like that of being charitable. A term which is absolute within its own type or level may be allowed to refer to entities of another type or level. However, if the absolute merely is, if it is without any determination, its being is without reference to lower level properties as well as same-level properties. The reason is that lower level properties, which particularize pure being, cannot be deduced from it. There are no further properties—such as all the properties of what has pure being other than pure being itself—referred to by the mere indeterminate property of being. To have all the virtues of a saint is to have some definite virtue which is not deducible from having some virtues of a saint. What is as pure being, by contrast, is not further determined. It is nothing particular.

From this realization the text[13] concludes that pure being is nothing at all. Merely to be without being anything in particular is not to be at all. This conclusion presupposes the tacitly introduced premise that what is in general must also be something in particular, must have some determinate property. To "be" in the indeterminate sense is to have some determinate feature.

In other words, being is determinable. Generally, the determination of a determinable occurs through another property that logically implies the determinable property without being implied by it.

The above premise is the first nonimmediate premise, the first "mediately discovered premise," of the *Logic*. Such premises are discovered within the scope of an indirect proof assumption, but since they are *premises* they survive that scope. The idea of a mediately discovered premise presupposes that a valid argument is possible without all its premises stated initially. The indirect proof assumption has a heuristic function in casting light on the mediately discovered premise. Thus, the indirect proof assumption, e.g., the assumption that you are merely what society expects you to be, first hides an undeniable contradictory truth: you are a seat of antisocial impulses. Yet, eventually the indirect proof assumption, contradicted by experience, helps you discover this truth.

Analysis of what it is to be merely in general shows that it is to be in particular. The more we attend to mere indeterminate being, the more our attention is directed to its *necessary* "other," the determinate property by which it is distinguished from what might be, and by which "mere" indeterminate being is contradicted.

The property of indeterminate being, of having some determinate property, is confirmed only by actually discovering a determinate property distinct from the entity's property of indeterminate being. Being determinate implies being indeterminate without contradiction because "being determinate" means "being indeterminate in and through instantiating some determinate property." Being is indeterminate, but it consists in having a further property that is not indeterminate.

Indeterminate being, as distinct from mere determinate being, is a true property of the absolute, insofar as what indeterminately is must have a further determinate property. This reanalysis of indeterminate being is in some way analogous to a shift from "gives" taken monadically to "gives something."

Feuerbach once observed that the dread of limitation is dread of existence.[14] Further, if to be is to be the value of a variable,[15] it is to satisfy a description attached to some variable; it is therefore—speaking in the ontological mode—to have a property. Existence is instantiation. Yet there must then be some property that is instantiated. That something has that property means that it instantiates it in particular, hence that it instantiates generally, hence that it exists. But, as we see, that it instantiates in general does not imply that it instantiates being this green field.

If indeterminate being is the instantiation of a differentiating determinate property, Parmenides's absolutization of what is apart from any other term is false. Hegel's dialectical-hermeneutic method consists in projecting oneself by hermeneutic self-alienation back into the most abstract (least self-differentiated) definition, and retraveling in thought the path by which our contemporary definition of the absolute reconstitutes itself. This method requires that, instead of rejecting the Parmenidean absolutization of indeterminate being externally, we allow it to refute itself internally.

By its internal dialectic, the theological absolutization of mere indeterminate being surrenders to its own discovery that indeterminate being is the indeterminate property of being distinguished by a determinate property. This mediately discovered premise is discovered by following up the cognitive dissonance in the implicitly contradictory absolutization of what indeterminately is as a monadic term. This premise allows us to infer that what merely has indeterminate being without further determination is nothing at all.

Yet the deduction of nothing remains in a Parmenidean orbit. The concept of being nothing at all is that of mere indeterminate being developed to the point of exhibiting its contradictoriness. Nothing is not a new definition of the absolute which no longer "assumes" (in the sense of indirect proof) the Parmenidean one. That there is one and only one absolute that is nothing means that there is an absolute and yet after all there is none at all. Strictly speaking we should not say "the absolute is nothing," any more than we should say "Santa Claus is nothing." We should say that being the absolute as mere pure being is uninstantiated, much as being Santa Claus is uninstantiated. To hold that the absolute is nothing is not to offer an alternate definition of the absolute; it is to express a theological skepticism parasitic on a self-negated Parmenidean definition. Within that tradition, it rejects the problem of defining the absolute as insoluble due to its inescapable self-contradiction.

3. Becoming

Not even the paragraphs on becoming[16] provide a truly post-Parmenidean definition of the absolute. Yet Hegel presents becoming, the alternation of being and nonbeing, as a definition of the absolute: "we
say, in place of the expression used by Heraclitus, that the Absolute is
the unity of being and non-being."[17] Becoming, like nothing, is indeed
a definition of the absolute distinct from pure being: the absolute is a
process of transition between mere being and nothing.

I distinguish basic definitions of the absolute from nonbasic ones.
Each basic definition of the absolute is a new assumption in a dialectical
indirect proof. Such an assumption presupposes that previous indirect
proof assumptions have been dropped. Pure being is a basic definition of
the absolute, and determinate being will be another. Becoming is a nonbasic definition of the absolute because it presupposes pure being as the
basic definition. It makes explicit what the absolute is if it is pure being:
the contradictory unity of being and nothing. Being ceaselessly passes
into and recoils from nothing.[18] Being as nothing is Parmenidean being,
i.e., the absolute as mere pure being. It is not yet an indeterminate being
harmoniously united with a determination that would make it something
and not nothing.

A distinction between "basic" and "nonbasic" definitions is not
explicit in Hegel's texts. I introduce it here in a rational reconstruction
of the dialectic as successive indirect proofs. Yet Hegel implies that
becoming is "nonbasic" by holding that it works out implications of a
Parmenidean fixation:

> Parmenides held fast to *being*, and was most consistent in affirming at
> the same time that nothing absolutely is not; only *being* is. As thus taken,
> entirely on its own, being is indeterminate, and has therefore no relation
> to an other; consequently, it seems that *from this beginning* no further
> *progress* can be made . . . and that progress can only be achieved by linking
> it to something extraneous [in external synthesis]. . . . The synthesis,
> which is the point of interest, must not be taken as a connection of
> determinations already *externally* there; the question is partly the genesis
> of a second to a first, of a determinate to an indeterminate first principle,
> partly however of *immanent* synthesis. . . . *Becoming* is this immanent
> synthesis of being and nothing.[19]

Becoming alternates between mere pure being and nothing. Nothing repeatedly determined as other than being appears as nonbeing.

Becoming is the circular repetition of being and nonbeing. This repetition is possible because the Heraclitean theology of becoming, like Gorgias's skepticism, remains in the Parmenidean orbit.

A truly post-Parmenidean successor to the Parmenidean definition of the absolute must supersede that definition, must no longer surrender it. Hegel says that becoming is the first concrete thought.[20] More precisely, it is a double concept. The absolute is alternately referred to under an implicitly contradictory description and the explicitly contradictory description that it implies: under a first definition as mere pure being, and under a second description arising through the self-negation of the first. The assumed first definition is false, but the second is true assuming the first. The Parmenidean error is not yet corrected, or even abandoned, but it is juxtaposed to its absurd reverse side.

The process of becoming does not define the absolute in the same sense as mere pure being. It is, we said, the alternation of that definition and its self-negation. The absolute is now pure being, now is not, and now again is. The transition from nothing back to being reflects a fixation on Parmenidean being. Without this fixation thought would effortlessly pass to determinate being, the next definition of the absolute; and the process of becoming would no sooner arise than immediately collapse.

Becoming is not necessary to the dialectical development. This can be seen by considering more closely the dialectical cycle of theological thought in its seven steps. This cycle is the form that thinking takes when it is determined, not by its variable objects or subjective environment, but merely by its nature as abstractive.[21] Dialectic is the rise and fall of abstraction. Consideration of this cycle will also provide occasion to note striking parallels between the Hegelian dialectic of the definition of the absolute and that of the Freudian self's narcissistic fixation on the abstract ideal ego, "the possessor of all perfections," a part-object preserving the illusion of infantile omnipotence.[22]

1. *Abstraction.* Thought begins its career, and each episode in its career, by abstracting an entity a from its context of other entities b or c, and from descriptions belonging to a in itself other than the description by which a was first abstracted for thought. Abstraction is the congenital act of thought.

2. *Term/Predicate Absolutization.* Since thought has not yet abstracted any b to which a is nonetheless related in the context, or any description G other than the description F under which a existing in itself (not merely for thought) is abstracted, thought absolutizes a apart from any b, and F apart from any G. This absolutization is, in the context of deductive logic, the introduction of a first assumption by indirect proof. (If a is one's own self, the absolutization represents fixation on an abstract self-concept, abstracted from b or G.)

3. *Defining the Absolute.* Theological thought equates some absolutized *a* with the all-embracing absolute. This is a second indirect proof assumption. (Theological absolutization, conceptually distinct from psychological absolutization of a self-concept, seems to distinguish the Hegelian science of logic. Yet absolutization of the ideal ego with perpetuation of an infantile illusion of omnipotence is preserved in theological absolutization.)

4. *Abstraction of Other.* Since an absolutized term *a* under an absolutized description *F* is what it is concretely only through some further term *b* or description *G*, *b* or *G* presents itself for abstraction. (An other productive of anxiety emerges into consciousness.)

5. *Negation of Other.* Since *a* is absolutized apart from any *b* or *G*, and since the absolutization of *a* and *F* refers thought to *b* or *G* for abstraction, the absolutization of *a* or of the description *F* is consistently maintained only by negating the existence of any *b*, or the true attribution of any *G*. (The other, *b* or *G*, and the anxiety it brings in light of one's absolutized but abstract self-concept are repressed.)

6. *Self-Negation.* The negation of *b*, or of the description *G*, necessary to maintain the threatened absolutization of *a* or *F*, is contradictory. When thought comes to recognize this contradiction, when it can no longer repress its *other*, it experiences its own self-negation. (The return of the repressed.)

7. *Negation of the Negation.* Thought overcomes its self-negation by negating its negation of the other, i.e., of *b* or some *G*; the other is then freed to be included in an expanded concept of *a*. But this concept, as explicated in statements of the form "R(elated) *ab*" or "*Fa·Ga*," is subject to renewed absolutization in a new dialectical cycle. (The unconscious is integrated into consciousness.)[23]

Among the above steps, step 5 (negation of other) expressed fixation on an absolutizing assumption. Becoming expresses an even greater fixation. It not only leads to negation of the other but also prevents passage from self-negation (step 6) to negation of the negation (step 7). The back-and-forth repetition between being and nonbeing stalls the dialectical development.

Parmenidean being as an object of fixation breeds becoming. Discovery of the contradictoriness of the Parmenidean position may lead to negation of the position. Yet it may also lead to repression of the contradictoriness, a retreat from incoherence into dogmatic reassertion the original Parmenidean position:

> The abstracting activity of the understanding is a clinging on to One determinacy by force, an effort to obscure and remove the consciousness of the other one that is contained in it. But if the contradiction is exhibited

and recognized in any ob-ject or concept whatever, then the conclusion that is usually drawn is: "*Therefore* this object is *nothing.*" . . . This dialectic does not go beyond the negative side of the result.[24]

We have viewed becoming as a circular thought process that fails to break out of the Parmenidean assumption. For Parmenides the absolute is mere pure being. For Gorgias, operating in the scope of this assumption, the absolute is not mere pure being, and thus is nothing. For Heraclitus the absolute is an inferential alternation between fixation on mere pure being and recognition that according to this fixation any description of the absolute as pure being must remain unsatisfied. If the absolute is mere pure being, it is not mere pure being, and so is nothing.

Yet it turns out to be nothing only on the assumption that it is after all mere pure being. Heracliteanism contains an explicit contradiction between the Parmenidean definition of the absolute and its self-negation. The absolute is both mere pure being and nothing at all. But because it cannot be both without contradiction, and because thought cannot rest with an explicit contradiction, the Heraclitean is driven in a circle between Parmenides and Gorgias. Let us listen to Heraclitus himself:

> War is the father and king of all things. . . . Men do not understand how what is divided is consistent with itself. . . . Opposition is good; the fair harmony comes out of the differences, everything originates in strife. . . . The good and evil are the same. . . . From all one, and from one all. . . . The way up and the way down are the same. . . . The living and the dead . . . are the same; the former are moved about and become the latter, and the latter in turn become the former. . . . In the same rivers we step and we do not step. We are and we are not.[25]

It may appear that Heraclitus is concerned with empirical becoming, not the purely logical becoming that Hegel has derived. However, his empirical images illustrate a logical point: the nature of things is grasped by the alternation of mutually contradictory descriptions, no one of which is true of them. The river merely at noon does not flow and thus is not even a river: it is the river at noon only by emptying itself into and becoming the afternoon river. The river merely at noon is not; or if it is, it is not what it is said to be.

Logical becoming is a process of circular inference oscillating between two contradictory claims. We step in the presumably same river twice and do not, we are and we are not. The good is successfully referred to as the good only by also being referred to as evil and hence not good. When, in the Heraclitean spirit, we pass to a Parmenidean theological opposition between being and nonbeing an analogous claim holds: the absolute is successfully referred to as mere indeterminate being only by also being describable as not being at all.

It is tempting to exploit Heraclitus's statement that "we are and we are not." Hegel places Heraclitus dialectically after Parmenides in the history of philosophy. Yet, with the support of Diogenes of Laertius, Hegel surmises that he was a chronological contemporary of Parmenides.[26] Contemporary scholars base themselves on Plato's claim that in his youth Socrates met with Parmenides to place Heraclitus before the great Eleatic.[27]

If Heraclitus had no knowledge of Parmenides, the Hegelian dialectical reconstruction of history differs from the historical order. Yet the rational reconstruction need not be invalidated by such a procedure (see the Introduction and final chapter to this work). Philosophers in the wake of Thales or Pythagoras reconstruct their tradition to see how their own positions develop out of a rational reconstruction and ordering of their predecessors. In such reconstruction nothing requires the rational order to be the historical order.

Apart from his appeal to Diogenes chronologically, Hegel appeals to Aristotle in holding that Heraclitus is a logical successor to Parmenides: "Concerning the universal principle, this bold mind [Heraclitus], Aristotle tells us, first uttered the great saying 'Being and non-Being are the same; everything is and yet is not.' . . . The universal principle is better characterized as Becoming, the truth of Being."[28] Aristotle himself writes: "For it is impossible for anyone to believe the same thing to be and not to be, as some think Heraclitus says. For what a man says, he does not necessarily believe."[29] Suppose—we cannot be certain—that Hegel is wrong and contemporary historians right in placing Parmenides after Heraclitus. Hegel may still be logically right about the Heraclitus of Aristotelian tradition. Aristotle preceded Hegel in undertaking a rational reconstruction of history. In any tradition in which successive members share a common aim, later contributors fill gaps in the common construction, on which all keep a steady eye as it advances toward completion.

If Heraclitus preceded Parmenides and Gorgias, the speculative logician's reply is that Parmenides returned to a hitherto implicit pre-Heraclitean assumption. Parmenides then developed that assumption—the absolute as mere indeterminate being—for the first time explicitly.

Parmenides's unconscious role would be that of a dialectical thinker retrieving a missing assumption in a still implicit indirect proof. Heraclitus—in saying "we are and we are not"[30]—would be the original thinker who asserted but did not dialectically construct the deficiency in what would later come to be called the "Parmenidean" definition of the absolute. Aristotle (and Hegel) then interpreted Heraclitus in this way by a partly revealing, and partly creative rereading, of fragment 81 in the light of Parmenides.

Heraclitus is open to different interpretations. The Hegelian-Aristotelian interpretation is one classical tradition of interpretation, attributing to Heraclitus a logical and not just cosmological intent. Some see in Heraclitus a Bergsonian cosmology of continuous process,[31] while others see a Whiteheadian cosmology of discrete momentary events.[32]

Hegel sees in Heraclitean speculation a critique of logical discourse. This critique locates a makeshift approximation to truth in contradictory but complementary descriptions of the absolute. Heraclitean becoming is a process without a continuing subject of change.[33] Mere being without further determination passes into determinate being, and thus into the contradictory of such indeterminate being. This is a process of the logos by which the cosmos is grasped, no merely natural process.

"Pure indeterminate being" survives today as a way of successfully referring to the absolute, but its passage into nothing shows that it misdescribes its referent. The alternation between being and nothing is between two false descriptions of a referent, one implicitly false (being), and the other entailed by the first and patently false (nothing). Parmenides held that "being" was identical in neither sense nor reference with "nothing." The Heraclitean position is that they are identical in reference but not in sense. Although "pure being" and "pure nothing" are "absolutely different [in sense],"[34] they are also "the same thing."

The paradox of Hegel's expression here is due, I suggest, to the fact that the Fregean idiom was not yet in use. Nothing is identical to mere pure being, but is so under the more developed description of being explicitly incoherent. Being is this same nothing, but under a foreshortened description concealing the incoherence.[35]

Theologians of mere being dialectically developed, we have argued, into theological skeptics, and through Heraclitus such skeptics retreated into theologians of being again—under the spell of Parmenides. Yet neither this development nor this retreat exists for the Presocratic philosophers. As Hegel says, for them being does not develop into nothing. It *becomes* nothing, gives way to it, passes through a transition into it.[36] The dialectical development takes place for us, and behind their backs.

2

The Anonymous Theology
of the Finite

n this chapter we take up categories of determinate being immediately beyond the "Parmenidean orbit." Except for the first—the absolute defined as having positive quality without specification of what particular quality[1]—these definitions are so pedestrian that no philosopher of stature has used any to define the absolute. These categories are at home in the anonymous world of what people think in general, without engaging the intellectual responsibility of anyone.

1. Positive Quality

Hegel says that there is not a sentence of Heraclitus which he cannot endorse.[2] Yet he is not a Heraclitean: the truth is reached not by adding to one false abstract description (pure being) its negation (nonbeing), but by developing the abstract description into a concrete one which neutralizes and includes its negation. There is no need to hold with Heraclitus that a stable noncontradictory definition of the absolute is impossible. If the absolutization of indeterminate being apart from determinate properties which distinguish one thing from another is dropped, indeterminate being can be reconceived free of contradiction as the indeterminate property of having some determinate property.

"Determinate being"[3] is not any specific determinate being, e.g., being water or human. Rather, determinate being is indeterminate being, evincing a universally predicable indeterminate property of having a nonuniversal specific determinate property, of being something (*Etwas*).[4] Even though the determinate-determinable distinction had to await the twentieth century,[5] we might more clearly call indeterminately determinate being determinable being. Because there is no genus outside the absolute which, in intersecting with the absolute, could constitute a determinate compound species of the absolute, particularizations of being are determinations of a determinable, not species of a genus.

If thought cannot rest with a contradiction, acknowledged contradiction is the motor of dialectical advance: "Generally speaking, it is contradiction that moves the world, and it is ridiculous to say that contradiction cannot be thought. What is correct in this assertion is just that contradiction is not all there is to it, and that contradiction sublates itself by its own doing."[6] Contradiction is overcome by dropping at least one contradictory assertion. Discovery that the absolute has a determinate property beyond pure being can be eliminated by regression to the assumption that the absolute merely is. But this is the very assumption that led to the contradictory conclusion in the first place. To break out of the circle and not fall again into the same contradiction, thought must deny that assumption, i.e., must negate its negation of the other. Such negation of the negation arises deductively by indirect proof in the claim that the absolute does not have merely indeterminate being. The absolute is only by virtue of a determinate property entailed in general but not in particular by its indeterminate being.

The self-negation of the Parmenidean position lies in recognition of the contradiction of absolutizing by assumption pure being. Negation of the negation negates the assumption by which determinate being was implicitly negated. It points to a new theological absolutization of being conceived as embracing the determinate other abstracted in the self-critique of Parmenideanism.

This dialectic by which the Parmenideans perish goes on, as we say, behind their back. The Parmenidean is a theologian of the abstractive "understanding." Such a theologian is stubbornly fixated on a single term or description. We may say that he or she methodically absolutizes absolutization itself in the seven-stage dialectical process introduced in the Introduction to this study. There is no awareness of the total process, of what mere indeterminate being is "in itself." "Being-in-itself is generally . . . an abstract way of expressing the Notion [concept]"[7]; it is not explicitly posited by the Parmenidean.

The new definition of the absolute as mere "determinate" (determinable) being retains indeterminate being as modified by a determinate property which implies it without being implied by it. The absolute is no longer absolutized as a single term of the property being. Being is a dyadic property referring to another term, to a determinate property. There is no contradiction between the absolute merely having indeterminate being and also having some other property. For indeterminate being is now conceived more concretely, and nearer the truth, as including reference to another property, though to none in particular. For the Parmenidean, merely to be is to be merely abstractly. Merely to be, more concretely understood, is now more than to merely be.

Hegel, we have noted, calls this more concrete form of indeterminate being "determinate being"—*Dasein*.[8] But the shift from indeterminate to determinate being cannot hide the fact that determinate being is a further determination of indeterminate being. What is indeterminate is not itself determinate. Rather, what is indeterminate has indeterminately some determinate property or other. Conjunction of indeterminate being and some determinate property is implied by the rule of absorption: "$p \supset q$" logically implies "$p \supset (p \cdot q)$." If the grass being colored implies that it has some particular color, then if it is colored it both is colored in general and has some particular color.

When what exemplifies being indeterminate refers to an undetermined determinate property, being indeterminate is a conjunct in the conjunctive property "being determinate." We may call it "being indeterminate and (hence necessarily) being determinate."

The absolute is now deabsolutized relative to some determinate property or other. But it may still be falsely absolutized relative to a further term. If "the right hand by itself" is an absolutized relative term, "the right hand with the left" is a deabsolutized relative term. By merging the idioms of formal logic and Hegel's "dialectical hermeneutics,"[9] the derivation of determinate being as a definition of the absolute is by introduction of an assumption in indirect proof.[10] For the most part we will not formalize. The deduction may be justified informally. Yet a distinction may occasionally be made between cases where formalization would be a pedantic exercise and those in which the refusal formalize conceals obscurity in the derivation.

Having some determinate quality is a universal supervenient quality of whatever is. It supervenes on the instantiation of any particular quality at all. Whether something is green or circular, it determinately is.

In its most immediate form, to have a determinate quality is to have "reality." More exactly, it is to have an implicitly positive quality.[11] Negative qualities explicitly imply positive ones, but a positive quality is ostensibly conceived as reality through itself alone, or rather through itself and the supervenient property of indeterminate being. An entity's negative quality of not being green is derived by exclusion of a positive quality, which thus intervenes between the entity and the negative quality. The dialectic of "determinate being" (indeterminate being through determinate quality) begins by abstracting and absolutizing implicitly positive (real) quality as the only kind of quality that an entity can have. Hegel calls such quality simply "quality," and—following Kant[12]—says that what exhibits quality is "real" (not "ideal").[13] Yet the "empirical reality" that for Kant is a category of the understanding is, taken as a theological category by Hegel, "a worthless existence."[14]

Positive quality becomes explicit as positive only by contrast to negative quality. But we first find the absolute defined as a real being free of negation, as exhibiting an implicitly determinate positive quality. For Hegel, Leibniz serves to anchor the point historically. The seventeenth-century philosopher, Hegel reminds us, denied all negation to divine attributes in his version of the ontological argument.[15] Divine mercy and divine justice, however different and even mutually negating they may appear to us, are in themselves a single imperfectly known perfectly positive quality:

> power and knowledge do admit of perfection, and insofar as they pertain to God they have no limits (Discourse I); . . . God alone . . . has the privilege of existing necessarily, provided only that He be possible. Now, since nothing can hinder the possibility of the substance which contains no limits, no negation, and hence no contradiction, this provides a sufficient reason for the knowledge a priori of God's existence.[16]

Since God is infinitely powerful and benevolent, power and benevolence are positive qualities, none of which negates the other. Leibniz's theism compels us to assume that God, necessary being, is only contingently a Creator. Only if we think the Leibnizian God apart from creation can it appear as absolute, not relative to anything else. Divinity is internally consistent, since the divine attributes bear no relation—and hence no relation of negation or incompatibility—to one another. An imaginary variation on Leibniz's God, an absolute entity conceived without a world but with an absolute positive quality, approaches a post-Parmenidean definition of the absolute as purely positive determinate being.

In fact, however, Hegel holds that there are no cases in the history of philosophy of positive or determinate being defining the absolute without the implied negative quality. Insofar as divine mercy and divine justice are one, they are unknown and indeterminate, not the determinate mercy or justice of the human concepts we know. "A philosophy which attributed veritable, ultimate absolute being to finite existence [determinate being, *Dasein*] would not deserve the name of philosophy."[17] For merely positive determinate being is patently contradictory.

A post-Hegelian philosopher who at first glance appears to define the absolute as *real* is Bradley in *Appearance and Reality*. Reality for Bradley has a positive determination that cannot be fully grasped in common-sense predicate-subject discourse. Reality does not exhibit motion, is not spatially or temporally extended, is not a thing or aggregate of things, contains no relations. Yet, since each of these "qualities" is incoherent, nothing other than the absolute has them either. Only appearance has them, which is to say that they are only apparent qualities. They are not open to exemplification. Reality as immobile does not lack a property which something else could have. What we can minimally say of the absolute, according to Bradley, is that it is coherent. But coherence is a determinate quality of reality only if is possible for something else to be conceivably, coherently, incoherent. Contradictory assumptions in indirect proof play that role. But a coherence that contrasts only to incoherence conceived as impossibility falls into indetermination. The "more detailed description" of reality that is unavailable, according to Bradley, is even more obviously lacking all determination in itself. That description is unavailable absolutely, not just for us. What exists in itself but is never determinate is forever an unknowable, completely indeterminate, and hence inexistent "thing-in-itself," nonbeing itself.[18] We conclude that Bradley falls back into a nineteenth-century illustration of the Parmenidean definition of the absolute, not truly an illustration of reality or merely positive determinateness as defining the absolute.

Not every category is represented in the history of philosophy. Water for Thales was no mere positive empirical determination; it was the essence[19] of things become determinate in a single fundamental "element"[20] over against other elements. The most natural way out of this paradoxical interpretation of Thales as holding that the essence of all particular elements and things is itself a particular element lies in viewing him as a symbolical thinker. Water is not a particular universal essence, but is a particular empirical symbol of a nonparticular universal essence of everything; "water, though sensuous, is not looked at in its particularity as opposed to other natural things, but as Thought in which everything is resolved and comprehended."[21]

As a symbolical thinker Thales fails to fully reach the level of pure imageless thought that Parmenides attains. But in another way Thales surpasses Parmenides and the whole logic of being. For he defines the absolute implicitly as essence, more specifically as determinate "matter" (ein Materielles)[22] or universal "substance."[23] If water is the one out of which things come, an implicit distinction is made between essence and existence.

Thales is an original thinker. This is to say he is not a dialectical thinker. He does not construct the category of essence dialectically— let alone reconstruct it by reflection on the history of thought. He abstracts the essence of things symbolized as water from nonphilosophical experience—which is how (as the chronologically first philosopher) he can leap ahead of Parmenides and the whole theology of being to the theology of essence. Original philosophy defies complete regimentation by dialectical order.

Water as an empirical quality is not determinate being or positive quality in general. If we take being water as a purely empirical positive quality, that the absolute is water is—if not a symbolically expressed theological essentialism—an empirical definition of the absolute, not a purely logical definition at all.[24] Not operating on the level of pure thought, the claim would not commit Thales to any claim on that level. In particular, he would not be committed to holding that the absolute is a mere determinate being in general which—because being determinate is still quite indeterminate—turns out to be water in particular. In short, Thales is not the speculative theologian of positive determinate being whom we have failed to locate elsewhere.

2. Negative Quality

Water is normally understood as determinate. It is water, not fire or air. Yet Hegel can admit Thales's water as a historically upheld definition of the absolute only if it is indeterminate (though not merely indeterminate, since it is determinable). Water as the absolute is not the water which puts out fires, falls on the earth, and is evaporated by air. Water is a metaphor for something beyond itself.

Any assumption to the contrary—namely, that water as a positive determinate being is an absolute description—collapses, as we see that such a determination is as negative as it is positive. A determinate quality lapses back into total indeterminateness if it is not also negative. Water as the absolute is the source of empirical air as well as empirical water, is not other than air, and thus it fails to be determinately water.

Spinoza saw clearly that determination is negation.[25] What is positively determined by a quality is negatively determined as not having another quality. Thus, yellow is determinate only as not blue, green, or red; and water is determinate only as not air. Someone who experienced no color but yellow could not distinguish between yellow and color in general. If the absolute has a single determinate property, there is a second such property that it does not have. To have any determinate property at all is not to have a second property.

This Spinozistic insight is the second mediately discovered premise generated by a basic definition of the absolute in the dialectic of being. The first, we remember, was that what indeterminately is has a particular determinate property which implies indeterminate being, but which is not implied by indeterminate being. The second is: what indeterminately is through some determination lacks another determination. The absolute has a positive quality only by the negative quality of not having some other positive quality. Indeterminate being made determinable by negative as well as positive qualities is a third concept of indeterminate being, beyond both Parmenidean being and indeterminate being of merely positive quality.

Since the absolute is all-embracing, the other positive quality which the absolute here and now lacks presumably must qualify the absolute at another possible time or place. An apple is sour and not ripe because it will be ripe, has been ripe, or might be ripe, but also because other apples are ripe. A human being is determinately irrational because he or she might be rational, but also in part because others are rational. But there is only one absolute. It cannot be determined as immediate because something else is not immediate, but only because it itself has been, will be, or sometime could be nonimmediate as a potential possibility.

3. Something

This third definition of the absolute incorporates a single positive and negative property into a more concrete definition. Hegel uses "something" (*Etwas*) to designate this new definition.[26] A determinate being is here determined merely as something that has this but not that determination. More explicitly, it has this determination but not that of something else. But if there is something else with a second positive quality, the first thing with a positive and a negative quality cannot encompass the absolute. If a first something had a positive quality and a negative quality along with a second positive quality *of itself*, the first positive quality together with the negative quality could not exhaust it without the second positive quality, and indeed an endless series of qualities. A cat grasped as being a cat and not gray but black cannot be fully grasped, since being black as positive requires negative determination, ad infinitum. This would not be a problem for the usual definitions, which are definitions of a species which lay no claim to exhausting the entity defined. But since in definition of the absolute as an all-encompassing single entity there is no specific difference derived from a genus other than an absolute, definition of the absolute is no ordinary definition. It is definition of a determinable entity by a series of self-differentiations which approach it ever more closely.

Something merely positive and negative, or even merely positive, negative, and positive still otherwise—is finite.[27] Hegel does not associate definition of the absolute as finitely positive and negative—or as merely positive$_1$, negative, and positive$_2$—with any historical philosopher. It is so patently contradictory that we may doubt, even more than in the case of pure determinate being, that it was ever defended as a definition of the absolute. At most, a superficial common sense[28] may define the absolute as a finite aggregate of things: this, that, and the other thing.

An example of definition of the absolute by something finitely positive would be: the absolute is something merely illuminated and not dark. It could not be determined as merely lit up except in contrast to something that is dark. If this second thing is outside the absolute, it is nothing at all, unless it is something imagined or conceived. And if something different has really been imagined or conceived, the imagining or conceiving of the second thing is also in the absolute, as distinct from what is illuminated. Since the object of imagination or conception is inseparably implied by the act of imagining or (assuming conceptualism) by the act of conceiving, defining the absolute merely as this illuminated thing to the exclusion of that thing as imagined or conceived is contradictory.

Not all definitions of the absolute necessary to the dialectical deduction need be historically defended. The category of something, however necessary to enumerative common sense and as a bridge category in speculative logic, is quickly rejected in the unpublished silent musings of public thinkers. This otiose third definition of the absolute is in the first instance the assumption that the absolute is merely something. It is a two-part assumption: first, the absolute is determined merely by one positive and one negative quality; and, second, this dual determination leaves it unrelated to any other term.

The two aspects of anything finite, its positive and its negative determinations, are distinguished by Hegel as its being-in-itself and being-for-another.[29] To be for another is to be for another thing. A first thing is not some other thing, and yet it owes an essential aspect of itself, its being-for-another, to the thing which it is not. Because *being-for-another* is essential to the *being-in-itself* also embraced in the thing, there can be no absolute yet mere positively determinate thing-in-itself. Kant was right that the thing-in-itself, divorced from all phenomenal being-for-another, is wholly indeterminate.[30]

To those already acquainted with Hegel's logic, the distinction between being-in-itself and being-for-another suggests the essence/accident distinction of the second book of the *Logic.* But within the logic of being, being-in-itself, like being-for-another, is a subordinate aspect held within the unity of something as a basic category. Such mere aspects are not correlative categories. They are not abstracted and absolutized apart from one another. This is why implied determinations of a thing such as being limited, being subject to a barrier, being alterable, and being finite now begin to arise in the dialectic without providing fresh definitions of the absolute.

Being-in-itself in the dialectic of essence is contrasted to being-for-self as to a logically independent description. The two descriptions are not, as with the present being-in-itself and being-for-another, internally related aspects of a single intuitively given whole. Being-in-itself as essence may lie partially concealed in the intuitively given being, may not be expressed in it. Being-in-itself in the dialectic of being is not essence in this sense. It is only the thing's intuited internal quality, as contrasted to its external negative quality discerned by contrast to something else.

4. Limit, Barrier, Finitude, and Contradiction

The contradiction of the absolutization of something as a term becomes explicit when it is realized that to be something in particular is not to be what something else is, has been, will be, or conceivably might be. Given something determinate, there is some other thing that positively has the determination which the first thing lacks. To be something does not merely mean to lack some positive determinate quality other than the positive quality it has. It also implies the being of something that has the other positive quality. "Something" (*Etwas*) must not be confused with a thing (*Ding*), which endures as a continuant through change. The latter is discussed only in the second book of the *Science of Logic*. Something may be momentary. Therefore, a thing's self-alteration or multiform self-display embraces something's external limitation by something else, by a determination exhibited by something else. To believe there is an alternative to the life we lead is to assign a negative quality to it. This life in the here and now is not paradise. But this life is not really paradise only if we believe it might be, that paradise is a possibly real world, that there are alternative lives to lead.

Merely possible worlds are interpreted by Hegel in a sense closer to Kripke than to Lewis,[31] though he ultimately rejects a logic of *mere* logically possible worlds altogether. In an account of mere logical possibility he first holds like Kripke that a mere possible world is an abstractly conceivable variation on this real world, which is marked by a concrete web of relationships. An example is a world in which the Pope is the Sultan (*Enc*, par.143, add.). (This example is given by Hegel in the logic of essence in terms of the more developed category of actuality. I adapt it to the category of reality. The possibility of being real is distinct from that of being actual, but it is still a form of possibility.) Yet, such a world for Hegel is as impossible as it is only logically possible. Referring to mere logical possibility, he writes: "there should be no talk in philosophy of proving *that something is possible* or *that something else is possible*, too."[32]

A "mere logically possible world" either lacks ontological status or is in fact the real world under a false description, such as a description by false abstraction: "in fact, i.e., in thought, actuality [or reality] is what is more comprehensive, because, being the concrete thought, it contains [nonactual or nonreal, merely logical] possibility within itself as an abstract moment."[33] If it is actually possible (e.g., or really possible and not just logically possible) that the Pope is the Sultan, then newly true descriptions of being the Pope and of being the Sultan single out the same individual. New realities can emerge in history, realities such as a Turkish conquest of Rome in which the Sultan, proclaimed Pope, renounces the divinity of Christ. A Sultan-Pope is thus potentially a real possibility. But if such a Sultan-Pope never emerges he remains really impossible. By his more concrete true identity as the Ottoman ruler who has vowed to convert all Europe to Islam, the Sultan, logically cannot really be, as such, the Pope who has vowed to defend orthodox Christianity throughout Christendom.

The sky is determinately dark only if it is alternately light, or if something else is so. Apart from daylight, the darkness of the night falls into indeterminateness. A twenty-four-hour Arctic night could be dark by contrast to a purely imagined daylight of the same night. When we learn the concept of something for the first time, imagination of something else which may never become possible is itself possible. In order to experience something presently real, such as day as different from night, it is often necessary to imagine the possibility of something impossible though potentially possible and real—such as night which limits, blocks, undermines, and displaces the day that is present.[34] A first something—e.g., day—becomes determinate only retrospectively in contrast to night, or simultaneously in contrast to reference to it by a conceivable misdescription. The rotating earth which is the setting sun is determinate by not satisfying that first description which nonetheless successfully if inaccurately designates it. And pure being (that which merely is) is determinate by not being the determinate being by which pure being is more concretely described.

The third mediately discovered premise, which will permit us to theologically deabsolutize the being of something, is: given any mere something, there is something else not identical to it.[35] This discovery warrants a fourth definition of the absolute as a pair consisting of something and something else. Empedocles's system of love and hate does not illustrate this, because love and hate are hidden essential forces, not intuitively given qualitative determinations of the logic of being. The same is true of Zoroastrian good and evil.

But a simpler dualism of light and dark might illustrate definition of the absolute as a pair of things. First we refer to something such that there exists something else, e.g., "indeterminate being" in the sense of being determinable as two alternate things with different positive qualities. What is, is light, dark, and their pairing. Light is light only by not being dark. Next we absolutize the pair light and dark to the exclusion of any further term. We then introduce by assumption a new definition of the absolute as what indeterminately is by being determinable merely as a pair of something light and something dark.

However, a pair of things either is itself indeterminate or has its determination by *not* having another determination belonging to still something else. Thus, theological absolutization of a pair yields to absolutization of a triad, quartet, quintet, etc., of things.[36] Yet, instead of pursuing such a repetitious dialectic note that, as soon as we have negative determination of one absolute thing by something else, the latter limits and deabsolutizes the original something.[37] If we live in an eternal Arctic day and know nothing of night, that day is of course not limited. But day for the rest of us is limited by night. There is a point at which day stops and night begins. Night restricts day to being day and not night.

Yet to say that the absolute is limited by something else, or that it limits it, is an explicit contradiction. Limitation is the contradictory relativity of something absolutized to what lies beyond the limit. Implicit in the concept of the absolute is an impulse to overcome any limit, to escape being blocked by any barrier (*Schranke*).[38]

Being blocked by a barrier is the concept of being limited made more explicit. Thus being limited, or subject to a barrier, cannot define the absolute; rather, it points up the contradiction of definition of the absolute as something. The absolutization of day implies an attempted negation of night. Night blocks day in its course. It is not only a limit but also a barrier. There is a point at which day stops and night begins, and the absolutization of day would override that point.

In the total system of philosophy as Hegel presents it, the logical idea has nature as the other for which it is. Nature limits and blocks the idea, which must override nature to vindicate its absoluteness. But the impossibility of something existing to the exclusion of another for which it inescapably exists means that its absolutization in negation of the other is in turn negated. The philosophies of nature and of spirit complete the science of logic. The logic overreaching nature becomes the philosophy of nature.

Night alters, modifies, adulterates, and corrupts day. It negates the absolutization of day. Day is modified (*so beschaffen*, "constituted")[39] through night. Night gnaws away at the heart of day, undermining it from within, until finally day becomes night. The concept of something absolute becomes progressively more explicit in the concepts of being limited, being subject to a barrier, and finally in the concepts of finitude, perishability, and self-contradiction (*Endlichkeit*, "the finite").[40]

The otherness of something else to which something prior owes its being-for-other—its negative determination, limit, and modification—implies that the limitations and modifications of what is prior are external to its internal positive quality. In itself something is determined as something positive; externally it is negatively determined as not being something else. However, since nothing has being-in-itself except by not being something else, something owes its internal quality to its external modification, to something other than itself. Thus, what is something else is not external to the original something. Since something has its internal being-in-itself only by not being something else, it contradictorily both refers and does not refer to something else. (Something is only subjectively and not in itself determinate by not satisfying a falsely attributed description; an earth rotation is not determined objectively or in itself by being referred to as a sunrise.)

The absolutization of something solitary is the absolutization of its being-in-itself apart from its being-for-other. But this remains very close to the already rejected absolutization of positive determinate quality, with the same result: a total loss of determinateness. The other for which a something has being, and by which it is limited to being what it is, is internal to it, is its own self-limitation. Something is what it is through what limits it, which thus no longer places a genuine limit on it. The other is no other; the barrier which blocks the first thing from realizing its own internal impulse is lifted.

What is necessary as something else to something original is in some sense not really "other." But the second something also limits the first to being what it is, and so is other. A barrier is a limiting other internal to something originally given.[41] What meets a barrier is contradictory; it both excludes and does not exclude what bars its way. It excludes it because the barrier limits it to being itself and not crossing the barrier. It includes it because it is what it is by not being a second thing, which is thus the first thing's own internal self-limitation.

This contradiction, like all contradictions, ought to be overcome. Either the given something's inclusion or its noninclusion of what limits it must be abandoned. Since the thing excludes its limit only on pain of losing its determinateness—of collapsing back into pure indeterminate being—the exclusion must be dropped if thought is to advance. But if it includes what limits it, it has gone beyond its limit. The limit no longer limits or bars its way. When something overcomes a barrier, it englobes the second something by which it was limited, thus expanding to constitute something new and more inclusive. Whatever overcomes its limit at once overcomes itself, ceasing to be something limited.

The contradiction in limitation and subjection to a barrier may be stated like this: if the absolute is merely something—indeterminate being with determinate positive and negative qualities—there both is and is not something else different from that something. Before we said that if being was indeterminate it had a further determination, and that if it was positively determined it was also negatively determined. The antecedent made no reference to theological absolutization.

Now we say something significantly different from such "mediately discovered premises." If something is theologically absolutized as something, there both is and is not something other than it. The consequent now is an explicit contradiction.

> [T]here are two somethings. . . . As *determinate beings* they are indifferent to each other, but this their affirmation is no longer immediate, each relates itself to itself only *by means* of the sublation [dialectical transcendence] of the otherness which, in the determination, is reflected into the [thing] in itself. . . . Something with its immanent limit, posited as the contradiction of itself, through which it is directed and forced out of and beyond itself, is the finite.[42]

We have arrived at the logical consequence of fixedly clinging to something qualitative, absolutized as a term in defining the absolute. Before we saw (with Hegel's and Aristotle's Heraclitus) that if the absolute is fixedly Parmenidean being, it alternately is and is not, it is in a state of circular becoming. The contradiction between being and nonbeing was not fully explicit, since the assertion and the denial that being is were not simultaneous. Now we encounter the immediate derivation of a fully explicit contradiction from a definition of the absolute.

Fixation on the theological absolutization of Parmenidean being was—in Western history (as contrasted with Sankara in Indian history)—purely philosophical. It was not institutionalized. Whereas in Hinduism something close to the Parmenidean position was institutionalized in the Brahmanist caste system, through Plato the West committed parricide against Parmenides, the father of metaphysics.

There is perhaps no view so common as defining the absolute as an aggregate of detached and yet mutually differentiating qualitative somethings. Heraclitus moved in the Parmenidean orbit. The view that the absolute is a bunch of contradictory somethings moves in the orbit of purely qualitative being in general. Yet just as Heraclitus offered no new definition of the absolute, neither does the concept of what is finite or contradictory offer such a definition.

A certain brittleness in the concept of something qualitative severs it from all connection with anything else, so that something might exist even if something else did not. Merely as something, day is separable from a prior or subsequent night. To view the world merely as this, that, and the other qualitative thing is to view it merely as an aggregate of qualitative beings related only contingently. Yet something is determinately this and not that only by being internally related to that.

Assuming that some explicitly both absolute and yet relative entity exists, we are led to a view of the absolute as contradictorily being both relative and not relative. This is not an entirely new definition of the absolute. Parmenidean thought has already inadvertently defined the absolute as implicitly contradictory. But now thought defines it as explicitly contradictory. The explicit recognition of contradiction, together with the ontological impossibility of contradiction, in the end moves thought—we shall see—to assign contradiction to discourse rather than mere being.

Throughout the logic of being the absolute is merely indeterminate universal being. Here it is, more specifically, merely indeterminate being with a positive quality, and with a negative quality which some other possible being has positively. Such indeterminate being conceived as something is absolutized as a term to the exclusion of something else, which it requires in order to have the determinate positive quality it has. It is contradictorily held to be both relative and not relative. When a fixation on the absolute as something or as an aggregate of somethings occurs, the speculative logician reflecting on the contradiction of this definition infers not that the absolute is contradictory (nothing is contradictory), but that it is said to be contradictory. The statement defining the absolute as merely something is contradictory.

The assumption that the absolute is something, together with the discovery that as something it is both relative and not relative, leads to the reflection that definition of the absolute as something is contradictory. Given a metalinguistic definition of contradictoriness as a statement's property of implying both itself and its negation, we have ascended from an object language in which we speak of the absolute to a metalanguage in which we speak of speech about the absolute.

Hegel uses "finite" to imply explicit contradiction.[43] What is finite (*endlich*) perishes: it is self-nullifying. Anything as contradictory or finite comes to be internally altered. Thus, youth exclusive of old age is insidiously altered by old age so as to perish in becoming old age. Only youth inoculated against old age by including a tincture of it within itself is not qualitatively altered by it, does not perish and become an old age devoid of youth. The dyad of internally related old age and youth is in this second case self-identically exhibited throughout life. To be old already in youth is for youth not to perish even in old age. Only youth as a detached purely qualitative being perishes. Youth is not an essential substratum which remains identical through accidental qualitative change, but is something purely qualitative which essentially includes its qualitative opposite. Anything suffering alteration in the sense of an adulteration of its quality simply perishes.

All false definitions of the absolute absolutize what is implicitly relative, whether a predicate, a term, or both. Yet the absolutization of what one explicitly knows to be relative can only occur with ironic intent, or with the skeptical intention of bringing more innocent thinkers to self-refutation. What is contradictory cannot be. If thought cannot rest with a contradiction, it is because it accepts the law of noncontradiction taken both logically and ontologically. A contradictory statement is never the end of the matter for thought: it "sublates itself by it own doing."[44]

Yet one of the most astounding propositions in the logic of essence is that contradictory things exist.[45] In terms of book I on the logic of being, the finite as finite exists as contradictory.

The theological absolutization of what is explicitly finite has not been defended in the history of philosophy. According to Aristotle, Heraclitus came close,[46] but even he was forced back and forth between contradictories. He never came to rest in contradiction.

To find a form of thinking that positively wallows in contradiction, we must look beyond formal and explicit philosophizing. The moral sphere provides such a spectacle. The absolutization to which the individual soul sunken in evil subjects itself is an example. Such a soul asserts itself apart from the relation which grounds it in the infinite divine will, the general will. It thus conceives itself as contradictory and finite. Here is the stubborn fixation of the hard heart upon its finite self, of the soul upon itself as fallen:

> Evil is not just the absence of goodness; rather, what is negative attains
> a positive reality in feeling, and yet one which itself is purely null. . .
> What the concept of evil demands of us is nothing less than that we
> think contradiction, which according to ordinary logic—the system of the

identity of the understanding—ought be impossible. In fact, evil is to be apprehended as the existence of contradiction.[47]

Hegel lived before modern formal logic. It was still permitted to disdain formal logic as trivial and scholastic. We no longer live in such an era. The dialectic, as W. T. Stace saw, advances only by intolerance of logical contradiction. "Reason *cannot* rest in what is self-contradictory."[48] When Hegel speaks of evil as the "existence of contradiction," this means, to those who take formal logic with today's seriousness, that the fallen individual soul persistently acts on the contradictory belief that it exists like an atom whose existence or good is detached both from that of other individuals and from the community of individuals in which it has been reared. Self-interest asserted to the exclusion of the general interest is contradictory.

To find a second example of an "existing contradiction," we may look to economic institutions. The absolutization of mutually external things is institutionalized in commodity exchange: one field can be bought and sold only if it is not a second field, but also only if it is not a forest, not marshlands, not a river bed. To buy a field that is qualitatively self-limited by neighboring marshlands, that is inseparably one with the marshlands and thus escapes finitude, is at once to buy marshlands which are not for sale.

Contradictory things "exist" not literally in that one and the same entity has contradictory properties, but in that the assumption that it has contradictory properties may become a mental or institutional fixation. They exist to the extent that self-contradictory descriptions fixated in private or public life succeed in singling out genuine referents, albeit under abstractly false descriptions. There are no circles that are square, but this does not prevent the description of being a square circle from being used to single out something noncontradictory.

This seems the most reasonable way of reconciling the law of non-contradiction as the motor of dialectical progress with the claim that there are "contradictory things." There are no contradictory things, but there are things stubbornly referred to under contradictory false descriptions. The assumption that the absolute is contradictory is constructed as the absolute's equation with a term which has suffered term absolutization despite its relation to another term, or which has suffered predicate absolutization despite the term's instantiation of a second predicate.

The implicit definition of the absolute as finite or contradictory may occur in moral and economic life with the absolutization of finite selfhood and of the world as an aggregate of things. It also occurs in the narrated history of philosophy insofar as different definitions of the absolute are determinate by mutual exclusion and hence mutual inclusion. Indeterminate being as defended by Parmenides excludes determinate being, and yet in the course of the *Logic* comes to be determined by this exclusion. We may wonder why the *Logic*—which reconstructs philosophical definitions of the absolute—concerns itself with the view that the absolute is finite. In part the answer is that the logic is a system of all definitions of the absolute, including those of ordinary life and not just formally philosophical ones. In part the answer is that philosophers, while renouncing contradiction, nonetheless persist in contradicting one another.

A further explanation lies in the connection between celebrating explicitly contradictory things and persons of the world as absolute and the theistic view of the absolute which does enter the history of philosophy. Though formal philosophy does not define the absolute as finite or contradictory, it has defined the absolute theistically as an infinite which transcends the contradictory finite. This theistic definition of the absolute does not define the absolute as finite, but it does presuppose a worldly sphere of contradiction or finitude which the absolute as infinite transcends. Definition of the absolute as a "false" infinite beyond the finite perpetuates "the world" viewed as contradictory through the absolutization of qualitative things, even while it denies the theological absolutization of that world.

3

Anaximander and the Germination of the True Infinite

1. The False Infinite

We have now laid the groundwork for an account of the "true infinite," one of the *Logic's* most characteristic concepts. Hegel was the first to refer to this concept under this description. But under other descriptions the concept was already at work in the prior history of philosophy. In undeveloped form it seems to ground a definition of the absolute as early as Anaximander.

In the *Logic* the true infinite is contrasted with the Hebrew false infinite—a contrast impossible for Greeks prior to the Hellenistic age. Though Hegel locates classical theism chiefly in the logic of essence,[1] he refers to a version of the theistic concept of God as the false infinite in the logic of qualitative being. The Lord of the theology of essence is a *dynamic false infinite*, one of infinite power. The false infinite of the theology of qualitative being is an *aesthetic false infinite* which is immediately beheld in a heavenly beatitude beyond this finite world, and which is thus contradictorily limited by this finite world:

> The infinite . . . is determined expressly as negation of the finite, and reference is thus expressly made to limitedness in the infinite . . . and the presence in the infinite of such limitedness is denied. . . . the finite remains as a determinate being opposed to the infinite, so that there are *two* [qualitative] determinatenesses; *there are* two worlds, one infinite and one finite, and in their relationship the infinite is only the *limit* of the finite and thus is only a determinate infinite, *an infinite which is itself finite.*[2]

We interpret the false infinite as a basic category. Thought realizes that the absolute is infinite or free of contradiction first by defining it to exclude contradiction, to deny the being of the finite. Only from this position can thought proceed to define the absolute as an infinite or free of contradiction so as to include the irrespressible finite within it. Our main theme in this chapter is the transition in ancient Greek philosophy from the "finite" (chap. 2) understood as including the false aesthetic infinite, to the true qualitative infinite. Other concepts—the dynamic false infinite, allusions to theism and Kant—are brought into this ancient Greek theme. But they are brought in from the outside for purposes of comparison and contrast, from our own post-Greek culture. Classical theism negates the worldly definition of the absolute as something and still something else, as aggregates of qualitative beings and individual egos.

But in the world itself, the stubborn apotheosis (theological absolutization) of what for speculative logicians is explicitly relative—e.g., something, the finite self—is general. Individuals who are both in and of the world absolutize what is only implicitly relative.

Yet the relativity of what they absolutize is often too close to consciousness for comfort. But because their theological absolutization of what is relative is an assumption in an implicit indirect proof context, even in the world there is no categorical contradictory claim. The categorical assertion is rather that things are fixedly referred to under descriptions which turn out to be contradictory. This assertion may be accompanied by external reflection on the concept of finitude used in reference to things in public and private life, things which in fact exist free of contradiction.

That a statement is an assumption in an indirect proof is not always clear to those making the assumption. If our understanding of Parmenides is right, Parmenides was not clear that the theological absolutization of pure being was such an assumption. He presumably took it as categorical truth. In the same way, any unreflective common sense which asserts the absolute to be finite may be oblivious to the role which its assertion plays in a dialectic. That dialectic may exist for speculative logicians, but not for all thinkers in the dialectic.

Dialectical progress from the finite to true infinite consists in realizing that any definition of the absolute as explicitly finite or contradictory is an indirect proof assumption in a dialectical process. It is possible to believe that the theological absolutization of what is only implicitly finite is categorically true, but not that absolutization of what is explicitly contradictory is categorically true. The contradictoriness of Parmenidean pure being is implicit; the contradictoriness of the finite as such is explicit: "Something with its immanent limit, posited as the contradiction of itself, through which it is directed and forced beyond itself, is the finite."[3]

If we start from the discovery made in the world that what has been taken to be the absolute is finite, the relativity of the finite to the infinite follows from the realization that the finite ought to transcend its contradiction, to be nonfinite or infinite. An explicitly contradictory definition of the absolute cannot be maintained with comfort. Thought cannot rest with a contradiction. We read near the start of the logic of essence:

> contradiction is the root of all movement and vitality [of thought]. . . .
> Thinking reason . . . sharpens . . . the mere manifoldness of pictorial
> thinking . . . into *opposition*. Only when the manifold terms have been
> driven to the point of contradiction do they become active and lively
> towards one another, receiving in contradiction the negativity which is the
> indwelling pulsation of self-movement and spontaneous activity.[4]

Of the contradiction that already appears in the logic of being, Hegel writes:

> This contradiction is, indeed, abstractly present simply in the circumstance
> that *something* is finite, or that the finite is. . . . Thus the finite has
> determined itself as the relation of its determination [*Bestimmung*,
> vocation] to its limit; in this relation, the determination [vocation] is an
> ought, and the limit is a limitation. . . . What ought to be is, and at the
> same time is not. If it were, we could not say that it ought merely to be.[5]

Kant exhibited the relativity of the finite to the infinite as practical, not theoretical. We cannot prove the existence of the infinite from that of the finite. Yet striving by a finite being aware of its obligation to overcome its finitude presupposes belief that its infinitude is possible. We recognize that contradictory things (and finite egos) exist. But by a categorical imperative of all thinking beings we ought be free of this recognition.

Ought implies "can" in the sense of real possibility. More specifically, the obligation to do something requires the real possibility of doing it. If contradiction ought be overcome, its overcoming is possible. This much we know from Kant. Furthermore, if the possibility of overcoming contradiction is to oblige striving to really do so, this possibility is not merely abstract or logical but is a real potential of the world as it is. Reality is the more concrete and comprehensive category from which the mere logical possibility of it is formed by abstraction (adaptation of *Enc.*, par. 143, add.). The real potentiality of overcoming contradiction lies in the noncontradictory character of the real, so that what must be overcome is but a contradictory description subject to our correction. Mere logical possibility consists in variations on what is free of contradiction as concretely real, or as potentially real alternate developments of what is concretely real. Mere logical possibility (e.g., the Sultan-Pope), being as impossible as it is possible for Hegel, is not a genuine possibility capable of imposing obligation. The nonfinite or infinite, being really possible, thus really is. What is merely possible and not real turns out impossible, but what is really possible (the Christian Pope taken concretely) actually is. What is truly possible is, concretely situated, real, since it is abstracted and reconcretized from a source in what is real. Flight to Mars becomes really possible insofar as it is abstracted and reenacted from real flight to Mars.

For classical theism, the being of the infinite was the conclusion of an exercise by theoretical reason. For Kant the being of the infinite is a postulate of practical reason, a condition of the possibility of any obligation to transcend the finite. If it is not only desirable but obligatory for the contradictions ascribed to things to not be ascribed to them, it is truly possible for them to be overcome, and they at once are really overcome in real role models and practices. If I ought to tell the truth, my truth-telling is not only possible but available for reenactment by me in real institutional practices.

We in the modern world ought overcome division, the young Hegel once implicitly argued. In classical Greece it has once already been overcome as an empowering example for posterity, and thus by creative imitation it can be overcome by us.[6] We ought reconcile the infinite and the finite, the divine and the human, he later argued similarly. For their reconciliation has broken through to reality in Christ.[7] As early as 1800 Hegel writes:

> contingencies . . . through being attached to the eternal lose their character as contingency. They thus have two sides, and the separation of these two sides comes through reason. In religion itself they are not separated. To religion, or better, to the religious, general concepts would in no way be applicable, for the religious is no concept. The question is here not of contingencies first made by reflexion. It is rather a question of contingencies which as objects of religion itself must stand as contingencies, which as something fleeting have a high meaning, and as something limited but sacred are to be worthy of honor. And indeed the inquiry is limited to seeing if such contingencies occurred already in the founding of the Christian religion, in the teaching, actions, and fate of Jesus . . . , to seeing whether in the immediate emergence of the Christian religion circumstances arose to make this emergence positive.[8]

In his Berlin lectures the motive of his concern with history is explained: "in and for itself the reconciliation is completed in the divine idea and then it also appeared; truth became certain for man."[9] Reenactment of this real historical event makes reconciliation truly possible for us.[10]

Kant had held that the striving by obligation to overcome finitude requires postulation of a transcendent noumenal infinite which can never in even infinite progress become phenomenal.

> It is this alternating determination negating both its own self [the finite] and its negation [the infinite], which appears as the *progress to infinity*, a progress which in so many forms and applications is accepted as something ultimate beyond which thought does not go. . . . What we have here is an abstract transcending of a limit, a transcending which remains incomplete because *it is not itself transcended*. . . . Progress to infinite is, consequently [no progress at all but only] the repetition of one and the same content, one and the same tedious alternation of this finite and infinite.[11]

Hegel's youthful studies had persuaded him that such practical striving presupposed belief in an infinite already manifest in the finite phenomenal world. Rolf Ahlers writes here:

> Hope is archaeologically anchored in history. The ship of life must have a leaden ballast if its sail—hope—is to pull with might. Future fruition of human hope must be seeded somewhere if it is to be more than merely postulatory. To overcome the postulatory emptiness of the desperate hope of Fichte, the specificity of history had to be acknowledged, and the central candidate to ground hope is the specificity of the historical Christ, who once lived in the past. To empower hope with its full practical potential, Hegel turns backward archaeologically. That movement was prefigured at the end of the Frankfurt period. . . . Reconciliation must have already happened if it is to be completed in the future. Futuristic non-archeological eschatology is powerless.[12]

For the finite genuinely to strive for the infinite cannot be to strive for what is a mere "ought." One can wholeheartedly strive only for what one believes attainable. If one believes that an ideal forever merely ought to be realized, one does not believe it to be really attainable. Yet the only proof that it is attainable is that is really attained. Striving to create without such proof is, however estimable, rather an adventure than an obligation. In the *Logic* Hegel attributes this insight, not to himself and his own youthful explorations, but to the absolute defining itself in the history of Presocratic philosophy:

> the unity of the finite and infinite is not an external bringing together of
> them . . . ; but each is in its own self this unity, and this only as a *sublating*
> of its own self in which neither would have the advantage over the other
> of having an in-itself and an affirmative determinate being. . . . finitude
> *is* only a transcending of itself; it therefore contains infinity, the other
> of itself. Similarly, infinity *is* only as a transcending of the finite. . . . The
> finite is not sublated by the infinite as by a power existing outside it; on
> the contrary, its infinity consists in sublating its own self.[13]

An infinite truly beyond this finite world cannot be attained by anything
or anybody in this world. The infinite is attainable because it is already
implicitly attained, i.e., "contained" in the contradictory finite. Realized
by predecessors or contemporaries, an act is open to abstraction and
concrete reenactment by any among us.

Hegel's insight can be restated with the help of the more recent
insight of Keith Donnellan that successful reference under a false (e.g.,
contradictory) description is possible.[14] What is successfully referred to
under a false, contradictory description must really exist under some
true noncontradictory description. Successful reference to something as
a square circle is reference to something designated as a square circle,
but it is also reference to what exists under another description. The contradictory description under which it is successfully referred to implies,
given the law of noncontradiction, some consistent description under
which it exists. Similarly, the absolute, successfully referred to as the finite,
is the absolute existing under the true description of being infinite. To
suppose that the "absolute as finite" and the "absolute as infinite" refer
to different entities because the descriptions are different is erroneously
to infer nonidentity of reference from nonidentity of sense.

The transcendent infinite that appears in contrast to the true infinite in the logic of quality must be distinguished from later concepts of
the false infinite. The qualitative false infinite is not the quantitative false
infinite that will shortly appear in the logic of quantity.[15] It does not aim
at the sublimity of infinite magnitude. Nor is it the dynamic false infinite
of essence, eventuating in the sublimity of infinite transcendent power. It
is an aesthetic or qualitative infinite, suggested by the positive sublimity
of Oriental pantheism.[16]

The false infinite as an end in view—whether qualitative, quantitative, or dynamic—must be distinguished from an operational concept of quantitative infinite progress ("progress to infinity").[17] Yet such
infinite progress is directed to the bad qualitative infinite ("spurious
infinite," "*das Schlecht-Unendlichkeit*").[18] If Bach's music sounds like a heavenly sewing machine, it offers a presentiment of something qualitatively

sublime and infinite which we only approach by infinite progress in the world.

Infinite progress, an endless approach to the qualitative infinite, takes us beyond a present finite limit only to lead us to fall subject to something else equally finite.[19] The infinite lies beyond each finite thing, but one no sooner gets beyond one finite thing than one falls subject to another. The finite now present perishes in the infinite, but the infinite becomes finite again. This Hegel calls the alternation of the infinite and the finite.[20] It is a new form of becoming: "And so again there arises the void, the nothing, in which similarly the said determinateness, a new limit, is encountered—*and so on onto infinity.*"[21] Thing and other, day and night, became each other because each relative term in the dyad was absolutized in negation of the other. The same is now true of the finite and infinite. The infinite which perishes to become the finite has never been inoculated by a tincture of the finite. Once inoculated, the infinite does not pass into the finite: it develops as the finite while remaining infinite.

2. The True Infinite and Anaximander

The above reciprocal annihilation of the finite and the infinite is not an identity of the two in which one is reduced to the other, or in which one is simply denied to exist. The true identity of the finite and the infinite is rather an identity under distinct explicitly contradictory and noncontradictory descriptions, the former passing dialectically into the latter. The finite as explicitly contradictory is the absolute under an assumed incoherent description negating itself in favor of a more coherent description. The absolute refers to its own description of itself as contradictory, so as to deny that description in indirect proof. To define the absolute by the true infinite is to do so under a dialectically constructed description resulting from negation of the negation. "This infinite, as the consummated return into self, the relation of itself to itself, is being—but not [pure] indeterminate, abstract being, for it is posited as negating the negation."[22]

Here the absolute first defines itself by self-reference, as thinking itself dialectically. The finite as explicitly contradictory is the absolute under a false description assumed within indirect proof. The true infinite is the absolute under a corrected self-definition which escapes contradiction.

The absolute at which we have arrived evoking Christ in history, strongly resembles Anaximander's infinite in the history of Greek philosophy.

> Anaximander . . . said that the material cause and first element of things was the Infinite, he being the first to introduce this name of the material cause. He says that it is neither water nor any other of the so-called elements, but a substance different from them which is infinite, and from which arise all the heavens and the worlds within them. . . . And into that from which things take their rise they pass away once more, "as is meet; for they make reparation and satisfaction to one another for their injustice according to the ordering of time," as he says. * . .23

The evidence for invoking Anaximander in connection with the true infinite is threefold. First, Anaximander refers to an infinite which is no finite or determinate thing. Second, this infinite includes the finite. Third, the finite is no static element in the infinite; the infinite includes the generation and destruction of the finite.

Yet Anaximander phrases himself cosmologically, not logically. He does not explicitly identify the infinite with a dialectical thought process. He is known for a proto-evolutionary view of human origins, and thus of human thought. Is Anaximander's infinite implicitly—in itself and for us but not for Anaximander himself—a dialectical thought process? Hegel thought so, though the historical grounds remain shaky:

> The advance made by the determination of the principle as infinite in comprehensiveness rests in the fact that absolute essence is no longer a simple universal, but one which negates the finite. At the same time, viewed from the material side, Anaximander removes the individuality of the element of water; his objective principle does not appear to be material, and it may be understood as thought. But it is clear that he did not mean anything else than matter generally, universal matter. . . . True and infinite being is to be shown in this and not in negative absence of limit [i.e., not in the transcendent infinite]. This universality and negation of the finite [i.e., the contradictory] is, however, our operation only: in describing matter as infinite, Anaximander does not seem to have said that this is its infinitude.24

That the absolute is thought, *nous*, does not seem to be explicit until Anaxagoras. Yet according to Hegel, Anaxagoras's principle is already implicit in Anaximander. Anaximander's infinite is one thing for Anaximander and something more explicit for us. In the light of Anaxagoras we grasp Anaximander's infinite more truly than in the one-sidedly natural philosophy of the historical Anaximander.

To recognize oneself as finite, as explicitly contradictory, is to strive to overcome this finitude and achieve release in a truly infinite noncontradictory being. Without belief in the real possibility of such infinite being, the finite person is under no obligation to overcome the contradiction. The person is permitted to wallow in contradiction, presuming that its overcoming is impossible. Only belief in the reality of the infinite—belief that something noncontradictory is encountered even if under a contradictory description—summons thought, caught in a finite description of the absolute, to define the absolute as infinite. Yet an absolutely infinite being excluding all finitude is contradictorily finite through its very exclusion of the finite. Striving for the true infinite can only be satisfied by an infinite being including the finite. To be explicitly contradictory for oneself is thus to strive for release in a noncontradictory being which includes contradiction. The true infinite cannot, on pain of contradiction, lie beyond the finite. The finite in disguise must be, or more exactly belong to, the infinite, referred to under a false description of being transcendent.

3. The Finite and the Infinite

We must think about what it means to say that the infinite, the noncontradictory, excludes or includes the finite. Noncontradiction which includes contradiction cannot include an ontological contradiction. There are no noncontradictory things with localized pockets of off-limits contradiction. There is nothing with truly predicable contradictory properties, nothing ontological finite, which implies the existence of an ontological infinite free of such properties.

However, we may distinguish between the ontologically finite and the propositionally finite. We may also distinguish between a categorical assertion and a conditional assertion in an indirect proof assumption. Noncontradictory discourse can, without being categorically contradictory, contain conditionally assumed propositional contradictions. Noncontradictory descriptions may arise by indirect proof through the introduction, explication, and criticism of contradictory assumptions. Since such assumptions, absolutizing what is relative, *negate* related terms and descriptions, negation of them is "negation of the negation."

If a statement implies a contradiction, it is false. Theological absolutization of a mere thing absolutized as a single term implies a contradiction. Prior to this point in the dialectic, discovery of a contradiction in a definition of the absolute led directly to negation of the definition by indirect proof. However, absolutization of a finite commodity thing (or aggregate of things) is institutionalized, and thus not easily abandoned. Though thought cannot rest with a contradiction, contradiction is entrenched in the world, where thought sleeps. Hegel wrote to Edouard Duboc:

> One of your reservations arises . . with regard to what results from my exposition of causal dependence. It seems to me that what struck you concerns not so much the nature of the concept itself as the consequences elsewhere for knowledge should the concept not hold up. I would note that it is indispensable in logic to consider concepts without reference to their application and consequences. The concepts must stand or fall entirely for themselves. . . . This inquiry [logic] is solely concerned to determine which thought determinations are capable of apprehending the truth. Thus nothing is lost when one or another concept shows itself to be inadequate for the [theological] purpose [of defining the absolute]. Such determinations are at home in the finite world.[25]

For in the finite world "there is a host of contradictory things, contradictory arrangements [*Einrichtungen*], whose contradiction exists not merely in an external reflection [for casual observers] but in themselves [in publicly, intersubjectively, objectively institutionalized arrangements]."[26] Speculative theological thought alone declares its independence of the finite world, experimenting theistically with an alternate definition of the absolute as merely the nonfinite, as the infinite apart from the finite.

Here, with things and persons, the dialectic of definitions of the absolute realized in the history of philosophy intersects with the secular history of what Hegel calls "civil society": "the substance . . . particularizes itself abstractly [falsely, contradictorily] into many persons . . . who exist independent and free as private persons . . . : for these persons as such have in their consciousness and as their aim not the [true] absolute unity, but their own petty selves and particular interests."[27]

We now encounter concurrent definitions of the absolute, a rigidly institutionalized definition, and the protest of a counterdefinition: it is not the case that the absolute is merely a worldly finite thing or things. The theistic definition of the absolute as the transcendent infinite is a protest hurled out at the "way of the world" and its struggle of all against all, "the unessential play of fixing in mind [*Festsetzung*] and dissolving singular beings [*Einzelheiten*]."[28] Thus, the starting point for theistic proofs are "empirical things, and the total aggregate of such things, the world."[29]

Theism is parasitic on a worldly definition of the absolute as an aggregate of fixedly absolutized things, finite objects. It is an alternate metaphysical culture, diverging from the definition of the absolute sanctioned by the world. The theistic negation of this worldly definition of the absolute denies that the absolute is merely an unrelated thing or aggregate. But the power of the world is such that the denial does not suffice to eliminate the contradictory assumption.

The absolute is not contradictory. To say that the Empire State Building is not a square circle is not to say that it is definable as what is not a square circle. There are many things other than the Empire State Building that are not square circles. But to say that the absolute is not merely a contradictory thing by itself, that it is not simply finite, is to say that it is nonfinite, infinite, or noncontradictory. Because the absolute is all-embracing, it is definable as other than what it is not. The absolute is not-something-finite, it is not something isolated or absolutized by itself (nor an aggregate of contradictory things).

Let us briefly retrace our steps. Let B_1 be Parmenidean being; B_2 may then designate positively determined being; B_3 is both a negatively and positively determinate thing; B_4 is being an aggregate of at least two contradictory things; B_5 is not being such an aggregate, thus not being contradictory. This yields a new definition of the absolute: the absolute is simply what is free of contradiction, i.e., what is merely nonfinite.

But is this new definition of the absolute coherent? "Noncontradictory" can be understood ontologically or logically. In the present definition of the absolute, it is understood ontologically. The absolute is nothing ontologically contradictory, nothing that both has and lacks the same property in the same respect. Only propositions are logically contradictory.

The infinite as excluding the finite is not relative to anything ontologically contradictory, since nothing is ontologically contradictory. The absolute as a noncontradictory infinite cannot be relative to square circles, since they do not exist. In this sense, it is coherent to speak of the infinite as excluding the finite.

However, "the finite," by which we have so far purported to refer to something or other, shifts in reference when we realize that such somethings, were they to exist, would as such be contradictory. "The finite" cannot succeed in referring to qualitative somethings as such, since they do not exist.

When after the Copernican revolution "the setting sun" no longer was thought to refer to a motion of the sun, it, too, instead of falling into disuse, found a different referent. It really referred, not to a real motion of the sun, but to a merely apparent motion of the real sun explained by our position as observers on a rotating earth. The reference to the setting sun merely by itself, absolutized apart from earth, occurred under a false description.

Similarly, "the finite," insofar as its alleged referents turn out to be contradictory, must also either fall into disuse or find different referents. "The finite" refers, not to things, but to what are called "things" but in fact are "posits" of thought. It does not refer to contradictory things which do not exist. It refers to what is falsely designated under the contradictory description of being "things" absolutized by abstractive thinking despite their relativity.

The stubborn appearance of contradictory things is an objective expression of thinking stubbornly contradicting itself. The true infinite— outside of which there is nothing—embraces an act of assuming the existence of contradictory objects. We can discover such acts by reflection on the dialectic thus far.

The noncontradictory false infinite is absolutized in negation of "things" as contradictory because it is absolutized in negation of noncontradictory acts of asserting contradictory things. The false infinite, limited by such acts, is itself finite and contradictory. However, if the infinite is conceived more concretely as embracing such acts, it is the true infinite. Contradictory things do not exist; the assumption of them does.

Such assumptions of what is contradictory do not occur in a dialectical vacuum. They have a context of abstraction, absolutization, abstraction of the other, negation of the other, self-negation, and negation of the negation. Thus, the true infinite which includes the assumption of contradictory things at once embraces the general dialectical thought process of the logic. This thought process now for the first time, in reflection on fixed contradictory absolutizations, is forced to reflect on itself.

The true infinite emerges here in Hegel's "objective" logic of being. With the true infinite the subjectivity of thought thus arises in the heart of objectivity. The absolute is defined as a logical coherence arising by negation of the negation out of what is contradictory.[30] This subjective thought process is not that of the dialectical logician's own subjectivity. Rather, it is the subjectivity of the object, of an objective infinity which we merely behold. Only in the "subjective logic" of the self-concept (book 3 of the *Logic*) will our own subjectivity be in question.

Yet the apparent change of reference occurring when "the finite" ceases to refer merely to entities that prove contradictory in order to refer to the false assuming of such contradictory things is illusory. The change is in our understanding of what is referred to, not in what is referred to. We always referred to the stationary sun viewed from the rotating earth, but once referred to it under a false description. Similarly, we always referred to the appearance of what is contradictory arising from the persistent contradictory thinking of the abstractive understanding. But we used to refer to it falsely as the objective reality of qualitative beings

4. Linguistic Ascent and the Dialectic

We pass from a statement which turns out contradictory to the metalinguistic reflection that such a statement has been made. There is a subjective turn from the naive assertion of the statement's truth to the reflective assertion that a contradictory assertion has been made. The source of contradiction is the abstractive, absolutizing understanding. Stubborn persistence in the world of contradictory assertions which do not yield to negation of the negation occasions an equally persistent definition of the absolute by such assertions.

We have reached the implicit absolutization of dialectical thinking itself. Dialectical thinking begins to think itself by thinking that point where in its objective unfolding it dysfunctions. One is normally unaware of one's liver unless it fails to operate properly. Dialectical thinking is unaware of abstraction and absolutization until they cease to function in a fluid process of dialectical indirect proof. Abstraction and absolutization of things call attention to dialectical thinking by their antidialectical rigidity in the world.

If "things" exist, and if as such they are contradictory, thinking has contradictorily absolutized them in their relativity. Given anything said to be contradictory, it is not contradictory if it exists; rather, thinking falsely asserts it to be so. Apparent ontological contradiction is reduced to logical contradiction. If there are "square circles," someone persistently says so, and we, too, may humor the person by saying the same. If there is an infinite which excludes contradictory entities, it is really a logical infinite which excludes the contradictory assumption of such entities. An infinite which excludes contradictory discourse itself contains consistent logical discourse. It is a logical (self-consistent) propositional infinite.

Definition of the absolute as an ontologically false infinite was plausible only as excluding ontologically contradictory things from the absolute. But now, after the above subjective turn, the exclusion of contradictory things would only be the exclusion of contradictory assumptions. Such assumptions, unlike what is ontologically contradiction, occur. The necessity of the exclusion seems completely to vanish.

That the absolute is merely a nonfinite (infinite, noncontradictory) discourse absolutized as a term by itself refutes itself. An infinite system of true propositions free of logical contradiction (a comprehensive consistent system of knowledge) is approached by logically contradictory statements in the world. In part by such contradiction in the history of knowledge, such science is gradually, dialectically constructed. The systematic truth is essentially a result.[31]

Such a system is not limited by contradictory things, but by contradictory judgments made by abstractive thinking. Given any complete science which is not contradictory, dialectical thought supposes a contradictory statement which indirectly helps prove that science.

Reference to contradictory beings, far from failing as feared, succeeds as reference to beings under contradictory descriptions imposed by abstractive thought. But if the finite is a logical rather than ontological finite, the correlative infinite is a logical infinite. The infinite is a consistent process of thinking which, to be truly infinite, must include the logical finite. It must include contradictory judgment. But consistent logical discourse which includes contradictory judgment is indirect proof. The true infinite must consist in indirect proof. The absolute is not simply contradiction-free comprehensive Aristotelian scientific discourse. It is not a false propositional infinite.

There is a non-Aristotelian propositional infinite, which does not transcend the finite. The relativity of the finite to the false infinite was expressed by saying that, because the finite was contradictory, the absolute is nonfinite. Because by the law of noncontradiction the absolute is not what ontologically cannot be, it is what ontologically can be. Because it is not ontologically contradictory, it is what is ontologically noncontradictory.

What is ontologically noncontradictory is admittedly not relative to what is ontologically contradictory. Yet what is propositionally contradictory may be relative to what is not. What is propositionally noncontradictory is now understood concretely as embracing the propositional contradiction of indirect proof, not abstractly as relative to an external such contradiction. The propositionally contradictory infinite limited by the finite is limited by the logical finite of propositional contradiction. Therefore, the noncontradictory propositional infinite results in a true logical infinite of consistent dialectical discourse embracing an inconsistent assumption.

The assumption that there are square circles limits any logical discourse assumed to be free of contradictory assumptions. But the new definition of the absolute at the end of the dialectic of qualitative being is that the absolute incorporates contradictory assumptions into an expanded concept what is coherent.

The relativity of the finite to this new propositional infinite, the true infinite, may be expressed by saying that, given any proposition which generates a contradiction and which is thus "finite," the noncontradictory, nonfinite negation of it is indirectly provable with the help of that proposition itself. We say "provable" rather than "proved" because a valid proof can exist without anyone finding the proof. The premises which logically imply a conclusion do not imply that the conclusion will be drawn.

We may also move from the logical or propositional infinite to the logical finite. If a noncontradictory proposition has been asserted by the mediation of dialectical thinking, there is some contradiction-generating assumption which led to its assertion by indirect proof.

The above paragraphs are proposed as a rational reconstruction of the following passage, in which Hegel himself identifies the true infinite with the posited, asserted negation of the negation resulting from the dialectic:

> The infinite is the negation of the negation, affirmation, being which has restored itself out of limitedness. The infinite *is*, and more intensely so than the first immediate being; it is the true being, the elevation above limitation. At the name of the infinite, the heart and mind light up, for in the infinite the spirit is not merely abstractly present to itself, but rises to its own self, to the light of its thinking, of its universality, of its freedom. The notion of the infinite as it first presents itself is this, that determinate being in its being-in-itself determines itself as finite [contradictory] and transcends the limitation. It is the very nature of the finite to transcend itself, to negate its negation and to become infinite. Thus the [true] infinite does not stand as something finished and complete above or superior to the finite, as if the finite had an enduring being *apart from* or *subordinate* to the infinite [e.g., as in classical theism]. Neither do *we* only, as subjective reason, pass beyond the finite into the infinite; as when we say that the infinite is the Notion of reason and that through reason we rise superior to temporal things, though we let this happen without prejudice to the finite which is in no way affected by this [escapist] exaltation, an exaltation which remains external to it. But the finite itself in being raised to the infinite is in no sense acted on by an alien force; on the contrary, it is its nature to be related to itself as limitation,—both limitation as such and as an ought—and [by a form of indirect proof negating the contradictory absolutization of what is relative] to transcend the same.[32]

One question we have not discussed is whether dialectical thinking eventuating in negation of the negation, which clearly emerges in a process, is a "quality." A quality for Hegel is immediate, intuitively given. But immediacy itself may not be immediate. It may be circuitously constructed. An expert can encompass a vast subject matter in an immediate glance, where this is impossible for a neophyte. The process of dialectical development, like the routine of driving home every day from work for an employee, becomes immediate for the experienced speculative philosopher. The process as a apparently long-lasting succession becomes a static and immediately intuited routine. Yet such thinking in all its concrete twists and turns, especially when it is blocked at absolutization of the finite, remains a surprising and long-enduring process, not a quality.

We return in conclusion to the question as to whether the true infinite is found as early as Anaximander. Simplicus, as well as Theophrastos quoted by Burnet above, also gives us the one reliable fragment remaining from Anaximander:

> Anaximander . . . said that the principle and element of existing things was the *aperion* [indefinite, or infinite], being the first to introduce this name of the material principle. He says that it is neither water nor any other of the so-called elements, but some other *apeiron* nature, from which come into being all the heavens and the worlds in them. And the source of coming-to-be for existing things is that into which destruction, too, happens.[33]

For Hegel to invoke Anaximander in the lectures on the history of philosophy as source of the true infinite is a hardy hypothesis. Certainly in the history of philosophy, where pure being is clearly associated with Parmenides, the "true infinite" verbally bears the mark of Hegel himself more than Anaximander. This is especially true in light of the contrast between the true and false infinite, which depends on a contrast of Greeks and Hebrews not available to Anaximander.

Yet the association between the true infinite and Anaximander is not without basis, especially if we view the logic of being generally as the logic of Presocratic philosophy. Recapitulating, tradition says that Anaximander invented the concept of the "infinite" and the identification of the infinite with the divine. His infinite is distinguished from water, air, or any finite "element" that certain other philosophers identified with the absolute. If the absolute were water, it could not be water in any determinate sense. The infinite is asserted to avoid logical contradiction. Thirdly, he held that finite things or elements like fire, water, and air emerged out of the infinite and returned to it. His infinite is thus not a transcendent one; it includes the finite.

The one clear respect in which Hegel does not merely develop but apparently contradicts Anaximander is, as we have noted, that tradition interprets Anaximander in a materialistic sense. Aristotle viewed Anaximander as anticipating his own concept of primary matter.

Yet Hegel in the logic of essence will reduce any radical dualism of matter and thought to differences of description, i.e., to the difference between describing something as it is in its potentiality or in itself and as it is actually or for itself.[34] We already find an anticipation of his effort to close the gap between matter and thought in the next chapter, where we take up atomism.

4

Classical Atomism:
Thought Thinking Itself
Multiplied

The last three chapters have reconstructed the logic of qualitative being up to being-for-self. In Aristotelian terms, we understand "being-for-self" as thought thinking itself. Yet for Aristotle thought thinking itself does not define the absolute, since it is relative to the material world. Being-for-self has a more primitive connection to the absolute defined as the infinite of Anaximander in the last chapter.

The present chapter concludes the logic of being in the narrow qualitative sense. It prepares the transition from the logic of qualitative being to that of "quantitative being." If the Hegelian "logic of quantity" is understood in a strict sense, it is the logic of pure immaterial quantity, and of the quantitative infinite—see book 1, section 2: Magnitude (Quantity). In this sense, the logic of quantity is treated in the next chapter. Yet, in a broader sense, the logic of quantitative being includes the logic of many atomistic ones preceding the logic of quantity in the narrow sense. Hegel notes that being-for-self, which precedes atomism, is "quality completed."[1] In this broader sense the logic of quantity also includes the Pythagorean logic of the quantitative measures and ratios of qualitative units, which is subsequent to the strict logic of pure quantity.

The subject of this chapter is, historically, atomism's repeated replication of being-for-self, of the one of ancient philosophy in its full development. It is the quantitative self-replication of being-for-self, and the breakdown of the absolute's self-definition as a *single* qualitative being-for-self. The atomism constructed in Hegel's *Logic* really turns out to be an idealistic monadology. The one it multiplies is a being-for-self whose "nearest example" is self-consciousness. Whereas the atomists of history identified the soul with a compound of atoms and denied the immortality of the soul, Hegel's atomist in the *Logic*, an immediate disciple of the Eleatics like Leucippus, seems to have begun by identifying with the Parmenidean one. But, unable to sacrifice the world of the external senses, he resorted to seeking immortality by an indefinite reiteration of the one.

The *Logic*, we see, is not a history of philosophy. Here it is an ideal reconstruction of how atomism would have proceeded if it had been conscious of the monadological implications of the many ones brought out by Presocratic monists who identified the one with being-for-self, thought thinking itself. Atomism in its rational form is a Leibnizian cosmology without a theistic God to distinguish externally the mutually exclusive perspectives of the many ones.[2] The monads truly conceived have in themselves being for one another as well as being each for themselves. They are intrinsically intersubjective. But "the atomistic philosophy does not possess the Notion of ideality; it does not grasp the one as an ideal being, that is, as containing *within itself* the two [indispensable] moments of being-for-self and being-for-it [for the other], but only a simple, dry, real being-for-self."[3]

1. The Collapse of Being-for-Self

Being-for-self is thought thinking itself in thinking the finite object. The finite object, referred to under a contradictory description, is the other which infinite thought, clinging to logical consistency, negates. Yet thought is internally related to the finite object through its very negation of it. We have seen in the last chapter how, by negation of the negation, infinite thought subsequently expands to englobe that object.

But, having constituted itself in this expanded form, being-for-self now contracts into a form of thought thinking itself empty of objective content. The objective content of being-for-self is expelled outside it: "The one is the simple self-relation of being-for-self in which its moments have collapsed in themselves and in which, consequently, being-for-self has the form of immediacy, and its moments therefore now have a determinate being."[4]

To say that its internal moments have become immediate determinate being means that they are no longer recognized as internal; they are projected outside the original being-for-self, since the latter has become internally undifferentiated. The internal content of being-for-self is projected beyond itself, onto an excluded atomic other. Being-for-itself abstracts itself from its moments, which are projected outside itself as other determinate beings. Our task in this chapter is to explain and evaluate the transition from the one of Presocratic cosmology to the many mutually exclusive atoms of classical atomism. This transition, generally recognized by historians of ancient philosophy, is reconstructed in Hegel's *Logic.*

The emergence of this abstract being-for-self contrasts with the emergence of abstract Parmenidean being at the beginning of the dialectic of being. The abstraction of Parmenidean being at the onset of the dialectic was from a context of determinations which remained still unabstracted. We may call this "first abstraction." The abstraction of Parmenidean being implies no projection of already abstracted internal determinations outside itself. Determinations not discovered and abstracted cannot yet be projected.

The abstraction in the transition from one to many beings-for-self is different. We shall call it "second abstraction." It is abstraction from a context of determinations in being-for-self which are themselves already explicitly abstracted. Abstraction no longer supposes obliviousness to such determinations. It is the willful exclusion of what is clearly present within the dialectically constructed concrete totality of being-for-self.

Even if what is clearly present to mind cannot be denied, its presence within oneself may be denied: it may be projected outside oneself onto another. Projection is a self-defense against what is noted but unaccepted in oneself. The Freudian language of repression, defense mechanisms, and projection is possibly the best way of making motivational sense of the transition from one being-for-self to many, which has made little sense to even excellent commentators.[5]

A Parmenidean comes to define indeterminate being, the one, as determinate because he or she is deductively obliged to do so. Thought comes to see the one as one among many because projection of the one on external determinate being is a way of finding the one again in what appeared to be alien to it. The atomist salvages something of his or her identity in an alien world.

Being-for-self is the qualitatively true infinite. But it is not the absolutely true infinite. It approaches a true definition of the absolute as closely as is possible within the categories of qualitative being—which are immediately given, even if after a dialectical construction. Hegel describes being-for-self as an infinity "which is still abstract,"[6] as an infinity which has "a determinateness which is still quite qualitative."[7] "Something is for itself insofar as it transcends otherness."[8] Being-for-self, at its present limited qualitative stage, is thus weighed down by an unassimilated otherness at which it balks. It embraces reference to a contingent determinate being which has not been dialectically deduced.

Thought does not yet realize—as it will begin to learn in book 2 of the *Logic*—that particular contingent nondeducible determinations are absolutely necessary and deducible in general within the genuinely and absolutely true infinite. Being-for-self, illustrated by self-consciousness in contrast to what is other than the self, here becomes fixated on the absolutization of an abstract self, hence on a merely purported "true" infinite: "Self-consciousness . . . is being-for-self as consummated and *posited*. . . . Self-consciousness is thus the nearest example of the presence of [the] infinity [of qualitative being]; granted of an infinity which is still abstract, yet which, at the same time, is a very different concrete determination from [the even more abstract] being-for-self in general."[9]

Being-for-self seeks to maintain its infinity by abstracting itself from the alien content which remains within it. The unassimilated and contingent otherness which being-for-itself finds within itself is disavowed as incompatible with the infinite character of being-for-self: "The [internal] *moments* of being-for-self have collapsed into the *undifferentiatedness* which is immediacy of being, but an *immediacy* which is based on the negating which is posited as its determination."[10]

What is disavowed does not vanish, but is attributed to some other being-for-self:

> The *ideality* of being-for-self as a totality [of internal ideal determinations]
> thus reverts, in the first place, to [the independent] *reality* [of external
> and separate determinations] and that too in its most fixed, abstract form,
> as the [internally collapsed] *one* . . . the unity of the one with itself is
> reduced to a *relation*, and as a *positive* unity it is a negation of its own self as
> *other, exclusion* of the one as other from itself, from the one.[11]

Postulation of another being-for-self like the first as the recipient of disavowed attributes external to the first's own identity reinforces a fixation on abstract being-for-self, which otherwise might yield to negation by its other. The logic of many ones, despite the approach of quantity, thus remains within that of the "true" qualitative infinite of being-for-self. It operates in the orbit of abstract being-for-self.

The logic of atomism (Leucippus), quantity (early Pythagoras),[12] and proportion or "measure"[13] all presuppose this same being-for-self as the *principle* of the absolute. The definition of the absolute does not remain being-for-self, but it go through a series of reiterations and orderings of instances of being-for-self.

Projection is crucial to the development beyond merely one being-for-self. It is a psychosocial mechanism leading to many ones. The appeal of many ones, of a crowd, is that they preserve the illusion of the one's true infinity despite unassimilated alien determinations. The concept of being the qualitatively true infinite remains throughout to define the principle or elementary unit of the absolute.

Hegel's account of the erasure and contraction of being-for-self into the abstract ego, the one, expresses thought's will to self-abstraction apart any encompassing concrete whole. This perversely egotistic will proves indispensable to the transition to many exclusive ones:

> Self-subsistence pushed to the point of the one as a being-for-self is abstract, formal, and destroys itself. It is the supreme, most stubborn error, which takes itself for the highest truth, manifested in more concrete forms as abstract freedom, pure ego, and, further, as Evil. It is that freedom which so misapprehends itself as to place its essence in this abstraction, and flatters itself that in thus being with itself it possesses itself in its purity. . . . The [subsequent] reconciliation . . . is only the letting go of the negativity of its being-for-Self in place of holding fast to it.[14]

Self-abstraction and self-separation lead, by the previous classical dialectic of being, to self-surrender and self-reconciliation with the other. But the fixation on the original one now excludes such self-surrender. The original one is projected on the other, which appears as the same one multiplied.

2. Transition from the One to the Many: A Logical Analysis

At the level of formal logic, this self-separation is a further contradictory assumption in an inferentially necessary process of indirect proof. The category of many ones does not assume the absolute as a single separate ego, but as an aggregate of egos each assumed to be abstract. In the last chapter being-for-self was theologically absolutized. This definition of the absolute is now deconstructed. Qualitative being-for-self encounters an alien world of objective determinations, which limits it.

Being-for-self is maintained, but not as the definition of the absolute. The original being-for-self excludes a limiting factor from itself and attributes it to a second equally finite being-for-self. This second being-for-self is assumed to exist as a kindred, tolerable limit upon the first.

There is a second being-for-self. But, given any first being-for-self, the second cannot be deduced, is not logically necessary. The second is asserted, so to speak, for comfort. Given the first one (or being-for-self), the second is contingent.

Yet the very contingency of different ones relative to one another is the reality of the many. To deduce this reality is not to deduce real other ones; rather, it is to deduce the non-necessity of such ones assuming the reality of the first one. The other ones can be asserted, but not deduced.

The transition from the one to the many is not an impossible deduction of other contingent instances of oneness; it is the deduction of this very contingency of merely asserted other ones. The assertion of many ones is deduced as a conjunction of the original real one and the necessary contingency of further asserted ones.

The successor definition to the previous definition of the absolute as being-for-self defines the absolute as an aggregate of ones or beings-for-self which are mutually exclusive. Being-for-self is no longer the being-for-self, but is a being-for-self.[15] There is no necessarily single "absolute instance" of qualitative being-for-self: being-for-self is freed from necessary absolutization as an instance by contingent alternate instances. Through the relation of mutual exclusion between beings-for-self, each is also freed from absolutization as a monadic term. And through the contingent properties that each being-for-self projects onto others it is likewise freed from the absolutization of its defining predicate: each being-for-self receives from the others properties beyond mere abstract being-for-self. The absolute is the collection of all beings-for-self. This collection includes at the limit one contingent one; if it contains two, neither logically implies the existence of the other.

The question must still be asked: What, beyond a radically contingent freedom of will, explains the "evil will" that abstracts from its own concrete content—which it projects outside itself onto a contingent alternative one? The innocence of the original abstraction of pure being at the start of the *Logic* is due to the fact that dialectical thought at its onset had not yet abstracted anything else. The present abstraction of the abstract one is not so blameless, since it abstracts from determinations which have already been dialectically constructed. If in truth the ego knows that it is what it is only through its world, its self-abstraction from the world is a knowing and deliberate plunge into falsehood.

Such willful abstraction and self-separation is an egotism—a fixation on the abstract ego which, in terms of religious representation, defines the Fall. It is moved by the lure of rebellion: an individual will rebels against the all-embracing universal will. The concretely universal will reconciles itself to all that it contains. The exclusive individual will, dominated by the abstractive understanding, repudiates part of its content.

3. The Hebrew Fall and Ancient Greek Materialism

It is again surprising from a historical perspective how divergent Hebrew and Greek concepts are brought together in the same dialectic in the *Logic.* The Hebrew Fall is suggested as the key to the dialectical construction of Greek atomism. The materialist view of the world as an aggregate of material points purportedly follows from a moral lapse. Confronting an alien, purely physical world is the cosmological price for an inward curvature of the soul.[16]

Empirical and dialectical history seem to diverge here. Atomistic philosophy arose in Greek history, while in the *Logic* the Biblical Fall lies at its origin. In fact the *Logic* depends at most on an affinity between classical materialism and egotism in a sense broader than the Hebrew sense. Being-for-self as the absolute abstracts itself from the knowable contingent content of the world, and the world left behind appears wholly alien to it.

At the limit of projection, God, in his utter transcendence—the absolute as the original being-for-self—is reduced to nothing, and the absolute is defined empirically as matter: "For Empiricism, what is true is quite generally what is external, and even if it concedes something supersensible, no cognition of it is supposed to be possible. We have to confine ourselves to what belongs to perception. The full working out of this principle, however, has produced what was later called 'Materialism.' "[17]

To recapitulate the position we have reached, the disowned objective content of thought thinking itself (being-for-self) reduced to the bare ego reappears as limiting it from the outside. The infinite thinking self then seeks to overcome its apparent external limit by projecting itself onto the other, replicating in it its own infinity.

Abstract thought thinking itself, fleeing alienation in the world, forms the logical concept of the many. "The plurality of ones is infinity as a contradiction which unconstrainedly produces itself."[18] The misery of contradiction enjoys company. Infinite being-for-self in its "explication"[19] is contradictorily acknowledged to be finite. The apparently alien other repudiated by a first abstract being-for-self is ascribed to a second.

Further selves or ones are not deduced but posited.[20] In Biblical language they are "created." An inference within the dialectic of determinate being—e.g., what is day is not night—is deductive. If something is determinately day, we infer that it is not night. For to be day is, necessarily, not to be night.

However, there is no possible deductive inference from the proposition that an abstract being-for-self exists to the proposition that there also exists an excluded second abstract being-for-self. Day is internally related to night, and is totally indeterminate without this negative determination. But infinite being-for-self is as such self-determined, not externally determined by a second being-for-self.

If two beings-for-self were internally related as day and night, being-for-self would be determinate like day. And then it would not be infinite. The exclusion or "repulsion"[21] of a second being-for-self by a first is not deductively warranted by any internal relation between them as beings-for-self. It is posited out of a need to escape alienation, but without a deductive ground.

Two atomic beings-for-self are qualitatively indiscernible—except that the first being-for-self excludes some alien element, which it projects upon the second. This distinction prevents the many beings-for-self from being wholly indifferent and external to one another. It retains them in the domain of qualitative limitation as an essentially internal limitation. It refutes the true infinity of atomic being-for-self, which is only the qualitative true infinite.

Truly quantitative being, by contrast to exclusive beings-for-self, is (as we see in the next chapter) determined in totally external fashion by a "limit which is no a limit."[22] Quantity in the restricted sense of counting has been present in the *Logic* since infinite progress of alternate qualities was introduced in the dialectic of determinate being.[23] But quantity is not pure quantity until what is counted are not exclusive qualitative beings or even self-consciousnesses, but qualitatively identical numerical ones. To the infinite progress of many finite beings is now added—in the logic of quantitative being taken broadly—that of many beings-for-self and atoms, and only then that of many qualitatively undifferentiated ones.

4. Four Faces of the One

We noted that being-for-self has its readiest concrete example in self-consciousness.[24] The atomic unit of matter[25] and the mathematical one[26] emerge as further determinations or descriptions of being-for-self. The difference between (1) the one as pure being-for-self (both the initial concrete identity of subject and object and the subsequent pure subject abstracted apart from the projected object); (2) the one as atom (the material one); and (3) the one as quantitative unit is this: the many (potentially self-conscious) beings-for-self and atoms all exclude one another and thus still determine one another negatively and qualitatively. Mathematical ones, on the other hand, coincide with one another precisely through this mutual exclusion, and thus are completely identical in quality: "Quantity is sublated [transcended] being-for-self; the repelling one which related itself only negatively to the excluded one, having passed over into relation to it, treats the other as identical with itself, and in doing so has lost its determination: being-for-self has passed over into attraction."[27]

Consciousness is a contrast effect. Abstract self-consciousnesses differ qualitatively through mutual repulsion, while mathematical ones differ only numerically. Regarding atomistic philosophy, we read that "the repulsion which shows itself in the concept of the One was assumed to be its [the absolute's] fundamental force."[28]

A distinction is made between "first repulsion" and "second repulsion." First repulsion is the original constitution and projection[29] of another being-for-self, a means of conjuring up company in an apparently alien universe—through a world whose alien character results from one's own choice in defining oneself in abstraction from it. Second repulsion is the mutual repulsion of already constituted ones.

The "mutual repelling"[30] of abstract self-consciousnesses, unlike that of atoms, is social, competitive, based on envy: two abstract egos cannot have the same honors, or own the same private property. Competition, whether atomistic competition for places or social competition for honors, upsets the repose of solitary being-for-self. The mutual repulsion of atoms, materialized beings-for-self, is spatial. Atoms cannot occupy the same place at the same time.

In passing from qualitatively distinct ones to ones whose distinction is purely quantitative or numerical, the distinction of ones eclipses all differences in qualitative determinations. Instead of excluding one another in mutual differentiation, ones are now entirely indifferent to one another.[31] They pass continuously into one another. "Quality is the first, immediate determinateness; quantity is such determinateness which has become indifferent to being, a limit which is just as much no limit, . . . a repulsion of many ones which is directly the non-repulsion, the continuity of them."[32]

Ones whose distinction is merely numerical contravene Leibniz's law that nothing can be numerically distinct without being qualitatively distinct. But the violation is only apparent. The identity of indiscernibles is assumed in dialectical logic. There is no secret difference of things unexpressed in their properties. This law Hegel calls the "principle of diversity":

We are told that on one occasion Leibniz propounded the principle of diversity when he was at court; and the ladies and gentlemen who were strolling in the garden tried to find two leaves that could not be distinguished from one another, in order, by exhibiting them, to refute the philosopher's law of thought. . . . But with regard to Leibniz's principle it must be noted that being distinct must not be understood as external and indifferent diversity, but as inner distinction [*Unterschied an sich*], and that to be distinct pertains to things in themselves.[33]

It is not in themselves, but only falsely and for abstract thought, that purely numerical ones exist as quantitatively but not qualitatively distinct. A purely quantitative distinction of ones is merely posited, not objective in the ones themselves. A purely quantitative distinction of ones would be gratuitous, ungrounded in any discernibility of qualitative properties. Purely numerical distinctions asserted in the sphere of quantity mark the incoherence of a purely quantitative aggregate; they do not indict the identity of indiscernibles. Quantity is an ontologically hallow castle in thin air. Yet the gratuitousness of purely quantitative distinctions is not apparent to speculative thought until the logic of quantity has been left behind for that of essence—from which the above quote is taken.

The transition from quality to quantity supposes an underlying identity of reference through a gradual erasure of descriptive differences. Four descriptions of the one—hence four stages in this transition—have been distinguished: (1) the concrete presocial psychological (self-thinking) one (original being-for-self); (2) the abstract presocial psychological one (abstract ego, one); (3) the purely material one (atom); and (4) the purely mathematical one (neither psychological nor material). To these four faces of the one a fifth will be added in the course of the dialectic. Historically it is found in Pythagoras.

5. Pythagoras and the Fifth Face of the One

Purely mathematical ones—numerically distinct and yet qualitatively indistinguishable—either are not really distinct, or are misdescribed as distinguished merely quantitatively. Insofar as the identity of psychological being-for-self with the material one and with the mathematical one is maintained underneath the incompatible descriptive differences by which we refer to them, the question of the true description of the one is posed. Its true nature turns out not to consist in being discernible from other ones merely by excluding them like the atom. Nor is it to be totally indiscernible from them like the purely mathematical one. Rather, it is to be discernible from them in the manner of a soul, by microcosmically including its relationship to them. As a soul, each one is a system of perspectives perceived from a sympathetic dominant perspective. Truly described, the psychological one, "being-for-self," is a not a presocial monad. A Leibnizian monad, being windowless, has no internal relationship even of exclusion to any other monad. The one truly described is rather a soul, capable of sympathetically internalizing within itself the perspectives of other souls in the world soul:

> They [i.e., monads, unlike souls as social selves] are not in themselves others to one another; the being-for-self is kept pure, and is free of the accompaniment of any real being. But herein, too, lies the inadequacy of this [Leibnizian] system. . . . If it is a third term [God] which posits their otherness, it is also a third which sublates [dialectically transcends] it; but this entire movement which gives them their ideality falls outside them [instead of within them as in the case of social or microcosmic souls].[34]

The one, truly described, is social: it represents other selves by distinguishing them from itself as from one another, and by identifying with them sympathetically within its own dominant perspective, thus transcending the fact of their being other. The one truly described is the social psychological one. This is the one under a fifth description. The *Encyclopaedia* simply calls it the "soul." As a soul it exists on the level of feeling, but on this basis the thinking subject will arise:

> The soul universal, described, it may be, as the *anima mundi*, a world-soul, must not be fixed on that account as a single subject; it is rather the universal substance which has its actual truth only in individuals and single subjects. . . . The soul, when contrasted with the macrocosm of nature, as a whole, can be described as a microcosm into which the former is compressed, thereby removing its asunderness. . . . While still a "substance" (i.e., a physical soul) the mind takes part in the general planetary life, feels the difference of climates, the changes of the seasons, and the periods of the day, etc. This life of nature for the main shows itself only in occasional strain or disturbance of mental tone. In recent times a good deal has been said of the cosmical, sidereal, and telluric life of man. In such sympathy with nature the animals essentially live.[35]

Admittedly this quote is from the philosophy of spirit, not the logic. The one as a social self cannot be well described by either the logic of quality eventuating in the category of asocial being-for-self, or by that of undifferentiated quantitative ones. It will be described more fully in the logic of the concept (self-concept, *Begriff*). This true one is a soul which identifies sympathetically with the constant novelty of the cosmic environment, under ever new astral, climatic, seasonal, and historical descriptions.

The soul conceived in terms of both cosmic sympathy and the mathematical one is Pythagorean. Aristotle suggests that Pythagoras issued two versions of his philosophy, the early Pythagoras (or Pythagoreans) defining reality as number and the later Pythagoras defining it as measure or proportion. Aristotle notes that "the Pythagoreans . . . were the first to advance this study [mathematics], and having been brought up in it they thought its principles were the principles of all things: [the absolute is number]."[36] But since the sensory world does not appear to be number, the Pythagoreans passed on to a revised and more daring version of their definition of the absolute, integrating sensory quality with quantity. Aristotle continues: "Since . . . in numbers there seemed to see many resemblances to the [sensory] things that exist and come into being, . . . they supposed the elements of numbers to be the elements of all things, and the whole heaven to be a musical scale and a number [the absolute as measure]."[37]

In attempting to construe reality mathematically, Pythagoras in the second version of his philosophy substituted a metaphysical use of applied mathematics for theoretical mathematics. The absolute is no longer conceived as purely numerical ones, but as specific ratios of qualitative ones, each ratio defining a qualitative determination of the given world, such as water.

Yet the Pythagorean one out of which ratios and measures of ones are constructed is not purely quantitative or mathematical. The original Pythagorean one is itself a ratio of the limited and unlimited. There is a resemblance here, perhaps too close to be accidental, to the way being-for-self is constituted out of the relation of the qualitative finite and the infinite. For Pythagoras, the essence of the one is that of the soul—what Simmias, describing the soul in the *Phaedo*, considered a "harmony" of opposites.[38] The Pythagorean principle of the unlimited is Anaximenes's airy world-soul which is breathed in by the body of the cosmos, the limited. The cosmos is ensouled by the breath of soul life. The individual soul is also a proportion of the limited and the unlimited. It is a microcosm of the macrocosmic world-soul. The Pythagorean one has quantitative aspects: it can be repeated and then counted. Yet it is not a purely quantitative concept. It also has qualitative determinations, namely, variable relations of the limit (finite) and unlimited (infinite), being-for-self. To say that it is a purely quantitative one would mean that it is qualitatively identical to—and thus at once indifferent to—other ones which may be externally juxtaposed to it. But without at least qualitative differences of emphasis between the ones, cosmic sympathy makes no sense as a means of Pythagorean assimilation to the cosmos.

6. Atomism

Being-for-self directly precedes, in the *Logic*, definition of the absolute by classical atomism. Thought forms the concept of the atom by reiterating itself and projecting itself onto the objective other, which it excludes from its own abstract being-for-self.

Atomistic materialism for Hegel thus has a latent psychological content. His account of atomism agrees in essential respects with Aristotle's. Atomism explains the sensory world other than abstract being-for-self by an absolute which is only being-for-self reiterated, abstractly put nothing but reiteration of the one of Parmenides. This one was from the start implicitly being-for-self insofar as thinking and the thing for the sake of which we think are the same for Parmenides.[39] Aristotle's account of atomism reads as follows:

> Leucippus . . . thought he had a theory which harmonized with sense-perception and would not abolish either coming-to-be and passing-away or motion and the multiplicity of things. He made these concessions to the facts of experience: on the other hand, he conceded to the Monists [to those who invented the One] that there could be no motion without a void. . . . for what "is" in the strict sense of the term is an absolute *plenum*. This *plenum*, however, is not "one": on the contrary, it is a "many" infinite in number.[40]

In sum, the atoms of classical materialism are the Presocratic one multiplied. But the Presocratic one, we know, is implicitly infinite self-thinking thought, embracing both the thought of the philosopher and the cosmos which is thought. The atom is being-for-self, hence a thought.[41] Thales's water, Anaximenes's air, Anaximander's infinite are also implicitly being-for-self. They are "thought [*Gedanke*] in which everything [finite] is [dialectically] resolved [*aufgelöst*, dissolved] and comprehended."[42] They are "true and infinite being" in disguise.[43] They are "soul" and "consciousness."[44]

The atomist seeks to overcome the phenomenal world's apparent negation of the absolute as abstract being-for-self by construing the world as the manifestation of many centers of such being-for-self. Abstract being-for-self, no longer limited by the phenomenal world, is limited only by other exclusive beings-for-self. These other abstract beings-for-self, not deduced, are postulated to reduce what is apparently other than being-for-self to manifestations of being-for-self in other instances.

If Hegel's account is adopted, the atom is an explanatory projection of abstract being-for-self. The multiplication of ones, following being-for-self's projection of its own internal content, maintains the universality of being-for-self in the face of any contrary appearances. Atomism derives "the infinite variety of the world from this simple antithesis [of the One and the Void]."[45]

Concrete being-for-self, thought thinking itself, becomes the atom first through contraction into abstract being-for-self, and second through self-projection onto the internal material limit of abstract being-for-self. In materialism a description in fact true of the thinking subject is attributed to its material object, and denied of the vanishingly abstract immaterial subject. The soul as such is denied, but the units of matter inherit its essential characteristics of immortality and indivisibility.

The identity and difference of atoms consist in their mutual repulsion and attraction. Two atoms exclude one another, limit one another's forward motion. But since in such mutual exclusion each does to the other what the other does to it, each coincides with the other, thus shedding the appearance of being qualitatively different in this respect. They become purely quantitative ones by the exclusive abstraction of their shared qualities. Thus, in the Hobbesian social atomism,[46] which multiplies abstract being-for-self much like metaphysical atomism, the state of nature is not merely a war of all against all. It is also a society in which each member can understand and identify with other members in a kind of fraternity of rogues. Their universal mutual hostility becomes a bond. The atomistic worldview yields temporarily to the illusion of a quantitative reiteration of the same experience.

We have noted that the identity of the soul with the atom is supported by characteristics they share: they are both indivisible, both immortal. Yet, in other respects they have different properties: the soul feels and thinks, the atom is insensate. The ancient atomists consciously considered the soul to be a mortal composite of atoms—despite the fact that the Eleatic theory of the one from which the concept of the atom is derived holds that "thinking and the thing for the sake of which we think are the same."[47] Burnet considers the multiplication of the Parmenidean one by the atomists to be "the most important point in the history of early Greek philosophy."[48] Yet, when all is said, the upshot of Hegel's view—namely, that the early atomists were latent monadologists—may seem more provocative than historically founded.

Leibniz argued in the *Monadology*[49] that, since what is physical ("composite") can be infinitely divided, the atom's indivisibility or oneness is possible only if it is not physical but soul-like. Hegel cites Leibniz as upholding the concept of being-for-self—more particularly the initial concrete but presocial concept of being-for-self, in which the self's nonsocial other (limit) is included as an ideal moment of itself.[50] Materialistic atomism is an abstract metaphysics of being-for-self in which the self suppresses its own nonsocial other and projects it outside itself: "The ideating being, the monad, of Leibniz is essentially ideal. Ideation is a being-for-self in which the determinatenesses are not limits, and consequently not a determinate being, but only moments. . . . The one in this form of determinate being is the stage of the category which made its appearance with the ancients as the atomistic principle."[51]

Whereas direct progress toward truth would lead from solitary Leibnizian being-for-self ever more concretely to social Pythagorean being-for-self, the dialectic of the *Logic* proceeds from Leibnizian being-for-self to the more abstract or impoverished being-for-self of the atom, and finally of the pure quantitative one. This two-stage progressive impoverishment is the clearest expression of the abstractive understanding, division, and the Fall. The truth is approached indirectly via its extreme opposite.

To argue that, since the concept of the atom was historically formed out of the idealistic concept of being-for-self, atomism viewed as materialistic is false would be a kind of genetic fallacy. The atom may resemble being-for-self, even be suggested by it, and yet not be compatible with it. Automobiles were suggested by carriages, but are not carriages. Classical atomism is materialistic in intent even if the concept of the atom was derived from the more concrete concept of the one as pure self-consciousness.

Yet, it is possible that the concept of the atom is not only abstracted from a Presocratic animistic concept of being-for-self, but also preserves traces of its nonmaterialistic origin, and that it can be made coherent only by resolving matter back into idealistic being-for-self. If so, there is no genetic fallacy—and no mere ahistorical provocation—in the suggested argument against materialism. A Hegelian interpreter would simply distinguish between the latent idealistic content and manifest materialist intention of atomistic discourse.

The atomist thus appears as a latent pluralistic idealist. The manyness of repeated self-thinking beings-for-self desensitizes us to the internal qualitative self-determination of a single being-for-self in the original concept of the true infinite as solitary being-for-self. The concrete dialectical process of the true infinite—abbreviated as "the one"—congeals, "collapses,"[52] sinks into a static and brittle subject of "unyielding rigidity."[53] Thought explains atomistically the immediate qualitative variety of the world by abstracting from the internal qualitative nature of each of the atoms. It thinks only their plurality, position, motion. Yet, inquiry into atoms (rather than into the world by means of atoms) recovers the fact that they are projections of thought's own being-for-self:

> In being-for-self the determination of *ideality* has entered. *Being-there*, taken at first only according to its being or its affirmation, has *reality*: and hence finitude, too, is under the determination of reality at first. But the truth of the finite is rather its *ideality*. . . . This ideality of the finite is the most important proposition of philosophy, and for that reason every genuine philosophy is *idealism*.[54] . . The most familiar example of being-for-self is the "I." We know ourselves to be beings who are there, first of all distinct from other such beings, and related to them. But, secondly, we also know that this expanse of being-there is, so to speak, focused into the simple form of being-for-self.[55] . . . The atomistic philosophy is the standpoint from which the Absolute determines itself as being-for-self, as One, and as many Ones.[56] . . . Since atomism is still held in high esteem nowadays among those natural scientists who do not want anything to do with metaphysics, it should be remembered in this connection that we do not escape metaphysics (or, more precisely, the tracing back to nature of thoughts) by throwing ourselves into the arms of Atomism, because, of course, the atom itself is a thought.[57]

No one has seen an atom. The concept of the atom formed in the logic is not abstracted from divisible sense objects. Sense objects in general have been left behind with the passage to being-for-self and the true infinite. The atom is the shrivelled, repressed concept of the atomist's own being-for-self. Encountering an alien universe, thought thinking itself loses courage. The wealth of the self's content collapses. In an attempted compensation, countless multiples of being-for-self thus impoverished are projected on the cosmos. Yet the Leibnizian critique of atomism, successful as a critique, itself succumbs to the corrosive effect of dialectical reason due to its own windowless isolation of monads.[58]

If the abstract unit of matter conceived by external relations (space, time, motion, energy) is given concrete content, if what it is in itself unfolds, it is being-for-self, self-consciousness, mind, thought. As Leibniz saw, the only way to give determinate content to what the unit of matter is in itself, thus preventing what it is in itself it from being nothing at all for us, is to assign it the content of our own mental life.[59] Hegel, himself in the panpsychist tradition, only adds this content is the very one which we have stripped from it in forming the originally puzzling concept of the atom.

5

The Theology of Pure Quantity

1. From Quality to Quantity

We now enter the logic of quantity. It does not further develop the logic of "quality" in the general sense of whatness or determination. This the subsequent logics of measure and essence will do. Rather, it interrupts such development. The logic of quality comes to a temporary stopping point in the original being-for-self, "thought thinking itself"—what in the previous chapter we called the concrete presocial thinking self. This is being-for-self prior to its collapse into an abstract subject, into an atom, and ultimately into quantitative one.

One misunderstanding of the logic of quantity is avoided if we realize how its concept of quantity and number differs from Russell's set theoretical construction of number. The transition to quantity from being-for-self shows that quantity and number for Hegel presuppose psychological concepts. They are constituted by abstraction from such concrete concepts. They do not merely presuppose set theory. Insofar as Hegel treats number at all, he subscribes to psychologism.

A basis for Hegel's essentially Pythagorean view of quantity exists in ordinary language and the history of philosophy. "One" is "oneself," "one person." Pythagoras, the founder of mathematics, identified the one, source of all numbers and things, with the limited soul breathing in the unlimited surrounding air.[1]

We conclude not that Hegel is right, but that he has a distinctive concept of quantity and number which is no longer conventional in the philosophy of mathematics. For Hegel, a quantity of ones is abstracted from qualitative differences, both from differences within one self and between ones.

Yet, underneath, the selves remain as that from which quantity abstracts. A minimal psychological content remains. The one, as for Pythagoras, has a cosmic and microcosmic qualitative content. This is not true of Russell's concept of number as a class of classes, which constructs quantity independently of any particular content, psychological or otherwise. Russell's class definition of number, unlike Hegel's definition, was constructed to avoid contradiction. On Hegel's definition a "number" is not a class. A class is eternal, surviving its members as they perish in space and time. The ones in Hegel's definition of the absolute as a number form not a class but a collection. A collection or aggregate has the space-time location of its members. The collection of ancient Egyptians exists no more, but the class of which they are members still exists.

For Hegel, a number is a collection of quantitatively distinct ones without any qualitative distinction. Given the identity of indiscernibles, this definition of Hegel's makes quantity contradictory.[2] Yet this is precisely what the *Logic* intends: we have nothing to learn positively from quantitative definitions of the absolute.

Hegel is not interested in the philosophy of mathematics for itself. That was one of Russell's main interests, not Hegel's. Hegel is not interested in exploring the conceptual underpinnings of "how mathematics is possible" as a first-order discipline (contra Pinkard).[3] Hegel's aim is to explore the availability of quantity and number for defining the absolute. Russell and Hegel work at cross-purposes. Russell says that Hegel understands little of mathematics.[4] But Russell understands little of the speculative, especially Pythagorean tradition and its view of mathematics as instructive even if not ultimately coherent.

The concept of quantity addresses a question that can only be addressed after a thing's quality has been defined. Only when we identify what, qualitatively, we are talking about can we ask how many things have that quality. Yet we may ask how many instances there are of a quality even if the quality is poorly defined. If the question of quality languishes for whatever reason, the question of quantity may keep inquiry from languishing.

Quantity is the determinate negation or "other" of quality. To be a quality is one thing; to be a quantity of its instances is another. That there be some quantity of instances is necessarily implied by any quality. But to ask "What?" is not necessarily to ask "How many?" We can ask "What?" assuming that the quality has only one or no instance. This is to assume rather than to ask for an answer to the question "How many?"

In other words, to ask "What?" is not necessarily to ask "What is it among how many instances of the quality?" It is equally true that to ask "How many?" is not to ask "How many instances of what quality?" For the quality must already be identified before raising the question of quantity. To ask "How many?" is to ask "How many instances of a particular quality?"

Quantity refers *explicitly* to a quality: a quantity is a quantity of instances of some quality. But quality only *implicitly* refers to quantity. It is possible to consider quality in Platonic fashion apart from any actual instances. But it is not possible to absolutize instances apart from any quality of which they are instances: "we consider things first from the point of view of their quality [abstracting from the quantity of instances]. . . . When we move on to the consideration of quantity, this gives us at once the representation of an indifferent, external indeterminacy, such that a thing still remains what it [qualitatively] is, even when its quantity alters and it becomes greater or smaller."[5]

2. The Purely Quantitative Definition of the Absolute

Things of the same *essential quality* (determination) can be numerically different. For they may be distinguished by *accidental qualities*. But Leibniz's principle requires that things of the same complete quality be numerically as well as qualitatively identical. Within the logic of immediate given quality, the absolute's immediate quality is assumed to exhaust its entire quality or determination. Exactly the same exhaustive quality repeated in quantity would violate the identity of indiscernibles.

Being-for-self is "complete [immediate] quality." But does complete, immediately given quality exhaust quality in general? Is there not perhaps another sort of quality, and hence a more encompassing sort of complete quality? If immediate being-for-self is complete "quality" in the most encompassing sense, and not simply "complete" in the limited realm of immediate quality, being-for-self excludes any further quality. And, by the identity of indiscernibles, it has only one instance. Immediate being-for-self can have more than one instance only if each instance is differentiated from others by nonimmediate qualities. This will be possible only when we pass from book 1 on immediate, intuitively given definitions of the absolute to book 2 of the *Logic*. Book 2 considers continuing essential, nonimmediate underlying qualities indirectly expressed in variable external, immediate manifestations.

As being-for-itself presents itself in book 1, it is qualitatively infinite or complete. It is the true infinite inclusive of all prior immediate determinations employed in the definition of the absolute.

But if being qualitatively infinite is a *kind*, the absolute cannot be merely qualitatively infinite. For the qualitative infinite does not embrace all that is. It does not embrace the number of its instances. This number is logically independent of it.

If there are two beings-for-self, neither can be the absolute. Yet perhaps the absolute is a many. Perhaps it is an all-embracing quantitative infinite. The logic of quantity does not propose that there are many absolutes. Yet, being-for-self may not be the absolute. The logic of quantity asks: "Are there many beings-for-self?" If there are, being-for-self is the quality or kind of which the absolute is so many instances.

In the logic of quantity, quality remains. But since it remains constant from instance to instance, it remains in the background. Counting instances abstracts from continuous quality. Quality becomes indifferent to the multiplication of its instances, and comes to be neglected in the course of reiteration.

A chair is unaffected as a chair by continued reproduction in series. If the original chair was unique, its character is affected by initial reproduction. Yet further chairs in the series are not unique as such and are not affected by multiplication.

Numbering lithograph prints by hand eventually is comic. Loss of uniqueness by a general quality is a change of quality. It inaugurates repetition of the same quality. Yet, looking closely, each print is unique, like each leaf for Leibniz's ladies of the court. Purely quantitative aggregates have being-for-us, by abstraction from distinguishing qualities of their members, not objective being-in-itself.

Consciousness is a contrast effect. We can be conscious of change, but not of a constant background such as Pythagoras's music of the spheres. The logic of quantity relegates the already articulated quality of being-for-self to a background. In this background, qualitative being-for-self is not noticed because the same "complete quality" is everywhere. This quality will return to the foreground only when the abstraction of quantity from qualitative change breaks down in the logic of Pythagorean measure.

The absolute as being-for-self is the absolute as the true qualitative infinite of Anaximander. This qualitative definition may be put quantitatively, as it was by Pythagoras: the absolute is the one.[6] Quality and quantity are internally related: each is not what the other is. The quantity of instances is not the quality which they share, and their quality is not the quantity of instances which that quality has.

At the same time, quantity is itself a quality. Quantity is not the quality of which it is a number of instances, but it is another quality. It is qualitatively other than the quality of being qualitative. Part of the quality of being-for-self is to have a number of instances, though not any particular number. Its quality is not to have necessarily but one instance. Yet it has but one instance if it is to define the absolute.

Atomism, which followed being-for-self in the last chapter, identified the absolute as being-for-self multiplied. The absolute was a contingent number of abstract beings-for-self. These beings-for-self excluded one another. In the limiting case, this number of beings-for-self is one. The absolute is then a single, infinite, unbounded instance of being-for-self (Anaximander).

Putting the definition of the absolute as being-for-self quantitatively rather than qualitatively highlights the contingency of the number of its instances. The number of qualitatively identical beings is not necessarily one. And given one one there is no second one necessarily implied by the first. There is a necessary number of three terms in giving: giver, recipient, and gift. But such internally related terms are qualitatively distinguished. Given any being-for-self, there is no necessary number of others.

Since being-for-self is a "complete [immediate] quality," nothing of any other immediate quality can be deduced. For deduction of one thing from another depends on an internal relation. Being-for-self and any qualitatively identical second being-for-self are not so related. An internal relation, e.g., the relation parent and child, implies discernible terms. The parent is qualitatively not the child. Indiscernible terms are externally related. Identity as indiscernibility is an external relation. The lack of distinction between terms leaves them without any ability to determine each other's quality. Clark Kent is discernibly qualified as Superman, but is indiscernibly identical with him.

Suppose the absolute is a collection of beings-for-self equal to one. There is nothing necessary about that. If there is a second being-for-self of the same quality, neither will be deducible from the other. Each will exist as if the other did not. Given a hundred beings-for-self, nothing would change qualitatively in any of them if there were a thousand.

The uniqueness of being-for-self is not necessary. When the qualitative true infinite is assumed to be the absolute, qualitative infinity has but one quantitatively infinite instance. But the uniqueness of this instance is not entailed by being qualitatively infinite. A being-for-self which does not include in its complete description being quantitatively infinite can lose its status as a definition of the absolute. It can be asserted to have a copy in a second being-for-self. The multiplication of identical ones is posited without any objective ground in those ones.

It is not necessary to a being-for-self that there be another. The being of the second is not deducible from that of the first. But its being may be deduced as non-necessary or contingent given the first. Definition of the absolute merely as necessarily one qualitative being-for-self seems false. For it fails to recognize that being-for-self, even if only one instance actually exists, is one of an aggregate of contingent further instances. Being-for-self under the quantitative description of being one implies being-for-self under the description of being limited by contingent if not actually existing copies of itself.

By the new quantitative definition, the absolute is an all-encompassing number of qualitatively identical beings. In the limiting case the number is one. The case of only one being-for-self, in which the logic of quality culminated, is now subsumed under the logic of quantity. But other cases, where the number of ones is multiplied, are not excluded as impossible merely by their contingency.

Hegel was tempted to attribute the definition of the absolute as a quantity of ones to Pythagoras: "Pythagoras . . . conceived number as the basic determination of things."[7] The Pythagoreans identified the absolute as number, and the quantitative one externally related to contingent other quantitative ones is the first number. Each number is defined by multiple external ones in "reciprocal exclusion."[8]

However, if all Pythagorean ones participate in a single cosmic One as its different ensouled microcosmic members, only at a certain level of abstraction are they identical in quality. The idea that Pythagoras represents the theology of pure quantity must be reconsidered. Hegel concluded that Pythagoras went beyond a purely quantitative theology. Pythagoreans distinguished between the purely numerical "one" (among a contingent many) and the cosmic "Monas," the prequantitative thought of oneness, "of unity, self-sameness and equality, . . . of the connection and sustaining of everything, of the self-identical."[9] The quantitative one is one of many. The prequantitative one is unique, though it is the source of many abstract purely quantitative ones.

An alternative to viewing Pythagoras as a representative of pure quantity is to hold that pure quantity is, like the incoherent qualitative finite, a category whose theological absolutization is unrepresented in the tradition. It is more plausible to construe Pythagoras as defending measure as the definition of the absolute, which is the definition to which the *Logic* turns after pure quantity. Pythagoras began by seeing the world of endless qualitative sensory differences (e.g., different musical tones) as an obstacle to equating the absolute with a cosmic Monas. He then took up the idea of defining every concrete qualitative determination by a quantitative ratio. In this ratio each term is a multiple of units which, viewed abstractly, are qualitatively identical. This order defined by each term of the ratio is quantitative. But the concept of quantity requires abstraction from the actual uniqueness of ones.

3. The Leibnizian Impossibility of Qualitatively Identical Ones

So far we have assumed with ordinary mathematics that many qualitatively identical ones are, though not mutually necessary, logically possible.

This assumption of possibility is part of any assumption that they define the absolute. However, given a collection consisting of one qualitatively infinite being, the identity of indiscernibles means that its quantitative limitation by other unlimited qualitative identical ones is impossible.

The numerical discernibility of qualitatively identical things would be ungrounded even if it were not contradictory. No sufficient ground exists for distinguishing things sharing all properties. This alone is a refutation of the absolute defined as a quantitative aggregate of many ones unlimited by any further ones.

The assertion of quantitative plurality is due to the fact that the juxtaposition of ones is contingent. No impossibility of this juxtaposition follows from this contingency. To say that many ones are not necessary is weaker than saying that they are impossible, necessarily nonexistent. Yet, in modal logic non-necessity, i.e., contingency, follows from impossibility.

If something is a square, it is not necessarily a circle. This implies that the square's being a circle is contingent, and its contingency does not exclude its possibility. The contingency of its being a circle is based on the fact that from squareness we cannot deduce circularity. But it can also be based on the fact that from squareness we can deduce the impossibility of circularity. A square is not necessarily a circle because it cannot be a circle. But if the weak understatement of contingency is retained, the impression may be given that the stronger statement of impossibility is denied.

The identity of indiscernibles is not brought in from the outside as an eternally known, self-evident truth. It is the self-negation of the assumption that the absolute is a number of instances of the same complete quality. If the identity of indiscernibles is analytic, to assume that things are quantitatively distinct is contradictory when they are not qualitatively distinct.

"Complete" quality—being-for-self[10]—is "complete" only in preserving the key determinations from all categories of immediate quality. Being-for-self as complete in this sense does not construct everything; it has not constructed Mr. Krug's pen. If being-for-self is thus not empirically complete, it is thought thinking itself but not yet "reason," not yet thought thinking itself in "all reality."[11] The supposition of two beings-for-self is then not contradictory by the identity of indiscernibles. Two beings-for-self can be distinct in their empirical qualities even if they are identical as qualitative categories. Suppose that being-for-self is not viewed in its empirical completeness. Suppose that the abstractive understanding in the logic of quality has absolutized it theologically as abstract quality. It has then falsely assumed abstract quality to be complete quality. Assuming this position of the abstractive understanding, we cannot suppose two beings-for-self without contradiction. A quantity of qualitatively determinate things may concretely be a quantity of qualitatively different things. But this is not the concept of pure quantity exclusive of qualitative differences developed by abstraction in the logic of quantity. Atomism is a doctrine of impure quantity inseparable from qualitative difference. Atomists make being-for-self into a kind with instances accidentally[12] distinguished by position, shape, direction, velocity, etc. The absolute is an aggregate of mutually exclusive atoms.

Atomism then passes into a purely quantitative definition of the absolute. The accidental mutual repulsion of ones becomes internal to them as atomic ones. In this way is each one is qualitatively indistinguishable from the rest.[13] Each one is qualitatively unlimited by any relation to a second. But the hypothesis of multiple ones at once becomes contradictory. The discovery that the mutual exclusion of atoms is a common quality, not a basis for qualitative distinction, at first sight points us away from atomism to a purely quantitative definition of the absolute. For all atoms are distinguished by position, shape, direction, velocity, etc.

But it is impossible to have position in general without position in particular. Atoms are qualitatively one since they all have some position in general. Yet they are qualitatively distinct in having different particular positions.

No two atoms occupy the same space at the same time. Passage from an atomistic perspective of mutual exclusion to a purely quantitative perspective depends on the abstraction of common or general qualities from distinguishing particular qualities, of essence from accident.

The quantitative one is obtained from the atom, not by retaining the full notion of the atom and then adding something, but by eliminating something. The dialectic of the logic in general is thought to lead to greater concreteness. Here we see it leading to absolutization of a more abstract description.

No purely quantitative aggregate really exists. If it did, each one would be qualitatively indiscernible from other contingent ones and thus could not be quantitatively distinct. Moreover, it suffices to restore the context from which we have abstracted to see that each one exists only as a uniquely qualified being-for-self.

The breakdown of any theology of pure quantity lies in the fact that multiplication of the one is revealed first as contingent, but finally as impossible. Purely quantitative ones are contingent . . . on an impossibility. They are non-necessary by being impossible. Their contingency in relation to one another defines them as quantitative. Only qualitatively distinct things like parent and child necessarily imply each other.

The impossibility associated with this contingency defines quantitative ones out of existence. Given any one, another one of same quality is not necessary. This non-necessity of a second unit of the same quality makes it contingent on an impossible, purely quantitative, nonqualitative distinction from the first unit.

There is a transition from the positive prospect of multiplied ones as possible (but contingent) to the impossibility of such ones. It starts with the prequantitative one and ends with the postquantitative one. The prequantitative one emerged at the end of the logic of qualitative being as being-for-self. This is the source of Presocratic pluralisms. The postquantitative one is Neoplatonic: the procession of many ones is reabsorbed into the one one.

The breakdown of pure quantity as a definition of the absolute is restated thus: Suppose that the absolute is merely the immediate qualitative infinite (the one). Suppose that the one's quantitative infinity (noncoexistence with other units of the same quality) is contingent though possible. The door is then open to an equally contingent but possible multiplication of ones. Pure quantity is enabled by this supposed possibility.

Yet by Leibniz's law what is qualitatively infinite cannot be quantitatively limited by other ones or units of the same complete quality. Its freedom from quantitative limitation is necessary. And so the door to multiplied ones is at once closed.

In the modal square of opposition there are two kinds of contingency: the impossible and the possible. The contingent may be impossible. To be contingent is to be non-necessary. And what is impossible is non-necessary and thus contingent.

4. From the Presocratic to the Neoplatonic One

The logic of quantity and of measure offers variations on the theme of the one. We distinguish first theological absolutization of the prequantitative one which emerged in the qualitative form of being-for-self, and which may be called the contingent one: it is not necessarily the only one, nor necessarily accompanied by others.

We can deduce from one being-for-self neither that there are no others, nor that there are others. From one egg in a carton we can deduce neither that there are others, nor that there are no others. That there is only one egg is contingent, since we cannot deduce the nonexistence of others. And that there is more than one egg is contingent, since we cannot deduce others.

Apotheosis of the prequantitative concept of the one in the definition of the absolute is Presocratic, illustrated by Anaximander. The question of the possibility or impossibility of a multiplicity of ones is unposed.

The Neoplatonic, postquantitative absolutization of the one, by contrast, is noncontingent or necessary. For multiple ones have shown themselves by the identity of indiscernibles to be not merely contingent but impossible.

After its detour through quantity, thought returns to the definition of the absolute as being-for-self, now conceived as the one and only one. Before the dialectic of quantity this definition was contingent. It was then exposed to the challenge of quantitative reiteration of the one. Afterwards the uniqueness of the one is necessary.

No argument is explicitly developed to support the self-contradiction of pure quantity in the logic of quantity, where one might expect it. Only in the logic of essence do we arrive at Leibniz's law that purely quantitative distinctions between things qualitatively identical are contradictory—that the discernibility of nonidenticals is necessary. Hegel writes that their discernibility is nonanalytic, that it must be proven.[14] Perhaps it is not explicitly analytic. But what can be proven is necessary. And given the premises by which it is proven, its negation is contradictory: "Everything is diverse," or "There are no two things that are perfectly equal to each other"—to be distinct pertains to things in themselves.[15] In the *Logic* we read:

> That everything is different from everything else is a very superfluous proposition, for things in the plural immediately involve manyness and wholly indeterminate diversity. But the proposition that no two things are completely like each other expresses more, namely, *determinate* difference. . . . The reason why this proposition is striking lies in what has been said [in the logic of quantity], that two, or numerical manyness, does not contain any *determinate* difference and that diversity as such, in its abstraction, is at first indifferent to likeness and unlikeness. Ordinary thinking, even when it goes on to a determination of diversity, takes these moments themselves to be mutually indifferent, so that one without the other, the *mere likeness* of things *without unlikeness*, suffices to determine whether the things are different even when they are only a numerical many, not unlike, but simply different without further qualification. The law of diversity [the indiscernibility of identicals, the converse of the identity of indiscernibles], on the other hand, asserts that things are different from one another through unlikeness.[16]

The context of the discussion of the impossibility of purely numerical distinctions is the concept of difference. The logical law of identity is $A = A$. Leibniz's law of identity (including two converse laws) includes the law of difference in the form of the qualitative discernibility of things numerically different, yet things are found objectively to be self-identical under descriptions that are qualitatively and not just numerically different: $A = B$. True identity in difference is identity in qualitative difference. "Now this [Leibnizian] proposition [not the Leibnizian law of identity] that unlikeness must be predicated of all things, surely stands in need of proof," since it [e.g. $A = B$] is a "synthetic" proposition; "this proof would have to exhibit the passage of identity into difference, and then the passage of this into determinate difference, into unlikeness."[17]

Identity and difference are concepts from the logic of essence, not being. The self-refutation of the theology of pure quantity thus appears to lie beyond the logic of pure quantity (and of measure, which as we shall see still rests on pure quantity). The quantitative concept of what is indifferent to all differences of quality slips into the logic of essence in book 2. Only then is it explicitly repudiated.

Hegel thus does not exhibit a self-refutation of the theology of pure quantity in the logic of quantity itself. He writes in that section of the *Logic* as an eye-witness reporter of a great parade of hollow concepts. The many ones flow from the one one at the beginning of the dialectic of quantity. And they return to it at the end of the dialectic of measure.

The Neoplatonic metaphor of a quantitative outward "flow" of what is qualitatively self-identical, and of a reverse movement back to the source, is an instance of picture thinking. Hegel fails to indicate the full cash value of this image in pure imageless thought. It appears as the rhetorical tip of a dialectical iceberg below the surface of the exposition.

Quantity does not present itself as a "necessary" definition of the absolute.[18] To be sure, once the quality of something has been identified, the question is automatically posed as to the quantity of things having that quality. If we apply this principle to the absolute, which is an individual rather than a kind, the quality in question becomes "complete" in the sense of exhausting all determinations. There could be nothing other than the absolute to account for possible "accidental" qualities. The quantity of its instances is then necessarily restricted to one.

It is possible to refute a definition of the absolute qualitatively by showing that it has been defined by a single term of a qualitative dyad. This sort of refutation is characteristic of the logic of quality. But it might also be possible to refute such a definition quantitatively, by showing that the absolute is falsely defined as the sole instance of a quality. This sort of refutation is experimented with in the logic of quantity.

The difference between the logics of quality and of quantity is this: in the former the refutation succeeds, while in the latter it fails. The absolute is determinate being and not just indeterminate being. But the absolute does not include a second being-for-self which is a replica of a first. Determinate being follows necessarily from indeterminate being. But a second being-for-self follows only contingently. That it follows at all is thus contingent on its possibility. But since it is impossible, it does not follow.

The supposition of a quantitative aggregate only serves to point up the necessary uniqueness of the being-for-self with which we started. The modal status of "The absolute is the one" rises from contingency to necessity. But the concept of the one is not otherwise expanded.

The logic of quantity and measure intervening between the contingency and necessity of the one's uniqueness tests the hypothesis that the absolute is one being-for-self. It confirms it dialectically by showing the contradiction of supposing two or more indiscernible beings-for-self.

That the absolute is being-for-self is established in two ways: first qualitatively and Presocratically by showing that being-for-self resolves the contradictions of other qualitative definitions of the absolute, such as pure being or being-in-self. And second quantitatively by showing that being-for-self (complete quality) cannot be quantitatively repeated.

Thus, at the end of the dialectic of quantity and measure, the hypothesis of many self-enclosed ones or beings-for-self is Neoplatonically retracted. The one of pure quantity multiplies in an emanation of ones. The one of indifference is the return out of multiplicity, a being above all determinate being.[19] The dialectic of quantity confirms that the absolute must be thought thinking itself, being-for-self. But it makes no contribution to defining the absolute beyond being-for-self.

The dialectic of essence in book 2 of the *Logic* does not preserve any discovery that the absolute is many beings-for-self. Rather, it takes up again abstract being-for-self, and deepens it qualitatively through essential being-in-itself which is at once being-for-itself, an underlying essential quality (being-in-itself) which is at once an immediately given quality (being-for-self).

This does not mean that the further dialectic of the logic denies manyness in the absolute. The absolute contains many categorial aspects that can be counted. It only denies that the absolute divides itself naturally into members of a purely quantitative series of selfsame ones. This hypothesis is not preserved in the further advance of the dialectic. The logic of quantity shows that, contrary to what is often assumed, not every position in the dialectic is preserved in being transcended.

To say that the absolute is the one, that there is only the one, alludes to a not yet excluded possibility of many ones. The procession of ones from the one, we have seen, is not logically necessary. Indeed, the plurality of ones is impossible, not just non-necessary. The deduction of quantity does not deduce a plurality of actual ones. Such a deduction would admittedly be "a little strained" (Charles Taylor).[20]

The deduction of quantity is of the contingency and then impossibility of multiple ones. Quantity is the multiplication of what is qualitatively self-identical and, by the identity of indiscernibles, after all nonmultiple. A plurality of indiscernible ones is contradictory if "indiscernible" implies "numerically identical." But even if discernibility is only a "synthetically" attached criterion of numerical nonidentity, indiscernible nonidentical things—a plurality of indiscernible ones—could only be asserted but never factually supported.

5. Practical Fixation on Abstract Being-for-Self

Fixation on multiple qualitatively identical things is motivated practically, not justified theoretically. Such a plurality, which is without sufficient reason if not contradictory, is merely asserted. Aggregates of qualitative identical ones are postulated in institutions of buying or selling or, more generally, measuring.

To measure a field requires a qualitatively constant, repeatable unit of measure. To measure time requires a unit of time. To buy and sell requires a repeatable unit of exchange. Yet any two real dollars are qualitatively different in purchasing power, according to time and place. Any two real days differ in duration, due to variations in the rotation of the earth.

Within atomistic and Pythagorean philosophy the one is multiplied to explain what is not reducible to a single one. Objectively, the dialectic of quantity shows that the absolute must after all be one being-for-self. Since the absolute cannot be the immediately given being-for-self of a finite person, it must be cosmic being-for-self.

Infinite being-for-self at the end of the logic of quality is infinite only in its own sphere, i.e., with respect to the categories of immediate quality uncovered in the logic of quality. With respect to the nonimmediate, underlying essential quality of the cosmos, this infinite being-for-self is finite. But its absolutization is maintained in the hardened position of the finite, fallen ego.

The logic of quantity is that of a being-for-self fixated on itself, resisting release in being-in-and-for-itself. The self resists release in the arms of the universe (essential cosmic being-in-itself). Being-for-self seeks to maintain a definition of the absolute constructed out of itself by construing the absolute as a repetition of itself.

Thought upon reaching being-for-self becomes narcissistically fixated on itself. The self which refuses release in the cosmos empties itself of its cosmic content. This content does not disappear. Rather, it is transferred to a second finite self posited outside itself.

This emptying supervenes upon reaching any stable but incomplete definition of a concrete whole. The internal differentiation of the whole fades as thought, passing to other matters, refers to it through the mechanical repetition of the same name. Despite the internal richness we find in spirit, repeated reference to it as "spirit" reduces it to an abstract and lifeless subject. Transfer of the term's qualitative content to another instance is an illusory attempt at preserving the content. As if we could compensate for lost concreteness by a multiplication of abstraction. In fact repetition, far from reversing lost concreteness, merely reiterates it.[21]

Thought now sees that a plurality of qualitatively identical ones is an ungrounded, even contradictory assumption. The plurality is purely posited, without any reality or being in itself. It might be replied that ones are not qualitatively identical, since they are distinguished as to order. The second one is second, not first. The second one is not just any one. It is the one which defines the number two. Yet, to be counted in order, ones first must first exist unordered as distinct from one another.

The logic of quantity and measure succumbs to this unsupported procession of ones, which is reabsorbed in a supraquantitative one, a being beyond qualitative and quantitative being. This is the point of indifference,[22] the substantial substratum of all, known intuitively rather than by universal attributes.[23]

The worldview of natural science, based on the quantification of phenomena, rests on an ad hoc hypothesis that is contradictory or at least unsupported. There can be no descriptive basis for distinguishing descriptively identical ones. The reason for the hypothesis of pure quantity has nothing to do with its intrinsic merits. It has to do with the transactions it underlies, with the measurements it makes possible, and with the scientific explanation, prediction, and control it affords.

6. Finite Quantity

We now take fuller note of this castle in the air, mathematics and natural science. First, the concept of a definite quantity, a quantum or number, emerges against the background of indefinite or pure quantity, a general multiplicity of ones.[24] Each number is generated within the infinity of hypothetical mutually contingent ones by selecting a single one and then adding a finite number of ones to it.

The indefinite infinity of ones orders itself into the natural number series. By virtue of their qualitative identity or continuity all ones in a finite series are collected together. And by virtue of their nonidentity or discontinuity each partial collection is detachable from the totality of ones.[25]

Unlike each one in relation to other ones, each distinct number is qualitatively, not just quantitatively, different from other numbers.[26] The number three is not "indifferent" to the number two or four like an unordered one is indifferent to any other one. Four cannot be deduced from three by itself (i.e., without further axioms of number theory). But from three by itself one can deduce two, since three is constructed by adding a single one to two. Paradoxically, with the arrival of number the dialectic of quantity falls once again into qualitative distinctions.

The qualitative determinateness of each number is clear when we see that each is a general quantitative ratio.[27] Two is, more explicitly, $2x/x$—where $2x/x$ defines a series of numerical ratios qualitatively different from $3x/x$. Each ratio is qualitatively determinate, though it remains quantitative in its construction out of two series of mutually external ones.

7. Quantitative Infinity

Every determinate number is determinate by relation to a limiting next higher number. To refer in number theory to a number as first is to refer to a number that is second, third, etc. Thus, to absolutize the first or second number in a series of ones is to fall into a contradiction. If the absolute should somehow be number, it cannot be the number two. For it is axiomatic in natural number theory that every number has a successor number.

We approach here the concept of an infinite mathematical progression. Every natural number is a limit imposed on magnitude. Five is five and not six. The absolute cannot be a natural number, since each is finite and limited by a higher number. Every quantitative limit breaks down and is transcended by a higher limit. The current limit is a temporary break in a relentless process of quantitative growth.

To say that the number of eggs in the refrigerator is only five is of course not to say that five eggs are surpassed by six eggs. But to say that the number of purely quantitative ones is only five is to say something contradictory.

A collection of physical units does not necessarily have a successor collection larger than it. Such a collection may grow, but not necessarily. But since every number is succeeded by another number one greater than it, the absolute can be no single finite number or quantum.[28]

If the absolute is not a finite number, we may consider the possibility that it is an infinite number. The dialectic of quantity will indeed result in the discovery of a true quantitative infinite. But the true qualitative infinite failed to include all reality and thus was a limited true infinite. So the true quantitative infinite will also prove limited. It is true in the realm of quantity, but not absolutely. The true mathematical infinite is clarified by distinguishing it from a number of other concepts of the mathematical infinite:

1. If there is an infinite number surpassing every finite number, the suggestion that the absolute is an "infinite" number is understandable in one clear sense of the term. But it is also clearly false. The number of natural numbers is infinite. It surpasses every natural number, which is finite. But the absolute cannot be this infinite number by itself. For, though this infinite number is the number of finite natural numbers, it is itself none of these natural numbers. The "number *of* natural numbers" is a relative expression. If the "infinite" is that number it cannot coherently define the absolute.

2. We pass now to a second sense of the quantitative "infinite." We may mean by this quantitative "infinite" an *infinitely great natural number*.[29] Such a number (unlike the number of natural numbers) would include all other natural numbers. But this is a contradictory concept of the infinite. For every natural number is finite, i.e., countable in a finite number of steps from zero and surpassable by a further count.

3. Third, there is the false infinite. The "false infinite" of the natural number series is the endless remainder of the infinite series of numbers lying beyond any given quantitative limit which has been counted. "This infinity which is perpetually determined as the beyond of the finite is . . . the spurious [*schlechte*] quantitative infinite."[30] But this infinite series of numbers beyond any finite number is itself finite, not all-embracing. For it excludes, and is limited by, the finite number to which we have counted. It is obviously contradictory if identified with the all-embracing absolute.

4. The false infinite in the sense just specified must not be confused with the infinite progression ("quantitative progress")[31] of forever falling subject to, and surpassing, a contradictory quantitative limit. This progression is a process. What is impossible is not the monotonous process of repeatedly falling into and overcoming a limit or contradiction. What is

impossible is getting to the end of such a process, exhausting the endless remainder.

The false infinite is a beyond which excludes the finite. The true infinite includes it. Given this distinction, an infinite mathematical progression is not false—though Hegel in speaking of the progression as bad or "spurious" was not always clear about this. Consider successive counts in the process of counting. Suppose the infinite is not (1) the number of counts (the number of natural numbers), nor (2) the highest count, nor (3) the remainder of potential counts. Suppose it is (4) the process of counting itself. Its infinity remains unrestricted even though one never gets to the end of counting. For the same act of adding one to what has already been counted, which is forever attained in the process, is already attained in adding one to the first one. We attain here the true and most coherent concept of quantitative infinity.

The infinity of the series can be grasped without getting to the end of the series. It is expressed by a finite number of counts expressing the principle of the series. Given a first member of the series and rule for generating a successor member to a given member, the infinite series also is given. The infinite is given "once and for all" in a finite reiteration of its steps: "Zeno rightly says (in Aristotle's report) that it is the same to say something *once* and to say it *over and over again*."[32]

The infinite series is a true quantitative infinite, free of contradiction from limitation by anything within the series. It is a finite quantitative ratio. Thus $1/x$ encapsulates an infinite series of fractions once and for all. "The infinite quantum . . . is in the first instance a ratio."[33]

Yet there is a difference between the true infinity of quantity and of quality. In the dialectic of quality, finitude is discovered but overcome in the true infinite. Within the dialectic of quantity finitude is never overcome. Even in the so-called "true" infinite of quantity (the infinite process of counting just mentioned), the quantitative ratios and qualitative measures are finite. For they presuppose various different series of contradictory qualitatively identical ones.

Hegel claims that a bad infinite of number viewed as a beyond was employed in the Hebrew definition of God as greater than the greatest mountain, the infinitely great.[34] But there is no infinitely great magnitude beyond all finite magnitudes, no infinitely great distance beyond all finite distances. Every size is measurable by a finite quantity of ones. An infinitely great size cannot be measured at all, and so is no size at all.

In one sense the "bad infinite" of natural numbers is an infinitely great natural number that cannot be reached by counting. But this infinite is incoherent even without being externally limited by other natural numbers. An infinitely great number is no natural number at all. There is an infinite number of natural numbers, but the number of natural numbers is not itself a natural number.

Yet even without the bad infinite in this sense, even without false absolutization of one number, the infinite series remains.[35] Every natural number, a quantitative ratio with a variable ranging over the number series, is an infinite series of numerical ratios: e.g., $2x/x$. It necessarily is surpassed by a new number, e.g., $3x/x$. But the new number appeared in the very series of ratios which defines the first number: e.g., $2x3/3$.

What surpasses a given number is thus a "moment" within that number itself. Thus three is an ideal moment in two. A true quantitative infinite is a variable numerical ratio (e.g., two, $2x/x$) expressing an infinite series of constant numerical ratios ($2x1/1$, $2x2/2$, $2x3/3$, thus including three as one moment).

There is nothing contradictory about such an infinite series once two is granted. The contradiction lies only in quantity itself, in the fact that two is constructed by adding one to a qualitatively identical one. One rabbit added to itself is still only the same one rabbit. But by a seeming magic resting on the contradiction of all pure quantity, the purely quantitative one added to itself results is more than itself, namely, two.

6

Pythagoras and the
Logic of Measure

1. Quantity and Measure

We have seen from the previous chapter that definition of the absolute as an immediate multiplicity turns out to be its definition as a numerical ratio expressing the number of members in the series. Thus, if the number of ones is infinity—i.e., no matter how many ones we have counted one more one is also countable—the number of ones is the ratio of the sum of all countable ones to one.

Implicitly a number is already a measure, complete with amount and unit of measure.[1] In this chapter we explore measure as a new definition of the absolute. It will here be considered as more than "number" in a purely quantitative sense. It will be considered as the Pythagorean cosmos, an order of qualitatively determinate measures or proportions that pass quantitatively into one another.

An interesting difference obtains between the logic of qualitative being and that of quantity and measure. The logic of qualitative being embraced numerous "categories" in the sense of definitions of the absolute: mere indeterminate being, being as positively determinate, something, a finite collection, the true infinite, and many atomic ones. The logic of quantity and measure, to be sure, contain numerous *conceptual distinctions*—e.g., indefinite quantity, definite quantum or finite number, intensive and extensive quantity, continuous and discontinuous quantity, the false quantitative infinite, the quantitative ratio or true quantitative infinite. But these distinctions are not *categorial*.

There are several qualitative definitions of the absolute. There is only one quantitative definition: the absolute is the true quantitative infinite expressed by a variable quantitative ratio $(x/1)$ ranging over all numerical constants. "The Absolute is pure quantity."[2] The distinction between number and the true quantitative infinite (quantitative ratio) is not between two categories, but between degrees of explicitness in a single category. Quantitative ratio is number made explicit.

> The infinite, which in the [falsely] infinite progress has only the empty meaning of a non-being, of an unattained but sought beyond, is in fact nothing other than [truly infinite] *quality*. Quantum as an indifferent limit goes beyond itself to infinity; in doing so it seeks nothing else than to be determined for itself, the qualitative moment, which, however, is thus only an ought-to-be. Its indifference to limit, and hence its lack of an explicit determinateness of its own, and its passage away from and beyond itself, is what makes quantum what it is; this its passage into the beyond [other] is to be negated and quantum is to find in the [true] infinite its absolute determinateness. . . . Quantum is thus posited as repelled from itself, with the result that there are two quanta which however are sublated, are only moments of *one unity*, and this unity is the determinateness of quantum. Quantum as thus *self-related* [to another term which is not really "other" insofar as it qualitatively determines the first quantum to be what it is—e.g. as "4" in "2/4" assigns to "2" the quality of being half] as an indifferent [quantitative] limit in its externality and therefore posited as qualitative, is *quantitative ratio*.[3]

There is likewise only one definition of the absolute as "measure," despite distinctions within the general category of measure. Hegel is nowhere so indiscriminate as to say that qualitative being is a definition of the absolute. But "measure, like the other stages of being, may serve as a definition of the Absolute."[4]

Yet, though only two new definitions of the absolute are to be eked out of the logics of quantity and measure, quantity and measure take up 191 pages in the Miller translation, almost twice as many pages as the logic of quality with its greater number of categories. Hegel expounds at length, in the logic of quantity and measure, problems in the philosophy of mathematics of his own time (e.g., the problem of infinitesimals), and problems of applying the Pythagorean concept of nature as a scale of measures to the natural science of his own time. These issues concern the history and philosophy of science more than the theological logic of definitions of the absolute central to his own project in the *Logic*.

Much interesting work can be done on Hegel in relation to the special sciences, and the *Science of Logic* is an indispensable sourcebook on these questions. However, our aim, like Hegel's own central claim, is different. We take up Hegel's treatment of mathematics and the natural sciences only as needed in illuminating definitions of the absolute. When we do refer to the sciences, we may often avoid matters that depend on arcane knowledge of the history of science. Suspecting Hegel of wishing in part to demonstrate his mastery of mathematics and science to contemporaries and colleagues—"Speaking of lectures, I hope you will approve of my taking over mathematics in the upper classes—Büchner does not understand a thing about algebra"[5]—we may use contemporary examples known to the reader, though not necessarily to Hegel.

2. The Absolute as a Cosmic Scale of Quantified Qualities

We noted that a quantitative ratio is already a measure. But such a quantitative measure is an amount of a purely quantitative unit, a numerical one not characterized by any specific ideal quality (e.g., force, mass) or real quality (e.g., water, salt). To maintain that the absolute is such measure, a purely quantitative ratio, is to deny such ideal and real differentiations of quality—which is drastic. The alternative is to select terms for quantitative ratios and units of measure ("specific quanta," e.g., a foot)[6] which are themselves qualitatively determinate and objective.

The Pythagorean definition of the absolute as measure, going beyond the original Pythagoras' view of the cosmos as finite, explores this second alternative. The cosmos is an infinite "number" in a sense larger than the strict mathematical sense: "the so-called Pythagoreans, who were the first to take up mathematics, not only advanced this study . . . but thought its principles [i.e., its root sources, the limited and the unlimited] were the principles of all things . . . and the whole heaven to be a musical scale and a number."[7] Number in the sense of a scale of ratios between qualitative determinations is the essence of things musical, aesthetic, sensory, or qualitative. The heaven or cosmos aesthetically enjoyed is essentially a number, a number under a nonaesthetic description which gets at its essential form. But only in a sense not purely mathematical can the absolute be merely a "number." The absolute for the Pythagoreans is a qualitative, aesthetic "musical" scale with a mathematical scale of quantitative ratios between qualitative determinations (and units of such determinations) as its inner structural essence.

Each quantitative ratio is in itself qualitatively determinate. The number two, i.e., two ones, is not three. But the unit of measure, the quantitative one that is multiplied, is not qualitatively fixed. This unit can be made qualitatively determinate by fiat, by saying: "Let the unit of measure be one foot." Depending on one's choice of a unit of measure, the amount with which one comes up in measurement will be greater or less. The milk in the refrigerator does not by itself measure itself as either a gallon or four quarts. The result of its measurement is objective once a unit of measure has been chosen. But the choice of that unit remains arbitrary.[8]

The discovery of Pythagoras was that the qualitative determinations of the cosmos naturally and spontaneously measure themselves off in objective units of measure ("natural measures").[9] This discovery remains today the basis of natural science.

A particular force measures itself as an amount of mass times an amount of acceleration. Mass is the first term of the ratio defining force. And it is measured by a subjective, arbitrarily chosen unit of measure. Acceleration is the second term of the ratio, and it is again measured by an arbitrarily chosen unit. The infinitely variable ratio known as "force"—i.e., *ma*—is an objective self-definition of force in general. And it is at once a general rule of measurement[10] for measuring and comparing different particular forces.

One measures the particular force of an object by measuring its mass and its acceleration and then multiplying the two factors. Such a general and objective self-measure of force, providing a rule for measuring particular forces, is an objective and infinite quantitative ratio of two quantified qualities, each of which must be measured in some arbitrary or subjective unit of measure.

The *Logic* distinguishes between ideal measurement by stipulated units of a universal physical variable (such as force) and real measurement by natural units[11] of a particular element or compound (such as water or salt). Ideal measures are found in physics, real measures in chemistry. Chemistry distinguishes particular material compounds, while physics (mechanics) distinguishes universal properties of matter everywhere. Matter varies discontinuously from compound to compound, and continuously in its universal physical properties.

The universality of ideal measures means that the qualities defined by their respective ratios remain unchanged throughout nature. Force is everywhere, and is everywhere the product of mass and acceleration. The force of a baseball in motion does not in fact belong to a scale of qualitatively different forces each defined by its own quantitative ratio: e.g., ma, $ma2$, $ma3$, etc. Even if we can imagine such a scale, it is not to be found.

It is difficult to see how there could be a transition from one type of force to another; such a transition would be between different world orders. A scale of types of force would be a scale of different logically possible worlds each with different laws of causation and empirically possible occurrences, but without causal or temporal transitions between these possible worlds.

The transition from one chemical compound to another within a single world occurs by the addition or substraction of atomic units in a molecule. The units are fixed by the objective order of nature, not by us. This makes an objective scale of compounds with transitions in time imaginable.

Since force and other physical variables vary continuously in quantity, there is no objective unit of force. Force is measured externally by us, using conventional units. A quantity of water varies discontinuously: there is a natural and objective unit of water, consisting of one objective unit of oxygen and two of hydrogen. This objective unit is multiplied a finite number of times in a given quantity of water. There are of course subjective units for measuring water, such as a cup. But the water molecule expresses an objective or natural unit of measure. Objective units of measure are associated with the atomistic principle.

Measures in which the factors (e.g., acceleration or mass for Newton) must be subjectively measured are ideal. The outcome of the measurement varies along an infinite continuum of ideal positions. Measures in which quantities are objectively measured are real. Those quantities exist atomistically for themselves along a discontinuous scale in mutual exclusion. This Pythagorean atomism of Leucippus[12] is not atomism at the simplest conceivable level. It does not define the absolute merely as a collection of mutually repelled atoms. Rather, it asserts that in its self-constitution each of the ordinary things or elements of the world spontaneously and unconsciously measures the right portions of its ingredient atoms.

The health and stability of a human organism, for example, depend on a series of quantitative compensations in units of one quality for quantitative changes in units of another. Such compensations maintain an overall quantitative ratio.[13] Exerting oneself physically, one breathes more deeply, etc. By contrast, the stability of water is not maintained by anyone even unconsciously measuring and maintaining a ratio of two hydrogen atoms to one oxygen. Water unconsciously makes itself by measuring hydrogen and oxygen in the right proportion. It is a natural self-measuring of a certain number of particles of one type to another.

The elementary particles on this model are not "self-measures" of different qualities such as hydrogen and oxygen. Rather, they are different ones. Each one is a distinct prequantitative ratio of the limited and the unlimited. Pythagoreans distinguished them geometrically as dots. The familiar but ephemeral things of the world (musical notes, eclipses, illnesses) are quantitative ratios or self-measures of ones. The Pythagorean absolute by its formal definition is a scale of proportions between distinct ones.

A first unrepeated prequantitative one may limit the unlimited more than a second one. But the two factors of each such one, the limited and the unlimited, are nonquantitative. Thus a prequantitative one—the root of all quantity—is a relation of nonquantitative factors. Postquantitative qualities of ordinary experience, such as water or health, define themselves qualitatively as ratios of ones. But each original one measures itself off as a ratio of extraordinary primitive prequantitative qualities, the limited and the unlimited.

The ones are various self-limitations of the unlimited. Quantity is the essence of ordinary quality. But an extraordinary qualitative contrast is at the origin of the whole cosmic process, and in the first place at the origin of quantity. This extraordinary contrast brings Pythagoras back into the orbit of Anaximander's true infinite. But apparent renaissances are often revolutionary. The return to Anaximander at once points forward to a historical neo-Pythagoreanism which merged with Neoplatonism.

An objective ratio of objective ones is identified with a determinate kind of thing such as a stone or portion of water. This identity appears due to historical Pythagoreans. For they viewed a thing as self-identical under two types of description: an immediate qualitative description, such as the taste of water, and a relational quantitative description, such as a ratio of types of atoms. There is no attempt to reduce the immediate qualitative description to its experimentally discovered description in terms of self-measure. Water merely under its immediate qualitative description is not H_2O. Yet one and the same entity is discovered to satisfy both descriptions.

The logic of measure, without abandoning quantitative ones of the same quality, retrieves the idea of qualitative differences which drops out in the logic of pure quantity. Qualitatively identical ones do not in aggregate define the absolute as in the logic of quantity. The logic of measure depends on the recognition of different quantitative aggregates which are finite and qualitatively distinguished.

Quantitative ones of different quality occur in the different terms of a ratio. In different proportions, these ratios are found to be identical to the various sorts of things under the immediate descriptions with which we are familiar. Ordinary qualitative things (unlike the limited and the unlimited) are no longer taken immediately as in the dialectic of quality, but now find their essence in various proportions between different types of ones.

Measure, Hegel writes, is implicitly essence.[14] But there is a distinction between Pythagoras's formal essence (self-measure) of things and of elements and the dynamic essence that is taken up in the second book of the *Logic* as a way of defining of the absolute. In the logic of measure, the chemical self-measure of water is an essence underlying water as an immediate quality. This structural essence is a formal, nonsensory qualitative being. It is surveyable by the mind as a configuration. A mathematically representable structural quality is experimentally found to be the essence of what first presented itself as an immediate quality. Yet the scale of structural essences does not define the absolute without the sensory qualitative beings they define.

In the logic of essence in book 2 of the *Logic*, the absolute defined as "essence" will no longer be an intuitable quality, structural or not. It will be a thought object, not an object of geometrical representation as in formulas for chemical compounds. It will consist in an invisible, nonrepresentable capacity manifested in interaction between other things. It will not be a static pattern of atoms.

We can taste the water, and represent to ourselves its molecular structure, but we can only think—not see or represent—water's capacity to make grass grow. We see the growing grass, not water's essential capacity. Similarly, in the logic of essence we can only think the absolute's essential power of self-manifestation. We can see its self-manifestation, but cannot represent its prior power as a formal structure.

Much in a quality can change. A note played on one instrument will not sound the same on another instrument or in a different octave. But it will still be the same note as long as the same ratio of thickness, tension, and length is maintained. This ratio is not the aesthetic quality. But the ratio and quality are each "harmonious" in its own way—the one intellectually and the other aesthetically.

The real presence of a qualitative determination, for Pythagoras, depends on an accompanying stable quantitative ratio which defines the object's intelligible essence. This distinguishes the theology of measure from that of quality. Qualities are now mediated by quantitative proportions. The overall quality of the sound—neither the note by itself, nor the timbre, nor the octave, nor the accompanying chord—is subjective if not accompanied by ratios belonging to physical factors. The quantitative measure gives the objective formal essence of the thing. By an immediate qualitative description we could not be certain the thing is not hallucinatory.

Each numerically variable ratio (e.g., $2 \times x$), and thus each variable measure (e.g., $2 \times$ the population of China), determines an infinite series of numerically constant ratios (e.g., $2 \times 1,000,000,000$, $2 \times 1,100,000,000$, etc.). But each variable ratio is in turn located in an infinite series of qualitatively different variable ratios. The amount x of the unit H_2O is a different variable ratio from the amount x of the unit H_3O.

No single quantitative ratio of different types of real units is absolute, since it contains the real potentiality of passing by quantitative
increments into a qualitatively different ratio. Here is the Hegelian source
of Engels's law of the transformation of quantitative into qualitative
change.[15] Only a single scale (a scale of scales) of all empirically possible
real and ideal ratios could function as the universal structural essence
of all particular elements, things, and events. The absolute is no single
measure, but rather a universal measuring scale conceived as including
all that it measures. Each particular thing, no longer posited as standing
on its own as in the logic of quality, is now a particular grade or "nodal
point" along that scale.[16]

A musical performance manifests different permanent possibilities
of the same unchanging musical scale. Throughout all quantitative and
qualitative changes in the world, the cosmic scale of scale alone remains
unchanged. However, the *Logic* concedes that natural science so far has
only found a disconnected assortment of more or less revealing scales.[17]
The progress of science in part consists in unifying phenomena within
ever more embracing natural scales (e.g., the theory of electromagnetism,
or Einstein's unification of energy and mass in the same self-measure, or
the search for a unified field theory embracing electromagnetism and
gravity, or a scale of elementary particles).

Science is a quest for intelligibility. Plotting an earthquake or eclipse
within a ratio or on a scale of ratios makes it more intelligible, surveyable
within a constant formal structure. It would make it most intelligible if
one formal structure were not discontinuous with others such structures,
but were the structure of structures. So far such a structure has not been
found in nature, and even less in the realm of spirit and history. In history
insipid quantitative measures are easily found, according to Hegel, but do
not reveal the profound essence of anything.[18] Marxists have disagreed
about history. The debate as to whether there is an overarching deep
mathematical scale in nature or history concerns natural and social
science, but it also concerns the definability of the absolute as measure.

The possibility of a single Pythagorean "musical scale" in nature,
history, or even both cannot be logically excluded. Hegel only points
to the failure of empirical science to find any thus far. However, such
empirical confirmation would not serve to establish the Pythagorean
definition of the absolute as final. For, as we shall see later in the chapter,
a universal scale of ratios logically succumbs to the category of an underlying essential substratum of changing ratios and notes along the scale.

It remains here to consider the bad infinite of measure. The dialectic of measure, like that of quantity, presents a new version of the
distinction between the false and true infinite already encountered in
the logic of quality. The bad infinite of quality is an all-encompassing

noncontradictory being that is contradictorily beyond all "contradictory" things. The bad infinite of quantity is also contradictory: it is a quantitatively all-encompassing remainder after subtraction of any finite sum. The bad infinite of measure is a contradictory all-encompassing measureless quality which escapes the quantitative limits (ratios) of measured qualities.

All ordinary qualities have measures or are units of measure. The measureless may in fact be subject to a measure that has not been found.[19] If we grant that the "measureless" has a measure that is a quantitative transformation of existing measures, the good or true infinite of measure appears: it is the scale of all scales that survives the passage between the different measures or ratios lying along it. Such a scale, conceived along with the things it measures, constructs the most coherent definition of the absolute by the concept of measure.

Hegel ascribes definition of the absolute by the bad infinite in general to the Old Testament worldview, in contrast to other positions in the dialectic of being ascribed to the Greeks. The Greeks held the bad infinite to be unfinished and thus imperfect, while for the Hebrews to escape finitude was an expression of divine perfection. The bad infinite beyond the finite must be distinguished from Anaximander's good infinite which precedes, generates, and cancels any independent finite being. Only the latter was used by the Presocratic Greeks to define the absolute. The former was used only as a transitional concept on the way from the finite to the good infinite, to the unlimited and the limited in composition.

The logic of defining the absolute is intercultural, not exclusively Greek. The "bad infinite" is invoked in Hebrew rather than Greek definitions of the absolute. The bad infinite of quality, e.g., a shimmering mirage of perfection beyond all finite achievements, is invoked in the Kantian-Fichtean version of an essentially Hebrew definition of the absolute. The bad infinite of quantity as a definition of the absolute is ascribed to Haller and Klopstock, who base themselves again on the Old Testament.[20] The bad infinite of measure is also ascribed to the Old Testament, in which God assigns to each finite being its measure,[21] implying that God, the measurer or judge of all things, is beyond measure. (Hegel says that God is the "measure" of all things, but his explanation shows that he really means that He is the measureless measurer.)

3. Transition to Essence

The concept of a scale of real as well as ideal natural measures is constructed by presupposing many atomic ones of a given kind (e.g., units of oxygen) which are qualitatively identical except for their mutual repulsion. Insofar as atoms are related only externally, their relational properties of position and velocity are accidental or external to them. They are essentially identical in quality.

But this presupposition of essentially identical atoms which are accidentally discernible is groundless. If atoms are only accidentally discernible, if their multiplicity is accidental, the truth and explanatory power of atomistic pluralism itself would be a contingent accident. And a cosmic scale of measures stands up as a definition of the absolute no more than the aggregate of atoms which it orders, and which we have seen to collapse into the quagmire of pure quantity.

Even if the idea of a cosmic scale were well-grounded, that it is good explanatory science would not make it good metaphysical theology. It would not justify it as a definition of the absolute. It is a mere hypothesis. If the grounds for supposing many qualitatively identical ones are insufficient, the Pythagorean definition of the absolute as a scale of measures is an unfounded construction.

The many ones which emanated by postulation from the one one vanish again back into it, returning to their source. The many ones of different types are necessary to account for all ratios or measures. They distinguish a ratio as a special type of ratio. As a specific ratio, a monogamous marriage is a ratio of one husband to merely one wife rather than to a possible two or more wives. The quantitative multiplication of the same abstract wifely quality, and of the same monogamous marriage, is possible. Yet, as a concrete relationship a given marriage is a unique and unrepeatable community of a unique husband and a corresponding unique wife. Quantitative repetition of this unique wifely quality is excluded.

The many quantitatively distinguished ones of a quality arise ("emanate") from the original prequantitative one one. They arise by postulation in order to explain the world of immediate experience. The history of natural science from Pythagoras's original explanation of different musical notes to present-day physics and chemistry shows the explanatory power of postulating many ones of each abstract quality in some set of qualities. But the incoherence of postulating many indiscernible ones, seen in the light of the identity of indiscernible ones, leads the many ones of a quality to vanish again back into the one one of that quality. There is but one cosmos, one marriage of this quality, and atom of hydrogen of this situation. But then there is no way this atom can enter into a quantitative ratio except by abstraction, simplification, distortion of its full concrete character. Pythagoras's cosmic scale of ratios relating countable units is but a simplifying approximation to the concrete cosmos and individual microcosms.

Many qualitatively identical ones are contradictory and gratuitous—contradictory insofar as the identity of indiscernibles is analytic, gratuitous insofar as there is never a sufficient ground for distinguishing indiscernibles. The dialectic of the logic finally views the identity of indiscernibles as analytic: "the very nature of things implies that [to be plural] they must be different."[22] There is no ground for qualitatively identical and yet different ones beyond the mere act of asserting them. If qualitatively identical ones are contradictory, they are impossible. And if their manyness lacks a ground in any qualitative discernibility between them, we have seen it cannot be reasonably affirmed.

The single one which remains after the collapse of the many is the "indifferent" substratum of the other ones,[23] and thus also of the scale of measures. "Indifference" is the general characteristic of all ones, the quality of which is unaffected by the addition or subtraction of any number of ones. The original one one is indifferent to both the purely quantitative procession of indiscernible ones from it and to the subtraction of ones from that procession, to both emanation and return, descent and ascent.

The indifferent one may be historically interpreted as the one of Plotinus, which sends forth an inferior many without being diminished or altered by what is less than it:

> Being is the abstract equivalence [*Gleichgültigkeit*]—for which, since
> it is to be thought of by itself as *being*, the expression indifference
> [*Indifferenz*] has been employed—in which there is supposed to be as yet
> no determinateness of any kind; pure quantity is indifference as open
> to all determinations provided that these are external to it and that
> quantity has no immanent connection with them; but indifference which
> can be called absolute is the indifference which, *through the negation* of
> every determinateness of being, i.e., of quality, quantity, and their at first
> immediate unity, measure, is a process of *self-mediation* resulting in a simple
> unity. Any determinateness it still possesses is only a *state*, i.e., something
> qualitative and external which has the indifference for a *substrate*.[24]

This one is thus beyond being. For being has been shown to be determinate, and determinateness is attached to the one only externally and quantitatively. The one one is the substratum of the cosmic process of many indifferent ones. These ones are not affected by their emanation from the one any more than the one is affected by their emanation from it. The one undergoes purely quantitative change in becoming a many. It is the substratum of a change which leaves it indifferent, not affecting it qualitatively.

The indifferent substratum fails to leave the logic of being entirely behind for that of essence. For, though it is essentially indeterminate, it is just for this reason contradictory: it is determinate precisely as indeterminate and indifferent.[25] The indifferent remains indifferent to the cosmic process, and yet refers to it through its very indifference. That process, including our own reflection on it, is the implicit internal self-differentiation of that substratum.

The substratum, if contradictorily affected by the process even in being indifferent to it, can be coherently conceived only by ceasing to be viewed as indifferent. It is cosmic being-for-self (being self-conscious) in and through our reflection on it. But only potentially or in itself, not actually. Yet by this very characteristic the indifferent substratum passes into essential being-in-itself.

We recall that in the logic of quality finite being-in-itself was contrasted to being-for-another. In the logic of essence infinite being-in-itself will be contrasted to actual being-for-self. Essential being-in-itself appears, under a logically independent description, as actual being-for-self. Finite being-in-itself was the internal quality of a thing. Essential being-in-itself is its potentiality for actual being-for-self. The absolute is not in itself just any quality. The quality which it is in itself or potentially is being-for-self, the "quality completed."[26] Actual being-for-self goes beyond essential being-in-itself by actualizing it. But the actualization of an essence, we shall see, can never be deduced from it; it can only be discovered historically. The identity of the absolute as essential being-in-itself and actual being-for-itself occurs under descriptions the second of which is logically independent of the first.

Discovery that the absolute is being-for-self, not just in-itself, occurs through the speculative theologian's reflection on her own theological inquiry. For this inquiry is either nothing at all or is situated in the absolute. If it is in the absolute, it is either an activity of the absolute or an activity of some part of the absolute. But the act of the part is always redescribable as an act of the whole in and through the part.

Theological description is implicitly the absolute's own self-knowledge. It is not some unimportant ripple of self-deception in a remote and isolated island of consciousness in the universe. Even if it is false, it still conveys a definition of the absolute. Further, this definition is the absolute's own self-definition if the speculative theologian, as part of the absolute, acts on behalf of the whole. Yet, he or she does so only if the absolute can have intentions, or at least be assigned putative intentions by its member-agents. This is the view to which the *Logic* tends.

Hegel's absolute, beyond any definition by pure thought, is in truth spirit, a cosmic community including us and our intentions as organs of itself. However, such a view is not vindicated at this stage of the dialectic. At this stage infinite being-in-itself is only asserted to be actual being-for-self, actually self-aware in and through us. This assertion is not yet confirmed in the immediate experience of the speculative theologian.

The Neoplatonic definition of the absolute goes beyond the Pythagorean metaphysics of measure, passing into the logic of essence. For the Pythagoreans the absolute was the essential structure of quantitative ones. For Plotinus the cosmic structure of many ones was not the absolute; rather it flowed from the absolute as from a source. The absolute was the essential prequantitative one from which the many falls away, and to which it returns in the form of the postquantitative one.

Historically, there is a well-documented relation between later neo-Pythagoreans and early Neoplatonists.[27] Plotinus thought of himself as a Pythagorean. Here a dialectical transition seems to conform to a transition in the history of philosophy.

4. Concluding Observations on the Logic of Being

Generally, the logic of being may be considered the logic of immediately given being in ancient philosophy. The logical order of historical philosophers examined appears to be: Parmenides, Gorgias, Heraclitus, Anaximander, Leucippus, Pythagoras, Plotinus. The historical order of these same individual philosophers appears somewhat different: Anaximander, Pythagoras, Heraclitus, Parmenides, Leucippus, Gorgias, Plotinus.

Even if this historical order is debatable in some respects, significant divergences remain between the logical and historical orders. However, the more significant order in the history of philosophy may not be an order of individual philosophers. If we understand it as order of philosophical movements or schools of thought rather than outstanding individuals, it is possible to discover a historical order which corresponds more closely to the logical Hegelian order. One suggestion is: Parmenideanism, Sophism (Gorgias), Heracliteanism (including Stoic cosmology), speculative cosmology (through Anaxagoras), atomism (through Epicureanism and Lucretius), neo-Pythagoreanism, Neoplatonism (Plotinus). The time of a movement's decisive impact in the history of philosophy may not coincide with the lifetime of its founder.

Of course the success of the *Logic* does not depend on finding a historical order which exactly replicates the logical order. History is a realm of contingency. Dialectical logic is at most the inner essence of idealized history, not the outer appearance of real history. Hegel is clear that demonstrations of contingent temporal and even causal succession do not prove the existence of a corresponding dialectical order:

> Does not the sublime Christian knowledge of God as Truine merit respect of a wholly different order than comes from ascribing it merely to . . . an externally historical course? I do not allow myself to be put off such a basic doctrine by externally historical modes of explanation. There is a higher spirit in it than merely that of such human tradition. I detest seeing such things explained in the same manner as perhaps the descent and dissemination of silk culture, cherries, smallpox, and the like.[28]

The discovery of the dialectic at work in real history is a happy find, which cannot always be expected. An absence of full correspondence between history and dialectic limits the rationality of empirical history, and the rational reconstruction of our empirical identity. But it need not limit the rationality of the dialectic, or the rationality of the essential concept of empirical history.

THE RISE OF PHILOSOPHIES OF NATURAL SCIENCE IN WESTERN THEISM

7

Neoplatonism and the Logic of Identity

1. Essence: Abstract and Concrete

If the absolute's being-in-itself implies some actual being-for-self deducible in particular and not just in general from it, its being-in-itself is a dynamic potentiality for just such actual being-for-self. "Being-in-self," a code term for "essence," is then a concrete essence which explicitly encompasses particular contingent manifestations—though perhaps not all eventual manifestations. It is a concrete potential for some particular realization. The genius of a mature artist who has produced recognized masterpieces is such a concrete essence, which is present in her works. But this concrete essence is also an essence which has been—*ein Wesen, das gewesen ist.* At present it is not merely abstract genius in general, but that of particular revealed past works. Suppose, however, that an author's works appear only after unfulfilled assurances of her genius: until these works actually appear the asserted genius remained the hypothetical abstract essence of a young prodigy—a mere promise of things to come. Even the genius of the master remains in part abstract while the master still lives.[1] But once those undetermined works appear, what essentially has been apparently expands in light of them, with an identity which is seemingly (but only seemingly) posthumous. Hegel is not an objective relativist—for whom the essence of a thing, what has been, changes according to how the future itself changes. Rather, it is more fully constituted and revealed by the future.

The historical being-for-self of the absolute in a speculative philosophical tradition is not independent of its being-in-itself in nature, of the general potential for that being-for-self slumbering from time immemorial in the cosmos. Suppose being-in-itself is asserted abstractly prior to its actual fruition in being-for-self. In the same way, not yet actual, still unidentified works of genius must be blindly posited as a condition of attributing genius to a young child. Understood on such an analogy, the absolute's being-in-itself is a mere "abstract" essence.

The distinction between abstract and concrete essence is crucial for understanding books 2 and 3 of the *Logic*. Definition of the absolute as essence in book 2 of the *Logic* remains in the sphere of abstract essence. The crucial passage, with parenthetical indications of the neo-Aristotelian reading I propose, is this:

> Essence is being-in-and-for-Self, but in the determination of being-in-itself [potentiality]; for the general determination of essence is to have proceeded from being, or to be the *first negation of being*. Its movement consists in [implicitly] positing within itself the negation or determination [the abstractly possible actualization of potential], thereby giving itself determinate being. It becomes as infinite [concretely actualized] being-for-self what it is in itself, thereby giving itself its *determinate being* and becoming as infinite being-for-self what it in itself. It thus gives itself its *determinate being* that is *equal* to its being-in-itself and becomes *Notion* [concept]. For the Notion is the absolute that in its determinate being is absolute, or is [actually] in and for itself. But the determinate being which essence gives itself is not yet determinate being as in and [actually] for itself, but as *given* by essence to itself, or as posited [abstractly implied], and is consequently still distinct from the determinate being of the Notion.[2]

The abstract essence cited at the end of this quotation fails to include its determinate surface manifestations. Abstract essence thus excludes immediate determinate being. Yet since it is the essence of such immediate being, the latter becomes the essence of the first transcendent essence. Genuine masterpieces are alternately the essence of genius (which is contradictorily abstract without them) and the mere manifestations of genius: "In Essence the determinations are only *relational*. . . . But, in the first place essence as simple to itself is being; while on the other hand, being, according to its one-sided determination of being *something immediate*, is *degraded* to something merely negative, to a shine [semblance]."[3]

Book 3, the logic of the concept, does not reject definition of the absolute as essence. It only rejects its definition as abstract essence. The logic of the concept is the dialectic of a living concrete essence including particular historical realizations as well as yet to be determined future realizations.

2. Being-for-Self as the Highest Potential of the Absolute

The postquantitative one reached at the end of the logic of being was interpreted as a Neoplatonic being-in-itself withdrawn into itself out of the cosmic process. The prequantitative one reached already at the end of the dialectic of qualitative being was taken as the Presocratic being-for-self of the same cosmic process.

In starting now from the postquantitative one we can retrieve pre-quantitative being-for-self by reflecting on the inquiry accomplished. The act of abstracting, from the now accomplished dialectic of being, the mere potential for actualization of its successive logical determinations (pure being, determinate being, etc.) regenerates before our gaze the series of those determinations. This is the deconstructive-reconstructive abstraction, from a known dialectical achievement, of its logical seed. It is a self-induced forgetting of the dialectical result, a reenactment of it, and contemplation of it in its reenactment.

Because being-in-act logically implies being-in-potency with respect to that act, passage from the dialectic of being "in act" to the same dialectic "in itself" is deductively grounded. "Does" implies "can." The desire to know oneself is a desire to relive one's dialectical history and behold its unfolding before one's eyes in a process of emanation. It is a desire for being-for-self which resides in being-in-itself.

Book 1 of the *Logic* was a dialectic of a being-in-itself which is now in act, and which knows itself in act. It comes to be in act for itself: the dialectic successfully accomplishes itself, and in its being-for-self knows it has succeeded. This is its forward movement: from mere being-in-itself to being-in-itself-for-itself.

The move from the logic of being to that of essence requires a reverse movement from being-for-self to being-in-itself, from act to mere potency. Since act proves potency, being which is actually for itself proves its potentiality to be for itself: it is in itself actually for itself. It is capable of thinking itself in its abstract Parmenidean beginning, and it knows itself by reflection on its achievement to be so capable.

The postquantitative one at the end of the dialectic of being is not the finite being-in-itself found in the logic of qualitative being. Rather, it is infinite being-in-itself, not being-for-self in act, but in potency, in itself.

Being-for-self is the one element of the true definition of the absolute which survives from the dialectic of being. Categories of quality preceding being-for-self proved contradictory because they absolutized qualitatively relative determinations within being-for-self. Categories of quantity and measure following being-for-self contradicted the identity of indiscernibles; they numerically distinguished ones that were qualitatively indiscernible.

At the end of the logic of being, the dialectic of infinite being-in-itself reenacts itself for itself:

> Absolute indifference is the final determination of *being* before it becomes essence; but it does not attain to essence. It reveals itself as still belonging to the sphere of being through the fact that, determined as *indifferent* [*gleichgültig*], it still contains difference as an *external, quantitative* determination; this is its *determinate being*, contrasted with which absolute indifference is determined as being only *implicitly* the absolute, not the absolute grasped as *actuality* [*my translation of this same clause from the German*: this is its determinate being, with which it finds itself in the contradiction of being determined, contrary to its own nature as indifferent, merely as the absolute as being-in-itself, not as being-for-itself].[4] In other words, it is *external reflection* which stops short of conceiving the differences [as they are] *in themselves* or in the absolute as *one and the same*, thinking of them as only indifferently distinguished, not as intrinsically distinct from one another. The further step which requires to be made here is to grasp that this reflection of the differences into their unity is not merely the product of the *external* reflection of the subjective thinker, but that it is the very nature of the differences of this unity to sublate [dialectically transcend] themselves, with the result that their unity proves to be absolute negativity, its indifference to be just as much indifferent *to itself*, to its own indifference, as it is indifferent to otherness.[5]

A flower in bloom implies a prior flower in blossom. Determinate being-in-act implies a prior determinate being-in-itself "which has been." A reverse motion picture offers for contemplation the flower in bloom returning to the blossom and then the mere bud. In an inferential thought experiment, determinate being-in-act is led back to its mere potentiality or being-in-itself.

In the full flower of maturity, one thinks to return to the blossom of youth only when one's powers begin to fade. Being returns in itself only upon succumbing to the incoherence of purely "external," "quantitative" determinations. Unfolding again as determinate being-in-act, being actualizes for us its various potentials for determinate self-manifestation, including the potential for appearing contradictorily to external reflection as purely quantitative, indifferent to quality. External reflection reflects on the cosmos as a single indifferent substratum.

The internal reflection of the self-concept in book 3 of the *Logic* sees that the absolute is for itself in being for the philosophizing subject reflecting on it. Internal reflection retrieves prequantitative being-for-self as the true definition of the absolute, except that the absolute's being-for-itself is now performed by the speculative philosopher. It is not, as in objective logic (books 1 and 2), a mere object which the philosopher beholds and reports.

Being-for-self, thought thinking itself, is the highest potential of the absolute. The absolute is more truly defined as "being-in-and-for-itself" than as merely qualitatively positive being-in-itself, being-in-itself for-another, being a scale of measures in itself, or being-in-itself indifferent. The absolute is of course qualitatively positive. Yet that is not all it is. That is not its highest potential.

Its highest potential is its most comprehensive potential, the one whose actualization presupposes the actualization of all other potentials. Being-in-itself-for-itself presupposes being-in-itself qualitatively positive, being-in-itself qualitatively negative, and the potential for all other more limited determinations of being.

Being-for-self is the highest potential of the absolute because it presupposes the discovery of all other potentials. It presupposes their actualization. The being-for-self which a being achieves is proportional to the range of potentials it actualizes, upon whose actualization it reflects. Only the actualization of potentials proves their existence: "essence, and inwardness as well, only prove themselves to be what they are by moving out into the domain of appearance."[6]

Thus, being-for-self is not all or nothing. The being-for-self afforded by a wasted life is not that of a Goethe. The actual self-consciousness attained by an idle individual is not self-consciousness in all presumed potentials. Yet, the potential for self-consciousness is still highest: it is consciousness of oneself in all other actualized potentials. The limits of one's potential self-consciousness are the limits of one's actualizable potential. Actual self-consciousness is the being-for-itself of one's actualized being-in-itself. It is a reflection on achievement.

The enacted dialectic of being returns in itself to be dialectically reenacted for itself. Upon its original expansion, it succumbed to an unforeseen accident in the contradictions of quantitative indifference. After the empire of its original innocent expansion in quality, quantity, and measure has collapsed, it expands a second time: it beholds the dialectical epic with its contradictions as upon a screen which depicts stages of one's own genesis which no longer inwardly touch one's present existence.

Reenactment of the dialectic of absolute being-in-itself at the end of the logic of being explicitly reposits the objective qualitative being-for-self ("absolute negativity") which faded with multiplication of the one.

This being-for-self is implicitly posited in infinite being-in-itself. Being in oneself all one's determinations is also being in oneself for oneself.

Yet the true actualization of infinite being-in-itself, in the theology of the self-concept, is subjective (self-positing, not merely posited) being-in-and-for-itself. The absolute is not known only externally to be for itself: it accomplishes its own being-for-self in its act of thinking itself: "The *thinking* of necessity . . . is rather the dissolution of this hardness; because it is its going-together with *itself* in the other. . . . As *existing for-itself,* this liberation is called '*I,*' as developed into its totality, it is *free spirit,* as feeling, it is love, as enjoyment, *beatitude.*"[7] For the first time in the dialectic of philosophy's history, the subjective thinking of the philosopher defining the absolute enters into the definition itself. A scholar may proclaim a posteriori the absolute's actualization of its potential being-for-self in a Spinoza or Schelling. A speculative philosopher accomplishes it a priori by her own act even without Spinoza.

3. The Principle of Determinability as the Main Positive Lesson of the Logic

Every universal determination implies further determinability through a more particular determinate property, but which more particular property is never implied. The property of being human is determinable as male or female, Chinese or Russian, young or old. Sex, nationality, and age are not external accidents of humanity, but its more particular and internal determinations. This is the principle determinability.

Only by attributing determinability to humanity can humanity be truly attributed to any individual. No one is human merely in general. Nor can a limit be set to a property's further determinability. As long as we count human beings we reduce humanity as determinable to some abstractly and hence falsely determinate but repeatable character. We of course intermittently do this in daily life. The Pythagorean definition of the absolute as a master scale of ratios between quantitative units errs by a definitive theological fixation on such an intermittent recourse.

The particular determination is itself a general determination relative to a still more particular determination. Chinese and male are also determinable. The particular determining the universal is thus itself a universal requiring particularization. "The true, infinite universal which, in itself, is as much particularity as individuality . . . *determines* itself freely."[8] For the universal determination to cease determining itself still further is to cease to be a living determination. The true universal is essentially self-particularizing or self-specifying.[9]

This principle appears in different forms in all three books of the *Logic*. In book 1 it is the principle that to be determinate in general is to be determinate in particular. In book 2 it is the principle of the necessity of contingency: "though the really necessary is a necessary as regards form, as regards content it is limited, and through this has its contingency."[10] In book 3 it is the principle of the universality of nonuniversal particularity, or the concretely essential nature of the inessential.

The essential character of a thing consists in an abstract essence, abstracted from its past. It is what it has been.[11] But what has a general essential character must, to exist, be in process; it must also assert itself in the present under accidental descriptions not logically derived from the essential description based on the past.

If there is a main positive doctrine throughout the *Logic*, this is it. It is the doctrine of positive reason over against the abstract understanding's claim that the thing is fully intelligible in its universal essence. It is equally asserted against negative reason's skeptical claim that, since the thing is not intelligible merely in its universal essence, it is not intelligible at all.

The application of this principle at present is: being-in-itself made determinate as a particular potential being-for-self implies some determinate being-for-self for which that potential is the potential. Cosmic being-in-itself is not fully determinate by virtue of what can be deduced from its mere being-in-itself. Cosmic potentiality as such is not fully determinate any more than the particular determinate character of an animal is fully given merely by being an animal. The genus implies species, but does not imply the particular species to which the animal belongs.

Going beyond the *Logic*, the entire system of philosophy for Hegel ends with a definition of the absolute as self-knowing spirit, a community of ever particularizable individuals, including vehicles of its self-knowledge. It is neither a species nor the genus of any species. A species is relative to other species in the genus. A genus is relative to another genus, the source of any external specific difference by which it becomes one species or another. Since there is nothing outside the absolute, it is not open to external determination. It is a self-determining determinable. It is not a single or undivided individual. It is a macrocosmic community including microcosmic internalizations and individualizations of itself. It is the macrocosmic community containing all individualizations by which it determines itself.

The same principle of determinability applies to each individual. A general description of an individual implies a further particular description, but does not imply which. We test a general description of a person by questioning, to uncover a more particular description. If there is no more specific description to be discovered the more general description is falsified. A dangerous disease of which no one has shown any ill effects remains unconfirmed as a dangerous disease. In the same way, an essential being-in-and-for-itself which is not expressed in any actual being-for-self remains a being-in-and-for-itself which is purely potential, and thus only abstractly essential. It is the potential for nothing fully determinate, hence for nothing at all. For what is, is determinate.

In the logic of being, abstract definitions of the absolute have only implicit objective reference to further determinations. In the logic of essence they refer explicitly, whether immediately or upon reflection.[12] It is only for us as philosophizing subjects, not for Parmenides as a philosophizing object, that pure being refers to determinate being. But it is for Plotinus as well as for us that the first category of essence to which we now turn, self-identity, refers to difference. Pure being becomes determinate being, giving way to it. But self-identity in no way disappears in difference.

What is not just abstractly asserted but concretely confirmed to be self-identical is reidentifiable under different descriptions. Columbus is concretely self-identical both as the Italian navigator who entered the Spanish service and the discoverer of America.

Yet we must distinguish between the abstract concept of identity-in-difference and the different particular descriptions in which it is expressed. Self-identity refers explicitly to difference in general, but not to any particular descriptive differences. These must be discovered, not deduced from self-identity.

The concept of identity at the beginning of the logic of essence is not the Leibnizian logical concept of identity through all a thing's properties; it is an epistemological concept of discovered identity under different descriptive referring expressions. Hegel calls it "reflection in self" (*Reflexion-in-sich*, "inward reflection").[13]

Abstract identity as a definition of the absolute at the onset of the logic of essence refers immediately and necessarily to difference, which in turn refers contingently to its concrete expression in particular descriptive differences. Concrete identity-in-difference belongs to the logic of the concept, not abstract essence. An abstractly essentialist definition of the absolute by abstract self-identity cannot hold out against a concrete conceptual definition—unless the latter retrenches into the contradictory absolutization of abstract self-identity apart from the descriptive differences under which alone a thing is concretely found to be self-identical.

Abstract essentialist definitions of the absolute are thus explicitly contradictory. They absolutize what they explicitly recognize to be relative.Insofar as the contradiction is immediate and explicit, they are indirect ironic assertions of the futility of metaphysics. Nonetheless, we may suppose that the contradiction, though explicit, is not immediately obvious but only becomes so when the speculative theologian reflects. In that case, if theological essentialists remain naively unreflective, their abstract essentialism may be intended sincerely. A gulf arises between the skeptical dialectical logic of the theology of essence, which is reflective, and the credulous theology of essence in itself.

Despite their distinction, the logic of the theology of being is discovered along with the theology of being itself—though not along with Parmenides—in the contradiction of absolutizing abstract terms such as pure being. Pure being *passes* into determinate being for the speculative theologian of being. It *develops* into determinate being for the logician of the theology of being who sees what goes on behind the back of individual theologians of being.

The reflective logician of essentialist theology, by contrast, does not discover but sees immediately the contradiction of abstract essentialism which essentialism does not see. Abstract essentialism is not skeptical. The dialectical logic of abstract essentialism's pretension to defining the absolute is inherently skeptical.

Being is immediate, while essence is reached indirectly, by mediation of another. An essence is a hidden potential that reveals itself in what is immediate. However, each term in the relation is mediated by the other. Immediate intuited being in the logic of being was absolutely immediate. In the logic of essence its immediacy is explicitly relative.

Thus, the majesty of nature in the Old Testament worldview not only mediates but is mediated by the greatness of God. The Hebrew cannot look on nature as given without thinking the inscrutable sublimity of its Creator. The immediacy of the absolute as essence is contradictorily relative to its mediation, and indeed even explicitly so.

Being-for-self in the logic of being is absolutely immediate. But being-in-itself as potentiality in the logic of essence can appear immediate only to thought that has regressed to a Parmenidean theology of pure being out of the determinate sensory manifestation of abstract essence. What the theology of being takes to be absolutely immediate being the theology of essence takes to be relatively immediate, to be being-in-itself relative to independent particular actualizations of its potential being-for-self. The absolute as being becomes the absolute as essential being insofar as being, coherently conceived as determinate rather than pure being, logically requires nondeducible accidental determinate expressions.

The explicit incoherence of abstract essentialism makes us ask how it could be more than the sport of skeptical irony. The reply is that, at the onset of the logic of essence, such essentialism is explicitly contradictory only upon reflection, not immediately:[14] "In the sphere of Being, relatedness [*Beziehung*, reference] is only implicit; in essence . . . relatedness is explicit. . . . In *Essence* the determinations are only relational, not yet as reflected strictly within themselves: that is why the Concept is not yet *for itself*."[15]

Cases of abstract essence include those in which it is institutionalized in world history, as the abstractly essentialist Hebrew worldview is institutionalized in Western culture. That the absolute is essence is epitomized in saying it is the Hebrew Lord of the universe.[16] The importance of this definition of the absolute in religious and political history from Biblical times through the ancien régime explains its importance in the history of philosophy—which in view of its intrinsic logical incoherence might otherwise to be difficult to explain.

Hegel's claim that theological essentialism is summed up in Biblical creationism reminds us that creationism already appeared in the logic of being. It appeared where the false infinite appeared. The theology of abstract essentialism is the triumph of the false infinite. The false aesthetic infinite of quality gave way to the true infinite of quality. The false infinite of quantity gave way to quantitative ratio. And the false infinite of measure, the measureless, yielded to the good infinite of measure, a self-contained cosmic scale of measures. In the logic of essence a contradictory false infinite of essence does not occur by name. But that is because it is implicit everywhere, not sporadically as in the logic of being.

No dynamic essence or potential survives as dynamic if it is exhausted by any *de facto* finite series of its historical actualizations. "The Essence must *appear*. . . . Essence therefore is not *behind* or *before* appearance."[17]

Force, we are told, is identified with its manifestations.[18] But this can only be identification of force with the full range of empirically possible manifestations, not merely with those actually observed. If a force had no merely possible manifestations, it would either expand to include new actual manifestations, and in its expression would lose its original identity; or it would retain its essential identity but lose the explosive character of making merely possible manifestations accidentally actual. In this second case essence would become flabby: it would lose its force and become the quiescent inner essence contemplated in already revealed manifestations, both actual and ideal.

This creation by which we know the Creator is a finite manifestation of an infinite Creator, who could have created other finite possible worlds. His power is not exhausted by this creation. The false infinite is a contradictory infinite excluding something finite. Every definition of the absolute as abstract essential being-in-itself to the exclusion of possible accidental expressions which would also manifest its essence succumbs to the incoherence of the false infinite.

4. Reflection

The form that dialectical movement took in the dialectic of being was transition, the passage of birth and death. The form it takes in the dialectic of essence is explicit reference, whether immediately or upon reflection. And the form it will take in the dialectic of the concept is development. Pure being perishes as such to become determinate being. It passes away, and passes into determinate being without explicitly referring to it, and without developing into it.

Contingent epistemological identity, the result of identification, refers explicitly to differences of description. But the discovered self-identity of Columbus as identifiable under different referring expressions, as discoverer of America and Italian navigator serving Spain, is not developed out of Columbus's abstract self-identity.

Explicit reference may, metaphorically speaking, occur upon reflection rather than immediately. Three kinds of reflection are distinguished. Since the movement of the logic of essence is from immediate to reflective reference, this movement is clarified by clarifying reflection itself. Hegel's analyses of reflection center around distinctions between (1) positing reflection; (2) presuppositional reflection, also called external reflection; and (3) determining reflection, also known as immanent reflection.

Clarification of these distinctions begins by considering use of the reflection metaphor in general. There is a literal sense of these terms in which we cannot talk of "reflective" or "speculative" thinking without picture thinking, in contrast to the pure imageless thought which allegedly distinguishes speculative thought. Recent Hegel scholarship has emphasized Hegel's inability to rid his work of picture thinking and rise to pure imageless thought.[19]All abstract terms have derived from concrete terms. "To abstract" originally means "to take from," etc. To say that Hegel falls into picture thinking is often a version of the genetic fallacy, the fallacy of supposing that "abstract" refers to something empirical or visual just because it once did so.

That "calvary" at the end of the *Phenomenology*[20]—or "reflection" or "speculation" in the *Logic*—evidences picture thinking is refuted by showing that the terms are used philosophically in a sense contrary to what their pictorial sense suggests. For example, the imageless reflection of pure thought, contrary to the physical reflection of light, is bidirectional. The upstairs light physically lights up the downstairs entrance. The upstairs light lights up in thought the downstairs entrance and vice versa.

The "calvary" of spirit refers to no visual scene on the hill; it does not effect salvation from sin. It is the self-negation of the absolutized individual for the sake of negation of its own negation as one individual separate from others, and for the sake of its concrete reexpression in a community of different individuals.

Reflection, a metaphor for the referential activity of thought, is rooted in a relation. It implies a light source, a first illuminated object off which light is reflected (a first reflecting object), and a second reflecting object on which reflected light falls. The second reflecting light is illuminated in the reflected light of the first object. This second reflecting object is second source of reflective illumination. In mirror reflection, the second object reflects the form of the first object.[21] The sun is a light source which illuminates the human form whose image is reflected in the shadow in the pond. For Hegel, the expression of essence is its mirror image. But whereas in the *objective logic* thinking looks in a mirror at a separate essence, in the *subjective logic* of the self-thinking concept thinking looks at itself in the mirror.

Positing reflection in the logic is not such physical reflection. It is the illumination of object *B* solely by the mental light reflected off object *A* from some source in the power of mental illumination. This object *B*, by way of "return,"[22] is illuminated solely by the reflected light of *A*. Bidirectionally, down is illuminated merely by up, which illuminates down. But down, unlike the elevator which is down, lacks concrete existence. Since everything existing under a single description—one-dimensionally and merely as posited—lacks concrete independent existence, positing reflection "is the movement of nothing to nothing."[23] In other words, it is the movement of "illusory being" (*Schein*).[24]

In reflection that posits, as that reflection is immediately given, there is not yet any mirroring reflection. Positing reflection proceeds between nothing and nothing. The positing activity is the one factor in such reflection that is not illusory being. Yet, if positing reflection flits back and forth between one nothing and another nothing lit up by it, without finding anything of multidimensional depth existing independently of its being posited, it indirectly lights up itself as mirrored in the play of "nothings." It lights up, beneath a superficial play of nothings, speculative thinking (negation of the negation) limited to a purely positing function: "the immediate or being, is only this very equality of the negation [the other of that being] with itself, the negated negation, absolute negativity."[25]

Superficial immediate illusory being (*Schein*) has positing reflection as its deeper essence: "Illusory being is the same thing as reflection; but it is reflection as immediate. For illusory being that has withdrawn into itself and so is estranged from its immediacy, we have the foreign word reflection. Essence is [external] reflection."[26]

Reflective thought first rebounds back and forth between one object to a second. A first object that one posits makes one think of a second. If we close our eyes and behold the color phantasms that circulate, a left-hand phantasm, by its internal relation to what is to the right, makes one think of the right-hand phantasms. To posit a left-hand phantasm as such is to posit a right-hand phantasm. A right-hand dot illuminates the left by the light that the right reflects on it. Yet, if the two are asserted to be independent, this assertion proves hollow if they have no other properties than those they are posited to have. They are illusory as independent beings. And like all illusions they cast a reflection on the reflective activity positing them.

The second type of reflection is presuppositional or external reflection. Let us again cite a concrete example. To posit oneself, e.g., to choose one's profession, is not to posit the country of one's birth but to presuppose that country as already posited independently of one's choice. Everyone has a country of birth, which no one chooses in choosing who he or she is.

To cite another example, to posit something as an animal is necessarily to presuppose some particular species of animal as given independently of its just being an animal. What must already be posited independently of what is first posited, without being deductively posited in particular by what is first posited, remains external to what is first posited. What we have called the principle of the necessity of contingency is here a principle of presuppositional reflection. The contingent form taken by one's general essence is necessarily posited in general along with that general essence. Yet, it is necessarily posited in general as being externally presupposed and not posited in particular. Because the presupposed species of an animal cannot be necessarily inferred from the generic concept of being an animal, presuppositional reflection is also called external reflection.

The standpoint of essence is that of reflection.[27] But the reflection in the theology of essence is that of an abstract essentialism which excludes accidental predicates.[28] It is external reflection. The essence of a triangle casts a totally external light on the school grade in which it is studied, assuming it must be studied in some grade or other. And the abstract essence of the absolute illuminates its accidents in a similarly external light. What is presupposed is encountered as an external and yet inescapable fate.

Earning a living presupposes having some occupation or other. Getting married presupposes deciding to marry someone in particular. To marry in general without marrying in particular is not to marry at all. An individual who sincerely decides to earn her living only in general without choosing any profession in particular will nonetheless confront, by external reflection, the alien necessity of having some particular occupation or other. Really choosing to earn one's living logically implies having some occupation. But if the individual experiences that occupation not as something she has posited, but rather as posited independently by alien chance economic circumstances, her choice to work in general will bear a constant and explicit external reflection on the particular presupposed occupation with which she ends up.

The object of presuppositional reflection is in some respects always surprising and unpredictable. Essence as reflection is an abstract essence reflecting externally on what is inessential. The absolutization of an abstract essence (e.g., parenthood in general) makes the concrete determination that it presupposes (having this particular child) external to that abstract essence.

Someone who chooses parenthood realizing only that to do so is to choose some child or other engages only in positing reflection. Being a parent posits having a child, which in return posits having a parent. Someone who claims to have chosen parenthood but who, when the child comes along, insists that he or she did not choose to be the parent of that child, disowns the external reflection on the actual child which is presupposed by positing reflection on a child in general. The child that comes along is a reminder that parenthood, having children in general, has as an external presupposition in the actual particular child that is had. Anyone who has chosen parenthood but rejects parenthood of the particular child that comes along attempts to reverse the original choice of parenthood. Presuppositional positing of this particular child is the only way to coherently maintain one's positing of a child in general, to avoid repudiation of one's original positing reflection.

And a spouse maintains his or her identity through the choice of marriage in general only through accepting, in marriage in particular, a concrete and freely evolving person whom he or she did not really choose.

A third type of reflection, determining or internal reflection, stems from presuppositional external reflection. A person's identity is no longer reduced to his or her choice or positing. A thing is no longer reduced to what is posited in it in originally identifying it. External reflection is characteristic of abstract essentialism, which posits an abstract essence, and then discovers the inessential particularization external to that essence. Some particularization in which the person or thing manifests itself under different logically independent descriptions is necessary to its universal essence.

To put it in the Hegelian manner, the "truth of presuppositional reflection" is internal or determining reflection. The particularization of the essence internally determines the abstract essence precisely in not being deducible from it. For example, being American or French concretely determines one's general choice of a profession, so that the country of one's birth, which was presupposed independently of one's choice of who one is, is part of what makes one what one is professionally. Both an American and Frenchman can choose to be a waiter. But the particularizing external presuppositions of the choice are different in a country in which waiters form a widespread unionized profession from one in which this is not so.

What one necessarily presupposes but does not posit in positing oneself belongs to one's concrete essence as much as what is posited. It makes one's choice possible as this particular choice, without itself being chosen. In much the same way, being green or red makes being a color possible though it is not posited by positing reflection along with the positing of being a color. External reflection on one's external fate thus becomes internal reflection on one's concrete character. Character is fate.

Positing reflection does not mark the theology of being, in which Parmenides, for example, posits pure being without immediately reflecting on determinate being. But it does mark the logic of the theology of being in which pure being, once it is lighted up, immediately reflects on (coposits) determinate being. External determination marks the logic of abstract essence, which on being illuminated presupposes an inessential accident not immediately coposited. Accident contradicts absolutized abstract essence. Internal reflection marks the logic of the concept: what is posited under an essential universal description is essentially rediscoverable under accidental particular descriptions which it does not immediately coposit. Accident expresses essence. And it thereby ceases to be abstractly "accidental" as it is in the logic of essence.

The objective universal character of a thing or person is particularized by its past, and particularizes itself in the present. The universal precepts of old age are particularized by the past experience of a lifetime. The same precepts spoken in youth either ring hollow and lack true universality or are even now particularizing themselves.[29] A man whom the police first identify generally as going through a red light is particularized retrospectively as being a much wanted murderer. The philosopher who taught Plato particularizes himself subsequently for himself as the philosopher who drank the hemlock.

We are now ready to examine the logic of essence. The last position in the logic of being defined the absolute as an indifferent substratum. Though Hegel mentions Spinoza and alludes to Schelling,[30] Plotinus's postquantitative one, into which the world of emanated many ones returns, is the most plausible original historical representative of this standpoint.

Consideration of the first standpoint in the logic of essence confirms this view. The indifferent one becomes the essential one when it appears as being-in-itself, with the potential for regenerating the determinations of being from which it previously withdrew in abstract indifference. The indifferent one is the Neoplatonic one of the return, of an ascendent dialectic. The essential one is the Neoplatonic one of emanation, of a descendent dialectic capable of generating absolute negativity, being-in-and-for-itself, or internal reflection.

5. Neoplatonism and the Theology of Identity

Hegel traces the transition from the logic of being to essence back to Anaxagoras's separation of *nous* out from the changing mixtures of this world. Yet the most abstract definition of the absolute as essence is more developed in the historically later Neoplatonism than in Anaxagoras. This definition holds that the absolute is abstractly self-identical to the exclusion of all differences of descriptions. It is self-identical under but one description, that of the indeterminate one. Whatever is immediately given as determinate is the indeterminate one—which reveals the determinateness of what is given to be illusory. "Essence is simple immediacy as sublated [transcended] immediacy . . . through which otherness and relation-to-other has vanished in its own self into pure equality-with-self. Essence is therefore simple identity-with-self."[31]

Neoplatonic identity is abstract identity because it excludes differences. Thus, Plotinus's negative theology of pure identity characterizes the absolute only as not temporal, not bodily, not mental, etc.[32] It is indescribable in positive terms. If all the "different" descriptions of what is allegedly self-identical in difference (under different descriptions) are negative, the differences in description prove illusory. They reveal no internal self-differentiation of the absolute.

A negative property such as not being green can reveal something positive and determinate about a thing only if it is the determinate property of not being green but some other color. But if the thing has no positive qualities, no color at all, not being green entails no positive quality. Generalizing, if all a thing's properties are negative, they are all identically indeterminate. The thing admits of no descriptive differences.

The concrete identity found under different descriptions thus collapses into the identity of indifference. Yet the Neoplatonic definition of the absolute as the self-identical one is not the Parmenidean definition as indeterminate being, since the idea of the one explicitly refers to the emanation of a many which it reabsorbs and cancels. The first ones to emanate from the original one lack qualitative identity with the original one. The initial one to emanate is qualitatively distinct as intelligence, by which the original one thinks itself through its emanation.

But the one resembles indeterminate being in that its attributes are indeterminate even if their designations are linguistically distinct. The Neoplatonic one is self-identical as the timeless and the unlimited. But since "the timeless" and "the unlimited" have the same purely negative and totally indeterminate sense, the one is thus tautologically self-identical: the timeless is the timeless, the one is the one. The indescribable is the indescribable. The one is tautologically self-identical merely as the indescribable.

Of Plotinus Hegel says:

> the absolute, the basis, is here . . . pure being, the unchangeable, which is the basis and cause of all Being that appears. . . . The true principle is not the multiplicity of present being, for really and truly their unity is their essence. . . . This unity has no multiplicity . . . it is unknowable . . . the soul must attain . . . the thought of this unity through negative movement, . . . which makes trial of all predicates and finds nothing except this One. All predicates such as being and substance do not conform to it . . . for they express some determination or other.[33]

Yet, this very quote shows the impossibility of resting with the claim that the one is merely self-identical under a single description according to Neoplatonism. The Neoplatonists themselves assert a "movement" of the soul, by which the one is identified with itself under linguistically different descriptions which are all true of it. The absolute is not only self-identical: it is discovered to be such by discovering the identical reference of linguistically different descriptions. It is truly "timeless," "uncreated," "undivided," etc.

If the absolute is self-identical merely as indeterminate, it has no being at all. To be merely indeterminate is not to be all. To be only abstractly self-identical is to be nothing at all. Everything is self-identical. What is concretely self-identical by contrast is distinguished only by determinate descriptions. The concrete essential self-identity of the Neoplatonic one is not just the identity of a (e.g., "the uncreated") with itself. Rather, it is its discovered identity with b ("the indivisible").

Abstract identity is expressed by $(\imath x)\ Fx = (\imath x)\ Fx$. Things are abstractly identical under the same description. Such identity is tautological, repetitive, without logical movement.[34] It is the identity of formal logic, expressed in the logical law of identity. It is known a priori, and is uninformative.

Concrete identity is expressed by $(\imath x)\ Fx = (\imath y)\ Gy$. Two things are concretely identical only under different determinate descriptions. Concrete identity is discovered a posteriori, though like all true identity statements it is true necessarily. It is found a posteriori that the discoverer of America is Columbus, and that the absolute in itself is concretely the absolute for itself. Identity as an essentialist definition of the absolute is the concrete identity of essential being-in-itself with a subsequent being-in-act positing itself within (and concretizing) this essence.

The definite descriptions under which things are said to be identical are incomplete descriptions of the whole thing. Each definite description need be only as complete as is necessary to identify the thing. (If every description used in referring to a thing were complete, concrete identity would revert to abstract identity.)

Concrete identity is either a known identity or a merely ontological identity not yet discovered. Known identity implies identification: individual a singled out through one description is identified with b singled out through another (e.g., "The lottery winner is the town mayor"). If the identity of a with b is discovered by a, a is self-identifying: through one of its descriptions a is for itself.

Concrete ontological identity may occur between a and b under descriptions from the past, but also between a under a description true at some past time and b under a new description not true at that past time. In such ontological identity, a develops, redetermines itself, particularizes itself as b (e.g., the identity between Columbus as baptized and as the discoverer of America). But Columbus, the discoverer of America, not only reveals but retroactively determines what Columbus is essentially or in himself. The discoverer of America was even as an infant what he is in himself.

A thing's identity is constituted by all its properties. The *Logic* works with the identity of indiscernibles.[35] The identity of a is inconsistent with the existence of something of the same complete description that is not a. An entity is indiscernible from itself, and only from itself. As discernible from what it is not, a excludes anything else having the same identity as itself. Even if it is identical with other things by its abstract essence, it differentiates itself from all else by its complete identity.

The notion of numerically different but qualitatively indifferent things is contradictory. A thing's identity, its self-equality under any complete description, logically excludes a purely quantitative distinction of things: "in quantity we have something which is an alterable, but which still remains [qualitatively] the same in spite of its alteration. As a result the concept of quantity turns out to contain a contradiction, and it is this contradiction that constitutes the dialectic of quantity."[36]

The self-refutation of any definition of the absolute by purely external, quantitative distinctions is implicit in Leibniz's principle. Such definitions have directly preceded the logic of essence. A purely quantitative repetition of ones results from abstract thinking, which falsifies the ones by abstracting from their concrete qualitative differences. This falsification may be justified pragmatically, but must be rejected in a coherent definition of the absolute.

A main result of the science of logic is to repudiate quantitative definition of the absolute, and to retrieve qualitative definition. But true qualitative definition must be reflective, not immediate. The absolute is not merely the qualitative being-for-self left behind at the end of the logic of quality. It is qualitative being-for-itself which is essentially (in itself or potentially) identical with itself under the further description of being-for-self in act—more particularly, being-for-self in act in and through us.

The logic of essence thus begins with a dialectical retreat from contradictory quantitative being into qualitative being. But to back into one's dialectical past is, with the benefit of hindsight, to rediscover in that past the potential for one's present. Qualitative being recovered is essential qualitative being-in-itself, concretely self-identical with qualitative being-for-self-in-act.

The absolute is currently defined with Plotinus as the self-identical and wholly indeterminate object a. But if something is self-identical merely as indeterminate it has no being at all. For to be is to be determinate. The absolute must be self-identical under different determinate descriptions.

The Neoplatonic dialectic of identity retreats from concrete identity to abstract-identity-under-a-single-description. Columbus is Columbus. Second, it proceeds back to concrete identity in general: the self-identity of a under some other description than the one used in identifying a. Columbus is reidentifiable under some description other than merely being Columbus. Third, we arrive at concrete identity particularized by the discovery of an actual second description. Columbus is the discoverer of America.

Fourth, what is self-identical under a particular description must be self-identical by the exclusion of a particular opposite description.[37] What is green is not determinately green merely by not being nongreen, but by not being red. Columbus is not the discoverer of America merely by excluding the contradictory description of not being that discoverer. He is this discoverer determinately only by excluding a specific contrary, e.g., being the discoverer of a route to India.

Fifth, since being the discoverer of America excludes the opposed description of being the discoverer of a route to India, the description of Columbus as discoverer of America incorporates the determinate negation of the opposed description. Elimination of the first description's determinate negation of the second would remove the specificity of the first. Being the discoverer of America loses determinateness if it is not opposed to being that alternative discoverer, and loses even more determinateness if it is not opposed to any other discoverer. Absolutization of the definite description we historically have of Columbus, the one who discovered America, apart from its determinate negation is contradictory.[38] The particular description is, contradictorily, no longer that particular description.

Sixth, since thought cannot remain with a contradiction, we must conclude that Columbus is the discoverer of America only by inclusion of his determinate negation of not discovering a route to India. The true description of Columbus includes a specific relation to a second, opposite description precisely by excluding it.

Exclusion of the second description by the first means that the second is not satisfied by the entity. Its nonsatisfaction is included in the first description. Columbus is the discoverer of America only by relation to a possible but nonfactual description of himself as another discoverer. The discoverer of America, who is contradictory if described merely as such, is grounded in a relation between the actual Columbus and a merely possible Columbus.

The concrete identity of *a* with *b* under *different* definite descriptions is maintained only if they are identical under descriptions which each specifically exclude an opposite description. Moreover, they are identical under descriptions each of which has its excluded opposite somewhere beyond the object *a* or *b*. What is concretely self-identical is drawn into a web of various different relations with other actual or possible things. It is but a moment in an organic whole of internally related things.

The *Logic* asserts contradictory things in the world.[39] We may take this to mean that there are things whose contradictory and hence false description is publicly shared and institutionally necessary.[40] Motion as analyzed by Zeno is contradictory. But it is at once an objective contradiction institutionalized in shared references to the external sensory world.[41]

The finite person or self is also a contradictory but existing being— but by a subjective fixation governing its private practice rather than by an intersubjectively institutionalized belief. The person's fixation on contradictory beliefs about what it can and cannot do is the motor of its self-transcendence and development.[42] The contradiction is that there is something which one both can and yet cannot be. It is rooted in the conflict between what one fixedly holds one can be in one's innermost essence and what one knows oneself to be in the outer circumstances of one's existence. This gap is not usually viewed as a logical contradiction. In the *Logic* a contradiction is seen in it because being-in-itself, essential being, is understood as that to which a return is made, a return from actuality to the potentiality for that actuality. As an adult's achievements expand, a long-past infant's concrete potentiality for these achievements equally expands. The past as the essence of the changing present is not changeless. The contradiction in the development of a person attaches to a potentiality never yet actualized, hence a potentiality for nothing determinate, for nothing at all:

> internal self-movement [development, self-transcendence] proper . . .
> is nothing else but the fact that something is, in one and the same
> respect, *self-contained* [*sufficient*] *and* deficient, *the negative of itself.* Abstract
> self-identity is not as yet a livingness, but the positive, being in its own self
> a negativity, goes outside itself and undergoes alteration. Something is
> therefore alive only in so far as it contains contradiction within it.[43]

For a tree to be known as potentially in bloom presupposes, for Aristotle, that it once was in bloom, or that other trees of the same kind have been in bloom. Being-in-potency is inferred from a prior being-in-act. We know we can do from what we have done. If we have never done what we say we can do, and if nobody has ever done it, claiming to know that we can do it contradicts itself no sooner than it is said, since we cannot successfully refer to what has not been done. Potentiality is the potentiality for receiving into oneself an achievement already in act, already actually past, not for actualizing a unique purely possible achievement to which no one can yet successfully refer.

If you say you can write a book, you are not talking about any book already written. You know that with perseverance you can rewrite *Gone with the Wind* if you want. But this is not what you mean here when you say you can write a book. You mean you can write a book never yet written. Yet you do not mean a merely indeterminate unwritten book, since merely indeterminate books do not and can never exist. A book which has never been written is not a fully determinate book which only awaits material realization in ink. It will become the book, with whatever determinate identity it will have, only in the creative process of being written.

You have a potential for writing a book already published. Your essential potentiality lies in what you have done, and in such a potential there is no contradiction. The contradiction arises when you say you have it in yourself to be what nobody has ever been, to do what no one has ever done. One's essence arises from a return of one's achievement into itself. One backs into reflection on one's determinate being-in-itself out of reflection on one's being-in-act. But the potential for doing what one has never done is the potential for creating a new identity, and a new past essence for oneself.

Actually writing the book temporarily eliminates (but does not resolve) the contradiction between saying that one can write a new book and the admission that it has not been written, between holding that one both does and does not have it within oneself to write a book. One first says that one has it within oneself. Only such brash confidence produces books. Yet, without an actual book yet in existence there is no book—no determinate book—which one has it in oneself to write. The actual book does not confirm but creates the concrete potentiality for writing that book. One's essence is not only revealed but also created by one's achievement. Potentiality without achievement is a contradiction and a sham.

A fifteen-year-old youth is merely in herself an adult, not an adult in act. She is potentially an adult. But what adult? No one can be an adult in general. Thus, the fifteen-year-old is potentially some particular adult. Which one? She is not potentially any past or present adult. Even if she should take her mother, father, or a historical figure as a model, she is not potentially her father, or some adult of history. Any adult she will be she must create. Such an adult does not yet exist. The potentiality for being what does not exist must await its creation even to be a potentiality. Potentiality is relational: it is for being something or other.

According to the Aristotelian tradition, what one is potentially must already be in act, in another if not in oneself. Hence, the potentiality can precede its actualization. In the logic, however, the youth's potential for being the particular adult she will be is created in and through her active or passive selection of a particular determination of the determinable adulthood suggested by past, present, and imaginable adults. Potentiality is a relation to an actualization. If the actualization is not eternal but historical, potentiality itself is concrete and historical.

One's potentiality for being somebody else who merely might have been is no potentiality at all. That merely possible person cannot be even singled out except by a general description applicable to other possible individuals as well. Potentiality is either mere potentiality for something in general or for something in particular. If it is for something merely in general, it is impossible, since nothing is merely in general. If it is for something in particular, it is also impossible, because the particular being it potentially is, but is not yet in act, does not yet exist.

Thus, no one can be an adult merely in oneself, but not in act. What she is merely in herself would be either impossibly general or still unactualized. To be an adult in oneself implies being an adult in act.

The definition of the absolute as ground—the successor definition to identity—is, like all essentialist definitions, introduced as concrete identity in difference. Specifically, it is introduced as an identity under determinately different descriptions each with its respective exclusion or opposition. "The resolved contradiction is therefore ground, essence as the unity of the positive and the negative."[44] A youth struggling to be a lawyer—the specific negation of what he or she now is—without contradiction both is not and is a lawyer. That youth lives, for the present, in the opposition of alternation between professional competence and incompetence.

The absolute as essence is self-identical as both being-in-itself and being-for-self, as the world and *nous* lying potential within it. Similarly, the essence of an adult human being is not merely the child with an unactualized potential for adulthood. Nor is it simply adulthood or rational autonomy. It is both an ever returning childhood (adulthood withdrawn into itself) and the adulthood every adult strives again and again to reenact. The absolute itself is both the world and *nous*, both being-in-itself and the being-for-itself—the being-for-self in which being-in-itself actualizes itself.

Being-in-itself for Hegel is not, as for Sartre, merely the unambiguous being of things that are what they are. Being-in-itself is, potentially, what actually it is not. It is potentially being-for-itself-in-act. And being-for-itself is not, as for Sartre, an impossible self-objectification of the present act of consciousness. It is the act's self-discovery under a different description in the object, in being-in-itself, in its own unactualized potential being. *Nous* finds itself in the world; the adult sees herself in the child she was.

The identity of mere being-in-itself and actual being-for-itself means that, contrary to Aristotle, mere being-in-itself actualizes itself. Being-in-itself is creative, productive of its own being-for-itself-in-act. Only creativity can eliminate the contradiction of an unactualized potentiality that is yet the potentiality for something in particular.

If we see ourselves in our child, it is not because the child receives externally and passively the education that we give it as the adults we are. Rather, the child in fits and starts recreates itself as still another adult.

The child does not give itself a general form of adulthood belonging to others which it does not have. It actualizes itself by creating a unique form of adulthood which no other adult has ever had, and in so doing creates its unique potential for realizing that form.

The essence of the adult, the adult's concrete ground, lies in his or her ever more determinate self-creative, self-actualizing potentiality circulating under mutually opposed descriptions as positive and negative, e.g., competent and incompetent. The child merely as a still potential adult is only the abstract material ground of the adult who will actually emerge. The actual rationality of educators and parents is only an abstract formal ground. The active child grounds itself by circulating in oppositions between levels of achievement.

The concrete ground is both material and formal. But the collapse of concrete essence into abstract essence under a single description, which we have seen with identity and difference, appears again in the logic of ground. This time it is a collapse of concrete self-productive ground—the self-concept itself—into tautological abstract ground: "Ground does not yet have any *content* that is determined in and for itself, nor is it *purpose*: so it is neither *active* nor *productive*; instead, an existence simply *emerges* from the ground."[45]

The logic of essence begins with positive speculative reason declaring the absolute to be concrete identity in difference. Were this stance maintained, the logic of essence would be that of concrete essence, which is the logic of the concept. Only repeated lapses into contradictory abstraction maintain the logic of the concept—and with it the end of history—still at a distance.

The Deterministic Theology
of the Explanatory Ground

1. The Retreat from Identity-in-Difference to Abstract Identity in the Theology of the Explanatory Ground

The logic of essence is distinguished from that of the self-concept because it fails to maintain the concept of a concrete essence embracing its particularization and self-actualization through self-awareness. Hegel expresses this self-concept as follows: "[Concrete] essence shines *within itself* or is pure reflection. In this way it is only relation to self (though not as immediate but as reflected relation): *Identity within itself.*"[1] In such a concrete essence, speculative thought can recognize itself. The concept of this concrete essence is that of the self-concept itself.

Within the middle book of the logic, this concrete essence is no sooner attained than reduced to abstract essence. "Formal identity or identity-of-the-understanding is this identity, insofar as one holds onto it firmly and *abstracts* from distinction."[2] As concrete and true, Identity is "first the *ground* and then, in its higher truth, the Concept."[3] The theology of essence in the more limited sense stems from the abstractive understanding rather than reason.[4]

> Being is accordingly determined [in the logic of essence as distinct from being] as essence, as a being in which everything determinate and finite is negated. . . . But in this way, essence is neither *in itself* nor *for itself*; what it is it is through external, abstractive reflection; and it is for other, namely abstraction. . . . But essence as it has here come to be [as it has emerged concretely and in truth at the start of logic of essence], is what it is through a negativity which is not alien to it but is its very own. . . . It is being that is *in and for itself.*[5]

The retreat from the emerging vista of speculative reason is from a concrete rationality already announced at the onset of the logic of essence as lying in concrete identity in difference.[6] The retreat is back to a theology of the abstractive understanding, which abstractly absolutizes identity apart from the recognition of difference.

At this point a division arises in the text between the theology of the abstractive understanding and the skeptical critique of that theology from the standpoint of dialectical reason. Curiously, Hegel seems unable to give expression to the standpoint of the abstractive understanding without polemicizing against it. It is difficult for him to look upon it nonpolemically, simply bearing witness to its own self-refutation as his own dialectical method requires.[7] The theology of abstract identity is no sooner stated than labeled "silly."[8] Even within the main text of the paragraph it is said to be long "discredited."

Yet, the return to the abstractive understanding in the logic of essence is not a return to the prereflective, immediate abstractive understanding encountered before the onset of the logic of essence. Rather, it brings us to a more developed form of the understanding, reflective understanding: "*reflective understanding* . . . in general stands for the understanding as abstracting, and hence as separating[,] and remaining fixed in its separations."[9]

Reflective understanding is an abstractive understanding which has already seen the light of reason. Miller's omission in the above translation of the comma from the original German gives the mistaken impression that "remaining fixed in its separations" follows as much as the "separating" from the act of abstraction. Only separation, absolutization, follows from abstraction.

If one thing is abstracted from a second that has not yet been abstracted, it can only be asserted to exist separately from the second. Remaining fixed in the results of separation does not follow. To remain fixed is for the understanding to dig in over against contradiction and self-negation. Such stubbornness is a free decision, whose alternative is negation of the negation, negation of the self's negation-of-itself through negation-of-the-other.

Such fixation is a regressive decision, to which Hegel refers in a Biblical vein as the "Fall." We encountered this Fall in the logic of being, in the transition from being-for-self to many ones.[10] In light of this parallelism, we may understand the claim that "in the *whole* of the logic, essence occupies the same place as quantity does in the sphere of being: absolute indifference to limit."[11]

The abstract essence excluding accidents is a contradiction. On the one hand, it is limited by what "posits itself" apart from it. On the other hand, it is indifferent to its limit because the accidents that limit it are merely "posited" by it and "reflected within it." What has an essence necessarily requires accidents, and is reflected in them. Having a right angle is an accident which reflects the abstract essence of a triangle. Yet it is excluded from that abstract essence, "positing itself" apart from it.

Similarly, being a woman reflects the essence of a human, while not being a part of that essence. But being right-angled is not a possible accident of being human. If we view essence abstractly, absolutizing it apart from the finite range of alternative accidents that would reflect it, it is contradictory. A three-sided closed plane figure which is neither right-angled nor not right-angled is a contradiction.

The accidents that contradictorily express an abstract essence are countless. A unique, never to be repeated eclipse of the moon, viewed as a concrete event incapable of complete description, emerges ("posits itself") as more than what the laws of physics and any description of a prior state of the universe can predict regarding its essence. Prediction of an event refers to it under a description, by a finite number of general attributes. Yet if, by the nonidentity of discernibles, events are each unique, the complete description of a unique event is never exhausted by a finite number of general attributes. For the conjunction of those attributes would be open to multiple instantiation by different events. No matter how great the finite number of attributes in a description of an event, further attributes are always necessary to reach a complete description closed to possible multiple instantiation.

If this is granted, any concrete event limits any proposed absolute essential explanatory "ground" understood as the totality of causal laws with a description of an antecedent world-state. The laws of nature together with any description of the antecedent world posit that there will be an eclipse of the moon of some finite general description open to multiple instances, but not that it will be this unique eclipse. The world, described as being in a certain state at time t^1 and being governed by certain causal laws, requires and yet does not specifically include a more precise description of the eclipse as this individual event. Yet, deterministic theology, defining the absolute as the abstract essential determining ground of every event, denies the existence of future events under such more complete descriptions.

Reductionistic determinism—defining the absolute as the ground of all—illustrates the reflective understanding. This is no naive act of the understanding. The limits of determinism lying in the inexhaustible descriptive richness of the present are recognized only to be programmatically reduced by the theology of ground. Determinism in particular, like abstract essentialism in general, is an infinite program. Yet, it stimulates endeavor only as long as the essentialist ignores the fact that the program is unrealizable. There is an unbridgeable gap between the fact that an explanatory ground grounds a future event under an abstract description and the occurrence of that concrete event. This argument underlies the self-refutation of the deterministic definition of the absolute in the *Logic*.

The reflective understanding is thus abstractive, but is also more than the abstractive understanding. It knows the contradictoriness of its position, but stubbornly maintains itself in that position. It refuses defeat. The reflective understanding is expressed in various forms of reductionism. What is "reduced" is the experienced manyness of a thing's properties. The multiplicity of the absolute's descriptions is reduced to a single essential description—"whether it be the case that a part of the manifold that is present in the concrete is *left out* (by means of what is called analysis) and that only *one* of these [elements] is selected, or that, by leaving out their diversity, the manifold determinacies are *drawn together* into one."[12]

2. The Dialectic of Abstract Essentialism: Ambiguity in the History of Philosophy

In the Neoplatonic dialectic of abstract identity and difference, the single reductionistic description was that of an indeterminate one with which the referents of all apparently determinate descriptions turn out to be identical. In the dialectic of abstract ground and consequent to which we now pass, there is also a single essential description of the absolute to which other descriptions are reduced. The difference is that this essential description is no longer indeterminate. The reduction of other descriptions to it no longer consists in finding the same indetermination lurking behind other descriptions.

The essential description is now determinate. As in Laplace's deterministic model of the universe, this description is a complete determinate description from which other determinate but partial descriptions are deducible. The Neoplatonic reduction of the multiplicity of predicates to a single predicate gives way to a deterministic reduction of successive states of the universe to a single all-explanatory state at some time, governed by universal causal law.

Plotinus appears as a pivotal figure in the history of speculative philosophy: he both concludes the theology of being ("indifference") and initiates the theology of abstract essence (contradictory identity explicitly divorced from difference). In its Stoic form, the theology of ground chronologically precedes Neoplatonism, though for Hegel the apotheosis of ground is dialectically post-Neoplatonic. In fact, on some interpretations the absolutization of ground appears associated with early Greek philosophy from classical atomism through Anaxagoras to the Stoics:

> Nothing occurs as random, but everything for a reason . . . and by necessity [Leucippus]. . . . All things so happen by fate that fate produces the force of necessity: of which opinion were Democritus, Heraclitus, Empedocles[, and Anaxagoras]. . . . Democritus denies purpose by saying, everything which nature uses reduces to necessity. . . . Democritus calls it resistance, motion, and impulsion of the material.[13]

The concept of fate, necessity, reason, or ground in these early philosophers reflects a philosophical tradition deeply rooted in ancient Greece that diverges significantly from the theology of being. The theology of being is pantheistic or panentheistic. The absolute is known by immediate intuition—whether mystical, intellectual, or empirical. The goal is to lose oneself in the absolute. From Parmenides through Pythagoras to Plotinus, this remains an Oriental tradition in Greek philosophy comparable to Sankara and Râmânuja in the Hindu tradition.

When Hegel writes that Anaxagoras inaugurated the metaphysics of abstract essentialism,[14] he is thinking of Anaxagoras's concept of mind or *nous* governing an inessential world. Elsewhere we find theological essentialism identifying the absolute with power and lordship.[15] In either case, the goal is no longer the Oriental one of losing oneself in the absolute but the Western one of expressing one's will to power as a finite self, metaphysically absolutizing one's finite self, or (by projection) identifying oneself vicariously with an invincibly divine will to power.

We must not interpret such an essentialism as an exclusively Hebraic or creationist theism. The idea is independently present in Greece from Anaxagoras through the Stoics: "[mind for Anaxagoras] is the finest of all things and the purest, and it has all knowledge concerning all things and the greatest power[,] and over everything that has soul, large or small, mind rules."[16] The lordship of the absolute in the logic of essence is clearly expressed here. If accordingly we take "theism" to be more general than creationism, allowing that infinite, transcendent divine power may be expressed in ordering the world, not just in creating it, we may thus distinguish a theistic as well as a dominant pantheistic or panentheistic tendency in ancient thought.

Thales's one out of which all things come anticipates in the poetic image of water the logic of essence more than that of being. In the *Logic*, we have seen, Pythagoras is treated as representing the logic of being, although God as a scale of ratios is panentheistic rather than "pantheistic" in the strict Parmenidean sense. What distinguishes the logic of being is more general than pantheism: it includes panentheistic definitions of the absolute as long as the absolute remains by such definitions intuitively immediate or given.

According to Aristotle, Pythagoras started with an essentialist view that the absolute is the source of number, the self-limitation of the unlimited in the limited—with the one as a harmony of the finite and the infinite, the principle of all things in the cosmos. But he then took up the panentheistic position within the logic of being with which Hegel associates him, defining the absolute as a cosmic scale of scales, of ratios of microcosmic ones to qualitatively different such ones. Whereas the one was the essential inner source of the many, a cosmic scale of proportions is an immediate absolute for philosophical contemplation. Yet, if the legend of Pythagoras's invention of the term "philosophy" has any truth in it, he ended like Hegel as a speculative panentheist philosopher of the self-concept or *Begriff*, a philosopher of philosophy. For among microcosmic individuals, philosophers are those who lead the macrocosm along a path to the achievement of contemplative self-awareness. Thus, the logics of being, essence, and self-concept are seemingly all represented in Pythagoras's legendary career. This great ambiguity of the first "philosopher" makes him at once the most inescapable of speculative philosophers.

Dialectically, the rival theistic tradition of divine transcendence, which poetically began with Thales's statement concerning water, begins in earnest (in closer proximity to pure imageless thought) with Plato and Aristotle, and with the pivotal, ambiguous figure of Plotinus. It then moves through St. Augustine and the great Scholastic thinkers of the Middle Ages, and culminates in Leibniz and the equally pivotal and ambiguous thought of Spinoza. The passage from ancient to medieval thought is not one from pantheism to theism, but from a theistic absolute that can be intuitively contemplated by us to one that cannot.

Plotinus's ambiguity is due to the fact that he arguably expresses both the category of indifference at the end of the logic of being and the category of abstract identity at the beginning of the logic of essence. Indifference is expressed in reabsorption of the contradictory many into the one, while essential identity is expressed in the one's role as the source of emanation of the many. In like manner, Spinoza's distinction between an underlying and unknown substance and its infinite essential attributes places him in the logic of essence, while the intellectual self-love of God at the end of the *Ethics* places him already at the threshold of the logic of the self-concept.

Historically, a Greek "theistic" tradition, challenging the dominant pantheism or naturalistic panentheism, begins with Anaxagoras and the atomists (see below). Passing through forms of Stoicism and the ambiguity of Plotinus, it extends to Leibniz and Spinoza, eventually combining with Hebrew creationism. A general theistic tradition may well go back to Heraclitus as the philosopher of the logos by which all things become, rather than simply as the philosopher of becoming. We have already given some reason to include even Thales in this tradition.

We encountered classical atomism in the logic of being. Due to the role played by fate or necessity in atomism, we encounter it again as a possible logic of essence. Atomism also contains an ambiguity. It fosters two different definitions of the absolute: the absolute as the simple plurality of exclusive atoms, and the absolute as the system of causal law which explains the configuration of atoms. As a definition of the absolute, the second type of atomism is only accidentally atomistic; it is essentially a version of the theology of the explanatory ground of all things.

As a theology of being, atomism held that the fixated being-for-self of the atomist rediscovers itself reiterated over and over again in natural phenomena, so as to avoid self-negation by an alien natural world. In the metaphysics of essence, the motivation behind atomism is different: it is to explain the phenomena. True explanation presupposes greater respect for the phenomena than taking them as but a series of mirror reflections of oneself. It implies an obligation to submit to them in their contingency, not to impose oneself on them.

In the theology of being, the leading question for the atomist was. Why is there a sensory world other than myself? The answer implied a projection or repulsion of one's own self-concept onto the other. In the logic of essence, the leading question for the atomist is: Why is the sensory world other than myself this contingent world and not some equally possible world? The answer here has to do with causal laws. Atomism as a theology of being attempts to explain why there is an external sensory world at all. Atomism as an essentialist theology takes the existence of that world for granted and inquires into the ground of it being thus and not otherwise.

Atomism as a theology of being implied no necessary role for natural laws and prediction. Atomism qualifies as a theology of essence because of the role played in it by deterministic laws of nature. If determinism were retained without the atomism (e.g., as in Heraclitus, Stoic physics, and Spinozism), the essentialist theology of ground would still find illustration. Heraclitus writes:

It is wise, listening not to me but to the Law, to acknowledge that all things are one. But although this Law holds forever, men fail to understand it as much as when they hear it for the first time as before they have heard it. For while all things take place in accordance with this Law, yet men are like the inexperienced when they make trial of such words and actions as I set forth. . . . Of all men whose accounts I have listened to, not one has got far enough to know that wisdom is divided from all [fleeting] things.[17]

However, if atomism were retained without determinism (as with Epicureanism's swerve), the absolute could not be adequately defined as ground by the concept of atoms.

Given atomism, the absolute as ground is a configuration of atoms governed by natural laws permitting the prediction of perceived phenomena. Such atomism is one illustration of physical determinism. The absolute is not just atoms, but atoms grounding seemingly ungrounded independent phenomena which are in fact completely grounded.

The nonatomistic theological determinism of Stoicism also defines the absolute as a transcendent ground. "Stoicism" implies resignation to necessity, the necessity of contingency, and finally self-reconciliation with fate. This fate includes impassioned and yet finally futile attempts at revolt against natural law, revolts determined along with all else by natural law itself. The impersonal God of Stoicism—reason, logos, providence, destiny, fate, natural law, and necessity—is an infinite essential power holding sway over events and persons, a power to which as rational beings we are obligated to conform. However, precisely because Stoicism asserted a single cosmic substance, it can also be interpreted nontheistically, i.e., panentheistically. The transcendence of reason, necessity, or God results for Stoics from a failure to understand and accept natural law.

There is a general point to be made concerning the relation of the dialectic to the history of philosophy. Neither Heraclitus, nor atomism, nor Pythagoras, nor Plotinus, nor Stoicism, nor Spinoza appears simply and clearly classifiable as belonging to either the logic of being, the logic essence, or that of the self-concept. Each philosopher just referred to is commonly if not definitively interpreted as falling under at least two of the three general ways of defining the absolute. It is not always easy to tell a philosopher of being from a philosopher of essence, or from a philosopher of the self-concept. At different stages of a career or system one can be all three.

This makes it impossible to argue that ancient philosophy is unequivocally centered around a pantheistic logic of being, medieval philosophy around a theistic logic of essence, and modern philosophy around a panentheistic logic of the self-concept. Pythagoras may have invented speculative philosophy of the self-concept; Hegel then at most invented its systematic development. Still there may be dominant ancient, medieval, and modern trends.

The progression from being through essence to the self-concept is chiefly logical. Yet it is not wholly ahistorical. Despite variation in the conceptions of individual philosophers, the ancient Mediterranean world on the whole found the absolute immediately at hand in aesthetic or intellectual intuition. The medieval European world basically strove to behold the absolute in a concealed essential kingdom of God beyond intuition. And the modern Atlantic world fundamentally strives through universal human rights to enjoy the once medieval beyond in present sensory intuition, to bring it down to earth. Atomism, Pythagoras, Plotinus, Stoicism and other philosophies are ambiguous in part because there are alternate ancient, medieval, and modern readings of them.

Interpreted by the ancient world, atomism is a philosophy of being, or more precisely one of many beings, all immediately available to contemplation. It is not concerned with causal laws. Interpreted by the theistic perspective established in Europe in the Middle Ages, atomism belongs rather to the logic of essence: it is a quest for a transcendent complete science of the causal interaction of atomic particles.

To take another example, Pythagoras interpreted according to the logic of being is a theologian of the cosmos as a scale of scales open to theoretical contemplation. Thus, Archytas of Tarenta (fifth–fourth centuries, B.C.) referred to the cosmos as the "whole," a whole in which Eurytos of Croton (fifth century B.C.) had distinguished in detail different species by different geometrical configurations of pebbles. Interpreted according to the medieval logic of essence, Pythagoras becomes a Neoplatonic theologian of number, more exactly of a mystical transcendent, prequantitative one (e.g., Moderatus of Gade, first century, or Nicolas de Cusa). Finally, interpreted according to a modern Hegelian logic of the self-concept, Pythagoras, the inventer of "philosophy" and "theory," appears as the first theologian of philosophy, of the cosmos assimilated to God by microcosmically thinking itself in philosophical contemplation. A Pythagoras for all seasons.

Yet none of these three interpretations is likely faithful to the historical Pythagoras, who with other classical Greeks viewed the perfect divine harmony (the cosmos) as finite, infinitely surrounded by air. Upholding a finite God, could Pythagoras have defended what we have called the "anonymous" position of defining the absolute as contradictorily finite? It is more probable that he distinguished between the divine and what Hegel calls "the absolute," and that he defined the absolute as an infinite chaotic whole (air) surrounding and sustaining a finite, divinely harmonious cosmos.

Stoicism provides further examples of the historical disambiguation of apparent ambiguity. Stoicism is pantheistic from the standpoint of ancient philosophers who were presumed to number among the wise, and who contemplated and embraced natural law. But Stoicism is theistic from the standpoint of fools or fallen medievals who abandon themselves to passion and discover natural law as something to be approached by resigning themselves through renunciation.

Neoplatonism may serve as a final example. From the medieval European standpoint of the fallen self preparing for a dialectic of ascent to the one, Neoplatonism is in a general sense theistic. Yet, from the ancient standpoint of a philosopher who has attained mystical intuition of the one it is pantheistic.

Determinism has enjoyed a long career, surviving classical atomism, ancient Stoicism, and Spinozism. No doubt determinism is possible without being a theology. But in the *Logic* it is developed as a theology of a Laplacean divine mind capable of explaining and predicting all, but also (for lack of immediately intuitive omniscience) needing an explanation of it. The Laplacean superscientist, surpassing the human ability, is the being-for-self of the ground that explains as well as determines all facts. Explanation is for a mind. The absolute enjoys, in and through the hypothesis of a Laplacean superscientist, being-for-self in the contemplation of its own laws and temporally indexed world states. The superscientist is not just a fantasy to explain determinism; though Hegel does not discuss Laplace in the logic of ground, it is this fantasy that would have to be realized for the theology of ground to hold true. This fantasy is also the last form assumed by the absolute as being-for-self, as the one, before it temporarily perishes in the face of the empirical world which it always sought to negate. After the logic of ground the empirical world will temporarily stand on its own in a new phenomenalist definition of the absolute, until this phenomenal world passes into actuality and generates the actual world's being-for-self from a source in the heart of the phenomenal world itself. (An alternative, nontheistic deterministic theology might equate the absolute with objectively determined events divorced from any necessarily known laws, subjective explanation, and prediction; but Hegel understands the grounding relation as one of "explaining from grounds.")[18] A deterministic theology of the one occurs wherever the absolute is described by the mind (being-for-self) of a superscientist as occurring under two successive independent descriptions, such that the second turns out to be deducible from the first. Since explanation is for a subject, the absolute as explanatory ground implicitly includes and even merges with the intelligence for whom the ground necessarily exists. Despite dominant ancient, medieval, and modern trends of thought, we cannot identify deterministic definitions of the absolute exclusively with any one epoch. Its antecedents predate Neoplatonism, and Hobbesian or Laplacean versions postdate it. It is essentially a floating doctrine, not a historical school of philosophy.

It is difficult to identify historical order with dialectical order when faced with definitions of the absolute whose life spring eternal. A definition of the absolute arises historically out of both intraphilosophical dialectical considerations and extraphilosophical influences, such as religion, art, technology, science, and commerce.

Ancient atomism as a metaphysics of being originally arose, for Hegel, under both psychological and dialectical conditions—as an attempt at preserving abstract being-for-self by multiplying it so that one's being-for-self does not lose itself in the cosmic other. Stoicism as an abstract metaphysical essentialism arose through both intra- and extraphilosophical religious influences. Contrary to Neoplatonism, the absolute is found to be self-identical under both a general description and different particular descriptions. One resigns oneself as a Stoic to the world under its present particular descriptions because one believes them grounded in (deducible from, dictated by) a universal essential description of a cosmos with which one religiously identifies.

Modern atomism may be distinguished from ancient atomism by falling under the sway of an outwardly directed Western will to power over an alien world in place of the ancient (and Eastern) release from such a will. The modern atomistic form of the theology of ground is likewise influenced by explanatory physical science and technology as well as philosophical dialectics. It generalizes from the modern physics to a definition of the absolute as a whole.

Stoicism and ancient atomism held a general belief in natural causal law but offered few particular laws with any power of explanation, prediction, and control. In the absence of an ability to explain the present and actively predict and control the future, Stoicism fostered passive acceptance. Modern deterministic theology, by contrast, fosters active intervention in nature.

Stoic deterministic essentialism highlighted Heraclitus's idea of a governing, omnipotent logos, and rejected Parmenides's denial of the sensory world. Neoplatonism restores (and thus modifies) Parmenides by reabsorbing the post-Parmenidean dialectic into the one. The dialectic of being begins with Parmenides and ends with Parmenides discovered anew; it proceeds from the predeterminate, prequantitative being of

Parmenides himself to Plotinus's postdeterminate, postquantitative one. This one is now beyond being because being has proven determinate.

Stoicism begins with a Stoic use of Heraclitus's logos. It begins with the idea of the passive acceptance of logos or necessity, and it ends with the Baconian idea of their active appropriation and use in controlling nature by knowledge of its laws. In the Stoic-Baconian appropriations of Heraclitus, a logos pervading all becoming is paramount.

The overarching transition from the logic of being to that of essence is from the will to self-release (release from attachment to the finite self) to the will to infinite extension of the finite self's power. In the history of philosophy the dialectic of self-release does not end before that of the will to power begins. But the former precedes the latter dialectically. The discovery of the self under different determinate descriptions, as distinct from the merely self-identical one at the onset of the logic of essence, refutes the illusoriness of differences. But the will to self-release, in Sankara or Parmenides, is based on the claim of such illusoriness. Recognition of the reality of the world of differences is the basis of the finite self's will to power over the equally finite world opposed to it.

3. The Retreat from Concrete to Abstract Ground

The transition from the Neoplatonic definition of the absolute by abstract identity to definitions by concrete identity-in-difference depends on mutually irreducible descriptions under which the absolute is found to be self-identical. Thus, the self-identity of a given day under the description of being sunny absolutely to the exclusion of even the memory of being overcast falls "to the ground."[19] A contradictory description points in its fall to an unfallen ground which is subject to true redescription: "Now the thing, the subject, the Notion, is inherently self-contradictory, but it is no less the *contradiction resolved*: it is the *ground* that contains and supports its determinations [both contradiction and its resolution]. . . . Finite things, therefore, in their indifferent multiplicity are simply this, to be contradictory and *disrupted within themselves* and to return to their ground."[20] The concrete ground is a referent supporting logically independent descriptions. Under a true description it grounds itself under a false description. Thus the Copernican sun accounts for what is referred to as "the setting sun."

A society which is the referred-to ground of absolute and thus contradictory wealth is in fact determinately wealthy to the exclusion of yesterday's poverty, poor to the exclusion of the neighbor's wealth. It has concrete self-identity only through the different oppositions entailed by its different determinate descriptions. Each of its different descriptions is differentiated by a different opposition:

> Ordinary consciousness treats the distinct terms as indifferent to one another. Thus we say: I am a human being, I am surrounded by air, water, animals, and everything else. The purpose of philosophy, by contrast is to banish indifference and to become cognizant of the necessity of things, so that the other is seen to confront *its* other. And so, for instance, inorganic nature must be considered not merely as something else than organic nature, but as its necessary other.[21]

The contradictory denial of these oppositions or exclusions would reduce all differences of determinate description to reiterations of the same indeterminate description. The referred-to ground to which contradictorily absolute wealth falls is a particular wealthy society in a relation of exclusion to a certain poverty. No concrete society exists merely as wealthy. It also exists under other determinate descriptions (e.g., peaceful or belligerent) with their respective exclusions.

What I have just called a "referred-to ground" is a concrete referent of different descriptions which are logically independent, and even opposed through their own different oppositions to other things. It is a concrete ground, the thing encountered as concretely self-identical under materially different descriptions. "The thing, subject, or Notion . . . is the *ground* that supports its determinations."[22]

A Fregean concept of reference is helpful in understanding the *Logic.* Suppose the description "nonrational human being" is contradictory inasmuch as the essence of humanity lies in rationality. The description is false. Yet, the false description can be successfully used to make reference to something. But that "something" must exist under some other determinate description that is true.

Thus, a nonrational human may be a concretely rational human referred to in a culture that falsely abstracts and separates reason from passion. The concretely rational individual is then a limited "concrete ground" of the contradictory nonrational human being. The contradictory description successfully used in reference "falls to its ground" in the consistent description that accounts for it.

The concrete ground at which we have arrived is not yet the self-concept, the subject that reidentifies itself under logically independent descriptions. But it does approach the self-concept:

When we say that ground is the *unity* of identity and distinction, this unity must not be understood as abstract identity, for then we would just have another name for a thought that is once more just that identity of the understanding which we have recognized to be untrue. So, in order to counter this misunderstanding, we can also say that ground is not only the unity but equally the distinction of identity and distinction, too [i.e., the difference between the single referent and the multiplicity of its independent properties].[23]

What now happens in the *Logic* resembles what happened at the onset of the logic of identity and difference. Concrete identity embracing actual difference collapsed into abstract Neoplatonic identity without difference. The concrete ground underlying contradictory descriptions of an individual now collapses into an abstract ground: "Ground [the above concrete ground], which we encountered first as the sublation [dialectical transcendence] of contradiction, therefore makes its appearance as a new contradiction. . . . Ground is ground only insofar as it grounds [offers explanation]; but what has come forth from the ground is the ground itself, and herein lies the [tautological] formalism of ground."[24]

The concrete ground underlying contradictory descriptions of an individual is not a sufficient all-explanatory ground of that individual. The concretely rational human whose rationality is essentially expressed in and through passion is but a partial ground of the same human being referred to as nonrational in a given historical setting. A sufficient ground, as distinct from this limited concrete ground, would account for all the facts about what it grounds. The concrete ground frustrates the will to explain all that happens, to see in what is grounded nothing more than a projected reflection of the ground itself: "But this determinateness [of a concrete event] is not posited *by essence* [*the concrete ground*] *itself*; in other words, essence is not ground [not the fully explanatory ground] except in so far as it has itself posited this its determinateness."[25]

When the absolute is viewed as a fully explanatory ground, the different grounding and grounded descriptions of the absolute are no longer retained as logically independent of one another. One partial description is taken abstractly to be the absolute ground, the imperious explanation of all the rest. For example, society under but one description is singled out as grounding all other descriptions alleged to be logically deducible from the first. If we ask why this fall from a concrete to an abstract reductionistic ground occurs, it may be recalled that the theology of essence is a theology of power. The will to uncover an absolute ground expresses a will to power or mastery. Control of the initial conditions and the rules of the game becomes control of the game in its entirety. The

Laplacean fantasy of complete explanation thinly conceals a fantasy of omnipotence or complete control. Laplace's superscientist, for whom the all-explanatory ground (with initial conditions) exists, and who requires deductive explanation of consequent facts because he does not enjoy an intuitive contemplation of all facts, falls short of the omniscience and omnipotence of the creationist God. But to theologically absolutize ground is not to absolutize grounding facts. Because grounding or explaining is an activity of mind, it is to absolutize a transcendent intelligence who knows these facts.

"Ground," put metaphorically, is a form of reflective illumination. Illumination, in contrast to a mere light source, is reflective: there is necessarily an object that it illuminates. Illumination cannot itself be posited without positing such an illuminated, reflecting object. A light source embodies potential, not necessarily actual illumination. If there is no object off which it is reflected onto a spectator, it loses itself in endless darkness.

The illumination of an object that is not self-illuminating is either immediate illumination or reflective illumination. What is immediately illuminated by a light source may indirectly, by the reflection it gives, illuminate a second thing. To directly illuminate wealth is to illuminate poverty in the reflected light of wealth.

The logic of essence is a dialectic of reflective illumination. To posit what is found to be self-identical in a Neoplatonic framework is to posit in its reflected light linguistically different descriptions under which it is reidentified by the same semantic content: the one, the indescribable, the eternal, the changeless, etc.

This Neoplatonic concept of a self-identity discovered under different descriptions turns out contradictory, since it implies that the descriptions are not different. Yet to the extent that the descriptions do differ linguistically even if not semantically, the Neoplatonic assumption of purely abstract identity discovered without descriptive differences falls to the ground as contradictory. For if a description includes the language used and not just supralinguistic sense, nothing is reidentifiable solely under the same ever repeated but totally indeterminate description. The one referred to as "indescribable" is not the one referred to as "eternal."

Definition of the absolute by abstract self-identity under a single description makes its last stand in the theology of ground. In this theology it is conceded, contrary to Neoplatonism, first that the absolute is definable only by a determinate description, and secondly that there are different determinate true descriptions of the absolute. But one of these descriptions maintains itself as the complete or sufficient description of the absolute by "grounding" the others; other descriptions are explained by deduction from it.

An explanatory or grounding fact implies an observable consequent fact, which it posits by "positing reflection." The explanatory ground includes an unobserved lawlike hypothesis. The consequent is an observed immediate fact that calls for explanation by a nonimmediate essential explanatory ground. There is nothing logically presupposed in the consequent beyond what is posited in the antecedent. Every consequent description is part of what is contained in the antecedent description, and is thus assimilable to the antecedent description. Syllogistically, supposing that Thales is Greek is an immediately given fact, the fact is grounded in, i.e., contained in, the fact that he numbers among Presocratic philosophers who are all Greek.

4. Explanatory Grounds: Sufficient and Insufficient

Leibniz stated the principle of the sufficient ground. For any event there must be a sufficient ground why it is thus.[26] An Aristotelian material cause by itself is not sufficient to explain the fact of the event's occurrence. The material cause may slumber forever unactualized.[27] The material cause is insufficient, though every event has an abstract essence, potentiality, or being-in-itself which in Aristotelian language is its "material cause."

Children are, among other things, the material out of which adults are made. The child is in itself the adult, i.e., is the adult in essence. But one truly has it within oneself to be an adult only after one has actually become one. The child that the adult once was is only in itself an adult or, more precisely, that adult. Hence the dictum according to which essence is what has been. The child who has been is essentially, in itself, this individual adult.

An adult who has forgotten herself, suffering momentary regression into childish conduct, also has it in herself to be an adult. But a ten-year-old who is told to be adult, and who is made to believe that she can be, is constantly confronted with the frustration of not finding it in herself to be such. The belief in one's essential adulthood guides one's effort, and the failure of the effort establishes the contradictory belief that one cannot, without a transformation of one's identity, be an adult. The child merely as a child might never become an adult. A child is in herself an adult only in the past tense, only if she has been in herself an adult but is now actually an adult. One is temporarily in oneself an adult only if adulthood is recoverable after a lapse.

An Aristotelian efficient cause, what Hegel calls a "real" cause,[28] is also insufficient. An educator can do nothing without good material to work on. There is always more in the effect than external efficient causes can account for. But the formal cause[29] is sufficient to permit deduction of the effect, though only at the viciously circularly price of restating the cause and thus explaining nothing. Either the ground is something other than the effect and thus is insufficient to explain it (and this is the case of material and efficient causes), or it is the same as the effect to be explained, and thus is incapable of providing the needed explanation except in a viciously circular fashion (and this is the case of the formal cause). This is the paradox of explanation: "The formal ground-relation contains only one content for ground and grounded; in this identity lies its necessity, but at the same time their tautology. Real [efficient] ground contains a diversified content but this brings with it the contingency and externality of the ground relation."[30]

Hegel sees irony in the fact that the formal causation which in modern times came to be so widely decried has appeared in a new guise in the form of tautological deductive explanation in modern science.[31] The only noticeable difference, which does not affect the comparison, is that the formal cause for Aristotle was a form, while the formal explanation proposed by modern science is a set of propositions from which is deduced the further proposition that the consequent event occurs.

The maternal instinct is invoked to explain the mother's tendency to care for her young. And my asking my neighbor for advice about the stock market is explained by redescription of my act as an act of asking my neighbor who is a stock broker for this advice. Between maternal instinct and the tendency to care for the young there is only a linguistic difference. The fact that I ask my neighbor for advice is logically included in the fact that I ask my neighbor-broker.

The more inclusive fact explains the included fact by being more self-explanatory to those who first know only the second fact. The cause is not the effect. A relatively self-illuminating ground illuminates a non–self-illuminating consequent. The fact of asking my neighbor-broker for stock advice is not identical with the fact of simply asking my neighbor. Nonetheless, the first fact formally implies the second, and so the idea of formal causation is retained. One fact about an event formally contains the other. The question is whether there is some complete fact about every event or thing that logically contains all other facts about it.

The ordinary concept of a thing (or person) differs from that of an event in that its essence survives change, an alteration of its Leibnizian identity, while an event (process, monad or four-dimensional "thing-event")[32] does not survive change. The event of a lawn party may have the unchanging identity of beginning on the lawn but ending indoors due to rain. We do not know what the event is until we know how it ends. It would not be the same party if it both began and ended on the lawn.

A thing can gain and lose accidental properties and still remain the same as long as it retains essential properties. It remains essentially the same thing, though by the acquisition and loss of accidental properties it will not remain fully self-identical. For a thing's Leibnizian identity comes through all its properties, not just a restricted set of essential ones. A thing retains merely essential self-identity through different sets of accidental properties. Its complete Leibnizian identity at one time does not imply that it has the same Leibnizian identity at a future time. If the house's identity as burnt down were deducible from its identity before the fire, the house would be a process with unchanging temporally indexed properties of being burnt at one time and not burnt at another; it would not be a changing thing.

Vindication of the concept of a thing as a definition of the absolute requires that we show the distinction between essential and nonessential properties to be objective and not merely arbitrary or pragmatic, varying with shifting subjective interests as at the outset of the dialectic of essence.[33] The thing must have its essence in itself, not merely for an external observer, not merely for us.

However, the thing has its own essence objectively only by potentially surprising and resisting observers in the actualization of this essence. Actualization of an essential potentiality proves the potential. That potential is, under a more explicit description, identical with that actualization. A potential is a potential for something, and the actualization shows what the potential is for. The sugar lump proves its essential solubility and sweetness by actually dissolving in the mouth, thus acting selectively in opposition to the action of the water and taste buds.

Because the actualization of the essence is a further specification of it, no description of the essence as unactualized can imply or explain the actualization. Every actualization is a new creation. Nor can a description of the actualization fully explain the essence. The dissolution of the sugar lump implies that the lump had the essential capacity for this dissolution. But the sugar lump did not exist prior to dissolution merely with an unactualized capacity for this dissolution. A potentially dissolved sugar lump is, apart from this potential, actually more or less granular or powder-like.

What has potentialities must also have actual occurrent properties. Without occurrent properties (e.g., location, time, size, shape, color, texture, solidity, etc.) it could not be identified, and it then could not be tested for its dispositional essential properties. Yet, no description of the sugar dissolved in water, it would seem, permits us to infer how granular or powder-like it was, or what its other occurrent properties were.

Our conclusion is that there is no single true description of a thing which logically implies all other true descriptions. If there were, ordinary things would be processes and not things. They would be four-dimensional events stretched out in time, each including temporally indexed properties as essential to being the event it is.[34] It may be replied that what we ordinarily call things are processes. It is tempting to view things and persons that are entirely past as event-processes. Napoleon no longer changes (except by acquiring posthumous properties such as inspiring the Second Empire), but is timelessly the Emperor who married Josephine at one time and the Emperor who married the Austrian Princess at another. Only a sound case for determinism, however, can easily convince us that Napoleon when alive did not acquire new temporally indexed properties over time, i.e., that Napoleon at one time was indiscernibly identical with Napoleon at a later time. Barring determinism, Napoleon did not already have in 1806 the property of being defeated in 1815—unless in 1806 his essence (though past) was not yet fully constituted.

5. The Self-Refutation of Determinism

It is relevant to Hegel's rejection of the reductionistic doctrine of the world's total self-explanation under a single description that he in fact rejects determinism. The repudiation is most explicit in his discussion of mechanism in the logic of the self-concept. But mechanism as an expression of the "objective concept" is examined in the section of the subjective logic of the concept that is closest the objective logic of essence:

> the object, like any determinate being in general, has the determinateness of its totality *outside itself* in *other* objects, and these in turn have theirs *outside them*, and so on to infinity. . . . it is the object's own nature that points it *outside itself and beyond itself* outside itself and beyond itself to other objects for its determination; but to these others their *determinate function* is a *matter of indifference.* Consequently, a principle of self-determination is nowhere to be found; *determinism*—the standpoint occupied by cognition when it takes the object, just as we have found it here, to be the truth—assigns for each determination of the object that of another object; but this other is likewise indifferent both to its being determined and to its active determining. For this reason determinism

itself is also indeterminate in the sense that it involves the progression to infinity; it can halt and be satisfied at any point at will, because the object it has reached in its progress, being a formal totality, is shut up within itself and indifferent to its being determined by another. Consequently, the explanation of the determination of an object and the progressive determining of the object made for the purpose of the explanation is only an *empty word*, since in the other object to which it advances there resides no self-determination.[35]

Determinism assigns to each characteristic of the object determination by another object, so that in all respects the object is determined by what is other than itself. But there is a self-determination of the object which determinism fails to acknowledge. Externally related objects are indifferent to one another. They cannot determine one another. They enjoy instead self-determination through each individual object itself. The object must opt in favor of some more particular determination or other to make any predictable general determination fully determinate, rather than merely determinable. Self-determination is the necessity of contingent self-particularization under any general description. Self-determination must be understood as a creative process, not as a Stoic acceptance of past necessity. This is the interpretation substantiated by Hegel's texts on the philosophy of ground.

Whoever speaks of determinism speaks of universal causal laws. Such laws subsume things and events under general descriptions, and explain them only insofar as they are subsumable. Complete explanation of an event assumes the event can be completely described by a finite set of causal laws along with a complete description of the world at some past time.

Fire is explained by oxygen, combustible material, and heat. But what is thus explained is only fire in general, not all particular features of this fire. Whether because each thing has an endless list of properties, or because it has certain unique nonuniversal qualities not open to multiple instantiation, it is never possible to exhaust the individuality of a particular fire in a statable general description, no matter how extended. For no matter how much we particularize the description, either the quality as unique cannot be captured in a general description, or the description as general is open to multiple instantiation, and thus is not the complete description of this individual as contrasted with some other individual.

The deterministic form of abstract essentialism, which reduces all true descriptions of the universe and events to a single description of the universe at some time, neglects any incompletely describable individuality of the universe at successive times. The absolute is self-identical under different descriptions, but its individuality at any future time is not reducible to any finite description appearing in the consequent of a hypothetico-deductive explanation. Any description, even a conjunction of descriptions, is we have seen open to repeated instantiation; it thus fails to exhaust what is unrepeatable or individual. No event can have a deductively sufficient ground in any statable, finite description of it.

The sufficient ground of what a person or thing is lies not just in other things, persons, and laws, but also in the presupposition of its own individual activity. The sufficient ground of the dissolution of sugar lies not merely in the active dissolving force of the water, but equally in the complicity of the sugar itself, whose secret force consists in allowing itself to be dissolved. The force as passive is active in its very passivity.[36] This is a kind of circular formal causality, which affirms the individual self-formation of the event of dissolution in response to the water. The search for a sufficient explanation external to the event always results in explanatory insufficiency, but acquiescence in a sufficient explanation internal to the event results in circularity. If the event needs explanation, we say, it cannot explain itself; and if it can explain itself it did not need explanation.

What Hegel calls the true sufficient ground of the event, being internal, is not an "explanation" as understood by philosophers of science. It is not a finite set of facts from which the fact of the event's occurrence is deduced. Only facts or propositions can be deduced, not concrete events. The sufficient ground according to Hegel is rather the self-determination of an event which can be partially described but never sufficiently "explained."

The next move in the logic is from an explanatory ground over against a consequent to an essential law recapitulating sensory appearances. It is a move from explanation to description as a model for science. The ground gives explanatory illumination of the consequent facts, but it gives an incomplete explanation of the existing thing or event (*Sache*) which is the topic of such facts. We explain that there is a storm, but not this storm.

Yet, even if determinism is false, natural law as the lawful inner essence of external sensory appearances provides a nonexplanatory descriptive illumination of them. It will illuminate them by condensing their indeterministic variety into a single "stable image."[37] (Even if future sensory appearances could be completely deduced deterministically from present sensory appearances and universal laws, because the laws themselves are contingent summary descriptions of appearances, there would be no strong explanation of events. Given either determinism or indeterminism, explanation collapses into description.)

As long as reflective illumination is deductive explanation—a form of positing reflection in which consequent facts about an event are deduced from laws and descriptions of the world at some past time—indeterminism means that the event itself, the topic about which these facts are facts, emerges into existence in part ungrounded. It posits itself beyond the description of any deduced consequent proceeding from an explanatory ground with conditions. (I translate Hegel's "*Sache*" by "event" or "affair" rather than by Miller's "fact". An affair is a selected, significant event. Hegel has in mind a concrete occurrence which emerges into existence at a certain time—an event about which changeless "facts" may thereafter be true. It is a changeless fact about yesterday's sunrise that it occurred at 6:15 A.M.) Distinguishing between explanatory grounds and merely factual conditions, the *Logic* holds that the event tautologically conditions itself—it cannot ground itself. Beyond the past conditions of the event's occurrence, the present concrete event numbers among its own conditions:

> The movement of the fact [event] to become posited, on the one hand through its [nonexplanatory] conditions, and on the other through its [explanatory] ground, is merely the *vanishing of the illusion of mediation* [the illusion that the event as a totality is what it is through external causes]. The process by which the fact [event, *Sache*, affair] is posited is accordingly an emergence, the simple entry of the fact [event] *into* [*occurrent*] *existence*, the pure movement of the fact to itself. *When all the conditions of a fact* [*event*] *are present*, it enters into [occurrent] Existence. The fact [event] *is, before it exists*; it is, first, as [having a predictable general] *essence* or as [having] an *unconditioned* [ground inclusive of nonexplanatory factual conditions]; secondly, it has [fully] *determinate* [*present*] *being* or is determinate, and this in the twofold manner above considered, on the one hand in its conditions and on the other, in its ground. . . . When, therefore, all the conditions of the fact [event] are present, that is when the totality of the fact is posited as a groundless immediate, this scattered multiplicity [of ground and conditions] *inwardizes* itself in its own self. The whole [present] fact [event] must be present in its conditions, or all the conditions belong to its Existence.[38]

A deductive explanation consists in a series of facts which are expressible in true statements that imply a grounded consequent fact expressible in a further statement. The materially causal fact that hay is combustible (together with presupposed conditions) implies the further fact that it actually burns. The formally causal fact that a medicine has soporific power implies (without further conditions) the fact that it tends to put people asleep. The efficiently causal fact that lightning struck (together with various presupposed conditions) implies that the house burnt down.

Formal causality, sufficient but circular, is expressed in tautological statements, while material and efficient causality (without adding conditions) is nontautological and insufficient. An insufficient explanation explains only subject to further conditions. It is, as Hegel says, a relatively unconditioned ground which presupposes external conditions.[39] It becomes an absolutely sufficient and unconditioned ground[40] only if these conditions are incorporated into the ground.

The ground, if understood abstractly as "positing deductive reflection," is sufficient to explain certain facts about events and things, but not to explain the full concrete existence (occurrence) of events, or existence of things. Everything in some respect is grounded by other things, and in some other respect remains ungrounded by them. The sugar lump grounds the sweetness of the water, but not the transparency of the water. It thus fails to fully ground the water by positing (deductive) reflection. It casts an external presuppositional reflection on the water. Similarly, the water grounds the dissolution of the sugar lump, but not its whiteness.

There is an absolutely sufficient set of external explanatory conditions for an event in itself, viewed as a fully describable potential event, but there is no such set for the same event in act. The necessary conditions of the event in act are in part contained only within the event itself. It conditions itself. To use Whitehead's term, it is the "concrescence" of its conditions: "when, therefore, all the conditions of the fact are present, that is when the totality of the fact is posited as a groundless immediate, this scattered multiplicity inwardizes [*erinnert*] itself in its own self."[41] Again, that all causal laws pertaining to fire and all relevant antecedent conditions hold explains only a fire of some general description, not this fire. Explanation is complete only if the fact that an event occurs can be deduced from the antecedent explanatory facts. But a fact or corresponding statement that is deduced gives only a partial description of a concrete event. The event of a house burning is infinitely richer in total quality than the single fact about it that it burns. What is explained is always a fact, but a fact is about an event-topic of numberless other facts.

If the house's burning were exhaustively described by stating a finite number of facts about it, nothing further could be empirically discovered about it. And this would mean that it could not manifest itself objectively, in itself, or independently of our predictions. The house would exist only one-dimensionally for us, not in itself. Since an infinite description cannot even be formulated, and thus can never be deduced, a concrete event which is endlessly describable cannot be completely explained. A finite description of an effect open to multiple instantiation, we have seen, leaves the concrete effect partially undeduced and unexplained.

The event in act thus emerges partially ungrounded from any alleged deductively sufficient ground. The event or affair (*Sache*) exists beyond its abstract explanatory essence.[42] Stubborn absolutization of an abstract and deterministic explanatory essence of the present event provokes discovery that the event in part occurs beyond the past, is insufficiently explained by it, and is externally presupposed rather than merely posited by its explanation. The only sufficient grounding of the event is a general ground or condition which requires the event to determine itself in particular. If we explain that there was in general a fire, we also demonstrate that in particular there was an event which was more than simply a fire. If we explain one fact about what concretely exists, we demonstrate that there are others not explained.

The definition of the absolute as abstract ground may be stated like this: the absolute is the object which has a deductively grounding property f, so that whatever property an object may have other than f that property is logically implied by f, and so that there actually is a property of the object other than f. This definition is illustrated by classical determinism, though the definition contains no necessary reference to time. The more general idea is that the absolute is defined by a single complete world description which logically contains all partial world descriptions.

The Neoplatonic logic of identity and difference began with the idea of concrete identity in difference,[43] from which it then fell away into abstract identity of indifference. This Neoplatonic identity of indifference invokes the ontological law of identity regarding all that is ("Everything is self-identical," "$A = A$").[44] It applies this ontological law to the absolute, that outside of which there is nothing: "The Absolute is what is identical with itself."[45] More particularly, Neoplatonism falls subject to Hegel's lamentation that "when the Absolute is determined as *essence*, the negativity is often taken only in the sense of an *abstraction* from all determinate predicates."[46] For "of absolute Being Plotinus . . . asserted that it is unknowable. . . . On this point Plotinus . . . recurs to the fact that the soul must really first attain to the thought of this unity through . . . [a] skeptical movement which makes a trial of all predicates and finds nothing except this One."[47]

The undifferentiated one is the undifferentiated one. But this Neoplatonic logic, at the point of transition to the logic of the ground, ends with a reassertion of the original idea of concrete identity in difference:

essential distinction, as distinction in and for itself, is immediately only distinction of itself from itself; it therefore contains the identical; so that essential distinction itself belongs, together with identity, to the whole distinction that is in and for itself.—*As relating itself to itself*, essential distinction is already expressed equally *as what is identical with itself*. . . . Ground is the unity of identity and distinction, the truth of what distinction and identity have shown themselves to be, the inward reflection which is just as much reflection-into-another and vice versa.[48]

The dialectic of ground starts out with the concrete identity discovered under different descriptions, an identity with which the dialectic of identity and difference ends. Yet, in the logic of ground thought again falls away from concrete identity and difference. Again, though in a different way from Neoplatonism, it reverts to abstract identity under a single description.

The difference is that this single world description is now compound rather than simple. Indeed, it is comprehensive enough to logically contain particular descriptions of the world under which empirically we also discover the absolute. The absolute is found under different descriptions as required by the self-refutation of abstract Neoplatonism, but since the different descriptions are all logically contained in a single conjunctive description the diversity of descriptions is reducible. To say of some individual that he is a bachelor, is unmarried, and is a man is only in appearance to give three descriptions. We really said it all when we said he was a bachelor. By explicitly repeating part of what we implicitly said we give only the superficial appearance of saying something more.

Where Neoplatonism denied the determinate empirical reality of this world, the deterministic theology of ground claims to recognize this reality as a consequent logically contained in the explanatory ground. In intention, then, the deterministic definition of the absolute is faithful to experience. The Neoplatonic category of indeterminate essence is replaced by that of determinate essence. But the determinate world-essence of determinism is in the end as indeterminate (i.e., determinable) as determinate being in the logic of being. Just as there are innumerable ways of realizing determinate being, so there are innumerable ways in which a predicted eclipse under any finite description (no matter how extensive) may be concretely realized.

The deterministic theology of a divine Laplacean superscientist is a dialectical advance beyond Neoplatonism's one, but only insofar as the absolute is considered to be completely described under but a single extended description. Determinism is ultimately not serious about the absolute under particular descriptions whose difference proceeds as far as mutual logical independence of the explanatory description. The advance over Neoplatonism is that many general facts about the empirical world and its various events are described, explained, and predicted from the superscientist's deterministic perspective. The limitation to this advance is that there is still more to this world and its events.

The indirectly discovered premise by which deterministic theology refutes itself is: given any object with a property f logically implying a further property g, that object also has a property h not implied by f. Whatever is has a particular property not deducible from any single true explanatory description of it; and what has such an unexplained, ungrounded property ex-ists, emerges out of its ground, over and above it. The immediately given consequent gives way to a partially apparent concrete existing thing. The one-dimensional fact gives way to the partially apparent, concretely existing thing—the thing about which the abstract fact is a fact. As the following chapter will show, an existing thing— a largely ungrounded topic of countless observable facts—is no single "consequent" fact of some ground.

9

The Phenomenalistic Definition of the Absolute

1. The Absolute as an Essential Sum of Interacting Things or Interpenetrating Elements

The definition of the absolute that now arises is phenomenalistic. The absolute is defined (or more precisely, it defines itself) as interacting things, properties, elements, and appearances. We find here the first new basic categories since being-for-self in the logic of being. These new basic categories arise from reflection on the approaching breakdown of abstract being-for-self (or the one) in the logic of being. All categories intervening between being-for-self and appearance have presupposed a fixation on being-for-self, and thus may be designated as nonbasic categories. The one as thought thinking itself or being-for-self, we recall, negated the sensory world. The one is now negated by the absolutized sensory world. The logic of appearance is the self-negation of being-for-self, a negation of absolute being-for-self called forth by the unrelenting negation of the world of appearance by being-for-self. In the logic of essence, beginning with appearance, the determinate other of being-for-self, the empirical world, defines the absolute to the exclusion of being-for-self. It does so until it is discovered that the sensory world, in its appearance and in its actuality, proves not only intelligible through law-governed manifestations but also capable of manifesting being-for-self within itself. This conclusion will open the way to the logic of the concept, in which abstract being-for-self, finally surrendering its theological self-absolutization, actualizes itself concretely as the self-awareness or being-for-self of the sensory world.

This chapter concerns the logic of appearing things, and their phenomenalistic dissolution into the appearances themselves. In considering determinism in the last chapter we distinguished things and events. In the logic of appearances, directly following that of ground, the notion of an apparent event or affair (*Sache*) passes immediately into that of an existing thing having many properties.[1] The apparent event turns out to be a thing. A flash of lightning exists independently in itself, but also has numerous appearing properties dependent on other existents in the changing environment. It touches ground, causes a fire in the forest, is caused by an atmospheric charge, is bright, progressively discharges electricity, etc.

By the last of these properties we see that even a flash is after all a "stable" subject of changing properties,[2] a thing. It passes from having discharged half the charge to discharging three-fourths. The lightning flash interacts with the charge, first reducing the charge and secondly being itself reduced by this very reduction. Events or affairs heat up and wind down. An existent thing interacts with other things. Bright to the eye, the lightning flash behaves thinglike by causing a disturbance of air waves whose thunder reaches even after the brightness has subsided.

The definition of the absolute superseding the concept of a deterministic ground at first glance seems to be a commonsense definition: the absolute is an aggregate of essentially independent things. Each thing exists in itself as the partial ground of others. And each is in part grounded by others, receiving from them its properties. The rain grounds the wetness of the earth, which grounds the rain's fall to earth.

The transition in the *Logic* from the thing which has many properties to a phenomenalistic definition of the absolute through appearances may now be considered. The absolute viewed as interacting things as presented in the *Logic* should not be understood as a particularly commonsensical definition of the absolute. For Hegel interprets properties as portions of material elements which a thing "has," meaning that the thing phenomenally contains them as compresent. This shows that he does not construe "properties" as universals. Having a property does not consist in exemplifying a universal. Material elements and their portions are nonuniversal individual entities, while in the practice of subject-predicate discourse properties are assumed to be higher-type entities, universals.

For Hegel properties as universal predicates emerge only in the logic of the concept, more specifically in the logic of judgment. Yet subject-predicate discourse is used by Hegel throughout the *Logic.* Thus, if the cake has a portion of the sweet by containing it, the cake has by exemplification the universal property of phenomenally containing a portion of the sweet. The property of sweetness as a universal predicate exemplified by one thing can be exemplified by a second without altering the first. But a cake would be altered if its portion of the sweet viewed with Hegel as an element, a "matter," were shared, part of it going to another cake.

A general transition from a definition of the absolute by the inter-action of things (or, more precisely, of elements) to sensory appearances has often been made by philosophers from Hume onward. The reduction of a thing's properties to elements was suggested by the natural science of Hegel's time, which had only recently rid itself of phlogiston, while continuing to envisage fluid caloric, magnetic, or electrical elementary matters.

Yet, Hegel's interpretation of interacting things is not entirely a relic of a bygone philosophy of science. A similar doctrine of things as sense objects was affirmed in Bertrand Russell in *An Inquiry into Meaning and Truth* (1940). Russell's interpretation of the phenomenal red as a scattered particular, which in the red rose is partially compresent with the smell of a rose and other scattered particulars, is essentially Hegel's in-terpretation of the thing in terms of matters. Yet Russell did not consider the view commonsensical. Hegel's phenomenalistic interpretation of the absolute as interacting things differs from Russell in that it leaves no place for the theoretical entities of physics. There is no hint of scientific realism. In the place of electrons or other unobservable things-in-themselves, Hegel contemplates electricity as scattered appearances of a quasifluid elementary electrical matter.

When we say rain grounds the wet sidewalk, the "ground"[3] is no longer the absolute under a sufficient deterministic description. It means a limited, relative ground. One thing and its properties are logically insufficient but necessary to the manifestation of another thing and its properties. For example, the phenomenal color of the grass is manifested only for eyes. That eyes exist is a logically necessary ground of another thing's color quality, but without being logically sufficient to explain that another thing exists in the full range of its properties.

A mere thing-in-itself without apparent properties is not a thing at all.[4] The dependence of a thing's necessary properties on other things independent of it means that the essential independence of the non-commonsensical thing-in-itself of Kantian philosophy would be contra-dictory. The thing receives its properties from other things.[5] Each prop-erty is independent of the thing which has that property as received from other things. It is not essentially its property; its property does not necessarily belong to it. It is brought to manifestation by other things, and it belongs to more than one thing.[6] Many things are bright, wet, or sweet. Brightness, we may say, is not an essentially "private" property.

Brightness is not essentially a "common" property either. We can imagine a brightness which is only accidentally a property of different things. In a single all-consuming burst of light it may escape being the property of diverse finite things. The "property" becomes an "element". A material element exists apart from any particular concrete thing, even from things in general.[7] Yet, portions of it may accidentally flow in and out of particular things.[8]

Elementary sweetness and whiteness in a thing are essentially independent of it. They are also mutually exclusive in relation to each other. The sugar's sweetness excludes its whiteness. This is expressed to the imagination by saying that the portions of different elements which "coincide" in the same space-time region in fact exist in the "interstices" of one another. Each element, excluding the other, is yet porous,[9] open to penetration by the other. The theory of interstices reduces "coincidence" to noncoincidence. It reduces the thing of many properties or elements to an aggregate of mutually external portions of elements.

An "element" is not the absolute by itself. Rather, it belongs to the absolute viewed as an essential sum of qualitatively determinate elements defined by mutual exclusion. Their accidental "coincidence," in different portions at different times and places, results in the different passing "things" of common sense.

The lump of sugar is the sweet understood as an element here and now coinciding—alternating in the interstices—with other elements: the crystalline, white, cubical, hard, etc. The absolute is an essential sum of qualitatively determinate elements, not of the ordinary things of which these elements define the "properties." The Kantian thing-in-itself, we noted, is contradictory. Ordinary things of common sense are equally self-contradictory. To be a thing of many properties is to be both one and many, i.e., both one thing and an many elemental portions which (not alternating in the interstices) actually coincide in space and time:

> But the further moment in the Notion of the [ordinary] thing [of many properties] is that in this thing one matter [element] is present where the other matter is, and the matter that penetrates is also penetrated in the same point; in other words, the self-subsistent is immediately the self-subsistence of an other. This is contradictory; but the thing is nothing else than this very contradiction; and that is why it is Appearance.[10]

The instantiation of two properties can without contradiction be at the same time and place. But portions of two material elements cannot. Yet, the sugar in one and the same place contains as a thing both a portion of the white and a portion of the sweet. There is no contradiction in saying the sugar instantiates both whiteness and sweetness. A contradiction arises only if the two properties, the white and the sweet, are materialized under the influence of natural science as blobs, "abstract"[11] masses with scattered portions. An ordinary commonsense thing then contradictorily consists in portions of different matters at the same time and place—as if a piece of pumpkin pie could also be a serving of vanilla ice cream.

But the reconstruction of properties as elements or matters is logically necessary. It is no contingent result of empirical science.[12] It is necessary because "properties" (e.g., wet) are only accidentally so. They mask elemental forces of nature capable of inundating and completely swamping "things," thus capable of being the "property" of nothing. The sweet, accidentally a property of a sugar cube, is essentially a determinate element in itself with a far more general power of sensory qualification than sugar or any thing can reveal.

In the *Encyclopaedia* the contradiction of the thing is matched by the contradiction of defining the absolute as Aristotle's primary matter.[13] The concept of primary matter is derived from that of properties and elementary qualities. Things have properties. Properties are accidentally properties of such and such things, but are essentially qualitative elements such as the sweet. Elements are amorphous material substances capable of invading ordinary commonsense things, and are mutually exclusive in space and time.

Elements or "matters" are eternal material substances formed from primary matter. They are different elementary types of formed matter, which in turn become the properties of ordinary things. The absolute cannot be unformed primary matter by itself. For primary matter is essentially self-formative.

The elements of Empedocles come to mind. Take water as an element. But even as an element, water resembles a thing with different properties which change in interaction with other things. It is not as simple as the sweet. Water is now dry ice, now wet, and now gaseous steam, as it undergoes quantitative shifts. The melting of ice is influenced by warm air, by interaction with another element.

Yet, water is still an element—simple or not. It is an amorphous, scattered, potentially pervasive "thing" whose presence knows no conventional limits of spatiotemporal extension, and which can enter the less amorphous limits of ordinary things. Water can change without limit in its distribution over time and space and still be water. A thing such as a car cannot undergo unlimited change in size or shape and still be a car.

An ordinary thing with definite natural or conventional limits can be insidiously attacked and engulfed by the amorphousness of an element. The fire in the hearth can burn the house. Flood waters may reduce the town to shambles. Earth may make dust of the human form, and humid air can rust out an iron bridge. Chemical elements and compounds are discontinuous amorphous poisons for things of common sense. Attacked by the elements, things perish. The house's property of being heated by a fire is grounded in fire as an element. But this property constantly threatens to revert to a mere element in a way quite fatal to the house. In an apparently innocent property lurks an element which can engulf the thing.

Different elementary substances have primary matter in common.[14] Through their mutual independence they become indeterminate, and so coalesce as formless primary matter. Definition of the absolute as a collection of elementary material elements fails as much as a definition as primary matter without form. It fails to recognize that the elements are elementary formations of the same primary matter. An aggregate which is a series of differentiations of one thing or material is essentially, in itself, that one thing or material.

Hence, to define the absolute as an aggregate of externally related material elements is contradictorily to define it not as an aggregate at all, but as primary matter. Yet, the absolute cannot be defined merely as primary matter because matter refers to more than itself. For it potentially contains all forms. And it cannot be defined merely as form because form does not (as in the historical Plato and Aristotle) subsist by itself, but actualizes the potentiality of primary matter. The absolute can coherently be defined only as primary matter and form, as self-formative matter.[15] Primary matter would be mere essential being-in-itself without being-in-act.

The definition of the absolute as primary matter, though suggested by the Milesians as seen through Aristotle, is as contradictory as its definition as pure form. Plato and Aristotle were both drawn to a definition of "god" distinguished as finite from the true absolute, i.e., distinguished essentialistically as pure form (beauty itself, thought thinking itself) contradictorily excluding the eros or matter which for Hegel is the being in itself of (the potential for) pure form. Pure form subsists alone in an initial theological absolutization of it, while matter is parasitic on it. Yet, both Plato and Aristotle are aware of the contradiction of equating beauty or pure form in Parmenidean fashion with the true infinite absolute, and both implicitly negate such a theological absolutization of the finite.

The full contingent historical development of forms not only actualizes but determines inner essence as the being-in-itself of just these forms. Had other concrete forms developed, had the Roman Empire never fallen in the West, humanity would have been a different particular potential for a different concrete form. The potentially for adulthood is never a potentiality for adulthood merely in general. Developed form constitutes and first reveals original essential being-in-itself as the starting point for that development. The essential being-in-itself of this form is what the form has been but only now reveals. Essence is constituted and revealed retrospectively—as what has been. Primary matter in itself is the aggregate of formally distinct things; this aggregate is matter in act.

2. Phenomenalism

The contradiction of ordinary thinghood has resulted in the aggregate of things, elements, matter opposed to form, and even form opposed to matter as possible definitions of the absolute. Because things as such are contradictory, the world of things is but a phenomenalistic world of mere passing sensory "appearances."[16] The world of things is the absolute as it merely appears under a contradictory description. In this world properties shift back and forth between unstable things.

In the world of mere appearance, laws rather than things give stability to unstable appearances.[17] The thing and its properties, being contradictory, are only the appearances of what is. They are what is, but referred to by conventional though incoherent designations. Things, being contradictory as such, provide only an apparent stability to the world. Its real stability lies in the fact that the behavior of things as appearances (as apparent, passing collections of sense impressions parading as properties and elements) can be described in abbreviated form by uniform empirical laws.

As long as things were supposed to exist in themselves, law was not needed as a source of stability. Being-in-itself inhered in each thing, which grounded in part the properties of other things. The rain (granting presuppositions, without by itself permitting deduction of what is grounded) grounded the pavement's wetness, and the earth grounded the revolution of the moon. Laws were the principles according to which things behaved in grounding one another. But now things have vanished into mere appearances or, as we shall soon see, into forces which, far from being hidden, become completely visible in appearances, and in the laws governing those forces.

Transitory unstable appearances have no essential being-in-itself. For being-in-itself is potentiality, and an appearance that passes immediately away has no unactualized potential. Though Hegel does not use the term "phenomenalism" in defining the absolute as the law of appearances, we may make the post-Hegelian relevance of this section of the *Logic* clearer by use of the term. In phenomenalism nothing abides with potentiality but the laws of phenomena, the stable intelligible images of unstable sensory appearances.[18] The law as the being-in-itself of appearances must expand into actual appearances if it is to be the being-in-itself of something. The laws do not illuminate phenomena like the mind-independent causal ground of scientific realism. Nor do they ground presuppositionally like things. Laws illuminate in summary descriptive rather than explanatory fashion. They are the abbreviated being-in-itself of appearances. The laws and appearances have the same content, but differ in form.[19]

In law appearance is reflected in itself, into its intelligible form; in appearance the law is reflected externally into its sensory form. The law illuminates appearance by epitomizing it, repeating it in intellectual condensation. "Every body has mass" encapsulates an exhaustive conjunction of conditional statements of the form "If x is a body it has mass." The sum total of appearances that any body turns out to be includes appearances of mass.

The above concept of the law construes it as the stable image of unstable appearances in a single stable world. We now see that law turns out to give a stable image of different unstable worlds.[20] Each of these worlds is an empirically possible world, one among alternative worlds consistent with the laws of nature.

What appears to be empirically impossible may of course conform to undiscovered natural laws. But since coherent hypotheses about natural law can be empirically falsified, not all logically possible worlds are empirically possible. Unless the law of gravity is not a universal law but is a special case of a universal law allowing mutual repulsion as another special case, a logically possible contrary world governed by a law of mutually repelling bodies lies beyond the range of alternative empirically possible worlds.

Each empirically possible world exhibits the world of laws by selectively exhibiting certain manifest forces to the exclusion of other latent forces. Unemployment in an economic depression is one manifest force, that of the demand for work. By lowering wages it causes demand for hiring. By the law of supply and demand, the force of job seeking converts itself into the opposite manifest force of hiring. The law stays the same, but the world of appearances dominated by one force transforms itself into a world dominated by the opposite force. The force of job creation manifests itself, invading and overcoming the opposite force of job seeking.

Another example of the opposition of empirically possible worlds is the self-manifestation of the force of general welfare by an "invisible hand" in the heart of the apparently opposite force of the selfish pursuit of profit. Other examples are cited in the *Phenomenology*.[21]

Gravity is an example of law as a stable image of unstable local worlds within a single empirically possible world. It expresses itself by triumphing over the very real opposite empirical force of mutual exclusion and repulsion between bodies. By gravity bodies rebounding on collision may collide again. A projectile failing to attain a velocity of escape eventually manifests gravity. Without mutual repulsion gravity would remain unmanifested.

The so-called steady state theory gives a picture of alternating worlds of mutual attraction and mutual repulsion. The law of gravity holds in both worlds, but in one world considered by itself its manifestation fails to be dominant. It comes to be dominant only in the opposite world. The manifestation of all forces, all laws, requires consideration of all apparently different (as well as actually different) empirically possible worlds. Though there is only one set of empirical laws of nature, and one actual empirically possible world, there are countless different empirically possible worlds which would satisfy the same laws. An earth with two moons defines one range of empirically possible worlds. But a single empirically possible world may give the appearance of embracing different empirically possible worlds if conflicting (but logically compatible) laws lead to the alternate manifestation of opposite forces.

There is no unmanifested force,[22] or unexemplified law. In this empirically possible world as it presently appears, a given force may be manifest or latent. An entire empirically possible world may also be either manifest or latent. The law states conditions under which the force manifests itself at other times and places in this empirically possible world.[23] But we must distinguish between the emergent manifestation of a force in this empirically possible world (e.g., the manifestation of gravity if the velocity of escape is not attained) and the permanent manifestation of this empirically possible world through all its emergent manifestations.

A "force" in one sense is a series of all local phenomenal manifestations in this empirically possible world, while in a second sense it is the series of all local manifestations in every empirically possible world. Given determinism, empirically possible worlds other than this one never emerge as phenomenally manifest worlds. In identifying force with empirical law, Hegel invokes the second above sense. A world with two moons around the earth is compatible with laws of this empirically possible world. Yet it may also be another empirically possible world, differing from this one by the inventory and description of what exists in it rather than by the causal laws at work in it. Or it may be our own empirically possible world in a manifestation we have not yet observed.

Given indeterminism, the exact future inventory of actual worlds discernibly emerging from moment to moment and even the laws that recapitulate that inventory remain ontologically fuzzy. Water is not just its self-manifestation today, but also its manifestation in the ice age, and in an imaginably more poluted future. It is the sum of its manifestations in conceivably different empirically possible worlds which are found in the past, present, or future, or which are never actual. Since the present empirically possible world varies from moment to moment, the absolute cannot be equated with any one such world. The range of phenomenal manifestations with which force is identical in this empirically possible world is epistemologically fuzzy. The range of phenomena with which force is identical in all empirically possible worlds is much more vast, and even less fully manifest. In identifying force with empirical law, Hegel includes within force its manifestation in an empirically possible world of two terrestrial moons which in our world will never become phenomenally manifest, though it may be manifest to imagination.

3. Wholes and Parts

Natural law as a whole is identical in content with the sum of all empirically possible worlds. This sum is a nonorganic or mechanical whole,[24] the result of addition. The whole is partially revealed in each empirically possible world. In a mechanical whole or aggregate there is nothing in the whole beyond the sum of its parts, though this need not mean that the whole does not exist. Sums exist. But they exist for the mind that adds them up, not independently in themselves. In itself, apart from the mind that holds it together, a sum divides and disperses into parts. The division of a whole/sum into parts reveals the parts as independent wholes on their own. The parts are parts only in relation to another. Essentially, in themselves, they are wholes.

We here take up a definition of the absolute which comes pair-wise. Each term of a pair is an alternate expression of the other term in the pair: the whole *or* its parts. We likewise encounter force *or* its manifestations, the inner *or* the outer.[25] Previously in the logic of essence we encountered the absolute as self-identity excluding its different properties, the ground excluding its grounded things, primary matter excluding form, or conversely form excluding matter. The absolute did not present itself as identity restated as difference.

Were the parts in themselves parts, they would essentially refer to one another as parts of an organic whole of internally related terms. No part would give an independent disclosure of the whole. Each would have its place in a single description of a whole in terms of relations between the parts. The brain would not reveal the organism apart from other organs. It would do so only as also revealed by the sense organs from which it receives messages, and through motor organs to which it sends commands.

The partial descriptions—the organism contains a brain, has sense organs, etc.—would coalesce in one whole description. The parts, conceived as organic terms, vanish into the whole, just as before the mechanical whole vanished into its parts to become wholes on their own. But an organic whole, which is not a whole of independently disclosed parts, is not a whole of parts at all. It is a whole of internally related terms or moments.

To define the absolute as the sum total of empirically possible worlds is to define it as an *indefinite sum* until the range of these worlds has been determined. The discovery of this range and its limits is the job of natural science. If we start from the view that the absolute is the sum whole of empirically possible worlds, the discovery of the laws of nature is a gradual division of the sum of empirically possible worlds into its individuated parts. The whole as a sum thus displays an explosive force by which it breaks asunder.[26]

Definition of the absolute as a sum whole is restated with its alternate, equivalent definition as the divided parts added together. The whole has parts, and the parts make a whole. The parts and the whole are identical in content. A whole dozen is nothing but the parts added together as parts, and the parts as parts (not as independent wholes) are nothing but their sum.

The same whole-part relationship is designated taking the first term, the whole, as the subject of the relation, and again by taking the second term, the parts, as subject of the relation. The difference between the whole and its parts is one of form, not of content. They represent different forms for expressing the same content.

Definition of the absolute as the whole does not exclude its definition as the parts in the same abstractly essentialist way in which its definition as Neoplatonic self-identity excludes its definition as difference. Instead of excluding the parts, the whole is repeated in them. The absolute is defined in one and the same definition as the whole either condensed within itself, in its simple essence, or deployed outwardly in the independent parts. Definition as the whole is reformulated in terms of the parts without altering the definition. Definition as a sum whole which cannot be reformulated as the added parts would not be definition as a sum.

However, to say that the same content of thought is expressed in different linguistic forms is not to say that the different linguistic forms express it with the same completeness. It is one thing to say that the absolute is an indefinite whole of undetermined parts that remain to be discovered. It is another to say that it is a *definite whole* already manifest in a precise range of empirically possible worlds. The whole and the parts as they initially appear have a single thought content that they repeat in alternate ways. The indefinite whole and the parts turn out to be incompletely repetitive.

We do not refer under exactly identical linguistic meanings to either the aggregate whole or the parts. We refer through a shift of meaning to the indefinite aggregate as the condensation of the parts, and to the parts as the extensive exposition of the aggregate. The choice of a manner of reference between the "parts" and the "whole" is thus not wholly indifferent. But one choice forces us on to the other choice. The aggregate is a sum of parts there to be separated out. The parts are parts of an aggregate holding them in unity.

An aggregate, lacking any necessary connection between its parts, naturally divides and disappears into its independent members.[27] These members in turn can be brought together as a sum whole again. But such a summation is an external operation upon the parts, while the division of a whole of externally related parts is internal to its nature.[28]

Because division and not summation is intrinsic to the aggregate whole, the whole is not as stable as it first seems, but disintegrates. It is a "force" which completely empties itself in independent manifestations. The whole, as a still concealed force not yet vanished into its parts, fails to express its content as fully as the parts into which it divides. Force and its manifestations are one in content. But unmanifested force does not reveal its content as fully as the manifestations.

Viewing the whole as an aggregate, however static it may at first seem, implies viewing it as a dynamic force that breaks apart. The absolute defined as force is not defined by any particular natural force. The force defining the absolute is the internally self-divisive force of any sum externally added together. When the external force of addition is released, the natural internal force of self-division takes over. The whole fully manifests itself in its parts.

This process is illustrated in the history of science. We recall that definition of the absolute as the whole (or parts) is a version of phenomenalism. It is a phenomenalism that recognizes apparently different empirically possible worlds besides the present one, and that views scientific law as defining the range of all such possible worlds, even without explicit reference to all of them. Knowledge of the body of scientific law performs the addition of an infinite sum, which remains determinate by the exclusion of many logically but not empirically possible worlds. (An earth with two moons is empirically possible because natural laws allow that it might be manifestly apparent, not because it is ever empirically apparent in this empirically possible world.)

In the history of science it is possible to reach such phenomenalistic philosophy of science before the conclusion of the history of science, before discovery of all the particular laws of nature. The absolute will then be defined as an indefinite or indeterminate whole of empirically possible worlds, since we do not yet know the exact range of such worlds. It will be defined as an epistemologically indeterminate, still undefined sum.

It is the nature of an indeterminate sum not to be divisible for us into its members, since its members are not yet manifest or known. Something merely known as a pile of eggs is in itself a definite number of eggs which divides into this, that, and the other actual egg. But insofar as we know it merely as an indefinite pile, we hold the eggs together in a subjectively indistinct sum. The progressive discovery of laws of nature in the history of science transforms an indefinite sum of empirically possible phenomena into a definite sum. The history of science is the progressive division of the whole.

An implicit distinction operates here between two intimately related wholes: the phenomenal whole of empirically possible worlds and the intelligible whole of empirical laws by which ranges of phenomenal worlds are recapitulated and distinguished as empirically possible or impossible. In general, an aggregate whole, falling apart into parts which emerge as wholes in their own right, is destined to disappear as a whole. This applies to both the above wholes. The whole of empirically possible worlds, if not held together in the conceptual grasp of complete science, disperses into those separate worlds for nonscientific observers.

Much the same is true of the sum whole of empirical laws. The sum of such laws, insofar as they do not necessarily imply one another, lacks the stability of a single law viewed as the tranquil image of unstable worlds of appearance. This sum, due to various discoveries in the history of natural science, breaks down into particular laws discovered at different times— various limitations on the possible ranges of phenomena. It is a force rather than a whole, the historically dispersive force of self-manifestation inherent in the intelligible world of law itself.

We have now reached a definition of the absolute as force or its manifestations. The identity of sense between the repeated disjunctive terms here becomes more complete than with the whole and parts. The whole imperfectly repeated the parts because it was negated by the independence of the parts. The sum whole and its members failed to fully affirm one another.

Force, by contrast, is conceived dynamically as determining and expressing itself in emerging manifestations. The independent manifestations of a force, for example the force of individual genius, do not contradict the existence of the force. Yet, from the concept of the genius of an author we cannot deduce the works he or she will produce. These works are logically independent of the abstract concept of the author's abstract force of genius. Still, that force must determine itself and manifest itself in some particular works or other.

The emergence of particular parts is the demise of the whole; the emergence of particular manifestations is the confirmation of the force. A force is not a mere aggregate: its manifestations all express and particularize a single universal character. A force is an inner tension which manifests its definite nature only in its external release. A whole breaks down in its movement into parts. A force is defined by the movement into its manifestations; it is a process.

Two processes may be distinguished: the original movement into the manifestations, and the reverse movement out of the manifestations back into the inner force. Once definite manifestations have been separated off from an indeterminate sum of manifestations, they can be added up again. But the concept of a definite inner force in which the manifestations are recollected is different from that of a force not yet manifest. A force in which the manifestations have been recollected is "the inner."

The inner is not unexpressed. It is an inner which, having manifested itself, is visible in the outer. It is one thing to discover the inner laws of nature, and another to contemplate them externally in the phenomena of nature—much as it is one thing for the self-definition of the absolute to manifest itself for us originally and progressively in the empirical history of philosophy, and another for that self-definition, having manifested itself, to remain quietly visible to us looking back on empirical history as speculative logicians.

The inner lacks the dynamic character of a force. It is the true repetition of the outer.[29] The whole as it first appeared was an imperfect repetition of the parts; it disappeared in breaking apart. Force also was imperfectly repeated in its manifestations; it was a dynamic inner still caught in the process of moving outward. Indefinite force is not perfectly identical in concept with its definite manifestations; rather, it passes into these manifestations.

Where the mere whole in concept may remain (unlike its parts) indefinite, force necessarily becomes more definite. The inner is a definite repetition of the same definite content conveyed by the outer, but in different form. In the outer it is expressed in different local phenomenal worlds, while in the inner it is expressed in the revealed laws of nature.

According to creationism, the content of the absolute in its inner and outer forms is not fully revealed to you or me, but only to God: "So those who [in the objective logic] regard the essence of nature [of the outer] as something merely inward [unexpressed to us outwardly] and therefore inaccessible to us are adopting the standpoint of those Ancients who considered God to be jealous [of contemplation of the inner in the outer and of the outer in the inner by us]."[30] The identical content of the inner and the outer here is given a theistic interpretation in the objective logic. God alone immediately knows all, the entire temporal process revealed in his laws, and his own laws all directly revealed to him in his contemplation of the temporal. Only in the panentheistic subjective logic of the self-concept do we come to participate in contemplation of the inner in the outer, and the outer in the inner.

Scientific Realism and Self-Manifesting Actual Realty

1. The Absolute's Self-Actualization through Self-Knowledge

The context out of which the logic of actuality arises in the *Logic* is in part theological, but it is also that of natural science. The Pythagorean logic of measure yielded a philosophy of science that mapped the sensory world on the panorama offered by a master scale of scales. Each of these scales was one of different ratios holding between quantitatively variable amounts of qualitatively distinct units. The deterministic logic of ground was a philosophy of science which reduced reality to the statable facts—*explanans* and *explanandum*—of natural science. The phenomenalistic logic of appearance gave an alternative philosophy of science, in which, in condensed form, scientific laws described rather than explained the concretely existing data of observation. The logic of actuality yields neither a deterministic explanation-based philosophy of science nor a description-based one. It implies instead a causally-based view of science. Any causal past of actual events (*Sachen*), irrevocable except for certain posthumous properties such as causally contributing to this or that in particular, lies behind the phenomena that—contrary to fantasy—we are condemned to perceive in a given situation. If Hegel were writing today, I surmise he would range himself among scientific realists, though he would recall that "reality" is not limited to the external world but in its actuality includes the scientist as well. "Real necessity is *determinate* necessity. . . . But this determinateness *in its first simplicity* is actuality. . . . This actuality, which is itself as such necessary, for it contains necessity as its *in itself*, is *absolute actuality*—actuality which can no longer be otherwise [like an empirically possible world of appearance], for its *in itself* is not possibility but necessity itself."[1]

"Ground" and "consequent," as we have considered these terms in the logic of essence, differ in reference as well as explicit sense. Yet they are correlative. A ground is a ground of a consequent, and a consequent is a consequent of a ground. "Whole" and "parts" are identical in reference but not in explicit sense, as is also true of "force" and "expressions." The "inner" and "outer" are identical in both reference and sense. They convey the same thought content, but are formally different. They are alternative linguistic forms in which the same sense or thought content is put.

One form, the "outer," highlights that content in its expanded and phenomenal form. The other, the "inner," highlights it in concentrated and lawlike form. We cannot quite say "the whole or—in other words—the parts." For the whole comes whole, not in parts. The whole is implicitly the parts, but explicitly it remains the whole of parts. Yet, it is perfectly correct to say, following Hegel's usage in the *Logic*: "the inner or, in other words, the outer."

To be sure Inner Mongolia is not Outer Mongolia. But the inner character of a person is the outer behavior in which it is seen. And the inner law of nature is the outer phenomena in which it is visible or at least imaginable. The "inner" to which Hegel refers is the transparent inner.

The inner and the outer law are not distinct as correlative concepts, like being up and down, or ground and consequent. Rather, they are correlative linguistic formulations of the same concept. The expansive phenomenal account contains other words than the abbreviated lawful account. "What is outer is, *first of all, the same content* as what is inner. . . . Secondly, however, what is inner and what is outer are also *opposed* to each other as determinations of the form; and as abstractions of identity with self and of mere manifoldness or reality they are radically opposed."[2]

The concept of a dispersed and ever incomplete account of the phenomena condensed in a lawful account provides the most coherent formulation of the phenomenalist definition of the absolute. It was articulated in the history of philosophy by Hume: "The same cause always produces the same effect. . . . This principle we derive from experience. . . For when by any clear experiment we have discovered the causes or effects of any phenomenon, we immediately extend our observation to every phenomenon of the same kind, without waiting for that constant repetition, from which the first idea of this relation [of cause and effect] is derived."[3]

Yet phenomenalism, even in its most coherent form, is still incoherent. The inner law cannot be truly identical with what happens to be external in the present phenomenal world. For, consistent with the descriptive law of possible worlds, another world might have presently existed. The law of gravity also includes its manifestation in a solar system without moons. The absolute, according to the phenomenalist definition, is the identity of inner law and all empirically possible external worlds, without implying this world as present.

Only one of these worlds is the existing world, and phenomenalism by itself does not explain which one it is. If there is presently a world there are also worlds inverted in relation to it, which do not at present exist.[4] Empirically possible worlds are alternative candidates for realization in the present world. The present actual world satisfies some disjunctive description as one among alterative worlds. Yet, if something satisfies a disjunctive description, it also satisfies a nondisjunctive description by one of the disjuncts. But which disjunct it satisfies is not implied by the inner world of law.

Phenomenalism is a form of subjective idealism. That this world and no other exists may be ascertained empirically. But it cannot be explained why this world exists, rather than some opposite world in the unstable totality of empirically possible worlds, except by a form of what we today call scientific realism—in other words, except by asserting a causally active, actual reality independent our subjective minds. The logic of actuality is as relevant to contemporary scientific realism as the logic of appearance is relevant to contemporary phenomenalism. A phenomenalist construal of cosmology, of the space-time world, may not be a theology or definition of the absolute—as Berkeley clearly shows us. And not all scientific realists uphold a scientific realist theology,[5] but those who do define the absolute as the aggregate total of the interacting theoretical entities of science, including the human mind/brain. Only in this way can we explain the fact that the world that phenomenally appears—often against our wishes—is this world rather than some other.

"Actuality is the *unity* [*not identity*] *of essence and Existence*; in it, *formless* essence and *unstable* Appearances . . . have their truth."[6] Appearances come conjoined or unconjoined, but they lack the causal energy or activity[7] of what is actual. The instability of phenomenal appearances is seen in the fact that natural laws of science are the only limit—a most loose limit—on the possibility of what may appear unless mind-independent actuality stabilizes appearance and imposes determinate form on essence (being-in-itself) actualizing itself. This mind-independent world will by the end of the present chapter turn out to consist in actual events (*Sachen*).[8] Unlike changing things, events—except for already cited posthumous properties like the event's capacity to affect the future in unpredictable ways—endure as self-identical (with temporally indexed properties of beginning, being half way to the end, etc.) by the identity of indiscernibles,

SCIENTIFIC REALISM

to which we have seen Hegel subscribe. In the logic of appearance, immediately existing events (*Sachen*) became phenomenal things self-mediated through changing properties.[9] Now, in the logic of actuality, things become mind-independent events (*Sachen*) in a recurrent process of actualizing real possibility.[10]

The presently existing world, which has already been considered in the transition from the logic of ground to appearance, is not all Hegel means by "actuality," the new basic category defining the absolute in the dialectic.[11] Seven characteristics of actuality (*Wirklichkeit*) may be distinguished.

1. *Actuality as actualization of the full cycle of possibilities.* The inner essence is actual only through the full external cycle of its alternative and exclusive empirical possibilities potential within it, thus only through a temporal process. It is not fully actual in the present world. One present dove does not an make an actual summer. One rational act does not make an actually rational animal. What is actual (effective, *wirklich*) has staying power. It is not only acts, but sustains its action over the course of its potential empirical possibilities.

Some empirical possibilities, as defined by consistency with causal law, are not potential possibilities given the actual world. The actuality of the absolute thus requires that its different potential possibilities at some time each manifest themselves in its temporal career. What is truly potentially possible must at some time be actual, since potentiality is potentiality for an individual actuality, which can only be individuated by its presence. However, potential possibility—often referred to as "real possibility"—is distinguished by Hegel from "mere possibility": "Since possibility is at first the mere form of *self-identity*, . . . the rule for it is that only that something shall not inwardly contradict itself; consequently *everything is possible*, for this form of identity can be given to every content through abstraction. But *everything* is just as much *impossible* too [as it is merely and abstractly possible]."[12] Potential possibility goes beyond what is actual, which must develop further to actualize it. Mere abstracted possibility falls beneath the present actuality from which it is contradictorily abstracted.

2. *Actuality as the self-actualizing potentiality.* Phenomenalism construes the inner law as a descriptive copy which remains placidly indifferent to alternative potentially possible external worlds, in each of which it is partially visible. The theology of actuality in the *Science of Logic* (contrary to Aristotle's insistence on external efficient and formal causes) construes the inner essence as a power (*Macht*) which not only can but does actualize itself in the full range of different worlds. "What is actual *can act*; something manifests its actuality through that which it produces."[13]

3. *Actuality as a causally produced outer manifestation inwardly containing future further possibilities.* Actuality is the alternation between the inner possibilities potentially contained in the present contingent outer real events and their effects in a future outer events. The inner is not a ground of consequent facts, such as we encountered in the logic of ground. That ground was a body of propositions selected by, and existing for, a subject external to the ground, in order to explain or encapsulate consequent facts. The ground now is the present outer contingent manifestation potentially containing the inner possibility of further such manifestations. It objectively causes its own development: "the contingent [outer manifestation] is the actual as a merely possible. . . . The contingent . . . has no [deductively necessary explanatory] ground because it is contingent; and, equally, it has a [temporally preceding objectively causal] ground because it is contingent."[14]

The inner and the outer, which were identical at the end of the last chapter, now acquire different contents. For the inner is an invisible causal activity visible in subsequent outer effects. What is actual is not indifferently the phenomenalistic inner world of law or outer world of sense impressions. Rather, it is the inner seed as dynamically manifesting itself in the eventual outer growth, and the outer as manifesting prior inner possibilities of the contingent past. It is also the outward manifestation of the past containing the inner possibility of creatively determining itself in its subsequent outer development.

The inner and outer are no longer alternative linguistic forms, the one abbreviated and the other unabbreviated, expressing the same thought content. They are successive stages in the content's objective development.

4. *Actuality as overcoming inactual, nonessential existence.* The absolute, as it contingently exists in the present world, fails to actualize all its essential potential. One warm day in January can exist, but it is ineffective in melting the ice or making the grass grow. It lacks the insistent overwhelming power of a swarm of warm days. "Real actuality . . . preserves itself in the manifoldness of pure Existence."[15]

The durability of what is actual is in part due to its refusal to remain fixed in a single incoherent manifestation. An actual state overcomes contradiction between the existence and essence of the state.[16] A sunny day in winter stands in contradiction to the essence of winter. What it manifests in act stands outside what it actually is in itself. Whatever it may actualize, it is not winter. In such a day winter falls outside itself. It exhibits being-outside-itself (*Aussersichsein*)[17] (God in the pre-Christian Hebrew era was "outside himself" in his creatures).[18] Such a day can occur in the winter, but only if winter has the power to overcome it. Essence must manifest itself,[19] but not every existent in the parameters of a given essence manifests it. Being-in-itself can lie outside itself, and not in act. Only cold days in winter contribute to the actualization of its essence.

We say "contribute" because a single inner essence cannot actualize itself in a single manifestation, which might be an aberration. The essence must particularize itself in a multitude of manifestations, which agree and actualize it collectively. The self-actualization of being-in-itself must be independently confirmable by repeated observation.

One counterexample does not prove being-in-itself to be inactual. One positive observation does not prove actuality. Actuality is the manifestation of protean creative power.[20] This power must manifest itself. But it must do so itself freely, not deterministically, nor necessarily in every situation. Such many-sided self-actualization is not refuted by occasional lapses.

Actuality is a further definition of the absolute. It defines it as conforming, in the overall range of its outer existence, to its inner creative essence. To say that what conforms in its outer existence to its being-in-self or essence is "in act" is to use quasi-Aristotelian language. "Actuality" is the preferred translation for Hegel's "Wirklichkeit"; it underscores the Aristotelian character of the dialectic of essence in its culmination. "Actuality is the unity of essence and existence":[21] the absolute is defined as actualizing its essential potential.

5. *The necessary self-actualization of actuality in the definition of the absolute.* The Hegelian twist consists first in applying the actuality/potentiality distinction to the cosmos as a whole, and second in saying that nothing, not even the absolute, can have an essential potential without actualizing it. A potential is for something determinate, and only its actualization determines what the potential is for. Being-in-itself, coherently conceived, implies being-in-act, the inner as concretely manifested in its outer. Unlike Aristotle, Hegel does not view pure actuality Neoplatonically as a separate substance or form. The absolute has a primary potentiality which actualizes itself.

6. *Actuality as self-actualization/self-manifestation to an observer.* A number of questions are raised at this point, pointing to further characteristics of actuality. First, what is the inner essence of the absolute which must be outer? The logic of appearance (phenomena) led to the conclusion that the absolute is a force which spends itself in manifestations, only to retire into an inner realm nonetheless visible in the outer. But a force becomes manifest, and the inner visible, only to an observer.[22]

However, if the absolute is a force, or an inner intelligible form, the observer to whom it manifests itself, and who observes the absolute as a whole, cannot be outside the absolute. Outside the absolute there is nothing. This observer can only be the absolute itself in one of its manifestations. The absolute is in itself a force or inner essence which becomes manifest to itself, not to another:

> we have to exhibit what the absolute is; but this "exhibiting" can be neither a determining nor an external reflection . . . on the contrary, it is the *exposition*, and in fact the *self*-exposition, of the absolute. . . . But the exposition of the absolute is, in fact, its *own* act, which *begins from itself* and *arrives at itself*. . . . the absolute is manifestation not of an inner, nor over against an other, but *is* only as the absolute manifestation of itself for itself. As such it is *actuality*.[23]

7. *Actuality as agent power of self-actualization.* A second question now virtually answered pertains to efficient causality: By the agency of what does the absolute force manifest itself? If there is nothing apart from the absolute, the absolute must, contrary to Aristotelian substances, manifest itself to itself by its own agency. A force which manifests or actualizes itself is not subject to the violence of an external force (*Gewalt*), but is tranquil power (*Macht*)[24]—compare to Spinoza's distinction between force and power.[25] "The effect is . . . necessary just because it is the manifestation of the cause. . . . Only as this necessity is cause self-moving, beginning from itself without solicitation by an other [force], and the *self-subsistent source of production out of itself*."[26] The absolute is a productive power of self-manifestation to itself. The outer does not pry open the inner; the inner actively manifests itself in the outer.

To say that the absolute is actuality is thus to say that it is the actualization of its own being-in-itself as referred to at the onset of the logic of essence,[27] the actualization of its potential for being-for-self. The absolute's essential being-in-itself is its potentiality for being-for-self.

In the logic of explanatory ground and of appearance, the absolute was alienated from what it is in itself. It was defined in abstraction from the *subjective intelligence* that discovers Neoplatonic self-identity, from the superscientist who grounds a consequent fact in explanatory facts, and from the observer to whom force manifests itself. The absolute, in its alienated and abstract essence, lay outside itself.

2. Necessity

A further question concerns how the absolute manifests itself. The absolute power of self-actualization manifests itself by encountering and overcoming the force of another opposed substance.[28] Of course, if the absolute is a sovereign power of self-manifestation, there can be no other force to which it is opposed.[29] Yet no force or power can express itself without being solicited by another. In the case of an infinite power, this other power must be simulated.

The infinite power of self-manifestation becomes actually manifest by overcoming the opposite force of the absolute in its state of self-alienation. Knowledge is made reflective by the correction of error. A force buffeted by a second force can manifest itself without manifesting itself to itself. One can show one's selfishness to others, without showing it to oneself. The absolute's self-conscious self-manifestation, its power of self-manifestation explicitly for itself and not just in itself, is a power of canceling the illusion and appearance of an alien power over against it.

An outside force, serving to stimulate the self's self-conscious manifestation to the other, is not different from the original force of self-manifestation. Self-manifestation becomes reflective or nonabsolute only by falling into an abstract thinking which projects a not-self over against itself. It then struggles to overcome the opposite force, the not-self, its self-loss in the alien other.

The self that defines itself by an abstract essence in abstraction from the world finds alien otherness in the world. It finds contingency, externality, mechanism, mere quantity, indifferent connections, necessity, finite passive substance. Infinite thought dialectically adopts the position of a finite mind limited by the necessary course of external events, blind necessity.[30]

The absolute manifests itself to itself implicitly, unconsciously, when it stands speechless in awestruck wonder before an alien necessary march of events it cannot comprehend.[31] Such unconscious self-manifestation is called "absolute actuality."[32] Self-conscious self-manifestation in all that is lies beyond, in the logic of the self-concept and its development in the whole system.[33]

Conceptual thinking discovers the actualization of its purpose in the cosmic march of events. It finds its own inner essence in external contingencies. By the "concept" we understand thought's explicit concept of itself in its other, of freedom realized in necessity. It is the all-embracing self-concept by which one consciously is what one is in whatever presents itself as other, in and through the constraints of one's world: "Mind is . . . in its every act only apprehending itself, and the aim of all genuine science is just this, that mind shall recognize itself in everything in heaven and one earth. An out-and-out other simply does not exist for mind."[34]

The history of science is the absolute's struggle against thought's self-induced counterforce, the illusion of confronting alien necessity.

What the external world of hard necessity lacks to be comprehended is not laws of nature or specific causal connections, but a disclosure of overall *purpose*.[35] The laws of natural science describe how phenomena succeed one another, but do not explain why. The objective logic of identity, ground, appearance, and actuality ignores final causality—that for the sake of which the world is what it is.[36] Only when the hard necessity of reciprocally interacting external substances at the end of the logic of essence melts into freedom and personality does the end-in-itself—that for the sake of which cosmic process occurs—appear.[37]

In the logic of the absolute as self-concept, thought discovers that the world is what it is for the sake of thought itself. The world and its necessity are the objective genesis of its own self-thinking ultimately realized in the act by which we ourselves, reading the *Logic* for example, subjectively think the world. Necessity does not "vanish,"[38] but comes to be understood as an expression of one's own self-construction in history.

Necessity manifests itself as the external history of freedom, and thought comes to recognize itself in this history. With this self-recognition in the object, the transition from objective logic to the subjective logic of the self-concept is accomplished. The thought of the speculative logician manifests itself explicitly to itself in the process of necessity.

We have seen in reconstructing the logic of ground from which concrete existents emerge how determinism was repudiated. The process of "necessity" to which the *Logic* refers is not deterministic. It is an alternation between really possible future events and contingent actual events, "an alternation of inner and outer"[39]—the necessity of contingency.[40] Each actual event determines itself on the basis of the real possibilities potential within its predecessors, and bears within it the further real possibilities of the future. To be "necessary" in the logic of actuality is not to be causally determined. Indeed, it is quite consistent with being "contingent" or "non-necessary" in the usual sense of these terms. For what is necessary ("really necessary," not "formally necessary") is what could once have been otherwise, but which is now past and beyond change.

What remains throughout formally (logically) contingent—such as losing an election—becomes the day after really necessary for the loser. What is necessary could have been otherwise but can now no longer be otherwise. It is water under the bridge, and the hopes and fears of the past now become an ineluctable fate for the present:

> Real necessity [necessity as we really contend with it in life situations] is *determinate* necessity. . . . The *determinateness* of necessity consists in its containing its negation, contingency [what could have been otherwise],

within itself. But this determinateness *in its first simplicity* is actuality. . . .
This actuality, *which is itself as such necessary,* for it contains necessity as its
in-itself, is *absolute actuality*—actuality which can no longer be otherwise,
for its *in itself* is not possibility but necessity itself.[41]

Each contingent event is the self-actualization of its own real possibility as inscribed in prior events. The prior event potentially contains its
own successor event viewed as really possible; the successor event is a prior
real possibility become actual. Such a distinction between real possibility
(not mere logical possibility) and actuality of course makes actuality
finite, the further particularization of past necessity. That possibility is
not merely impossible possibility falsely abstracted from present actuality
(mere logical possibility)[42] but is potential in present actuality opening
itself to "the advent of the future."[43]

3. Spinoza and the Transition from Necessity to the Self-Concept

Reference to Spinoza is prominent in the discussion of actuality.[44] His
concept of substance is understood as the concept of the external spatiotemporal process of necessity.[45] But it is also interpreted as a halting articulation of the absolute's power of self-actualization and self-
manifestation to itself.[46] These are the two known faces, extension and
thought, of Spinoza's substance. They are the two known attributes of
substance, one external and the other internal, one material and the
other mental. The absolute as extension is necessity, while the absolute
as thought is self-revelation.

The correspondence between the two attributes in their unfolding
in Spinoza's philosophy means that thought manifests itself to itself
in the march of external necessity—whether or not it is not aware of
doing so. It becomes aware of doing so only by discovering the laws of
correspondence between extension and thought.

In the *Logic,* as arguably in Spinoza's own philosophy, the distinction
of substance and attribute gives way to a distinction of substance and
accident.[47] According to Hegel, a Spinozistic attribute manifests the
essence of substance, but it is an abstract description of it established
externally by the "intellect."[48] The substance ends up as an unknown
substratum underlying its attributes, which are external and thus accidental to it. Since there is an infinity of attributes, no known attribute or
finite collection of them is the essence of substance. An attribute is but
one way in which the intellect perceives the essence of substance.[49]

Each attribute is in part a subjective accidental manifestation of an underlying unknown substance. Yet each attribute manifests something objective about substance by being, like the substance itself, infinite and conceivable only through itself. Thus, each is a logically independent description of the same substance. For this reason, no attribute is internally opposed to any other, and neither extension nor thought has its determinate negation in the other.

We note an important difference between being-in-itself (Hegel) and extension (Spinoza), and between being-for-self (Hegel) and thought (Spinoza). In the *Logic* essential being-in-itself is a return out of actual being-for-self, and being-for-self is an actualization of being-in-itself. Being-for-self is a reflection on an individual's or nation's historical achievement, on its established being-in-act. This does not mean, as Kierkegaard wrongly inferred, that the individual loses him- or herself in a past essence, foreclosing the possibility and even necessity of making new choices unto death. It means that the authentic, existential being-for-self of a free individual builds within a tradition, on the established historical being-for-self which scholarship may reconstruct. Whether from the past to the present or from the present onward, there is a development, a creative self-particularization proceeding from being-in-itself (nature, matter) to being-for-self (thought, spirit) which Spinoza did not fully recognize.[50]

Cosmic being-in-itself, initially abstract and not targeted on any particular being-in-act or actual being-for-self, develops concretely to encompass some particular being-for-self. Merely abstract being-in-itself, a cosmic potentiality not yet determined as a potentiality for anything in particular, is (if conceivable at all) conceivable through itself alone like a Spinozistic attribute. In fact it is not coherently conceivable, being an incoherent fiction of the understanding. Yet, because concrete being-in-itself implies some nondeduced contingent being-in-act or other, it cannot be an attribute in Spinoza's sense of a self-intelligible nonrelative property.

The absolute as we see it defining itself in the *Logic* is self-identical under initially logically independent descriptions of established being-in-itself with a determinate realized potential and contingently emerging present being-for-self. But the self-particularization of a determinately realized potential cancels the potential's logical independence of its particularization. A young person with his or her present achievements is first capable of choosing a particular profession or other, and secondly chooses. No one can choose a profession merely in general. When one has chosen a profession in a particular historical context, one becomes the more concrete potential for that particular choice.

Past being-in-itself comes to include already particularized being-in-act; but as long as the absolute retains creative being-in-itself at all, being-in-itself is not exhausted by its realized being-in-act. That the absolute has creative (not merely past) being-in-itself implies that there will be a further particular being-in-act, but not necessarily this or that being-in-act. We thus distinguish between two aspects of being-in-itself: (1) past being-in-itself, the definite potential for the actual present. This is the essential being-in-itself which has been, i.e., "past Being." From this must be distinguished (2) present being-in-itself, the incoherent, contradictory merely asserted potential for a concrete future which has not yet determined itself.

If the absolute still has life,[51] it has present as well as past potential being-in-itself. It falls into the contradiction of knowing itself in its inner essence to be what it is still incapable of fully manifesting in its outer existence. If a finite individual, or the absolute, no longer has life, it enjoys the coherence of merely past being-in-itself. Life yields to repeated reconstruction of an acquired identity.

Spinoza's duality of substance and attributes is one of an underlying unknown substratum and accidental manifestations perceived as essential attributes. Substance-attribute duality conceals substance-accident duality. The substance, without an objectively known essential attribute, passes into the accidents.[52] But then accidents are not really accidents of any substance, and so are not accidents at all. Either there are accidents and there must be a substantial subject which does not dissolve in them; or the substance does dissolve, and there are no accidents, because there is no underlying substance. "Substance" is merely posited to support the illusion that actual contingent events in the process of necessity are "accidents." Accidents are events that happen to a substance. The dissolution of substance into accidents, we now see, is the dissolution of "accidents" into objective events (*Sachen*).

Before, in the dialectic of ground, finite events turned out to be enduring, changing, interacting things. Now the infinite and hence non-interacting substantial thing dissolves into events:

Inwardly the necessary is *absolute relationship* [objective past *conditions* serving as the basis for present *facts*—think of Whiteheadian actual occasions][53] . . . , in which relationship sublates itself equally into absolute identity. In its immediate form it is the relationship of *substantiality* and *accidentality*. . . . As necessity substance is the negativity of this form of inwardness, and therefore it posits itself as *actuality*. . . . the actual, as immediate, is only *something accidental* which in virtue of this [very status of] mere possibility passes into another actuality; and this *passing over* is substantial identity as *activity of form*. Substance, therefore, is the totality of accidents; it reveals itself in them as their absolute negativity.[54]

For substance to dissolve into accidents is for it to dissolve into the cosmic creativity running through events that resemble what the post-Hegelian Whitehead called actual occasions. This creativity or "form-activity"[55] is not a substantial subject. The accidents are not really accidents, since substance in its blankness has dissolved them into fleeting events in the process of necessity, not as accidents *of* a substance.

The logic of the self-concept is in sight, first objectively or for us, then subjectively or for itself. The actual self-manifestation of the absolute to itself is first asserted abstractly as an external reflection on the cosmic process of "outer necessity"[56]—a reflection which we make as speculative logicians.[57] We see that the absolute can manifest itself only to itself.

Secondly, the process of necessity, the substantial power expressing itself in "accidents"—contingent "free actualities"[58]—is constructed as the stage on which the self-conscious self-manifestation of the absolute to itself arises. It arises concretely and self-consciously only after having contrived to conceal and break its own movement in the display of external necessity.[59] The process of necessity—substance dispersed and dissolved into a spatiotemporal extension of events—sets apparent limits to self-knowing thought. The "blind" process of necessity, the endless arising and passing away of contingent current events—including wars, revolutions, depressions—seems to drift aimlessly until the gift of sight allows it to see itself.[60] "The *blind* transition of necessity is rather the absolute's *own exposition*."[61] But for the absolute to grasp alien necessity in thought is to melt away the "hardness" of such necessity.[62]

This blind causal power of cosmic substance, manifesting itself in effects, is infinite. But the causal power of cosmic substance presupposes a passive substance[63] on which to act. The infinite substance thus becomes a finite active substance presupposing a finite passive substance. The passive substance which limits the power of the active substance more properly has "force" rather than power. Force (*Kraft*) depends on something else for the solicitation of its expression and is thus passive as well as active.[64] Power (*Macht*) is sovereign and self-manifesting.[65] Infinite substantial power manifests itself by contending with the apparently external force of a passive substance.[66] It consents to a contrived contest of forces. The passive substance is being-in-itself, or matter, while the active force is being-for-self or thought. But the active force, being-for-self positing itself only on the basis of being-in-itself, is itself passive; and the passive force is at once active.[67] Being-for-self recognizes its own activity in matter, and recognizes material passivity in itself.

The power of substance thus appears to itself under two guises. We have here, historically, merely an approximate reconstruction of the Spinozistic duality of substance and attributes out of the foundation of substances and accidents. But the duality is no sooner reconstructed than restricted. Contrary to Spinoza, past being-in-itself and present being-for-self, extension and thought, imply each other in Hegel's logic as stages of a single developmental progression.

The transition to the logic of the concept now requires us to see two things. First, the progression of being-in-itself to being-for-self is a development of being-in-itself which continues to remain within itself. Secondly the objective development of being-in-itself in the world of necessity includes the actualization of our own subjectivity. The objective act by which the cosmos thinks itself is the subjective one by which we think the cosmos. Necessity, being-in-itself, does not vanish.[68] Instead it manifests freedom, and that is its meaning and purpose. The necessary march of events in the world reveals itself as the construction of our own identity as agents of the absolute's self-knowledge on the crust of the earth.

Spinoza is a pivotal, ambiguous figure in modern philosophy, much as we found Plotinus to be in ancient philosophy. Though the concept of substance as an unknown substratum underlying "accidental" manifestations in thought and extension suggests that Spinoza still falls in the objective logic of essence, we conclude with the famous last pages of the *Ethics*, which suggest that he himself passed from the logic of essence to that of the self-concept.

> The mind's intellectual love of God is the same divine love by which
> God loves himself. Not insofar as He is infinite, but insofar as He can be
> explicated by the essence of the human mind viewed under the aspect of
> eternity. Put otherwise, the mind's intellectual love of God partakes of the
> infinite love by which God loves himself. . . This love by the mind . .
> is an activity by which God, to the extent that He can be explicated by
> the human mind, esteems Himself to be accompanied by the idea of
> Himself.[69]

4. Does the Dialectic of Defining the Absolute Have a Conclusion?

We have completed a reconstruction of definitions of the absolute in the *Logic* from pure indeterminate being to the self-concept. (We shall use "self-concept" to translate "*Begriff*" because it implies self-reference, and because at the very beginning of book 3 of the *Logic* Hegel explains the concept as being-in-and-for-self.) The remainder of the *Logic* introduces no further definition of the absolute. Rather, it explicates what is contained in the absolute idealist definition of the absolute as the self-concept, more precisely the absolute idea. The reader who wishes a recapitulation of the entire dialectic of definitions of the absolute from being to the concept may refer to the penultimate chapter of this book.

Whether the list of twelve basic definitions in this account is complete is an important question. An answer depends on an answer to two other questions. Must the dialectic begin with the category of pure being? Must it proceed in a single rationally motivated line of deduction to the category of the self-concept?

The previous chapters have developed Hegel's own positive reply to both questions. Should this reply prove satisfactory, an important implication follows concerning the speculative tradition in the history of philosophy which the science of logic reconstructs. If the number of categories Hegel distinguishes is complete, this tradition has a conclusion, not just a beginning and definite development. Post-Hegelian members of this tradition (e.g., Schopenhauer, Nietzsche according to the Heideggerian interpretation of him as a metaphysician, Bergson, Whitehead) must be interpreted as developing a definition of the absolute from the *Logic*. Yet the possibility that post-Hegelian definitions of the absolute develop the science of logic by stubborn fixation on categories on which Hegel suggests no fixation must be left open. Further, as the summary recapitulation of the dialectic of essence shows below, Hegel himself vacillated on the question of whether to include primary matter as a basic category. There is nothing magic about the number of twelve categories. All that is necessary is that the introduction of every category be well motivated by reflection on the self-negation of a previous category.

5. The Logic of Essence in Review

In the dialectic of essence, the absolute is defined as an abstract essence that explicitly refers to its necessary correlate as contradictorily being unnecessary to it. We theologically absolutize entities under explicitly contradictory solutions. We are fixated on self-negation, on a definition of *A* explicitly in negation of *A*'s necessary correlate.

1. Abstract *self-identity* as the absolute is self-identification explicitly under necessary different descriptions which are diverse, like and unlike, and opposed, and which are contradictorily excluded from the absolute.

(The absolute defined as being-for-self, the one, survives in the logic of essence.)

2. The abstract *ground* of explanatory facts (including primary matter$_1$ and pure form$_1$ as two explanatory factors—see acount in *Logic*) is the absolute explicitly separate from the existing things of which it is only an incomplete ground. But abstract explanatory ground, due to its inability to explain everything about existing things, perishes as existing entities proceed from its demise. Due to the self-refutation of determinism, nothing is retained from ground in the subsequent dialectic, just as in the dialectic of being nothing positive is retained from the contradictory multiplication of ones. The dialectic continues from the explanatory ground to define the absolute by what is left over after the ground perishes, namely, existing things. (What perishes is the definition of the absolute as the being-for-self of the Laplacean superscientist.) Things are the absolute conceived as abstract *things-in-themselves* to the explicit exclusion of their necessary distinguishing properties.

3. Because things perish in favor of their independent *property-elements*,[70] they have no positive contribution to make to the subsequent dialectic. The dialectic continues from things to define the absolute as the remaining correlate of things, as properties reconstrued as interpenetrating elements. Properties as material *elements* (scattered particulars) are the absolute in explicit negation of the things that would have those properties.

4. The *primary matter$_2$* in which different apparent material elements coalesce through their common independence and indetermination is the absolute in explicit negation of form$_2$ understood as the plurality of different determinate elements—an *Encyclopaedia* category absent in the *Logic.* Is this category necessary? Elements must be viewed most abstractly for them to coalesce in primary matter. If they are seen as determinate in relation to one another, the category of primary matter will not arise here. I suggest that it be viewed as an optional category whose inclusion is not necessary; it does not do any significant work in the subsequent dialectic.

5. *Laws* describing the interpenetration and separation of material elements (formed matter) define the absolute to the explicit exclusion of the laws of another epoch of this world, or possibly to the exclusion of the laws of another empirically possible world with different laws—there were no laws of biology before the evolution of biological organisms.

6. The *laws of all empirically possible worlds or world states* form a whole in explicit negation of its own parts necessary to its being a whole, i.e., in negation of the separate concrete phenomenal appearance of any one law. (The parts are reformulated as the whole.)

7. The absolute is the *inner force* of the whole or totality of laws

to the explicit exclusion of itself in its necessary outward dispersed manifestations. (The force is reformulated in its expressions.)

8. The absolute is the *inner realm of statable law* to the explicit exclusion of the outward phenomenal realm which that inner world requires to manifest itself. (The outer is an alternative formulation of the inner.)

9. The absolute is the *actual world* in which the inner real possibility or potentiality allowable by law and the character of the past actualizes itself outwardly and concretely in actual happenings, but in explicit negation of an observer to whom these happenings manifest themselves.

10. The absolute is an actual *world that manifests itself to itself* (being-for-self, which went under with the abstract ground, is retrieved!) in explicit negation of the necessary march of past events in the world.

11. The absolute is *actuality that manifests itself to itself precisely in the march of necessary past events*—the absolute is the self-concept.

EMANCIPATION FROM NATURE IN THE INFINITE FREEDOM OF PERSONS

11

The Subjective Self-Concept and Its Passage into Judgment

1. Introduction

Perhaps surprisingly, the third part of the *Logic*, the logic of the concept is, according to Hegel, not the most difficult.[1] Once the logic of being and essence is understood, the logic of the self-concept simply harvests the fruit of the most nearly true logical definition of the absolute.

The absolute is defined in the logic of being as immediate thought thinking itself (being-for-self), which speculative thinking there posits as objective, i.e., outside itself. Speculative thinking, in positing it, limits itself to its function to the abstractive understanding. It thus posits under but one description, as mere being-for-self.

Such a definition is the culmination of a pantheistic cosmological theology. Progress occurs from one definition of the whole absolute as immediately given (e.g., pure indeterminate being) to another, until an explicit and relatively stable definition of the absolute as being-for-self (the one) is attained.

In the logic of abstract essence, the absolute is again defined as objective, as lying external to speculative thought. Beginning in the logic of things-in-themselves in interaction and of phenomenal appearance, it is defined as being-in-itself without any explicit reference to potential for being-for-self.[2] The thing-in-itself in the logic of essence of course refers explicitly to something, namely, to its properties. Its potential being-for-self lies concealed in its being for us: abstract being-in-itself exists for itself in existing for us as speculative logicians. But only by passing into the logic of the self-concept will a definition of the absolute arise that recognizes this.

The theology of abstract essence succumbs to negative reason. Negative reason offers a skeptical critique of the contradiction of defining the absolute apart from something else posited as absent. The absolute as essence is, in the end, as contradictory as any object conceived apart from its knowing subject.

In the logic of the self-concept (*Begriff*, personality conceived as grasping itself in a spatial and especially temporal world that it constructs) into which we now enter, reason becomes positive, speculatively constructive: I first define the absolute objectively as a being that is both potentially and hence actually for itself. Thus far, the logic of the self-concept repeats that of essence. But, second, the absolute is actually, and not just potentially, for itself only insofar as I myself actualize this objective potential being-for-self subjectively by my very act of defining the absolute. The absolute is subjectively for itself insofar as we ourselves accomplish this being-for-self in thinking it. It is this being-for-self of the *Begriff* that justifies speaking of the "self-concept" instead of the "notion" or simply the "concept."

In the logic of being there are transitions from one definition of the absolute to another only implicitly contained in the first. In the logic of the abstract essence each definition explicitly refers to something it leaves out, hence to an alternate correlative definition. In the logic of the self-concept there is only one definition of the absolute: the absolute is personality, the self-concept, which develops without ever even unintentionally falling outside itself.[3] Thus does the Kantian transcendental ego survive in the logic of the self-concept.

The logic of being is based on a transition into something not deducible merely from the assumed but unexplicated definition of the absolute as mere indeterminate being. From the mere concept of the absolute as pure indeterminate being, without the added indirectly discovered analytic premise that to be is to be determinate, we cannot deduce determinate being even in general.

The logic of the self-concept, by contrast, is one of immediate deductive self-analysis. Thus, a concept contains terms[4] which explicitly stand in internal relations to one another. A right-hand dot essentially related to a left-hand dot is a left-hand dot essentially related to a right-hand dot. Each term of a concept is inseparably one with every other.[5] The distinction of terms is but one of highlighting.

The self-analysis of the concept is for Hegel the work of German idealism. This historical movement was united by a single definition of the absolute from Kant through Fichte and Schelling to Hegel himself.

The historical allusions in the logic of the self-concept are more transparent than they often are earlier in the *Logic*. The self-concept in self-development analyzes itself into the subjective, objective, and absolute concepts (the idea). The theology of the subjective concept is ostensibly Kantian (and Fichtean); that of the objective concept draws on the Schellingian philosophy of nature, while that of the idea, with which the *Logic* ends, is realized in Hegel's own absolute idealism.

The logic of the subjective concept first takes up the concept as such, in its most abstract sense. Secondly, it treats it as judgment, and thirdly as syllogism. Yet, throughout this apparent treatment of classical formal logic—of definitions, propositions, syllogisms—Hegel continues the *Logic*'s preoccupation with theo-logic. The *Logic* is the subjective science of the objective logos of the absolute or God. It is certainly not a usual formal logic. Hegel undertakes a hermeneutic study of formal logic in its hidden theological meaning, a meaning that formal logicians as such can hardly be expected to appreciate.

The "self-concept" in the first abstract sense is its immediate form. The abstract self-concept analyzes itself as universal, as particular, and as individual. The self-concept as individual is the concrete self-concept constructed out of its abstract universal and particular descriptions.

The universal, particular, and individual self-concepts all belong to the self-development of one concept. Hence, they cannot be treated separately like indeterminate being, determinate being, and being-for-self. The universal concept is not the abstract universal. It is the concrete universal which is explicitly identical with the concrete individual, but which is referred to under an abstract description.

The dog described as "the dog" (*a* under the description *F*) refers to an individual by an abstract or universal description. The dog described as "the collie" (*a* under the description *G*) refers to the same individual by a more particular description. And the dog as "the dog who is the collie" (the *a* as *F* under the description *G*) refers by a concretely universal, individual description. Analogously, the objective cosmos is the objective cosmos, the objective cosmos is the self, and the cosmos is the cosmos which is the self. It is itself, is other than itself, and is itself in being other than itself.

2. The Self-Concept: Some Main Points

Several preliminary points about the self-concept must be kept in mind.

1. *Being in general implies being in particular.* What exists under a universal description must, to exist under that description, particularize itself. The world to be the world cannot merely be the world.

2. *Relativity of universality.* Being a dog is universal relative to being a collie, yet particular relative to being an animal. The particularization of a universal description creates a new universal which, to survive, must be particularized again.[6]

3. *The general concept has no species.* Particularization is the determination of a determinable, not the specification of a genus. The universal "color," for example, is determinable as green. Color is not a genus. There is no species of color defined by the intersection of that genus class and a second differentiating class. Green is a color. But it is not analyzable as a species of color uniting a genus and specific difference. Any true description of the absolute is also determinable, not generic. If particularization of its general description were the specification of a genus, the absolute could never be particularized. For any class of entities beyond the absolute, with which it could intersect, is necessarily empty.

4. *The concept of the absolute is a self-concept.* An individual (concrete) concept is necessarily a *self*-concept, and not just a concept, when it is the concept of the absolute as a whole. To recognize a dog as a dog even in being a collie gives a more concrete concept of what it is to be this dog. But it implies no self-concept including the thinker who would think him- or herself in thinking the dog. Yet to know the absolute (and not just the dog) is to know it, among other things, in and through the knower who knows the absolute from a perspective within the absolute itself. This concept does imply a concept of the cosmos as a self-concept.

5. *This self-concept is the Kantian transcendental ego.* This self-concept as a definition of the absolute first historically appears in Kant and Fichte.[7] The transcendental ego is the absolute as general or universal. It is particular in the finite phenomenal world that the universal ego conditions. And through transcendental reflection on itself the universal transcendental ego is individual. It recognizes itself in its phenomenal particularization. The self-concept as individual is at once universal and particular.

6. *The self-concept enjoys the absolute power and rights of personality.* The self-concept is personality.[8] Personality as a definition of the absolute is the truest purely logical definition of the absolute in world history, and hence in the history of philosophy. The cultural dominance of this definition of the absolute at the end of history is the spiritual reformation that completes and consolidates the revolution of 1789. The human person, the highest achievement of the cosmos, is currently backed up by the force and might of the cosmos. Substance becomes subject, but subject in return develops as substance.[9]

3. Judgment

A concept is a "germ."[10] Appearing first under its general description, it develops and particularizes itself into an individual. In the opening sections of the logic of the self-concept, universality, particularity, and individuality are distinguished, but not separated. They are held within the self-development of a single concrete self-concept.

In the logic of judgment (*Urteil*) which follows, these determinations become separated. They fall apart. A judgment is a faculty of thought developing out of a concept. First, judgment is potential in each concrete concept. The concept of the dog as a collie, for example, is potentially the judgment (true or false) that the dog is a collie. To utter the judgment is to take the immediate content of the concept (as also the self-concept) and put it discursively.

Second, the judgment develops outside the concept, i.e., beyond the limits of the concept: the inseparability of the three determinations of the concept, though recognized to be inescapable, is also denied. "The dog is a collie" does not preserve being a collie as a particular determination within the individual "the dog." The dog is set up as a subject of predication apart from its particular predicate—otherwise the statement would be uninformative. This leap into the error of discursiveness is a foil for the systematic reconstruction of the immediate concept in the form of explicitly self-mediated immediacy. Self-mediated immediacy unfolds after the logic of the judgment, in the logic of the syllogism.

Systematic philosophy does not forsake judgment to cultivate the silence of mysticism. Nor does it reconstruct the self-concept of the absolute as an axiomatic system of propositions. It reconstructs it as a process of judgments arising and passing away in self-contradiction.

For example, a subject of predication is set up in abstraction from its universal predicates, which are subsequently attributed to it.[11] Only when the subject is not initially conceived in and though its predicates is there a point to attribution. The result of attribution is to reconceive the subject through its predicates. The destiny of attribution is to lapse back into the pointlessness of an identity statement. Repetition of even the most interesting judgment ends in boredom. For the prior abstract view of the subject can no longer be maintained. The abstract subject of predication is replaced by a concrete concept of the subject inclusive of the predicate.

J. N. Findlay has said that Hegel's *Logic* was written before the distinction between the "is" of predication and the "is" of identity was clearly established in modern logic.[12] Yet, this distinction is already explicit in the *Logic,* even if not christened terminologically. Hegel recognizes the difference between predication and identity in his presentation of the logic of judgments. The "is" of predication yields to the "is" of identification:

> At the level of its thought, the subject is first of all the singular, and the predicate is the universal. What happens in the further development of the judgment is that the subject does not remain just the immediate singular, nor does the predicate remain just the abstract universal; next the subject and predicate also acquire the significance of the particular and the universal (in the case of the subject), and of the particular and the singular (in the case of the predicate).[13]

The subject of predication develops from being an abstract instance to being a concept, a concrete universal. The predicate starts out being an abstract universal, and develops into that same concrete universal. The subject-predicate judgment thus develops into a judgment of identity.

The rose is red. There is at first no presumption that it is identical to the red. This subject-predicate structure, with its nonidentity of terms, underlies meaningful nontautological judgment.[14] The predicate term, the red, in extension goes beyond the subject term. And the subject term, the rose, in its full description goes beyond the predicate term.[15]

Of course some identity statements can be formally nontautologous. "The rose is the most beautiful flower" may be illustrative. If so, assertion of the statement requires "judgment" in the sense of discernment. It requires taste.

The assumption of an abstractly conceived rose absolutized apart from its universal and particular determinations is contradictory— whether that assumption be contained in a nontautologous identity statement or in a subject-predicate statement. The rose is what it is through its various properties. "The rose is the most beautiful flower" can be reconstructed without contradiction only as: "The rose which is among other things the most beautiful flower is the rose which among other things is the most beautiful flower." A nontautologous identity judgment is coherently stated only as a tautologous nonjudgment.

The logic of judgment begins with nonidentity in both reference and sense between the terms in the simple subject-predicate judgment. For example, consider "The absolute, outside which there is nothing, is mere indeterminate being." If the absolute is, and if nothing is mere indeterminate being, subject and predicate differ in reference as well as sense. The logic of judgment proceeds to identity of the subject and predicate terms in reference but not sense—e.g., "The absolute as universal is identical with the disjunction of its particular forms." And it ends with the identity of these terms in both sense and reference: "The absolute which is true to its concept in the particular conditions of its historical realization is . . . true to its concept in the particular conditions of its historical realization"—a tautological identity statement which dispenses with any labor of discerning judgment.

Statements such as this third one, however, capture the truth of the matter. Judgment falsely absolutizes abstract subjects or predicates. The identity statements which most closely capture the truth are those in which the faculty of judgment loses interest. For tautologous identity statements repeat the same description in the predicate term as occurred in the subject.

As the dialectic of judgment develops, it is increasingly the description under which terms refer rather than the judgment itself which attracts interest. Immediate descriptions of determinate being (e.g., "is red") and of reflection (e.g., "is expensive") give way to self-mediated conceptual descriptions (e.g., "is self-identically human in general in being Napoleon in particular").

Humanity in general is self-mediated by its particular determination. Interest shifts from statements, identity statements which show no judgment, to self-mediated definite descriptions (e.g., "the a which remains self-identical in being identical to b") which the statements merely repeat.

This self-mediated description, maintaining self-identity in general through being other in particular, is a "description under a description": truth is claimed for a general description only if a second more particular description is also true. Using an example suggested by Donald Davidson,[16] a trip can be slow under the description of being an automobile ride, but not slow under the description of being a bike ride. The absolute is what it is in general only under a second description that particularizes the first.

Interest shifts, in the course of the dialectic of judgment, from judgments back to concepts. It shifts to self-mediated universal, particular, or individual definite descriptions, each of which maintains its identity in reference only by sharing that identity with descriptions of the other two types. For example, a is a Socrates who is Socrates only by being a human being. The concept of the human species shares reference with the disjunction of its particularizations. The individual is the species only by satisfying one of its particular forms. These forms exclude one another. But by doing so they, in another sense, include one another. Each form is what it is by not being the others. Plato is not Socrates. Yet Plato is Plato only through Socrates. Socrates is a specimen of the human species in general, but only by being the Greek philosopher who drank the hemlock in particular.

The logic of judgments reconstructs the whole concrete concept of which the subject-predicate judgment is the original self-division (*Urteil*).[17] We have seen that in the end the concept of the absolute is a self-concept. It is an act of self-thinking accomplished by a rational being or person. Kant's basic insight is that the rational subject grasps itself in grasping the objective phenomenal world. The division of this concept in judgment is a division of the absolute into a purely thinking transcendental subject over against the world viewed as dead matter devoid of subjectivity.

Judgments need not be overtly expressed in sentences. As Errol Harris reminds us, perception is already judgmental.[18] The phenomenological act of seeing a cow includes the judgment that a cow is before one. The act includes positing a subject of predication, and predicating the universal being-a-cow of the subject. For the faculty of judgment, the world is an aggregate of subjects of predication, things of many properties. But when the judging subject describes the objective world as an aggregate of fixed abstract subjects of predication, the dialectical movement of subjective judgment toward, through, and beyond fixed abstraction is excluded from its description of the world. Thus, the distinction established by judgment between the subject of discourse and its predicate implies more fundamentally a division within the absolute between thinking and the objective world, subject and object.

Mind-matter dualism plausibly emerged prehistorically in the fall into patriarchal conditions and in labor.[19] It was not originated but only reconstructed by Descartes. The Cartesian "metaphysics of the understanding"[20] has, for us even if not for Descartes, a place within the speculative philosophy of reason and the concept. "The judgement is the self-diremption of the Notion [self-concept]; *this unity* [of subject and object, universal and particular] is, therefore, the ground from which consideration of the judgement in accordance with its true *objectivity* begins. It is the *original division* of what is originally one."[21]

Judgment is a heuristic denial that the absolute is self-thinking thought, a denial arising within the very definition of the absolute as self-thinking thought. Aristotle's thought thinking itself descends to earth at the dawn of modern philosophy as Descartes's *cogito*, which truly thinks itself, its own existence, in thinking its error of judgment, its fallibility.

Descartes ostensibly defines the absolute by the logic of essence as infinite lordship transcending both nature and the finite mind. Yet, under the cover of this theism he anticipates a Fichtean definition of the absolute as the self-concept.[22] His initial assertion that the world and divine mind transcend what is known by subjective thought thinking itself points up common fallible judgments by which the self reconfirms its own existence. To say that Descartes's dualism is really an absolute idealism is to say that the Cartesian philosophy never gets beyond the *cogito*.

The *cogito* is the center of Hegel's interest in Descartes. Cartesianism in its manifest form is a "metaphysics of the understanding," which in its result refers to mind under the single description of being thought, and to body under the single description of being material.[23] But at a deeper level the Cartesian philosophy is Fichtean:[24] "The spirit of his philosophy is simply knowledge as the unity of Thought and Being. . . . The first of the fundamental determinations of the Cartesian metaphysics is from the certainty of oneself to arrive at the truth, to recognize Being in the Notion of thought. But because of the thought 'I think,' I am an individual, thought comes before my mind as subjective."[25] Mind/matter dualism is the result of judgment. Judging implies a division of the infinite self-thinking subject. It is first divided into (1) a subject of thinking (conceiving/judging) and (2) objective topics of judgment. Second, it is divided into (3) objective topics (subjects of predication) and (4) their predicates.

These divisions are a temporary self-negation (death, crucifixion) of the absolute as self-concept. The judging self is alienated, incapable of recognizing itself in the mechanistic world of abstract subjects of predication that it creates for itself. A true definition of the absolute is possible only when the judging self becomes a syllogistically reasoning self. The objective material world then becomes the "middle term" by which the subject is related to itself (cf. next chapter).

If the self-concept manifests itself to itself in an apparent world of alien necessity which turns out to be the world of the self in disguise, it does so through a particular world which cannot be completely deduced from the initial self. The concept separates into universal and particular concepts, and then cancels this division.

Because every explicit description of the absolute is subject to further particularization, no definition of it can be a complete explicit description of it. Because particularizability belongs to the true definition of the absolute as the self-concept, a true definition of the absolute is incomplete as an explicit description of it. This would pose no problem if essential and accidental properties could be neatly separated. But it is essential to the absolute that it particularize itself by accidental properties. Having accidental properties in general is an essential property. And since it is impossible to have accidental properties in general without having them in particular, some particular accidental properties or other are also essential.

A thing's individual identity is determined by its individual essence. Its species identity is determined by its species essence. Leibniz's identity of indiscernibles is individual identity, and it makes all properties essential. If something has an accidental property, it can retain its species identity while losing that property. But it cannot retain individual Leibnizian identity while losing an accidental property. A completely explicit definition of the individual essence of the absolute would be an complete description of it—which is impossible. All individual definition of the absolute—even as the absolute idea at the end of the *Logic*—diverges from the traditional logic of definitions, which is a logic of species definition requiring every definition to be completely statable.

A human in general must have some particular age, some sex, some cultural origin. One cannot be human in general without being a human in particular, essentially specified by a particular age, sex, and cultural origin, etc. But such endless specifiability places unwelcome limits on logical discourse. Davidson's objection to a relational descriptive predicate implicitly containing an "indefinitely" great number of places[26] is that it makes explicit description incompletely statable, an infinite task. Description becomes irrevocably "elliptical." As Anthony Kenny observes, "we can make 'Brutus killed Caesar' into a sentence which describes, with a certain lack of specification, the whole history of the world."[27]

What is true of describing a human being here is true of the absolute. The *Logic* does not try to give a successful definition of the absolute by the classical logic of definitions, or even by any other standard of definition. Yet, this is not a failure of the *Logic*, or of the speculative tradition that it reconstructs.[28] For it does not prevent it from doing what it undertakes to do: to lead thought to an experience of the true absolute which thinks itself in the system of categories, but which cannot be absolutized merely as that system of categories abstractly conceived.

A definition of the absolute as close to the truth as any that pure thought explicitly constructs remains empirically determinable. The definition is absolutely true only if it is incompletely explicit. Only if it encompasses empirical determinations that even the philosophies of nature and spirit and the positive sciences make only partially explicit.

The essence-accident distinction collapses because every substance requires accidents essentially and not accidentally. Second, the distinction collapses in theoretical science because the individual accidents that the substance has cannot be objectively demarcated from its essential properties. This demarcation is determined by practical interests. It is the practical interest in the rational potential which determines rationality and not two-leggedness as the specific difference of humanity. Rationality, not two-leggedness, perfects human happiness. The essence-accident classification of properties cannot be justified from a theoretical standpoint. From such a standpoint, an absolutely true definition of the absolute must contain a complete description of it. But even a definition inspired by practical commitment must include all its properties if to be rational in general is to be particularized as rational through some nationality, some region, some local neighborhood, some relationship to particular others. Definition of the absolute by practical interest in the category of absolute spirit goes quite beyond definition by the logical idea. But it remains abstract unless taken to be implicit. It does not contain a complete explicit description of it in all its richness.

True individual definition of the absolute in the *Logic* cannot fully succeed. It cannot succeed because it cannot be judged by the standard of classical species definition, in which accidental differences can be ignored. The purpose of defining the absolute as an individual essence is to disclose a self-developing absolute that never leaves behind the activity of ever more particular self-definition. Speculative thought moves beyond the logic as beyond the shadow realm of "an isolated system of abstractions" that remains "confined within itself."[29] It at once moves beyond the whole system of mere pure thought. Only the system understood concretely is truly the absolute. This is the system overreaching the empirical wealth of the absolute.

Since definition, once accepted, is analytic, and since judgment is nonanalytic, no judgment can be a definition. Judgment fixes a subject to which predicates are externally attached. The full individual essence of the absolute as the self-realization of the self-concept is not explicitly grasped by judgment, in which subject and predicate differ in sense. But once a true definition has been grasped, the absolute as a subject of wit and judgment is recast to satisfy the definition. Judgment gives way to tautology. The absolute as the self-realizing self-concept is the absolute as self-realizing self-concept.

To judge of anything as a fixed subject of predication is to characterize it from an external point of view, by comparison and contrast. Wit and discernment are at home in more sophisticated worldly circles, where superior taste and good breeding reign supreme. This is not the world of philosophy. In the world of taste and discernment, each connoisseur endeavors to set herself apart from all peers, to shine by her own light. The ground of philosophical definition and concepts is absent.

4. The Dialectic of Judgments

The above general reflections on judgment prepare the way for a reenactment of the dialectic of judgments. Hegel seeks to show that types of judgment in a complete table of judgments "follow necessarily" in the definition of the absolute.[30] We shall see, however, that this necessity is not strictly deductive.

The types of judgment distinguished by Hegel approximate closely the Kantian table of judgments in the *Critique of Pure Reason*. The *Logic* distinguishes judgments of the following description: (1) qualitative judgments, (2) quantitative judgments, (3) contingently reflective or relational judgments, (4) necessary reflective judgments, and (5) conceptual modal judgments.

Qualitative judgments are used in the logic of being: e.g., "The absolute is mere indeterminate being." Quantitative judgments are used in the logic of quantity: e.g., "The absolute is many ones." Contingently reflective judgments appear in the logic of essence: e.g., "The absolute is the ground that comes to appears in its grounded consequents." Later in the logic of essence necessary reflective judgments of are prominent: e.g., "The absolute is the inner law manifest in the outer world." Finally, in the logic of the concept, conceptual modal judgments appear: e.g., "The absolute is necessarily true to itself in the particular conditions of its existence."

Qualitative Judgments: Positive, Negative, and Infinite

Qualitative judgments are those whose predicates are either positive and immediate (e.g., "red");[31] negative (determinate negations of such predicates, e.g., "not red but some other color");[32] infinite (indeterminate negation of predicates, e.g., "not red but without necessarily being anything in particular other than red").[33]

The positive judgment "The rose is red" is false if understood to mean "The rose is merely red." This falsehood warrants the negative judgment "The rose is not merely red." Thus, by supposing positive and negative judgments to contain the implicit absolutization of the predicate expressed by "merely," the positive judgment is an assumption by indirect proof whose contradictoriness implies the truth of the negative judgment. "The predicate [of the positive judgment] . . . as this *universality* which [in fact] is not real or concrete but *abstract* . . . contains only *one moment* of the subject's totality to the exclusion of the rest."[34]

> The [positive] judgment merely enunciates [the falsehood] that the subject is [exclusively the] predicate, or, more definitely . . . that the individual is universal and vice versa [the abstract universal, falsely viewed as the subject's totality to the exclusion of the rest of the predicates, is posited as the concrete individual]. By virtue of its purely logical

content the positive judgment is not true; but has its truth in the negative judgment. All that is demanded of the content is that it shall not contradict itself in the judgment; but as been shown it does contradict itself in the above judgment.[35]

Further, if the rose is not merely red, it has some undetermined property other than redness. This serves to deduce the infinite judgment.

Such qualitative judgments appear in the logic of qualitative being. The first definition of the absolute contains absolutization of the property of indeterminate being taken as immediate: the Parmenidean claim that the absolute merely is absolutizes this property. The claim starts out as a judgment ("The absolute merely is"), and upon repetition ends up as a tautological identity statement when the subject of the judgment is reinterpreted in light of the predicate ("The absolute which merely is, is the absolute which merely is").

Quantitative Judgments: Singular, Particular, and Universal

The so-called "*quantitative*" judgments treated by Hegel are admitted to be not purely quantitative.[36] "All men are on earth" invokes the qualitative determinations of the extensions of two classes. So does the judgment "All ones are qualitatively identical." Such judgments are "quantitative" only insofar as they proceed by quantification of the propositional function of some singular judgment.

Hegel treats quantitative judgments together with "contingent reflective judgments"[37]—which he distinguishes shortly after from necessary reflective judgments. We shall treat these judgments separately in the next section.

The progression of quantitative judgments starts with the singular judgment whose subject is only one entity.[38] The progression then passes on to particular judgments,[39] i.e., to existential quantification of a propositional function. Yet, a Hegelian existential quantification differs from today's existential quantification by the insistence that the predicate has at least two instances, not at least one: the subject of a particular judgment is "*these* or a *particular number of individuals.*"[40] And, finally, the progression proceeds from existential quantification to universal quantification.[41]

A dispositional predicate in quantitative judgments is successively instantiated by one and only one member of a class, by more than one, and by all members. The transition from "one and only one" entity of a given description to "some" ("at least two") is clearly not deductive. The transition lies in the introduction of the false assumption that indiscernible entities can be nonidentical, distinguished quantitatively though not qualitatively. "Particularity . . . must be merely an [assumed] extension of the individual [with its selfsame quality] in external reflection."[42]

Given the identity of indiscernibles, the assumption of two entities each completely described in the same way is false. Yet an assumed quantitative reiteration of a single complete description in at least two and eventually all members of a class alone serves to construct the quantitative definition of the absolute in the logic of being. The absolute is the summation of all ones. The transition from some instances of a given quality to everything having that quality appears as a further indirect proof assumption. It may be taken as a conjecture open to logical self-criticism and correction, rather than as a weak induction.

Contingent Reflective Judgments

Having considered quantitative judgments, we take up contingent "reflective" judgments. Hegel includes them in the classification of judgments, and places quantitative judgments under the rubric of contingent reflective judgments. Yet, we have reason to doubt that contingent reflective judgments constitute a distinct type of judgment. They are "reflective" because of the nature of their predicates, not because of their propositional structure as judgments: they have predicates that are illuminated only in the reflected light of independently existing objects.[43]

An example is "Some roses are expensive," meaning that they would exchange for a relatively greater rather than small number of currency units essentially independent of the rose. Or "This vase is fragile," meaning that it will break if dropped on a hard surface—where it and the reflectively illuminating surface are essentially independent of each other, each being capable of existing without the other. The vase's fragility is discovered empirically and hence contingently, not by analyzing essence of the vase.

The vase could exist and be fragile even if there were no hard objects apart from it, though its fragility would go undetected, unilluminated by whatever reflected light such objects would cast. Even if "The vase is fragile" is necessarily true by virtue of the nature of the vase, it cannot be known to be true a priori. Dispositional properties, unlike qualitative properties, cannot be discovered by direct inspection of the object. Nor are they analytically contained in the concept of the object. They are discovered only by observing the thing's interaction with externally related things. They manifest themselves in the reflected light of independently existing things.

Judgments of reflection are prominent in the logic of essence ("All things found to be self-identical are different from other things").

Concepts of quantity are illustrated in the logic of being ("All ones are qualitatively identical"). It is possible for a quantitative judgment to be purely quantitative and thus nonreflective, through repetition of a nonreflective predicate. But it may be impossible for a reflective judgment supported with evidence to lack a quantitative dimension. A single living human being is identified as mortal by being placed in a class with more than one member, where one or more members are deceased.

While qualitative judgments are judgments of inherence, contingent reflective judgments are judgments of subsumption.[44] Redness inheres in the rose: it is brought within the scope of the rose because it is open to immediate inspection on the rose's surface. The dispositional property of being perishable does not inhere in the living rose in this way. Rather, this rose is subsumed under, brought under, perishability by virtue of being one of many members of the class of roses.

Redness is an immediately observable property. Perishability is a reflective property. A rose which has not perished is not identifiable as perishable by any direct inspection of it. Rather, it is known to be perishable in the reflected light of other roses in the same class. In judgments of inherence the predicates revolve around a subject which immediately displays them to intuition. In judgments of subsumption the individual subjects fall under universal dispositional predicates after comparison with other similar subjects.

Contingent reflective judgments bridge books 1 and 2 of the *Logic*. They refer to the logic of quantity in book 1 by their more or less quantitatively "extended" subjects. They belong to the beginning of book 2 by their experimentally detected dispositional predicates.

The quantitative and qualitative dimensions of contingent reflective judgments are connected. Suppose a vase is placed in a quantitatively extended class of vases, some but not all of which have shown their fragility by actually shattering. What was but a qualitatively determined vase is then not only quantitatively determined (one of some or all of a class of vases), but also reflectively determined, e.g., as brittle.

"All vases are brittle" need not be viewed as an induction.[45] Suppose the concept of a vase is expanded by reflection beyond its immediate qualitative determination. Suppose that membership in the class of brittle things is included in that concept. Vases are then essentially brittle. The reflective concept of a vase has replaced the qualitative one, and "All vases are brittle" becomes "The vase is brittle."

What we call "the vase" here is of course no particular vase. It is an idealized universal vase standing in for all individual vases. The vase's brittleness, which before reflective judgment was external to it as a particular vase, now belongs to its universal being-in-itself.

"Everything is a one, an aggregate of ones, or an aspect of a one." This statement shows it is possible for a judgment to be quantitative without expressing the reflective illumination of different entities by one another. It is also possible for reflective judgment to lack a quantitative dimension.

The Neoplatonic definition of the absolute is: "The absolute is the one and only one *x* found self-identical under a show of different descriptions which are really nothing but the same description of being the one." The different descriptions by which reference can be made to the absolute are really the same.

"The absolute is the beautiful" means no more nor any less than "The absolute is the one." The one is the one. The different descriptions under which the absolute appears are an illusory show, but the reflective light cast by this empirically surface show illuminates the absolute as self-identical under a single description.

The absolute, unlike the vase, cannot be placed in a quantitatively extended class of absolutes. Attempts to refer to the absolute under any description but a determination of "the one" prove self-refuting. No doubt, "The absolute is found to be merely self-identical under the single description of being the one" is reflective, since it cancels the show of identity under different descriptions. (By contrast, "The absolute is mere indeterminate being" contains a purely qualitative description.)

But a contingent reflective judgment, like qualitative judgment, is a type of subject-predicate judgment. The reflective element lies in the structure of the predicate, not in the form of the judgment. Thus, from the standpoint of logical form, quantitative judgments represent a type of judgment distinct from qualitative judgment, while reflective judgments properly speaking do not.

Necessary Reflective Judgments: Categorical, Hypothetical, and Disjunctive

Beyond quantitative judgments lie necessary reflective judgments. "All roses are expensive" is an a posteriori judgment about all members of a class. Yet, the truth thus expressed may well be a necessary truth which is not yet known a priori, but which is arrived at by an empirical induction. If a universal statement is not in fact groundless, if its truth is not a matter of accident and coincidence, the ground of its universality lies in a necessary statement about the nature of all members of the class. Either "To be a rose is necessarily to be expensive" is true or "All roses are expensive" stands ungrounded, or incompletely grounded in a finite number of empirical observations.

It is hard to deny that some universal propositions are grounded in necessary judgments. For example, "All bachelors are unmarried" is grounded in "To be a bachelor is to be necessarily unmarried." But surely not every universal proposition is grounded in a necessary proposition. As we have just seen in the case of the vase, the *Logic* distinguishes between prereflective and postreflective entities. When reflection upon a qualitatively determinate entity first arises, the reflected predicate is external to the entity. The qualitatively determinate rose is only accidentally expensive. But after reflection the attribute is posited across the entire membership of the class of roses, and the rose's essence is expanded and determined more concretely as necessarily expensive.

The contingent universal truth "All roses are expensive" becomes a necessary universal judgment grounded in the nature of roses. "The rose is necessarily expensive." Hegel associates necessary judgment in its first stage with the category of substance.[46] The universal, quintessential rose is a total substance from which being expensive is analyzed out in one of its attribute.

The judgments of necessity are first the categorical subject-predicate judgment, in which the subject is an actually existing kind containing the predicate. The absolute is the cosmic substance which necessarily exists, which is infinite, and which possesses other necessary attributes such as being material or thinking.

Second, there are hypothetical judgments, which are universally quantified conditional judgments: "If anything is a rose, it is expensive." "If something is the cosmic substance, it necessarily has the attribute of being material." These two propositions state that if something has a universal form, it has a given particular determination of that universal. The rose is considered as a universal kind, and being expensive has been reflected into the rose's nature as one of its particular forms. The hypothetical judgment diverges from the categorical judgment in that categorical assertion of the substantial subject's existence is withdrawn. What remains is only the predicate's dependence on the subject even if the subject should not exist.

Disjunctive judgments, the third type of necessary judgment, consist in exclusive disjunctions.[47] They assert identity between a disjunctive series of particular descriptions and the referent of an abstract universal description. If the referent of a particular description exists, so necessarily does the referent of the universal description. But if what is referred to in universal terms exists, it need not be referred to merely by one particular description. Other particular means of reference are also available. "Expensive is merely fine clothes, or if it is not it is exclusively fast cars . . ."

"The cosmic absolute is exclusively matter, or rather exclusively thought, or if not then exclusively some other attribute." In fact the substance has many attributes. The mutual exclusion of the disjuncts comes from absolutizing each particular as the only true particular description. The number of the disjunctions is the number of possible particular descriptions that can be selected for predicate absolutization.

Disjunctive judgment expresses a truth about any abstractly universal concept. For the abstract universal is the exclusive disjunction of its logically possible particularizations. Still, the range of possible particularizations does not imply which particularization is actual. The concrete concept of an individual is its self-identity found under an *actual* particular description as well as an abstractly universal description. Hence, disjunctive judgment falls short of expressing the concrete concept.

Modal Conceptual Judgments: Assertoric, Problematic, and Apodictic

The final judgments are modal conceptual judgments. They are essentially value judgments. The subject of the disjunctive judgment just considered was an abstractly universal definite description, which was said to have the same reference as one or another exclusive particular description. The subject of a modal conceptual judgment is an individual which embraces both universal and particular forms, and which is thus identical to the concrete concept.[48]

Modal conceptual judgments attribute value predicates such as truth, beauty, and goodness. They assert, question, and ground correspondence or harmony between a thing's particular conditions of existence and its concept. "The absolute is true (to itself)" means: in the particular concrete historical conditions of its development it actualizes its universal concept—the concept of being the self-identical cosmos which, in particular, thinks itself in a finite subject.

The first modal conceptual judgment (e.g., "The absolute is true") is an assertoric judgment.[49] It asserts that the absolute in whatever real existence it has satisfies its concept. But the judgment makes this assertion dogmatically, without any ground.

The absence of evidential ground opens the assertoric judgment to doubt. It is possible that the absolute after all does not satisfy its concept. We thus have a problematic judgment.[50]

The third and final modal conceptual judgment is the apodictic judgment: doubt is overcome by a ground in the empirical conditions of the concept's historical realization. "The house constituted so and so is good."[51] The absolute satisfies its concept because of the demonstrable conditions of its development in history. The conformity that defines the beauty of the rose, or the truth of the absolute, is not between factors internal to a partly abstract concept, but between the abstract concept and real conditions that particularize it.

5. Judgment Transcended

In conceptual judgment, judgment itself with its explicit distinction between subject and predicate falls away. There is nothing in the subject not explicit in the predicate, and nothing in the predicate not explicitly received into the subject. "Subject and predicate have the same content."[52]

When we say "The rose actualizes beauty, its internal concept, by such and such particular conditions of its existence," we state a definition of the individual, not a judgment. The definition is reflected back into the term defined. "The beautiful in such and such particular (genetic, mineralogical, climatological, etc.) conditions of its actualization is identical to the beautiful in such and such particular conditions of its actualization." The "rose" abbreviates the concrete individual identified with the totality of its universal and particular factors.

We recapitulate by listing the following sequence in the development of forms of judgment. Quantitative judgments are considered, as for Hegel, to be a subspecies of contingent reflective judgments.

I. Contingent Qualitative Judgments of Inherence
1. The rose is merely red
(Judgment of a quality's inherence in a subject. Indirect proof assumption)
2. The rose is not merely red
(Negative judgment of inherence inferred by indirect proof)
3. The rose has some quality beyond that of being red
(Infinite positive judgment of inherence)

II. Contingent Reflective Judgments of Subsumption under a Dispositional Predicate
4. The (one and only) rose is (discoverably) perishable
(Singular judgment of subsumption)
5. Some roses (in the class of all roses) are (discoverably) perishable
(Particular judgment of subsumption. "Existential generalization" following from 4 only on modern interpretation of such generalization)
6. All roses are (discoverably) perishable

(Universal judgment of subsumption. An apparent induction)

III. Necessary Dispositional Judgments

7. The essential rose is (necessarily) perishable
   (Necessary categorical judgment. Reconstruction of concept of subject in 6 to include dispositional predicate, so that 6 is not really an induction)

8. If something is a rose, it is (necessarily) perishable
   (Necessary hypothetical judgment. Suspension of the assumption of the subject's existence)

9. What is perishable is (necessarily) either the rose or is some other living thing
   (Necessary disjunctive judgment. Transformation of dispositional predicate in 8 into subject)

IV. Modal Axiological Judgments

10. It is the case that the rose is beautiful
    (Assertoric modal judgment, with axiological predicate)

11. It is possible that the rose is not beautiful
    (Problematic modal judgment with axiological predicate)

12. It is necessarily the case that the rose is beautiful because it is red and perishable
    (Necessary or apodictic modal judgment with axiological predicate)

We have noted where this progression appears to be deductive. It does not appear so everywhere. However, this failure of deductive development does not mean that the *Logic* as a sequence of definitions of the absolute is not deductive. For, unlike the category of the self-concept as a whole, no judgment is by itself such a definition.

The progression of judgments begins with contingent qualitative predicates (1–3). It moves to dispositional predicates (4–9), and finally to necessary axiological predicates (10–12).

On the subject side, it begins with singular empirical subjects (1–3). It then moves to quantitatively generalized subjects (5–6), to universal essential subjects (7–9), and finally to modally determined subject-predicate judgments (10–12).

Clearly this is not a purely formal—let alone deductive—logic of judgments. Where Hegel might be most suspected of doing formal logic in the traditional sense—the logic of judgments and syllogisms (next chapter)—that is not, it turns out, what he is doing. For his logic of judgments distinguishes judgments according to the content of terms, not simply according to logical form. It moves from inherence to subsumption, to necessary conceptual analysis, to modally determined value judgment. Inherence passes into subsumption by arbitrary quantitative reiteration of the subject.

Seemingly arbitrary universal subsumption passes into necessary conceptual analysis by the objectification of reflective activity, i.e., by building into the subject the results of subsumption under quantity and external reflection on the subject. And conceptual analysis becomes modal axiological judgment by judging the consistency with which a concept realizes itself in an individual.

Of the four functions of judgment that Hegel distinguishes—immediate description (inherence), mediated comparison (subsumption: this rose is perishable by analogy with other members of the class of roses), analysis, and evaluation—evaluative claims come closest to stating "truth" in the philosophical sense: e.g., an individual state is a true or good state because the universal concept of a state consistently realizes itself in its particular circumstances. It fails to state truth completely, we shall see, only because philosophical truth is dialectical, a process of establishing itself indirectly over against error. Hegel's logic of judgments is a presentation of judgments on a scale of their progressively more coherent speculative use. Yet, even the most speculative use of judgment falls short of a dialectic of speculative theological definitions. And it is only a small part of the development of the true definition of the absolute as the self-concept.

Theology of the Rational Syllogism

1. From Judging to Syllogistic Reasoning

Judgment emerged in the previous chapter out of the self-concept, which is as true a definition of the absolute as the logic can attain. The theory of judgment does not establish a new definition of the absolute. It only develops what is contained in its definition as the self-concept. Since definition of the absolute is a theological task, the *Logic* presents a theology of judgment, not a formal logic of propositions or judgments. Recalling this helps reduce impatience with a text which, by classifying judgments and syllogisms, retains in part the appearance of a formal logic manual—perhaps the manual which Hegel in Nuremberg had been commissioned to write by the Royal Bavarian Government.

Nonanalytic and nontautological judgment, we have just said, has a theological function. Suppose that the absolute is the self-concept. Judgment then effects the absolute's self-division into a subject of predication and an independent predicate. The subjective self-concept falls apart in judgment as a condition to its subsequent reconstruction in contrast to judgment as a "rational" syllogism. Such a syllogism concludes with tautological statements in which the subject and predicate terms are each the same concrete individual. In both cases this individual satisfies an abstract universal description by satisfying a more particular description.

Despite Hegel's claim that the section on essence is the most difficult of the whole science of logic,[1] the section of the *Logic* on the syllogism is probably the most difficult in the entire book. We must be satisfied if the following account is at least somewhat more straightforward and understandable than the original, without being misleading.

Judging begins by abstracting and separating off a subject of attribution from a subsequently predicated attribute. Judgment predicates an abstractly separated attribute of the abstracted subject. True predicative attachment of a attribute to a subject presupposes its prior detachment from that subject.

The subject of a subject-predicate judgment is a *logical subject* abstracted and absolutized by itself under some description. Such a subject may also be a *thinking* subject. For thinking may be the description under which the logical subject is singled out.

If the logical subject is a thinking subject, *judgment* in its discernment requires that the predicated attribute be logically independent of the attribute by which the subject is identified. The thinking subject (subjective self-concept), abstracted and absolutized by itself, has the discernible predicate of thinking some particular object.

Judgment discovers in itself a peculiar syllogistic process by which the separation between subject attributes and predicate attributes is overcome. Suppose the judgment that John has the logically independent predicate of being merely German. But to be German is to be European. Therefore, by the law of absorption, John is both German and European. The conjunctive predicate "German and European" is more concrete, less incomplete, than the predicate "merely German." It more closely coincides with the John's full nature. The conjunctive predicate is thus so much the less external to the subject. Expanding conjunctive predicates come ever closer to reproducing the subject in analysis.

The science of logic contains a theology of the syllogism in definition of the absolute. Again, the reader who expects formal logic of the syllogism will be exasperated. To the *syllogisms of the understanding* familiar to us from formal logic Hegel adds the *rational syllogism*. As the existence of hypothetical and disjunctive syllogisms in propositional logic shows, the concept of syllogisms is somewhat elastic. It is not restricted to classical categorical syllogisms. The syllogism in its rational form demonstrates that the subject of the concluding judgment implies a middle term which is preserved in the predicate attributed to that subject. For example: "The absolute is merely positively determinate. What is positively determinate is at once negatively determinate. Therefore, the absolute is not merely positively determinate, but is positively determinate and at once negatively determinate." The absolute is the minor term, the subject of the conclusion. What is positively determinate is the middle term. The major term is what is positively determinate and (hence) what is negatively determinate. There are three simple predicates prior to the conclusion, and none but those predicates appear in the conclusion. The major term is a compound predicate, formed by conjoining a universal middle term and the predicate by which the middle term is particularized.

The rational syllogism is distinguished from the usual categorical syllogisms of formal logic by including in the major term conjoined predicates together expressing the particularized middle term. It is also distinguished in that its first statement is an indirect proof assumption, an assumption dropped in the concluding statement. Without an indirect proof assumption, a rational syllogism would cease to be rational: "The absolute is positively determinate. What is positively determinate is at once negatively determinate. Therefore, the absolute is positively determinate and at once negatively determinate." This syllogism is valid, but it is not rational because it lacks the heuristic, error-correcting feature of indirect proof. Rationality is essentially the ability to correct error.

Ultimately, the rational syllogism will lead, by repetition, beyond the syllogism, and indeed beyond all forms of judgment. It leads to tautology: the absolute as positively determinate and negatively determinate is the absolute as positively determinate and negatively determinate. The individual which is universal by being particular is the individual which is universal by being particular.

2. Syllogistic Thinking and the Absolute Idea

The rational syllogism plays a role in the remaining two parts of the logic: in the logic of the "objective self-concept" and of the "absolute idea" (absolute self-concept). Eventually it plays a role in the entire system of philosophy, including the philosophy of nature and of spirit. (See sec. 4 below on pansystematic syllogisms.)

The object is the developed subjective self-concept returned within itself, into an undifferentiated form. The objective self-concept is a collapsed subjective self-concept. An objectively given rational syllogism lying dormant in the history we inherit is a once living subjective syllogism withdrawn into itself. Our own subjectivity is concealed in our objective world. This objective world expresses in immediate form an entire dialectical history of rational syllogisms by which we have become what we are. By projecting ourselves into our world and bringing it back to life in subjective thought, the dialectical, syllogistic process concealed in the object unfolds again on an epic scale such as we have seen in the history of philosophy.

When the object reveals itself as the self-reconstruction of a past objectively given subjective self-concept, the original self-concept appears as a *subjective* self-concept.[2] The objective self-concept is a limit on the subjective self-concept, which is overcome through the rebirth of the object into objectively realized subjectivity. The objective self-concept is the obstacle which the subjective self-concept must overcome to realize itself objectively. This obstacle is the subjective concept's own collapsed self awaiting dialectical reinflation.[3]

The objective self-concept is first the developed subjective self-concept reduced to and concentrated in its undeveloped immediate source. It is "the *syllogism,* whose mediation has been sublated [erased, *ausgeglichen*], and has therefore become [reverted to] an immediate identity."[4] The point of the rational syllogism is: the absolute as merely universal is individual by not being merely universal, but by being particular as well. Stated otherwise, the absolute merely as universal is the absolute as universal and particular. The absolute as universal is not purely universal; it is both universal and particular, i.e., individual.

The erasure of differentiation between universal, particular, and individual determinations results from repetition of the rational syllogism reducing it to a tautology: the absolute as universal and particular is the absolute as universal and particular. Here there is no judgment, and no false indirect proof assumption that the absolute has but one determination. In this statement of the form "$a = a$," there is only "immediate identity." This objective self-concept is the immediate object into which the articulated self-concept vanishes. The subjective self-concept encounters an object which is the dead remnant of that very subjective self-concept, a remnant left over from its incipient historical self-construction.

The objective world we encounter is different from that encountered in other times and places. For the present world has produced us. It potentially contains us and not persons of other ages. The successful labor of the self-concept's past self-construction in history withdraws upon completion into an objective world confronted by the living self-concept.

Through historical reconstruction of the subjective self-concept out of the objective world (out of the concealed, objective self-concept), the absolute idea (absolute self-concept) arises. The subjective self-concept discovers itself in the syllogistic process of its object, and thus ceases to be merely subjective. The reconstruction of the object is self-reconstructive —eventuating in self-knowledge in knowledge of the object.

Self-loss in the objective self-concept's immediate starting point is a fall from "self-mediation" to immediacy in the subjective self-concept's discovery of the collapsed objective self-concept. The concrete process reverts to its abstract objective source, out of which it regenerates itself. The objective concept is the seed back into which the subjective concept is concentrated.

The collapse[5] of the subjective self-concept into its origin in immobility and rest is a conceptual deconstruction of the subjective self-concept, preparing its self-reconstruction. The objective self-concept is an apparent not-self which is actually the self in disguise. The objective self-concept—the departure point for self-reconstruction of the subjective self-concept—is the middle term, the abstractly universal "other" by which the subjective concept is concretely mediated with itself.[6]

The objective world, in which you do not immediately recognize yourself, is your own self still concealed within itself. The subject existing concretely for itself is actually what the object is only potentially, in itself.[7] The objective concept is the self-mediated subjective concept reduced to its mere potentiality, to "immediate individuality."[8] The phases of its reconstruction into concrete individuality will be examined in the next chapter. The logic of the self-concept, we have noted, is connected for Hegel with German idealism. The return from the subjective self-concept to the objective self-concept underlies the development from Kant to Schelling's philosophy of nature.[9] Schelling saw that nature as the total object haltingly constructs itself into a self. And it does so independently of our logical reconstruction of the process.

Hegel, endeavoring to formulate himself in the *Logic* on the level of pure thought, treats the subjective concept instead of subjective spirit, the object (objective concept) instead of nature, and the logical idea instead of absolute spirit.[10] On this logical level, he claims that syllogistic reconstruction of the object's original self-construction pursues that self-construction beyond the external object to completion in the self-knowing idea. The cosmic object in general is, in particular, the object reconstructing itself in and through individuals such as us.

The self-reconstructive objective self-concept is the particular middle term between the universal subjective self-concept and the individual concrete self-concept (absolute idea). The dialectical process of the objective self-concept is an objectively historical syllogistic thought process.[11] Objectivity begins, we have noted, with the collapse of self-mediation into immediacy: "this subjectivity [of the concept] . . . is subjectivity itself which, being dialectical, breaks through its own barrier, and opens itself up into objectivity by means of syllogism. This *realization* of the *Concept* . . . which through the sublation of the mediation has itself as *immediate* unity, . . . is the *Object*."[12]

Tautologically, the subjective self-concept (which reconstructs itself in the objective self-concept) is identical to that which reconstructs itself in the objective self-concept (which is the subjective self-concept). Such an *identity statement* transcends *judgment*. Yet it retains a referential function. "Socrates is Socrates" is uninformative. But we successfully refer to

Socrates by its use. The preceding identity statement directs us to the self-particularizing self-concept. It shows that the distinction of terms in a "rational syllogism"[13]—in this case universal and particular terms—is reproduced in each term.[14] By the concrete concept of Socrates, Socrates (the individual) is analytically Socrates as mortal (the universal) only by being human (the particular). And the individual concrete self-concept is analytically the universal subjective self-concept only by reconstructing itself as the particular objective self-concept.

We now see how the syllogism functions in the balance of the logic. The mediation of universal and individual extremes occurs by a particular middle term: The subject is (by hermeneutic self-alienation with indirect proof assumption of another standpoint) merely the subject reduced to the object. The subject reduced to the object is (by its dialectical self-reconstruction) also the object remaking itself into subject. Therefore, the subject is (concretely), not merely reduced to the object, but both the subject reduced to the object and the object remaking itself subject.

This illustrates the rationally self-propelling syllogism that is Hegel's concern. Judgment in the conclusion of an ordinary formal syllogism separates a universal subject and individual predicate. In *rational* syllogistic thinking this is not the case. Such thinking uses the universal middle term (e.g., subject reduced to object) to abstract a particular term (e.g., object remaking itself subject) which, conjoined with the middle term by the law of absorption, concretely defines the subject in the major term. Superficially opposed universal subjective and concrete subjective self-concepts are identified. The subject of the conclusion reproduces itself, in a conjunctive analysis of itself, in the predicate, by retracing the self-construction of the objective concept into the concrete subjective self-concept.[15]

3. The Theological Logic of the Syllogism

Hegel's logic of judgments turned out in the last chapter to be one of different uses of judgment—description, comparison, analysis, and evaluation. Evaluation used judgment most conspicuously for purposes of theological logic. Yet, the evaluative judgment that the absolute is true because its concept is actualized in the particular conditions of its existence was not deduced. The theological logic of the syllogism now provides for deduction.

In the logic of the "subjective concept" Hegel comes closest to treating traditional formal logic. The biographical context of the text helps account for the apparent hesitation in this last book of the *Logic* between a survey of formal logic for its own sake and an exploration of the theological import of the logic of judgments and syllogisms.

Hegel, we have noted, was "commissioned" to write a logic manual for Bavarian secondary schools, and the *Science of Logic* was the result of this endeavor.[16] The official who commissioned him was Friedrich Niethammer, an early follower of German idealism. Niethammer accepted Kant's transcendental interpretation of the table of judgments contained in formal logic. According to this interpretation, the categories of the understanding are expressed in the different types of judgment. *Judgment* expresses the abstractive *understanding* because it separates the subject of predication off from the predicated attribute. Judgment is never correct in the sense of conforming to the nature of things. It is never more than an approximation. For things according to their nature are not separated from their predicates or properties. Rather, judgment makes things conform Copernican-like to the abstractive nature of the understanding.

By syllogistic inference, *reason* reunites what the understanding has separated. If judgments correspond to categories of the understanding, the rational syllogism corresponds to the categorial structure of reason. For the syllogism contains a middle term by which the concept of the minor term is, as the judgment becomes a conclusion, concretely defined in the concept of the major term. The syllogism is to the Hegelian categorial structure of reason what the table of judgments is to the Kantian categories of the understanding. But the syllogisms of classical logic fail to satisfy this purpose. For the middle term in them remains external to the major term.

Hegel uncovers a neglected form of the syllogism, which we call the rational syllogism of indirect proof: "Assume *S* is merely *M*. To be *M* is to be *P*. Therefore, *S* is not merely *M*, but is *P* as well: *S* is *M* and *P*." This truly rational (i.e., error-correcting) syllogism indicates the single true category of reason. The syllogisms of formal logic are only syllogisms of the understanding. Because the middle term is not contained in a compound major term, the major term *P* in classical syllogisms fails to define the *S*. The major term "*M* and *P*" in the rational syllogism provides such a definition. The truly rational syllogistic form expresses the category of the self-concept, most concretely, the absolute idea.

Book 3 of the *Logic*, interpreted chiefly as a theo-logic, is yet a logic. It is certainly not logic for the sake of logic. Rather, it pursues logic for the clues it offers as to the category of reason (the self-concept) and its codification in reasoning. As a formal logic manual, Hegel's *Logic* can be faulted for being written with an ulterior agenda. Ordinary formal logic is evaluated according to he degree to which its various forms conceal or reveal the category of reason. This category of reason, which defines the absolute, reveals itself as more than the private invention of Hegel and other German idealists. It is publicly if implicitly institutionalized in syllogisms, and preeminently in the truest form of the syllogism. This form of the syllogism has enjoyed historical use, even if it is not recognized in the table of syllogisms in manuals.

Hegel classifies figures of the syllogism.[17] But he does not classify them by the ordinary figures and moods familiar to us from formal logic. Instead they are classified by the order of individual, particular, and universal terms in each syllogism. This is something which in standard formal logic is a matter of *content*, not *logical form*.

Thus, in Hegel's Individual-Particular-Universal (I-P-U) syllogism, P stands, not for a *particular judgment* but for a *particular middle term* mediating a individual term I and a universal term U. I-P-U is shorthand for a syllogism of the three successive judgments I-P, P-U, I-U—each distinguished according to whether its subject and predicate term is individual, particular, or universal.[18] The I-P-U is illustrated by the following nonrational syllogism: "Socrates is Greek (I-P), Greeks are human (P-U). Therefore, Socrates is human (I-U)."

Rational syllogisms serving to define the absolute in the *Logic* have the form I-U, U-P, I-UP. An illustration is the following syllogism: "1. The immediate individual absolute I merely has the universal characteristic U of power (I-U). 2. For something to have power U in general is in its particularity to have P (U-P). 3. Therefore, the absolute I does not merely have power U, but manifests itself as P as well (I-U, U-P, I-UP, i.e., I-U, U-P, I-I)." The form of this syllogism may be abbreviated as I-U-UP (I-U-I). This form appears nowhere in Hegel's classification of syllogisms. I propose to view it as an informally developed contribution by Hegel to syllogistic logic and formal logic generally, representing a potentially notable contribution to even today's formal logic texts.

Abstraction is made in Hegel's classification of syllogisms from formal considerations of the *quantity* and *quality* of judgments.[19] That his classification is not formal is clear from the fact that two formally distinct arguments can both be I-P-U syllogisms: "This sense quality is greenness (I-P). Greenness is the thing's color (P-U). Therefore, this sense quality is the thing's color (I-U)." "Nothing that is this sense quality is greenness (I-P). Greenness is the thing's color (P-U). Therefore, nothing that is this sense quality is the thing's color (I-U)."

The rational syllogisms that retain Hegel's interest have singular terms. Hegel's particular terms (e.g., "the capital") and universal terms (e.g., "the city") are really, for him, singular terms which refer under more or less particular descriptions. "Human" refers ostensibly to a universal class. Yet, on pain of contradiction no one, we have seen, can be human in general apart from being some human in particular. So "human" is coherent only as an abbreviation of a determinate singular description ("human by being Greek; human, and hence Greek . . .").

"That which is green" refers to a singular individual, but under a less universal description than "that which is colored." So-called particular or universal singular referring expressions are descriptive singular referring expressions under more or less abbreviated descriptions. In ordinary non-Hegelian logic "the man," "the animal," and "Socrates" are singular terms. That one such term refers by narrower description than another is of no concern to formal logic. Statements are particular or universal within usual logic, but not terms.

The *Logic* designates the predicate terms, not simply statements, as "universal" or "particular." Hegel thus imports into the logic of the syllogism differences of generality between terms which Aristotle reserves for the logic of definitions. Definition and syllogistic reasoning merge.

Yet, for Hegel the Aristotelian distinction between genus and specific difference is, we have seen, replaced by the distinction between a general determinable and its particular determinates. For an Aristotelian, specific difference implies the intersection of two genuses. The genus "animal" intersects with the genus "rational being" to produce the human essence with rationality as the specific difference. But the absolute as one genus, we know, cannot intersect with a second genus, since there is no other genus. The absolute must therefore be a self-determining determinable. The source of its determination is within itself.

The *Logic* introduces into the standard logic of definitions a concern to define individuals, ultimately that individual which is the absolute. The goal is not, as in the traditional theory of definition, to define species. The result is a classification of syllogisms by the definitional function of terms rather than by the deductive form of the argument.

"The philosopher" is a general singular term used in defining Socrates as the philosopher who drank the hemlock. "He who drank the hemlock" is a particular singular term. Each term connotes one component of a more concrete individual description. In syllogistic definition the particular term is a singular term used to refer to an individual under an (incomplete) particular description presupposing an unstated more universal description.

The syllogisms that concern the Hegelian science of logic have only singular terms, we hold, because the dominant theological interest of the *Logic* is the defining of the absolute. Absolute spirit exhibits most concretely infinite individuality ("singularity").[20] It is never subject to a general description except by satisfying a further particular description. Thus, absolute spirit falls under the general characteristic of thinking itself in all reality only by virtue of its particular characteristic of overcoming limitation by the external world.[21]

Hegel's statement that the absolute itself (and not merely definition of the absolute as considered so far) is a syllogism[22] at first seems outrageous. Yet, the statement does not go beyond definition of the absolute as the self-concept. It only develops the meaning of that definition. The absolute daily determines and particularizes itself under a merely general abstract description in order to develop under a more concrete description, including the particularization along with the general description.

The logic of judgments in the last chapter ended in evaluative judgment. Socrates is true to his essential humanity by the particular circumstances of his life. The absolute is true to its general concept of being logical thought thinking itself by satisfying a particular description of passing outside itself and actualizing itself in objective nature.

The predicate of the evaluative judgment explicitly invokes universal and particular descriptions. But it does not explicitly mention a concrete individual satisfying these descriptions. Lying beyond judgment and syllogistic reasoning, definitions of a term make explicit reference to this individual: "The absolute is defined as the concrete individual which satisfies a universal concept by satisfying some more particular concept." Instead of a grounded judgment of the absolute's truth or genuineness, we have here an individual equated (in the definiendum of a nonjudgmental identity statement) with the same individual defined by a particularized universal concept. Compare to: "Socrates is defined as this concrete individual who is in general this man by being in particular this mortal." This is offered as a definition of an individual. The referring expression to the right of "is defined as" is descriptive. But it refers to Socrates by description showing traces of this syllogism: "All who are Socrates are merely this man. But to be this man is in particular to be this mortal. Therefore, Socrates is this man who is this mortal."

The absolute is not merely the universal absolute self-concept, but is both this self-concept and the natural world from which in particular the logical self-concept is abstracted. The absolute is the absolute self-concept which by being actualized in nature is spirit. This shows the fundamental form of the rational syllogism.[23] It is grounded in the necessary or apodictic judgment: The I which is U actualized as I by being that which is P.[24] In this necessary judgment we have "something singular that relates to its universal, i.e., to its concept, in virtue of its constitution. Here the particular appears as the mediating middle between the singular and the universal; and this is the basic form of the syllogism."[25]

4. The Three Pansystematic Syllogisms of Speculative Philosophy

Syllogistic inference provides the form in which the absolute attains self-definition.[26] The end of the *Encyclopaedia* distinguishes three syllogisms by which the absolute defines itself through the entire system of philosophy—including the philosophies of nature and spirit as well as the logic.[27] Examination of these pansystematic syllogisms illuminates the role of the syllogism in the *Logic*, and of the logic throughout the system.

All three pansystematic definitions presuppose that the absolute is the self-concept. Each differs by beginning at a different point on the same circle—the circle of conceptual universality, particularity, and their resultant individuality. Since every point in circular motion presupposes all prior points, to break into the construction starting at any one point requires abstraction from presupposed prior points.

None of the three pansystematic syllogisms is a syllogism of the understanding (of traditional formal logic) in which the middle term is external to the major term. All are rational syllogisms in which the "subject [of the conclusion] is by means of the mediation [middle term] coupled [identified] with itself [in the conclusion's predicate term preserving a universal middle term with the particular term in definition of the minor term or subject of the conclusion]."[28]

Discovery of the rational syllogism incorporating indirect proof—contrary to the usual syllogisms of formal logic—belongs to Hegel. The traditional syllogisms of formal logic are syllogisms of the understanding which retain the separation of particular, singular, and universal terms. The rational syllogism is based on an alleged self-contradiction in the assumption of such separation, so that the compound major term becomes possible. The absolute is power and hence its self-manifestation; it is *UP*, i.e., *I*.

The rational syllogisms in which the system constructs itself allow only a provisional, heuristic, or expository separation of terms. Yet, the usual formal syllogisms of the understanding conceal a rational syllogism of indirect proof at work in the objective world of falsely absolutized things:

> In the following examination, the syllogism of the understanding is expressed in its subjective mode, according to its ordinary current meaning. This mode belongs to it when we say that *we* make these syllogisms. And, in fact, the syllogism of the understanding is *only* a *subjective* syllogizing; but this has also the objective meaning that this syllogism expresses only the *finitude* [contradiction] of things. . . . In finite things their subjectivity—as a thinghood that is separable from

their properties, from their particularity—is equally separable from their universality.[29]

A subjective syllogism is one that we arbitrarily choose and externally construct. An objective syllogism makes itself, propels itself forward to overcome the contradiction resulting from the abstraction and separation of a universal term from another term that particularizes it.

A rational syllogism is a nonimmediate argument of three terms. As its recurrent form we have found: (1) The absolute is merely U. (2) To be U is to be P. (3) Therefore, the absolute is not merely U but is both U and P. Contrary to categorical syllogisms in formal logic, the middle term, we have seen, has a second occurrence in the conclusion in the major term. Example: (1) The absolute is merely ground. (2) All grounds have consequents. (3) Therefore, the absolute is (conjunctively) both ground and (hence) that which possesses a consequent, not merely ground. Or, nonconjunctively, it is a ground particularized by having a consequent. The minor term or subject of the conclusion is the absolute, an individual. The middle term is the ground merely in general. The major term is the ground and consequent, the ground by way of the consequent in particular. This is how the middle term is preserved in the major term, which is the syllogistic self-definition of the minor term.

We see that P in the above paragraph is not the entire major term. Unlike the syllogisms of classical logic, the middle term U is also part of the major term UP. The three terms of a rational syllogism are not major, minor, and middle. The three terms are an individual minor term, a universal middle term, and a particular term conjoined with the middle term in the major term. The middle term does not, as in Aristotelian syllogisms, drop out as a purely external means to the conclusion; it is internal to the conclusion itself, to the major term. "What happens in the rational syllogism . . . is that by means of the mediation the subject concludes *itself with itself* [is identified with the predicate term including the universal term and its particularization]."[30] Secondly, propositions (1) in the above paragraph are not premises as with Aristotle, but are indirect proof assumptions. Only indirect proof is a deductive argument which, as required of rational syllogisms in paragraph 182 of the *Encyclopaedia*, we do not make. It makes itself in escaping contradiction.

The three pansystematic rational syllogisms, each developing individuality through particularity from universality, are as follows:

1. *Logic, Nature, Spirit.*[31] This is Hegel's first pansystematic syllogism at the end of the *Encyclopaedia*. It is the syllogism followed by his own exposition of the system of philosophy. It starts with the absolute (the minor term) asserted to be merely the logical idea (absolute self-concept

as the universal middle term). We then first encounter nature as it particularizes the universal logical idea negatively, as the determinate and negated other of the absolutized idea. The theologically absolutized idea is not nature. But to be the absolute idea is to be actualized in nature. Therefore, the absolute is not merely the absolute idea in general, but is the idea actualized in nature. Ultimately the idea is actualized in the natural historical existence of philosophers, i.e., in spirit and not just in nature. (1) The absolute is by assumption merely the absolute idea. (2) To be the absolute idea is to be such in and through nature (and spirit). (3) Therefore, to be the absolute is not merely to be the absolute idea, but is to be such through nature (and through spirit, which is nature in its true form). The system in this form is a dialectical panlogism in which the absolute idea of logic is actualized in nature, its apparent other. The idea (cf. chapter 14) is the universal middle term by which the absolute, as a subject of predication, receives as predicates that very middle term conjoined with its particularization.

2. *Nature, Spirit, Logic.*[32] Depending on the starting point of the rational syllogism, nature is either more particular[33] or more universal[34] than the logical idea. Nature as the other of the mere idea and as the actualization of the deabsolutized idea is more particular. Nature in the second pansystematic rational syllogism presented below—viewed as the "proteus" which contains the idea in potency—is more universal.

The logical idea, nature, or the spirit, can each become universal by an expository fiction, by an indirect proof assumption within the system in one of its expositions. By a rational syllogism, the assumed contradictory absolutization of the subject under any merely abstract, universal description eventually exhibits the self-negation of the assumption.

In itself nature is not more universal than the logical idea. But if we assume nature merely under an abstract universal description to be the absolute,[35] this assumption shows itself to be contradictory. For spirit and the absolute idea as they develop concretely in world history and the history of philosophy also belong to nature. They particularize it.

In this second pansystematic syllogism, we abstract from (eliminate from mind) the logical point of departure of the first syllogism. Nature— not yet grasped concretely by the philosophy of nature, which applies categories of the logic to the interpretation of nature—ceases to particularize the absolute idea taken as the universal term. Nature not yet grasped by thought becomes itself the universal beginning of the system of philosophy. Yet nature falls into self-division through the emergence within it of the abstractive understanding. The understanding is responsible for an abstract subject opposed to an abstract object, an abstract ego over against a non-ego. The division into which the absolute falls through the understanding is overcome through reason, i.e., through the logical idea. Yet, since the initial and continuing logical subject of the system posited here is nature, not logical thought, the system becomes a dialectical naturalism.

Recapitulating: (1) The absolute is by assumption merely nature in general. (2) To be nature in general is to be objectified by an abstractive understanding which falls into opposition to nature, and which overcomes this opposition by actualizing the logical idea (absolute spirit, philosophy). (3) The absolute is not merely nature in general, but falls into a division between a subject and an objective nature, and overcomes this self-division by actualizing the logical idea (philosophy).

This second exposition—nature, spirit, idea—seems to follow the non-dialectical temporal order of nature in itself, evolving in succession both the abstractive understanding and rational self-comprehension by concepts. Yet this evolution from a (a) pre-biological *nature before abstraction* to (b) *nature for abstraction* as the object of the understanding, and to (c) *nature after abstraction* for rational thought cannot be dialectical. For this evolution of original nature, giving birth to abstraction rather than presupposing it, at once gives birth to dialectical thought. The second dialectical exposition cannot properly begin until nature exists for abstraction. Nature as an abstracted object over against an abstracting subject is nature for abstraction, incorporating a relationship to its abstracting subject.

Nature before abstraction, not yet "in the idea," would be a point of departure for an external, non-dialectical, genetic account of the idea. Nature for abstraction but oblivious to this abstraction is the starting point of a dialectical account. This account abstracts from nature in the first exposition, where it manifests itself as the other of the absolute idea. The second exposition generates the logical idea in the form of nature thinking itself. The self-concept, the idea as thought thinking itself, is nature's actualization of its own potential.

The first exposition of the system—logical idea-nature-spirit—proceeds from the point of view of speculative philosophy. It starts with the logical self-concept that arises from the history of philosophy, passes over into the opposite of the self-concept (into nature), and at last through the philosophy of nature finds itself in nature, in the form of spirit viewed as nature in its true form.

The second exposition—nature-spirit-logic idea—starts from nature taken immediately by the abstractive understanding as things in external spatial relationships. As it first exists for the understanding, as it is first thought, nature does not yet contain any more concrete thought determinations than this. Nor is it the abstracted other of the logical idea.

The second philosophical exposition detaches nature from the congealed logical culmination of philosophy in the logical idea. Nature in itself, viewed neither as the other of logical thought nor as actualized for itself in self-knowing spirit, is an objective starting point in space-time process. Nature in itself, neither posited as having been abstracted by thought its other nor as actualized for itself in self-knowing spirit, is an objective starting point in time and space. But nature then proceeds to reveal itself through logical categories used in natural science. It finally reveals itself in spirit, absolute spirit, and the logical idea—all potential within itself.

The temporal process exists, but it exists in truth in its result, not in its purely natural starting point. If we seek to abandon ourselves to the life of the natural object, to a point of departure in the arms of nature in itself, our progress becomes dialectical only when nature enters and passes through its fallen state over against the understanding to emerge finally as absolute spirit, the understanding reunited with nature by the logical thought of reason. Substance manifests itself as subject, nature as self-knowing; "a capital misunderstanding . . . is that the *natural* principle of the *beginning* which forms the starting point in the *natural* evolution or in the *history* of the developing individual, is . . . the *truth*, and the *first* in the notion."[36] The first exposition, beginning with the logical self-concept or idea, is scientifically closer to the truth because it begins with the self-concept of nature, with what nature ought to be by its own internal essence and standard. Nature ought to complete the achievement of all it can achieve by an awareness in and through beings such as us that it has indeed achieved it.

We grasp and express "the True, not merely as *Substance* but also a *Subject*."[37] Hegel also writes that "the True is actual only as system."[38] Science actualizes and even perfects nature, its substantive basis. But science does not exhaust nature any more than contemplation exhausts the life of a rational animal. Once, before Parmenides and all his now forgotten predecessors, the absolute was unthought, and yet existed. Even now nature ceaselessly extends its range of phenomena and particularizes the system of science.

3. *Spirit, Logic, Nature.*[39] The absolute here is first a spirit undifferentiated from nature. Spirit proceeds to separate itself from nature in the "Fall," with which human career history commences. This spirit surmounts its separation from nature through religion, ultimately through German idealism and its logic of the absolute self-concept (logical idea). Spirit releases itself from the final stage of logical abstraction in what Göschel with Hegel's approval in 1829 calls "love."[40] Spirit is concretely actualized in nature, which is an other which is not really other. This time the system, with a different starting point in a prehistorical human

spirit that falls into separation from its home in nature, is a dialectical idealism. (1) The absolute is merely spirit in general. (2) To be spirit is to overcome by means of the logical idea its separation as a fallen subject from an external nature. (3) Therefore, the absolute is not mere spirit; it is in particular spirit overcoming by means of the logical idea its separation as a fallen subject from nature.

We must note that the transition from spirit to the logic—i.e., the explicit presupposition of spirit by the logic that is prominent in the second and third expositions of the system but not in the first—arises even in the first exposition (logic-nature-spirit). For the logic is an ideal reconstruction of the history of philosophy, and the history of philosophy from which the logic is abstracted belongs to the realm of spirit grasped by the philosophy of spirit. The dialectic of definitions of the absolute is abstracted from history and spirit. When the self-concept arises at the end of the logic of essence through the speculative philosopher's grasp of herself in grasping the object, philosophy (through German idealism), history, spirit, and the philosophy of spirit in particular explicitly infiltrate the logic itself. Pure imageless thought, preparing the transition to *Realphilosophie*, begins to absorb elements of the real context from which it has been abstracted. Further, when the first exposition of the system is repeated, the original logic will follow the philosophy of spirit in a repetition of itself only by a purely artificial forgetting of the entire system of philosophy that itself has already been explicitly abstracted. Giacomo Rinaldi's critique of B. Lakebrink thus seems correct:

> The concept of *self-consciousness* [and more generally spirit] . . . plays a crucial role not only in the *Phenomenology of Spirit* but also in the *Logic*. . . Completely erroneous and misleading appears to be one chief assumption of B. Lakebrink's Hegel interpretation, i.e., that "consciousness" would be an "element" essentially alien to Hegel's Logical Idea. . . . the process of thought set forth in the *Science of Logic* is not merely "ideal-objective" in character . . . but at the same time expresses the essential form of concrete human self-consciousness.[41]

5. Classification of Non-Rational Syllogisms

When Hegel classifies syllogisms in the *Logic*, we have remarked already he does not include the *I-U-UP* rational syllogism at the heart of the *Logic*'s own dialectical movement. The syllogisms in his classification are, more or less, those of ordinary formal logic, even though his classification is based on the universality, particularity, and individuality of terms rather than on the quantity or quality of propositions. Instead of proposing an entirely new syllogism, he seems to want to discover the rational syllogism lurking in the background of the commonly accepted syllogisms of formal logic: "the syllogism . . . is in the first instance *immediate*; hence its determinations (*termini*) are *simple, abstract* determinateness; in this form it is the [nonrational] *syllogism of the understanding*. If we stop short at this [traditional] form of the syllogism, then the rationality in it, although undoubtedly present and posited, is not apparent."[42]

Hegel's desire to show traces of the rational syllogism in ordinary syllogisms of the understanding is probably responsible for his classification of syllogisms by different sequences of individual, universal, and particular terms instead of types of proposition. For the absolute is not a proposition, judgment, or series of propositions. It is an infinite individual that is forever defined by a universal description through being at once defined by a more particular term. The absolute is spirit through being the absolute self-concept actualized in the natural space-time sensory order.

The *Logic* classifies syllogisms as qualitative, reflective, and necessary.[43] Qualitative syllogisms of "determinate being" ("of existence"[44]— *des Daseins*) are syllogisms of the abstractive understanding, containing abstractly designated universal, particular, and individual terms. Like Aristotle's categorical syllogisms, these syllogisms are based on relations of terms. Such syllogisms are "qualitative" because "the terms are thus immediately and abstractly determined."[45]

There are six possible types of qualitative syllogism. While in a rational syllogism the middle term is universal, in arbitrarily constructed syllogisms of the abstractive understanding the middle term may be either particular, universal, or individual (singular). The middle term as particular either determines a universal term (*UPI*) or is abstracted from an individual term (*IPU*). "Greek," designating a particular term, determines the universal term referred to as "human," and is abstracted from the individual term "Pythagoras." The middle term as universal either is a necessary condition of the particular term (*PUI*) or is abstracted from an individual term (*IUP*).

Being human is a necessary condition of being Greek but being human is abstracted from Pythagoras. Being Greek as abstracted from Plato may be technically designated as being Greek$_2$ in contrast to the being Greek$_1$ abstracted from Pythagoras. It is good to recall that Hegel is a nominalist, that is, a conceptualist: "in thinking things we transform them into something universal; but things are singular."[46] The various qualities of different cases of being Greek may be taken as distinct and individual.

The middle term as individual either completes a universal term by particularizing it (*UIP*) or is the source from which may be abstracted the universal term presupposed by a particular term (*PIU*). Pythagoras contains the particular term "Greek" which completes (or helps complete) the universal term "human" (*PIU*). And Pythagoras contains the universal term "human" which determines itself through particular term "Greek" (*UIP*). "All humans identical with *A* are Pythagoras; Pythagoras is a Greek, therefore, all humans identical with *A* are Pythagoras, who is Greek."

All terms in a rational syllogism are identical in reference. The developed rational syllogism makes this explicit by exhibiting identity of description as well as reference: "What is referred to as merely the absolute logical concept and yet is not merely this concept but is spirit by also being actualized in nature is what is referred to as merely the logical concept and yet is not merely this concept but is also spirit by also being actualized in nature."

This tautological "perfection" of the syllogism was anticipated by Gottfried Ploucquet.[47] It transcends the syllogism as a subjective conceptual process of inference, which gives way to an objectively self-determining concept.[48] The concept is subjective and fluid: one term—universal, particular, or individual—is abstracted apart from the rest, but not stubbornly absolutized apart from them. In the tautological syllogism the abstraction is thus overcome.

A necessary syllogism of tautological *statements* replaces a non-necessary syllogism of *judgments*. Hegel calls the tautological syllogism "quantitative."[49] We may understand the tautological syllogism by beginning with an ordinary formal syllogism of the understanding in which the determinations of terms are abstracted from one another: "All humans are mortal. Socrates is human. Therefore, Socrates is mortal." When we reflect that each of these three descriptive determinations is concretely inseparable from the other two, this ordinary syllogism is replaced by the following tautological syllogism: 1. All humans$_1$ who are mortal$_1$ and Socrates are mortals$_1$ who are human$_1$ and Socrates. 2. All cases of Socrates who are mortal$_1$ and human$_1$ are humans$_1$ who are mortal$_1$ and Socrates. 3. Therefore, all cases of Socrates who are mortal$_1$ and human$_1$ are mortals$_1$ who are human$_1$ and Socrates.

The above may be distinguished from the following parallel syllogism: 1. All humans$_2$ who are mortal$_2$ and Pythagoras are mortals$_2$ who are human$_2$ and Pythagoras. 2. All cases of Pythagoras who are mortal$_2$ and human$_2$ are humans$_2$ who are mortal$_2$ and Pythagoras. 3. Therefore, all cases of Pythagoras who are mortal$_1$ and human$_1$ are mortals$_1$ who are human$_1$ and Pythagoras. Each statement in this syllogism is an identity statement by the law of association in conjunction. But reversible conjunction is replaced by "necessary conjunction" in this version of the rational syllogism: 1. All humans$_1$ who are mortals$_1$ and hence (by this hemlock-related mortality) necessarily Socrates are mortals$_1$ who are human$_1$ and hence necessarily Socrates. 2. All cases of Socrates who are mortals$_1$, and hence necessarily human$_1$, are cases of mortals$_1$ who are Socrates and hence necessarily human$_1$.

A concrete concept of this particular Socratic mortality implies the identity of any such "mortals" with Socrates and with a concrete case of humanity. Therefore, all cases of Socrates who are mortal$_1$ and hence human$_1$ are mortals$_1$ who are human$_1$ and hence necessarily Socrates. This formulation expresses the dependence of an initial abstract universal description on a subsequent particular description. Apart from such dependence the initial description "human" is abstractly universal precisely because it is initial. Thus, a first universal description of being human is not true of Socrates unless it is conjoined with a second more particular description of being mortal. But if being human is first and hence abstractly universal, being mortal or being Socrates is necessarily subsequent and particular. Thus, the reversal of order in conjunction here at once reverses the universal or particular status of a term within the syllogism. But outside the syllogism Socrates is absolutely individual.

Of course, being mortal is relatively general even if it particularizes being human. And so being human must necessarily be particularized further to be more than approximately true of the individual Socrates.

The above formulation of the rational syllogism in terms of necessary conjunction may be abbreviated without conjunction through the following "by" construction: 1. All humans who are mortal by being Socrates are mortals who are humans by being Socrates. 2. All cases of Socrates who are mortal by being human are humans who are mortal by being Socrates. 3. Therefore, all cases of Socrates who are mortal by being human are mortals who are human by being Socrates.

The ordinary syllogism with which we began above is non-necessary because being Socrates, abstractly considered, does not imply being mortal. Yet, Socrates concretely considered as universally mortal and particularly human does imply Socrates as universally human and particularly mortal. Going from the first usual syllogism to the rational syllogism depends on seeing that "humans" in the first syllogism means concretely but implicitly "humans who are Socrates and (hence) mortal."

If we think of mortality as universal, we think of humanity as relatively particular, and of Socrates as individual. In the objective order, this is so: Socrates is an individual who is in general mortal by being in particular human. Socrates the individual is not simply mortal; he is mortal under a particular description. If we treat a mere unparticularized mortal as an individual we falsify its universal character.

Particular and universal determinations both belong to each individual. "All humans are mortal" without subscripts detaches such determinations from their context in individuals. The individual has a universal determination by having a more particular determination. The determinations of the concrete individual are each what they are through the others. The universal is what it is through the particular, and conversely. The particular determination is a particular determination of just that universal.

"All humans are mortal," a judgment, begins by absolutizing humanity apart from mortality. Otherwise it would express not a judgment but the identity statement: "All humans who are mortal are humans who are mortal." Humanity must first be absolutized apart from mortality for information to be conveyed by attributing mortality. Yet, the absolutization is contradictory, since humanity is what it is only as a particularization of mortality. The tautological syllogism of course proves nothing. As a syllogism it is a dead end. But it does prominently exhibit the individual concept that it tautologically repeats.

Of the various "reflective" and "necessary" syllogisms that remain in Hegel's classification of formal syllogisms, the disjunctive syllogism comes closest to articulating the concept. For it identifies the universal concept with mutually exclusive particulars.[50] Reflective and necessary syllogisms include common types of nonrational syllogisms of the understanding.

The *Logic* distinguishes three types of reflective syllogism: (1) The syllogism of allness, without a individual middle term: "Socrates is a Greek. All Greeks are human. Therefore, Socrates is human." While qualitative syllogisms are classified by the succession of terms (in this case *I-P-U* for Socrates-Greek-man), reflective judgments are classified by a consideration of quantity: the middle term in the above syllogism is all members of a class (e.g., all Greeks).[51] The defect of the syllogism of allness, it is said, is that the universal major premise presupposes the individual conclusion. The universal premise must first be established by inductive argument: (2) The inductive syllogism: "*A* is a Greek and a man, *B* is a Greek and a man, etc. (some Greeks are men). Therefore, all Greeks are men." Inductive arguments of course are not conclusive. This defect is said to be removed by analogical argument, by which the universal is seen in the individual case: (3) The analogical syllogism: "*A* is a Greek, and he is human. *B*, who is Greek, is therefore also human."

The *Logic* distinguishes three syllogisms of necessity: categorical, hypothetical, and disjunctive. In the categorical and hypothetical syllogisms, the simple propositions are analytically necessary. Such syllogisms are "necessary," not merely by logical form, but by their component statements. Examples are as follows: (1) The categorical syllogism: "a subject is united with *its* predicate through *its substance* [essence]."[52] "All triangles are three-sided. A right-angled triangle is a triangle. Therefore, a right-angled triangle is three-sided." (2) The hypothetical syllogism: "If bachelors are unmarried humans, and if unmarried humans are humans, bachelors are human." (3) The disjunctive syllogism: "The stop sign is either red or green. But the stop sign is not red. Therefore, the stop sign is green."

Let us suppose the first disjunctive premise in this last syllogism is necessarily true. The premise depends on a disjunctive analysis of its universal subject into exhaustive mutually exclusive particular states.[53] This premise approaches the individual as the particularized universal. What the individual can be in particular is limited by what it is in general.[54] But the exclusive disjunction of particularizations categorically affirms none.

This disjunction is still only the abstract universal. The concrete universal, the individual, is not such an undetermined disjunction. It is determined by the decisive negation of all but one exclusive disjunct, by the further particularization of the abstractly universal disjunctive determination through a nondisjunctive particular determination, through a single disjunct. Which disjunct by its actuality further particularizes the disjunction is determined by a nonabstract, concrete consideration of the disjunction itself. Being green or red by being green is not being green or red by being red.

6. Constructive Syllogisms

We reconstruct the established past, but we construct the future. A rational syllogism of formal logic discovers an established particularization of an abstract universal. An individual who is human in general is discovered to be human by being male in particular. Another human being who is either male or female is discovered to be female. But a child who is neither a baker nor a butcher makes him- or herself into a butcher. Construction of the future makes a universal characteristic more particular than a preceding such characteristic of the individual.

Such constructive particularization may be negative or positive. One particularizes a general description negatively by choosing against a particular description. Thus, one may choose to differ from one's parents. This type of self-construction is expressed by an objective disjunctive syllogism such as: "I am either only what my parents are, or I am something else. I choose not to be what my parents are, so I am something else."

Negative particularization leaves the field of positive determination open. An individual may particularize a general self-description positively, by yielding to the positive attraction of a particular description. In either case, we invoke an extended sense of "syllogism": individual development is itself syllogistic, whether qualitative (*I-U-PU*) or disjunctive.

"Everything is a *syllogism*, a universal that through particularity is united with individuality; but it is certainly not a whole consisting of *three propositions*."[55] Everything is a self-constructive rational, objective syllogism—a process in which a chosen particular determination makes the general description of the individual more particular and concrete than it was. One daily constructs oneself by particularizing anew one's established humanity. In this sense Socrates or the absolute indeed has claim to being a "syllogism." They are not syllogisms of formal logic. Yet their completion makes possible reconstructive syllogisms of formal logic.

The disjunctive syllogism of formal logic concludes Hegel's classification of syllogisms contained in the logic of the subjective self-concept. The disjunctive syllogism of the formal logic is retrospective: if the premises are true, the conclusion is already true. If you are either married or single but are not single, you are already married.

The disjunctive syllogism of the objective self-concept, of the individual particularizing its universal concept objectively at the present time, survives as a living process: "The individual has the mere potentiality of being either a butcher, or a lawyer, or a teacher. The individual decides not to actualize a potentiality for being a lawyer, or teacher, etc. Therefore, the individual decides to actualize a potentiality for being a butcher."

Such a disjunctive syllogism is objective. It produces itself objectively in the world, independently of any observing subject. But, since it ends with attribution of a particular predicate, it is not rational. It does not conclude with an expanded, more concrete predicate that corrects the attribution of merely a single predicate.

This disjunctive syllogism may be set alongside the following syllogism, which is not only objective but truly rational: An employee has merely some occupation in general. To have some occupation in general is to have a particular occupation. But this is as far as our rational syllogism gets. To have some particular occupation is not to have any occupation in particular. The choice of a particular occupation between various alternatives goes beyond formal syllogistic inference. Our employee has made himself be a butcher and not a baker. Therefore he does not merely have some occupation in general but by decision is a butcher in particular. Objective positive self-particularization is implicitly negative self-particularization within a range of alternatives, within an objective disjunctive syllogism.

A nonobjective *I-U-PU* rational syllogism of formal logic reconstructs past conceptual development. An *already actualized universal concept*, conceived abstractly as excluding all particularizations but one, is first conceived abstractly as excluding that one, and then reconceived concretely to include it. An objective *I-U-PU* rational syllogism, in which the present determines itself, particularizes an *unactualized abstract universal concept* in which no particularization is yet excluded or negated.

The Objective Self-Concept

1. From Formal Syllogisms of the Understanding to Rational Syllogisms

Classical syllogisms, though a subjective process of inference, have long been viewed as one of the most "artificial"[1] topics of all philosophy, "an object of universal derision and disgust."[2] As mechanical constructions temporarily retained only by rote memory, they are no sooner academically regurgitated than they are forgotten and collapse into an apparently undifferentiated (but implicitly still differentiated) object.[3] In the last chapter, however, we found a "syllogistic" form of thinking that is no arid contrivance of formal logic. A rational syllogism was found, unlike the usual "syllogisms of the understanding,"[4] to have an independent, self-moving, and hence objective life of its own. The rational syllogism of indirect proof, like any syllogism that remains in actual use, escapes collapse into a lifeless object.

Reason as a rational syllogistic process "rises above the finite."[5] Yet, it is not "the empty abstraction from the finite, not the universality that lacks content and determinateness, but the universality that is fulfilled or realized."[6] Since the finite is contradictory,[7] syllogistic reason rises above the contradiction of absolutizing a limited thought object (e.g., being a right-hand dot). Yet, it preserves that object unabsolutized: "the rational is nothing but the syllogism."[8] But a syllogism which propels itself forward by its repugnance for self-contradiction, which corrects the contradictory absolutization of a limited determination while learning how that determination is preserved within an infinite whole, is what we have called a "syllogism of indirect proof."

By including such a "rational" syllogism in the logic of syllogisms Hegel stretches the range of syllogisms beyond what is recognized in traditional formal logic. The syllogism of indirect proof qualifies as a syllogism only in the sense of being an argument with three simple predicates. Yet the predicate of the conclusion conjoins the predicate of the middle term and of the third more particular term. (Recall the syllogism of Parmenideanism: "The absolute is mere indeterminate being—an assumption fixed in the understanding. But to be mere indeterminate being is to be some determinate being in particular. Therefore, the absolute is not mere indeterminate being but is both indeterminate being in general and determinate being in particular.")

The dialectical history of such self-moving, living, rational syllogisms of indirect proof predates formal syllogistic logic in the history of philosophy. According to the Hegelian science of logic, such syllogisms governed the history of speculative theology defining the absolute well before Aristotle. After Aristotle, rational syllogisms continued to govern definition of the absolute by the self-corrective abstractive understanding. They continued to do so up to reason's grasp of the absolute in the German idealist logic of the subjective self-concept. In this new logic the absolute ceases to define itself syllogistically *by* the abstractive understanding. Rather, the absolute is defined *as* a syllogism, not as a concept or judgment but as a self-moving, living syllogistic process.

Now, in the logic of the objective self-concept, thought again fixes itself in the position of the abstractive understanding, which we thought it left behind with the transition to the logic of the self-concept. Definitions of the absolute by the understanding were relegated by the logic of the self-concept to the objective logics of being and essence. Thus, the categories of essence were distinguished as "products of the reflecting understanding."[9] The understanding is the abstractive and separating faculty of thought.[10] It abstracts and separates one partial object from another—e.g., force from its expression. But, in contrast to the self-concept (*Begriff*),[11] it is also abstracts and separates the total object from the subject that thinks it.

The first two books of the *Science of Logic* rationally and syllogistically unfold definitions of the absolute by the abstractive understanding. The understanding is a faculty of pure thought, thought thinking itself, i.e., thinking the universal categories of thought ranging from pure being to essential substantiality. Yet, it is not the concrete self-conscious thought of reason. When the rational syllogism no longer unfolds objectively in the history of philosophy in the logics of being and essence, it exists for itself in the self-concept. The understanding places itself in the context of reason (negation of the negation, i.e., negation of negation of the inseparable other).

2. The Mechanical Object: An Object of the Understanding Recollected as Comical

The paradoxical return to fixation on the understanding in the midst of conceptual thought, in the logic of the objective self-concept, is a feigned or "mechanical" return. It is mimicry. It does not restore the naive conviction that this fixation originally carried. Every great event, it is said, is condemned to occur twice—the second time as farce. In recollecting Parmenides's definition of the absolute as pure indeterminate being, for example, reason conceives being as mechanical object. Its syllogistic development is arrested. An object or motion is "mechanical" when it is artificially and yet incompletely detached from the process in which it is known to exist, and is parodied. The thought process fixing on such an object is also mechanical:

> A *mechanical style of thinking, a mechanical memory, habit*, a mechanical way of acting, signify that the peculiar pervasion and presence of spirit is lacking in what spirit apprehends and does. Although its theoretical or practical mechanism cannot take place without its self-activity, without an impulse and consciousness, yet there is lacking in it the freedom of individuality, and because this freedom is not manifest in it such action appears as a merely external one.[12]

In being recollected by a follower of Zeno the Eleatic, the commonsense belief in motion is "mechanical." Spirit is no longer present in it. It is viewed without being fully detached from its dialectical fate. The belief in continuous motion is mimicked. An object fixed in mind by the understanding is liable to becoming mechanical the second time around. It may elicit a "here we go again" feeling. The second time appears as a parody of the first, wooden and halting. Parmenides's indeterminate being, recalled with a background knowledge of its dialectical fate, becomes a mechanical object, the first effect of which is to make Parmenides comical. Despite its original place in the life of a self-moving rational syllogism of indirect proof, it becomes a subject of humorous anecdote—a kind of automaton. Hegel himself significantly contributed to ending the traditional anecdotal tradition in the history of philosophy represented by Diogenes Laertius,[13] and by those who followed in his footsteps through the Kantian Wilhelm Gottlieb Tennemann.[14] According to this tradition, the history of philosophy is a collection of curious opinions by more or less odd individuals divorced from common sense.

We thus now meet the view that is usually taken of the history of philosophy which ascribes to it the narration of a number of philosophical opinions as they have arisen and manifested themselves in time. This kind of matter is in courtesy called opinions; those who think themselves more capable of judging rightly, call such a history a display of senseless follies, or at least of errors made by men engrossed in thought and in mere ideas.[15]

Yet, instead of seeing past philosophers as mechanical marionettes with opinions frozen in uncommon poses, we can also identify with the grandeur of a Parmenides, so completely reliving that definition that one temporarily forgets the dialectic of his self-refutation. When that self-refutation appears, Parmenides may appear as a tragic hero of thought. However, Hegel himself brought great historical thinkers back to life as epic heroes. This was his innovation upon the anecdotal tradition. A tragic hero embodies a value detached from one's everyday life, a value which one admires but with which one does not fully identify. An epic hero has contributed to making one's present-day everyday life possible, so that identification with such a hero is more complete. Because an epic hero has helped form one's own identity, she is taken nonmechanically and noncomically, with the same seriousness with which one takes oneself. The life of a mechanical person is recounted anecdotally. Such a person is a topic of comedy. Mechanical treatments of both nature and history are possible. We shall see how the mechanical objectification of past human history, as contrasted to nature, makes comedy of it. Finally, we shall see how a subjective identification with history as epic elicits its serious side, and how the continuation of current history constructs an equally serious objective disjunctive syllogism before our eyes.

When one abandons oneself to a definition of the absolute, one relives its heroic dialectic. But when one recollects the foibles of past standpoints without even temporary abandonment to their allure, the recollected experience is that of a comically mechanical object. Indeterminate being, as a detached mechanical object of recollection, is a comical replica of Parmenides's original indeterminate being when we judge its bizarreness from the perspective of common sense. Parmenides is tragic when, realizing the sublimity of his definition of the absolute, we know the dialectic of its self-refutation but do not yet realize that Parmenides is the epic origin of our own identity. If the science of logic is a philosophy of the history of philosophy, the logic of the objective self-concept begins by treating the pre-nineteenth-century anecdotal stage in the narration of the objective history of philosophy, of the self-concept. The philosopher lost in distraction mechanically loses his shoe without knowing it, like Hegel himself reportedly did.[16] The sublimity of thought thinking itself is deflated to the level of a mechanical misstep for the common hilarity to onlookers. The logic of the absolute self-concept or idea in the next chapter treats the Hegelian concept of narrating philosophy's history as part of epic world history—or, more accurately, we shall argue, world-historical tragi-comedy.

An object abstracted by the understanding is separated from other objects, which form at most an aggregate with them. If the understanding abstracts and separates an object, it abstracts and separates it even from itself. Reason overcomes the separation of one partial object from another, e.g., force from its expression. Reason is at work in the logics of being and essence, correcting the understanding's absolutization of partial objects. It is also at work in the transition to the logic of the self-concept, correcting the understanding's absolutization of the object apart from the thinking subject. Unlike the understanding, reason includes itself in its definition of the absolute as the self-concept.

The understanding was always part of the life of reason. Parmenides's definition of the absolute in the "objective logic" as mere indeterminate being was the work of the abstractive understanding. It occurred within the total life of reason as the generation and self-correction of the understanding.

3. The Autobiographical Prehistory of the Self-Concept

Rational thought at the end of the logic of the subjective self-concept, in the logic of the objective self-concept, recalls prior fixations of the understanding. Objects of the understanding now appear as mechanical as the first steps of an infant about to fall down again. From such recollection conceptual thinking returns to the present in the absolute self-concept, incorporating in its self-concept its dialectical roots, and identifying with their results.

The interest motivating the transition from rational syllogistic thought at the end of the subjective self-concept to the "objective self-concept" eventually becomes genealogical, not just curiosity or high-brow comedy. Since this genealogy is of no single individual but of thought through the generations, it takes epic proportions. Reason recalls its ancestry in fixations of the understanding. Yet, it does not lose itself in this origin, but contemplates its own self-construction out of ancestral objects perceived as developmental instead of defective and mechanical.

Not only the childhood but even the ancestry of an adult belong to its autobiography. The abstractive understanding fixed upon abstract objects belongs to the ancestral prehistory of concrete conceptual thinking. The self-concept in book 3 of the *Logic* (in the *subjective logic*) has overcome the opposition between thinking and its object that marked the object as an object of the understanding in the *objective logic*. Yet, conceptual thinking now recollects its prehistory in the abstractive understanding. It appropriates its origins.

The solar system is presented by Hegel as a mechanical process, a process of mechanical objects. We inherit such a process as objectively given from Newton's construction of a chapter in the history of natural science. Mechanical objects are contradictorily interdependent in their mutual independence. They are interdependent in their mutual attraction, and yet nothing prevents one from existing independently by itself without others to attract it or be attracted. The solar system illustrates the mechanical syllogism in the physical world. Thus, an independent but dependent celestial body like earth receives its velocity and position from the sun (and secondarily from other celestial centers of attraction) by gravity.[17] Gravity is here a universal middle term which, when particularized by the velocity and position of all secondary centers of attraction, reduces the first body falsely assumed to be independent to dependence.

> Here, then, we have the manifest *contradiction* between the complete
> mutual *indifference* [independence] of the objects [e.g., celestial objects]
> and the identity of their *determinateness*, or the contradiction between
> their complete *externality* in the identity of their *determinateness* [relative
> to one another]. This contradiction is, therefore, the *negative* unity of a
> number of objects which, in that unity, simply repel one another: this is
> the *mechanical process*.[18]

The syllogism of the mechanical process, the process of the mechanical object, is visible in spiritual as well as material processes.[19] According to Bergson, the mechanical treatment of the spiritual is precisely what provokes laughter.[20] The recollected syllogisms of the history of philosophy defining the absolute include fixation by the understanding on abstract, mechanically detached objects. Yet, these syllogisms are self-correcting rational syllogisms of indirect proof. The rational recollection of such syllogisms, long blocked by anecdotalism, eclipses the comical spectacle of artificially independent objects of the abstractive understanding—such as indeterminate being, merely positive being, merely positive and negative being, etc. Indeterminate being and other objects from rational syllogisms in the logics of being and essence are no longer recollected, as wooden and mechanical.

4. Mechanism and Atomism

For mechanism, the absolute is an incoherent, dependently independent mechanical object or collection of such objects. Such a definition, arising in the logic of the self-concept, is mocked by metaphysical skepticism or negative reason. But organic conceptual thought no longer thinks mechanistically when it discovers its origins in superficially anecdotal preconceptual thought, in the once amusing pratfalls from the lives of the philosophers.

It is common to restrict mechanism exclusively to materialism. But, as we see in recalling Parmenides, a mechanistic view of thought and its objects is equally possible.[21] Mechanism, a purely logical concept, is not restricted to objects of any one branch of the sciences. We have seen that philosophical distraction mechanically causes, to the general amusement, a loss of ordinary awareness of one's surroundings—dependent independence.

Atomistic philosophers such as Hobbes[22] and scientists such as Newton[23] were doubtless unaware of being "mechanists" in Hegel's developed and polemically critical sense. They were unaware of representing a position that subjective German idealists would recollect and parody as incoherent until the same idealists appreciated its development into objective idealism. Yet, the original mechanists construed the independence of objects as categorical truth, not as a heuristic way station in the construction of idealism.

Mechanism, defining the absolute as mechanical object, is alien to the logic of the self-concept if it is not taken as a term of some abuse. It asserts "the absolute *contradiction* of the complete independence of the [distinct moments] that are manifold and of their equally complete dependency."[24] Being contradictory, it is interpretable by its dialectical result more than by the original intentions of its authors.

Mechanism in the logic of the concept resembles the atomism of the logic of being, and the reciprocal interaction of "things" and "substances" in the logic of essence. The contradiction of mechanism (as of atomism, interactionism, and the theology of quantity) is that it asserts a mutual independence of objects which yet are interdependent.[25]

Yet, the logic of mechanism, unlike atomism and interactionism, presupposes the subjective self-concept. Mechanism is atomism or interactionism, but first as a comic standpoint to which a subjective idealism, unmindful of its origins, regresses prior to its Schellingian development into objective idealism. The objective idealist defines the absolute as a living or ensouled object. But the concept of the living object arises out of the contradictions of the mechanical object.

A difference between atomism and mechanism is that mechanism is not a new category or definition of the absolute. Objective idealism in general and mechanism in particular belong instead to the development of the self-concept as the reigning definition of the absolute. Definition of the absolute as the absolute object[26] conceals its real definition as an absolute self-concept.

For Hegel, Leibniz's panpsychist monadology best illustrates mechanism in the history of philosophy.[27] What is mechanical (and contradictory) in the monadology is the mutual externality of windowless monads that each seem to mirror all the others, and yet do so without mirroring one another at all, but only by the puppetry of external divine agency. In a perfect mechanism, interdependence is orchestrated from above.

From Leibniz we see again that mechanism is not necessarily materialism. It is a possible perspective in the human as well as physical sciences. Hobbes and modern civil society give atomistic or mechanistic models of human life.[28] Yet, mechanism is as deterministic as puppetry. It can be as comical as the routine of a mechanical mime. What a thing is, is determined by other things.[29]

5. Chemism and the Common Pursuit of Different Goals

Chemism stands between mechanism and organicism[30] as a transitional concept. A chemical aggregate is one in which the elements are independent and yet selectively drawn into bonds with one another. Mechanism is not exclusively illustrated by the natural sciences, and chemism is not restricted to chemistry.[31] For many the elective affinity between friends or lovers illustrates the chemism of the logic better than chemistry.[32] When the attractive "tension" or "affinity"[33] between two elements or individuals eventuates in bonding, it is neutralized,[34] only to be reborn with renewed separation.[35]

In chemism a "contradiction"[36] implicit in mechanism becomes explicit: explicitly contradictory mutual independence and mutual dependence between individuals. This contradiction is overcome by teleology,[37] i.e., the logic of value and purposefulness. If we seek a term parallel to "mechanism" and "chemism" to indicate the interpretation of nature by goal-directed activity, we can do no better than "organicism." (Hegel does speak of "life" in connection with teleology.[38])

In chemism there is a bonding of individuals who continue to have different goals or needs. The aggregate has no single overall goal. The individual members simply help one another. Thus, the "chemistry" of partners in marriage and other individuals in community does not consist in subordinating either member of the partnership to the goal of the other, but in a reciprocal, natural, uncalculated desire of each to help in the attainment of the other's goal. The contradiction of chemism is resolved by the fact that the individuals involved are essentially independent but only contingently interdependent. Thus, the chemistry of love may dissolve into a pure mutual independence of the parties.

6. External Teleology or Goal-Directed Action

In chemism there is solidarity between individuals pursuing different goals. In the goal-directed activity of a single organism, on the other hand, we have a hierarchy of individual organs. One dominant organ unconsciously sets the goal for the others. When the individual who sets the goal consciously calculates the adaptation of other individuals as servants in the attainment of the goal, we have "external," "subjective," merely "finite" teleology.[39] All conscious external action directed to realizing a goal illustrates "finite teleology."

In external goal-directed action, the goal is first abstracted in its momentary realization in the actual world; "the content of the [finite, external] purpose [Zweck] is just as much restricted, contingent, and given as the object [over against the purpose] is particular and given in advance [ready at hand]."[40] The "end" as merely found is not yet served by means, but it does represent a value.

What eventually becomes a goal pursued by external action is first simply *found* as an unintended value: "actuality is what is more comprehensive [between actuality and possibility], because, being the concrete thought, it, contains possibility within itself as an abstract moment."[41] The goals we pursue as real possibilities—love, justice, peace—were first momentary facets of a more complex actual world, that happily took us by surprise. Once abstracted and detached from its original context, a value becomes a goal—an end-in-view pursued by more or less appropriate means. It becomes an object of recollection and fixation. It is absolutized in negation of its original situation, independently of any real situation, which becomes the external obstacle to its realization.

The goal-directed agent negates itself as goal-directed, and it negates its goal as unrealized, in negating the existing world from which its goal has been detached, and through which the goal was only momentarily realized. The goal is relative to an actual context from which it has been abstracted ("The content of the purpose . . . is . . . restricted, contingent, and given").[42] The way to overcome the contradiction of assigning independent status to an unrealized goal is to particularize the goal anew, to conceive it more concretely, to replace it in a new precise context, to find it once again already actualized. The separated extremes of the unrealized end and the objective world are each negated through inclusion of the other.[43] Goal-directed action, preceded by a momentary found value in past experience, finds the same general value reparticularized in a new context. This is the secret of the passage from the external reflective teleology of goal-directed action to internal teleology.

The telos, end, or value of internal teleology is a general end already consciously or unconsciously realized without being pursued by a calculation of any particular means or end. An example of such an end is the normal breathing of an organism.[44] If the internal teleology is infinite, the value is permanently and pervasively realized throughout the objective world. An example would be the goodness of the universe overcoming all evil. An end of external teleology is any particular end that is initially unrealized and subsequently realized only by goal-directed action, a conscious calculation of means. The particular end may particularize a general end of internal teleology—as for example the end of breathing with an open window particularizes breathing in general. On a theological scale, the calculated pursuit of evil is capable by a ruse of reason of transmuting itself into good.

Internal teleology is a concept borrowed from Kant.[45] A *finite internal telos* of a single organism is an uncalculated value of the exclusive individual living being which is first found without being pursued. An *infinite internal telos* is the value of the world as a whole viewed as alive with the spontaneous realization of value. Hegel calls a finite goal "subjective end."[46] The found value of the whole world is the "objective end."[47] The end has already been realized. Its realization can be consciously pursued by a calculation of means only after its realization has been discovered without such pursuit. The pursuit of an internal end as an external end adapts it to new objective conditions.

The dialectic of external goal-directed action is a rational syllogism in which the absolutization of an abstract external end is tested and rejected: (1) The external end is independent or absolute. (2) To be that end is to be related to an external objective world. (3) Therefore, the external end is not independent, but is related to an external objective world. External goal-directed action arises when thought insists on the assumption in (1). Thought then attempts to abolish the objective world insofar as it prevents the end from being truly absolute: "End . . . is the subjective notion [self-concept, *Begriff*], as essential effort and urge to posit itself externally . . . its activity is directed against external objectivity."[48]

Internal purpose is realized by a modification of this syllogism, without the calculation of external action and means. It is realized when the detached abstract end is conceived concretely as including the objective situation, and the objective situation as including the end. The understanding absolutizing the end apart from the real situation is unblocked. Neither the end nor the objective situation is conceived abstractly in opposition to the other. By negation of the negation, the conception of the end as absolute in negation of the objective world from which it is abstracted is negated.

7. Internal Teleology

Mechanism views the objective world out of which subjective conceptual thinking emerges as something alien to it. It recollects contradictory mechanical objects or aggregates as conceived by a fixation of the abstractive understanding, and it mocks them insofar as they belong to the human world. As Bergson would argue at the turn of the century, the comical consists in what is the human and living assuming the guise of an automatism. The process of the solar system is not comical, but a pratfall or slip of the tongue is. The mechanical object is the first form of the object recollected in the logic of the objective self-concept. It is followed by recollection of the chemical object, and of the organic object. There is no life in a pure mechanical object to which the subjective self-concept can empathetically abandon itself. Conceptual thought *recollects* the mechanical object as a thing absolutzed by the understanding; it *identifies* with the organic object, and with the living human being who causes laughter by behaving as a mechanical object.

Mechanism, the contradiction of the inwardly dependent independent object, is superseded first by chemism—the solidarity of mutual assistance—and finally by organicism, by an infinite non–goal-directed purposefulness. "Life"[49] takes the absolute to unite objective syllogisms of the abstractive understanding, which risk a breakdown in detached objects, and the fluidly self-advancing syllogisms we shall call subjective syllogisms. The subjectively conceptual, purely rational thought of the present brings to fluid self-moving life the mechanical rational syllogism of the past blocked by fixations of the stubborn understanding. Subjective syllogisms of the present reconstruct and mobilize positions frozen in objective syllogisms. They dispel the comedy of life turned mechanical.

The dominant member of an organic aggregate is not windowlessly adjusted to other members from the outside like Leibnizian monads. It is a dominant microcosm of all others, internalizing them sympathetically within itself and reflecting their common impulse. The dominant microcosm finds its goal already realized in its members without any conscious intent. Thus, self-preservation of a whole organism is realized without conscious intent in the functioning of the various organs:

> But in fact the object is *implicitly* the Concept, and when the Concept, as purpose, is realised in the object, this purpose is only the manifestation of the object's own inwardness. So objectivity is, as it were, only a wrapping under which the Concept lies hidden. . . . The accomplishing of the infinite purpose consists therefore only in sublating the illusion that it has not yet been accomplished.[50]

This dialectical argumentation on behalf of infinite teleology, the sudden discovery of purpose already realized in the world, need not be conservative or quietistic. Take, for example, the purpose of human rights and its pervasive if unintended place in the post-World War II world. To absolutize the ideal of human rights abstracted from the existing international world order, or to absolutize the existing world order abstracted from the ideal of human rights, is to view the world order as failing to live up to its principal self-imposed standard proclaimed by the 1948 United Nations human rights declaration. It is thus to view the world order as objectively contradictory, as combining both institutionalized affirmation and denial of human rights as an independent goal. The world is not, in the outer accidental conditions of its existence, what it is in its inner self-imposed essence. But since a self-imposed abstract essence must somehow express itself in the accidents of its existence, it essentially is what it is not, and is not what it is. The human rights ideal is most pointedly affirmed in the ever increasing media exposure and condemnation of atrocities.

Perceived contradiction is painful. External purposeful action seeks to remove the contradiction from the postwar world order, and from the ideal of human rights thus abstracted from a more complex world and absolutized apart from it. But what, according to a dialectical argumentation, can purposeful action accomplish? It can only conclude that the ideal of human rights cannot be coherently realized so long as it is defined abstractly. It is internally related to the existing world order from which it is abstracted. Its realization consists in replacing it concretely in the context of this order.

Human rights and the present world order are inseparably one. The goal of universal human rights is on the agenda of world history only because the concept of such rights has been abstracted positively from real examples in this world of what human relations can be, as well negatively from the century's atrocities. The pursuit of the human rights ideal cannot be purely tactical action against the world as it is; it must be strategic action on behalf of the world's own institutionalized will to realize that ideal in a morass of accidental tactical compromises that are actually quite essential to it.

The reflective pursuit of human rights as an unactualized ideal meets with frustration. The frustration is relieved only by finding human rights already realizing themselves in a century's struggles and institutions. Goal-directed action (external teleology) is an expression of internal teleology. If the century's atrocities did not exist, its commitment to human rights through goal-directed action would not exist either.

The present rational "syllogism" of indirect proof[51] does not end with acquiescence in what is. In negating the contradictory negation of the world by an absolutized abstract ideal, it may lead to very energetic goal-directed action. However, this action will not be on behalf of one's own merely subjective goals. It will be on behalf of the "objective end,"[52] of the world itself which has allowed abstraction of one's conscious subjective goal. Goal-directed action will no longer be external. The agent will find her goal open to actualization in the realizable alternatives of the world as it actually is.

This is goal-directed action on behalf of unconscious "internal purposiveness,"[53] ultimately of the "infinite purpose."[54] It is not the inevitably frustrating sort of goal-directed action that seeks to actualize an abstraction. It is a concrete goal-directed action that expresses the revolutionary struggle of the world. Its success is not guaranteed to go uncontested. The world may have other goals as well, or even tire of goals. The world may undergo a sea change. But action directed toward realizing a value already found to be represented in the institutions and struggles of one's times is free of total frustration and failure.

8. Internal Teleology and the Objective Disjunctive Syllogism of Exclusive Choice

At the beginning of the chapter we recalled a first extension of the meaning of "syllogism" to include the rational syllogism of indirect proof. Definition of the absolute as indeterminate being or atoms is definition by the understanding as distinct from reason. But the syllogisms of Parmenideanism and atomism are rational. Yet, they are not conscious in the independent self-understanding of the mechanistic Parmenideans (e.g., the Megarians) or atomists of history. It is only subsequent speculative historians of philosophy, not Parmenideans, who grasp the syllogism of Parmenideanism. Only postatomistic thinkers grasp the syllogism exhibiting the contradiction of atomism.

Rational syllogisms in the history of philosophy are objective syllogisms constituted by the past philosophers who have stumbled over fixations of the abstractive understanding. Other objective syllogisms with interdependent objects frozen in a false independence by the understanding arise in the history of science—as in the Newtonian concept of the solar system.

The concept of the internal telos or end points to the still broader concept of objective syllogisms. Syllogisms now include objective syllogistic processes of self-determinative exclusive choice. The concept of syllogisms expands beyond the realm of mere judgments. We pass on to the syllogism of the present deed. Such a syllogism is *irreducibly* objective. A reducibly objective syllogism finally consists in judgments that can be rethought subjectively. An irreducibly objective syllogism places the thinking subject before a choice that emerges without being inferred from the disjunctive premise and its alternative possibilities.

A rational syllogism of judgments is a self-determining, self-corrective process of reasoning, a version of indirect proof. The major term may include a disjunction imposing a choice, not just an inference. "This fetus is merely human. To be human is to be of one nationality or another. Therefore, this fetus is not merely human but is both human and either of one nationality or another." This subjective reasoning points to an objective process of self-determining activity resulting in a decision for a single nationality.

From the above syllogism it cannot be determined whether the fetus is French or German. Maintaining its humanity by determining itself as not French, it determines itself positively as German. An objective self-constructive disjunctive syllogistic process of choice and deed determines the choice between alternatives which the disjunctive premise leaves open. If one is merely employed one has some occupation, either this or that. But only the selection of a "subjective end," not inference, can determine that one is a baker and not a butcher:

> end is . . . essentially in its own self *syllogism*. It is the self-equal universal . . . indeterminate activity. . . . On the one hand this reflection [of this activity] is the *inner universality* of the *subject*, while on the other hand it is a *reflection outwards*; and to this extent it is still a subjective end and its activity is directed against external objectivity. . . . End is . . . the urge to realize

itself; the determinateness of the moments of the Notion is externality; but their *simplicity* in the unity of the Notion [self-concept] is inadequate to the nature of this unity, and the Notion thus repels itself from itself. This repulsion is in general the resolution [*Entschluss*, decision] of the relation of the negative unity to itself [the subjective self-concept], whereby it is *exclusive* individuality [exclusive choice within an irreducibly objective syllogism of disjunctive possibilities].[55]

An internal end realizes itself spontaneously and unconsciously, without obstruction, in the fluid passage from absolutization of an abstracted (e.g., recalled) end, through negation of the objective situation and negation of the contradictory absolutized abstract end, to reconcretization of the abstract end to include the new objective situation. The end as merely abstract is not merely abstract but is concretely realized again in the world.

This nonobstructed, hence nonobjective, rational syllogism of an internal end of life is joined to an irreducibly objective, disjunctive syllogism when that rational syllogism is blocked at absolutization of the abstract end. But to choose consciously between alternatives is to discover the internal end of the life-activity of choosing, realized without that end being pursued as a goal.

For example, to pursue consciously the goal of private pleasure abstracted and absolutized apart from a social context of unpleasant constraints is first to place the goal back in this general context of constraints from which it has been separated. Second, it is to articulate the disjunctive choices that the objective context allows, and to develop that context by making one choice or another. The context allows space for alternative incremental increases and decreases in private pleasure. One maintains life within this totality by renewed particular choices. The disjunctive whole preserves itself by ever new particular choices made between its real possibilities:

> this reflection that the end is reached in the means, and that in the fulfilled end, means and mediation are preserved, is the *last result of the external end-relation*, a relation in which that relation has sublated itself, and which it has exhibited as its truth. . . . The moment of the end has now reached the stage where the moment of externality is not merely posited in the Notion [self-concept], where the end is not merely an *ought-to-be* and a *striving* to realize itself, but as a concrete [infinite] totality is identical with the immediate objectivity. This identity is on the one hand the simple Notion and the equally *immediate* objectivity, but on the other

hand, it is just as essentially a *mediation* [a possibly conscious goal-directed action by external means].[56]

The internal end of the living organism, i.e., survival itself, is in general a syllogistic process of self-determination by choices. Life, to maintain and reproduce itself, must particularize itself in an ever changing environment. Goal-directed action generally is re-specification of the goal's general realization. Discovery of an original particularization of a general end does not require goal-directed action. Unintentionally discovering with delight the taste of strawberries illustrates an internal end discovered without external goal-directed action. Development of the goal's original particularization through reparticularization is the model for realizing an unrealized goal by such action. A goal once realized in one particularization is realized in a new particularization.

To pursue pleasure in general without pursuing any particular pleasure is to pursue nothing at all. For neither pleasure, nor wealth, nor happiness, nor any other goal exists merely in general. The immediate form in which an abstract goal exists is the form from which it is abstracted in the concretely existing world. Human rights, for example, exist realized in the form in which we know them in the United Nations, international courts, and voluntary monitor organizations. Without this partial realization of the goal further realization could never be entertained. To pursue human rights is to recognize their particular realization in the existing world and pursue further such particularization. It is to lend one's services to the world's further self-development based on its established identity.

By exclusive choice the person escapes the incoherence of being human merely in general but not in particular. The human person, as a term in an irreducibly objective disjunctive syllogism, "appears . . . as exclusive individuality."[57] The recognition that *mere* humanity is contradictory passes into momentarily hesitant choice between forsaking humanity and the nondeducible choice of a particular form of humanity.

In the *Logic* "individuality" is understood in two senses. The universal as the nonexclusive disjunction of its particularizations is a nonexclusive individual. An exclusive individual, by contrast, constitutes itself by excluding certain disjuncts. The first individual is universal and macrocosmic, both male and female; it is "the genus disjoined into its species."[58] The second individual is microcosmic, e.g., either male or female but not both, "the particular as individuality to the exclusion of the others."[59]

An object at the start of the logic of the objective concept was a collapsed subjective syllogism whose internal differentiations were forgotten and submerged: "the object is . . . the *syllogism*, whose mediation has been sublated and has therefore become an immediate identity."[60] At a later stage this object comes to life again in chemism and organicism. Such an object is not irreducibly objective. It is the subject withdrawn within itself to be unfolded anew.

Yet, we have now introduced the irreducibly objective syllogism of choice. The universal, as the inclusive disjunction of its possible particularizations, is the coincidence of universality and exhaustive possible alternative particularizations. The universal term becomes indistinguishable from the disjunctively expanded possible particulars, and hence from the *inclusive individual* as identical with universality and all-sided particularity. This coincidence is all-sided objectivity, "that which is in and for itself, and free from limitation and opposition."[61] The *exclusive individual* is established by one-sided actual (not merely possible) particularity, by choice and sacrifice.

Microcosmic exclusive individuality emerges by exclusive choice between alternative exclusive possibilities. It is possible to fantasize endless occupations, but a professional makes an exclusive commitment to a single occupation. In this choice the coincidence of the universal, particular, and individual terms is abolished by assertion of exclusive individuality. The merger of universal judgment ("*a* is human") with disjunctive particular judgment ("*a* is married or single") prepares the way for an established social identity won not through further judgment, but through an exclusive individual decision.

The disjunctive syllogism of deed in the *Logic* must be exclusive to express a syllogistic process of choice and sacrifice. The disjunction contained in all-sided objectivity is inclusive. All-sided objectivity becomes an exclusive disjunction when the different disjuncts become incompatible predicates attributed to the same subject at the same time. The exclusive individual is one-sidedly particular. Only over time is it potentially a multi-sided, universal, inclusive individual.

9. Constructive and Reconstructive Syllogisms

In objective disjunctive syllogistic processes, the disjunctive premise "*p* or *q*" is not already truth-functionally true, but is made true by decision. Such processes are not subjective syllogisms of formal logic and reason. They are objective, self-constructive syllogistic processes, which make subsequent reconstructive subjective syllogisms possible. Hegel refers to such irreducibly objective syllogisms in the discussion of goal-directed action.[62] He distinguishes them from reconstructive syllogisms which "represent" teleological action.[63]

Either there will be a sea battle tomorrow or there will not, though this is not truth-functionally true today. The battle has not yet been decided. The sea captain then decides against a battle. So there will be none. This objective disjunctive syllogism is an objective process of particularizing an disjunctive universal by deciding for one disjunct: "its [the Concept's] *universal nature* gives itself external reality through *particularity*, and in this way . . . the Concept makes itself into the [exclusive] singular."[64] No conclusion is deduced. Rather, decision makes a particular disjunct true, and thus makes the disjunctive premise truth-functionally true.

In the *Logic* the subjective syllogism of formal logic ended as the disjunctive syllogism. It then passed into an irreducibly objective syllogism of self-determination. The process of self-particularization, on completion, is reconstructed by a subjective disjunctive syllogism.

There are reducibly objective constructive syllogisms in natural and human history prior to hermeneutic reconstructive syllogisms. Reducibly objective syllogisms essentially consist in subjective judgments. These judgments can be unfrozen and brought to life in subjective reconstruction. Subjective syllogisms of formal logic which define the absolute in the *Science of Logic* subjectively reconstruct objectivity. They are not purely subjective or arbitrary. They are a reflection of objective historical syllogistic processes. The passage from the subjective self-concept to the subjectively reconstructed objective self-concept is necessary if subjective syllogistic thinking is not to remain finite and merely subjective.

The idea with which the *Logic* ends is the correspondence between the subjective self-concept and the objective self-concept. This correspondence will be analyzed in the next chapter. It consists essentially in a subjective syllogistic thinking reliving its own epic autobiography, beginning with mechanical objective syllogisms from the history of philosophy and science in which it cannot at first identify itself. The absolute as the universal self-concept, thinking itself concretely and in particular, must be objective as well as subjective.

From the fact that a person falls under a finite self-concept we cannot deduce that the self-concept is objective. A finite person is not infinitely actualized. But from the fact that the absolute falls under an infinite self-concept we infer that the self-concept is objective, not merely subjective.

Such reasoning suggests to Hegel the ontological argument.[65] The absolute conceived as the infinite self-concept would not be infinite if it remained merely an abstract concept in the understanding ("the untrue notion"),[66] unactualized in the objectively existing world.

Yet, Hegel historicizes both Anselm's argument and God's objective existence. He construes Anselm's subjective concept of the absolute existing "in the mind" as reconstructive. The objectively existing concept that is in the world—to which the ontological argument proceeds—taken as creatively self-constructive. Natural and historical construction particularizes and individualizes speculative thought, testing its truth as a reconstruction.

In the object (*Gegenstand*) viewed over against the subject,[67] the distinctions internal to the subjective self-concept collapse into "immediacy."[68] The subject for which the object exists abstracts from distinctions buried in that object. In such an immediate object, the constructive process of self-determination shrivels to a fixed point. The object is the subject, but it is the subject merely in itself, not yet actually for itself, or for us. The subject knows the object as mechanical. But it does not know that the object contains its own subjectivity in seed. It does not yet appreciate that it itself, the subject in its objective historical self-construction, has actualized the dialectical potential of that object.

10. Subjective, Objective, and Absolute Idealism

The subjective idealism of Fichte remains fixed at the subjective self-concept.[69] The transition from the subjective to the objective self-concept was historically undertaken by Schelling, who expressed it vividly as a transition from intelligence to "petrified intelligence."[70] To conceive the stone and other mechanical objects as "petrified" intelligence implies that intelligence is the reference point, that mechanical objects as such do not causally precede intelligence (the rational self-concept). Rather, intelligence causally precedes objects perceived as mechanical.

Parmenides mechanically absolutizing indeterminate being preceded modern conceptual self-comprehension. But this absolutization appears "mechanical" only as recollected by that self-comprehension. Through self-fragmentation by the abstractive understanding, reason produces itself in petrified, mechanical disguise. Philosophical reason in the logic of the self-concept, unlike the abstractive understanding by itself, sees through this disguise. It produces the disguise to rediscover itself dialectically in the mechanism of independent objects, in the chemism of individuals subject to selective mutual attractions and repulsions, and finally in infinite life.

For the subject to lose itself in a mechanical other come to life is to find itself. The life of the object is the self-construction of the very present standpoint from which the subject alienated itself. This self-reconstruction passes in the *Logic* from "mechanism" to "chemism," "teleology," "life," "theoretical cognition," to the "practical idea," and finally to the "absolute idea" (next chapter).

The living, self-moving reconstruction of the petrified mechanical object—passing through chemical objects and life to the idea—derives from the empathetic understanding of hidden subjectivity by subjectivity. For reason in the logic of the self-concept, the veil of objectivity is lifted, revealing subjectivity to itself. The absolute idea is both theoretical and practical reason, the theoretical reconstruction, promotion, and completion of historical emancipatory practice. Epic theoretical reconstruction of past practice is at once the theory of current practice, which in turn further confirms the theoretical reconstruction of the past.

> it is only the will itself that stands in the way of the attainment of its goal, for it separates itself from cognition, and externality for the will does not receive the form of a true being; the Idea of the good [more concretely, historical moral praxis] can therefore find its integration only in the Idea of the true [theoretical reconstruction]. . . . Accordingly in this result *cognition* is restored and united with the practical Idea. . . . The absolute Idea has now turned out to be the identity of the theoretical and the practical Idea. The absolute method [of cognition] . . . does not behave like external reflection but takes the determinate element from its own subject matter [practical striving], since it is that subject matter's immanent principle and soul.[71]

The absolute idea is the substantive identity of theory and practice as the concrete result of the reconstructive method. The *Logic* reconstructs in pure thought the empirical history of philosophy defining the absolute. But the history of philosophy emerges within the practical context of world history, within the halting progress of freedom in the world. The history of philosophy itself is the dialectical self-reconstruction and self-comprehension of universal freedom on the level of pure thought. The *Logic* stabilizes universal freedom. It makes good the French Revolution's lack of a Reformation—a lack cited by Hegel at the end of the *Lectures on the Philosophy of World History*. Theoretical reconstruction completes practical construction.

14

The Absolute Idea:
The Career of Freedom
Grasping Itself in Pure Thought

1. The Absolute Idea

The absolute idea with which the logic concludes is that of the identity of the subjective and objective self-concepts.[1] It is not the idea of this identity projected into the future, but is its actuality in the present,[2] the objective realization of the subjective self-concept. It is the subjective self-knowledge of the objective absolute. In its immediate form Hegel calls this idea "life." He does not mean by "life" merely the biological life or even the logical concept of such life—including mortality and reproduction of the species (and for us the entire Darwinian biosphere) as well as individual sensibility and motor response. Life is here a logical concept of pure thought[3]—the concept of a subjective internal end of the entire objective world spontaneously actualizing itself. We have examined this concept of an internal telos in the previous chapter.

The subjective self-concept no sooner completed its self-construction in concepts, judgments, and syllogistic thinking than it recollected the comedy of its infancy in the theology of the abstractive understanding from Parmenides onward. Parmenidean being is recollected as the objective self-concept in its most abstract form. This objective self-concept is the subjective self-concept reduced to the conception of its first halting "mechanical" steps.

The objective realization of the subjective self-concept occurs when the subjective self-concept returns to itself out of its recollection of mechanical objects, and out of products of the abstractive understanding generally. This return occurs when the subjective self-concept, as it forms the objective concept of an unforeseen internal telos, recognizes itself in a suddenly subjectified objective self-concept. It no longer laughs at itself. Life is the process of an internal end which is as subjective as it is objective.[4]

The absolute idea, including life as its immediate form, has two sides. At the immediate level of life, these two extremes are (as Schelling had said) sensibility and irritability,[5] the receptive sensory faculty and the active motor faculty of response. At more developed reflective levels, these same two extremes are theoretical and practical, cognitive[6] and moral.[7] Life, as concretely embracing these extremes, is continuous self-reproduction and self-preservation through theory and action.[8] Life maintains itself in a dynamic equilibrium of sensibility and irritability, theory and action, inquiry and belief.

An expository account of the absolute idea is analytic, not synthetic or heuristic. The text constructs neither the concept of life nor that of the absolute idea by showing the contradiction of abstracting and absolutizing knowledge apart from moral action. Rather, the definition of the absolute as life or the absolute idea is already given at the onset of Hegel's treatment of the absolute idea.[9] It is given in the identification of the subjective and objective self-concepts. Progress in the whole sphere of the self-concept is an analytic process of making explicit of what is implicit:

> The progression of the Concept is no longer either passing-over or shining into another, but *development*; for the [moments] that are distinguished are immediately posited at the same time as identical [inseparably one] with one another and with the whole. In the sphere of *being* the dialectical process is passing over into another [definition of the absolute], whilst in the sphere of *Essence* it is shining into another. In contrast, the movement of the Concept is *development*, through which only that is posited which is already implicitly present.[10]

The sections on the objective self-concept and the absolute idea develop and make explicit the fuller content of the self-concept. They do not do this by a dialectic that expands to encompass externally appearing determinations. Rather, they do so by analyzing a Kantian development—the Copernican revolution—internal to the infinite self-concept. This revolution consists in a development from the autonomy of theory to that of practice, from independent cognition to infinite volition including self-cognition.[11]

Thus, the discussions of "cognition" and of the "good" are a progressive but internal analysis of aspects of the single category of the self-concept, life, or the absolute idea. The sections on the objective self-concept immediately prior to examination of life and the absolute idea specify explanatory models by which the positive sciences interpret nature, beginning with mechanism and ending in a teleological model of explanation as self-explanation.[12] Thus, the acorn explained by the oak tree is ultimately explained by what is implicit in its own self, by its own internal telos.

The teleological model of explanation cancels the distance between subjective and objective self-concepts because the subjective self truly identifies with the objective self-determining, self-explanatory process of the internal telos.[13] The subjective self-concept understands nature in its logical concept as realizing its own teleological activity, its own receptive, responsive, self-productive, self-maintaining life.

The sections on cognition with which discussion of the absolute idea (absolute self-concept) begins[14] treat sensibility raised to scientific cognition. Instead of treating objective explanatory models like a mechanical aggregate or chemical whole, they treat the forms of subjective nonphilosophical scientific exposition. The externally limited finite cognition[15] of mathematics and of the natural sciences falls short of the all-embracing speculative cognition of philosophy.

Thus, the *Logic* treats definition as finite, subjective, arbitrary, and exclusive self-definition.[16] This is so even though the purpose of the *Logic* has been for the absolute to render its own infinite self-definition. The lion objectively defines itself by its claws.[17] An individual person defines herself by the subjective, exclusive choice and execution of a particular project. The absolute objectively defines itself in the *Logic* by dialectically transcending partial self-definitions.

Consistent with the section on definition by finite cognition is the nonspeculative focus of the section on theorems,[18] which discusses the geometric method rejected by the dialectical method.[19] Finite cognition is nonphilosophical theory detached from its object, and from any relation to ethical practice. The infinite cognition of speculative philosophy presupposes and completes such practice.

The passages on finite cognition break scientific discourse down into analytic and synthetic statements, definitions, classifications, and theorems. They absolutize cognition apart from moral practice only to make explicit the indispensability of cognition to moral striving for the good. The indispensability of sensibility to irritability (motor response) in life is well known. That practical reason is indispensable to theoretical knowledge was discovered by Kant in the Copernican Revolution. For Hegel, taking his stand on this Kantian ground, it is a question of exhibiting and expounding the truth that "cognition is restored and united with the practical Idea."[20]

A morally good will is as necessary to cognition as motor response is necessary to the stimulation lying in the contrast of sense experiences. Cognition is constructed by the practical will for the latter's own purposes. It guides action, as in the Marxist or pragmatist alternation of theory and practice. Yet, such alternative cognitive and practical pursuits develop in succession, each by itself. Each presupposes a finite subject either cognitively determined by, or practically determining, an independent object.[21] But this is not the unity of theory and practice that Hegel chiefly has in mind.

The objective realization of the subjective self-concept is achieved only by the "absolute idea" (absolute self-concept). This idea is the absolute identity,[22] and not the alternation, of practical and theoretical reason. The self-concept in the absolute idea constructs not only the process of its own finite knowledge of external objects, but also its own practical activity in world history.

This construction of historical practice—concretely, narrative historical practice in the story of freedom—brings that practice to completion in reconstructive infinite self-knowledge. The absolute idea is, placed in its most concrete context, the self-knowledge of the absolute cosmic spirit awakening in history. Indeed, the passage from finite theory limited by external objects to volition is, indirectly, theory's passage into an infinite theory of the volition it contemplates. Volition passes into unlimited self-knowledge. "The passage . . . means that the universal, to be truly apprehended, must be apprehending as subjectivity, as a notion self-moving, and form-imposing."[23]

2. Human Rights

We now draw some conclusions from the view of the *Logic* given in previous chapters. Some writers have been tempted to view the work pan-logistically, as the autonomous self-construction of absolute truth. Others have assimilated Hegel to a Neoplatonic tradition, viewing the *Logic* as an asymptotic approach to a transcendent theistic divine vision.[24] We have viewed the absolute idea hermeneutically, as a rational reconstruction of practical striving in history, and hence as an epic discovery of our own identity through history.

More especially, we have viewed the history of philosophy—of which the *Logic* purports to reconstruct the rational kernel—as a reconstruction of world history in essence. We have in turn viewed world history, spirit as the truth of nature,[25] as an extension of natural history, as an achievement of nature itself. Philosophical logic, taken subjectively by the philosopher as a presuppositionless starting point, finds its external other in nature. It overcomes that alien otherness through development as the philosophy of nature and spirit. Nature is the other of the absolute logical self-concept, but the philosophy of nature is the development of that concept within nature itself.

Theologically, we have interpreted the absolute neither as a pantheistic divine logos positing itself, nor as a theistically conceived timeless divine spirit which partially escapes our inevitably dialectical and hence temporal grasp in this world. We have inferred from the Hegelian concept of the true infinite that the absolute must be conceived panentheistically. The absolute is no finite construction such as the *Science of Logic*. Nor is it merely beyond anything finite. Rather it contains the finite while being irreducible to it.

We have interpreted the *Logic* as the autobiographical epic of the world spirit constructed (unlike the philosophy of history) largely on the level of pure imageless thought. Of course there can be no epic of the world spirit as poetic art in the strict sense.[26] For art speaks to the senses and to imagination, while the transnational world spirit is primarily an object of thought.

But this leaves open the possibility of a philosophical epic of the world spirit. Royce once suggested that the *Phenomenology* was biography. Biography is usually understood to take an individual human life as its subject. Yet Royce understood the *Phenomenology* as the biography of the consciousness of everyman. There is little difference between such a biography and an epic of the world spirit. The Homeric literature consists in the epics of the Greek nation, but it at once may be considered as belonging to the biography of every Greek.

The *Logic* is the biography of everyman defining the absolute. The qualification which remains is that this biography is more strictly autobiographical; it is the self-narration of the absolute defining itself through the agency of philosophers on behalf of everyman.

At one time Hegel, in the Berne-Frankfurt period with Hölderlin, believed in poetry as a reply to the divisions of the modern world (e.g., Earliest System-Programme).[27] Authors like Klopstock aspired to give an epic poetry of Homeric stature to the Germans. However, modern civil society convinced Hegel that epic as a poetic art form was dead, and that the need to reconcile the divisions of the world could only be met by pure thought, by philosophy.[28] No modern nation has found its Homer because, given the interdependence of nations, no nation can confidently muster a sovereign Homeric sense self-congratulation.

For Hegel the French Revolution needed to be philosophically reformed through self-comprehension.[29] The philosophical epic contained in the *Science of Logic*, though abstracted from any individual historical event, is interpretable as the scientific basis of the spiritual Reformation and completion of the French Revolution. We have interpreted the *Logic* as intending an imageless reconstruction of the history of philosophy, and indirectly of the world history of which philosophy is a self-comprehension. The distinction between theoretical reason ("cognition") and practical reason ("the good") in the logic of the idea becomes a distinction between theoretic reconstruction and the world-historical sociopolitical story of freedom. Neither political world history nor its theoretical reconstruction arose within the history of philosophy per se. Rather, science and world history develop the logical category of the absolute self-concept in infralogical spheres of the real world.

The absolute idea is realized by historical understanding in an epic identity between ourselves as subject and the struggles of the world spirit we share as object. Generally, epic has two functions: self-congratulation and exhortation. It serves to celebrate victory over past contradictions, but it also sets an example for renewed struggle against the contradictions of the present. But our contradictions are in us, in our past, while epic poetry in the Homeric tradition celebrates victory over an external enemy. A struggle against internal contradictions is properly tragi-comedy, not epic. The struggle has a tragic aspect because once living voices from the past perish from their own logically fatal flaws. And it has a comic aspect because those who negate their negation of others survive to mock, unintelligently, those who did not let go of their self-absolutization under abstract descriptions.

Yet the *Logic* gives the appearance of epic because of Hegel's own perception of its relation to the history of philosophy and world history. He views world history as a struggle of Western liberty against Oriental despotism, and the logic as a struggle of a Western definition of the absolute as subject to triumph over an Oriental concept as substance. In fact, the panentheistic "Western" definition of the absolute as personality appears in the Orient (e.g., Râmânuja) as well as the West, and the "Eastern" pantheistic definitions appear in the West (e.g., Parmenides) as well as the Orient. But this objection of ethnocentrism directed at the *Logic* is eliminated once we reconstrue the *Science of Logic* as a tragi-comedy, and only superficially and ideologically as epic. Epic by definition is aimed at a foreign enemy, while tragi-comedy reflects a civil war (and final reconciliation) internal to the human spirit. The use, with Hegel, of mostly Western philosophers to concretize definitions of the absolute (especially truer ones) reflects an effort to communicate by familiar reference points. It would be dangerous to take this practice as necessary or assign to it any deep meaning.

The tragi-comedy of the *Logic* is pure celebration within its own

domain if we grant that the definition of the absolute with which it concludes is logically unsurpassable. The philosophy of history, by contrast, is
a tragi-comedy of the world spirit—but not at the level of pure imageless
thought—and does not necessarily eventuate in an unsurpassable conclusion. It is in part exhortation, not pure self-congratulation. Even if the
logical idea undergoes no further purely logical self-particularization, it
is empirically particularized in new ways depending on time and place.
Concrete absolute knowledge in the system is to be sure knowledge of
the absolute, indeed its self-knowledge, but it is far from omniscience.
We know the past attainments of freedom, but the confidence they give
in future attainments is limited. Knowledge of the past yields at most
rational faith in the future, an exhortation lending orientation to practical striving. Hegel claimed no knowledge of world history including the
future as well as the past and present. History being a qualified character
reference for human nature, faith in the future is necessarily qualified.
Yet, future failure cannot erase the monuments to past success.[30]

The philosophy of history, compensating for the great difficulty of
the logic, expresses essentially the same tragi-comedy more concretely,
not in the purely logical mode of imageless thought. World history as the
story of freedom is the exoteric tragi-comedy of the world spirit which,
in Europe and Asia as in America and Africa (perhaps with the current
exception of some branches of Islam), is gradually superseding different
national and local epics of the past.

The *Logic* is that same tragi-comedy in its conceptually stricter
but esoteric form. Insofar as pure thought presupposes the imagery of
world history stored in our minds, the *Logic* is the ghostlike reflection of
events of the flesh and blood. Esoteric tragi-comedy in the *Logic* shows
the conceptual basis of Hegel's philosophy of history in an inferentially
necessary development of definitions of the absolute. Definitions of the
absolute proceed both logically and historically from (1) pantheistic
definitions in which the thinker's selfhood is submerged in the immediate
object, through (2) theistic or panextheistic definitions in which the
thinker find's his or her selfhood in bondage to transcendent power,
to (3) panentheistic definitions in the logic of the self-concept, where
the knowing self is free, determined by cosmic power known to be none
other than the substantial basis of itself.

The absolute self-concept that conclusively defines the absolute in
the *Logic* is rational personality. Hegel insistently defines the absolute as
all-encompassing freedom—as infinite self-awareness or *personality*:

> The absolute Idea [absolute self-concept] has shown itself to be the
> identity of the theoretical and the practical Idea. Each of these by itself

is still one-sided, possessing the Idea itself only as a sought-for beyond and an unattained goal. . . . The absolute Idea, as the rational notion [self-concept] that in its reality meets only with itself, is by virtue of this immediacy of its objective identity, on the one hand the return to *life*; but it has no less sublated this form of its immediacy, and contains within itself the highest degree of opposition. The notion is not merely soul, but free subjective Notion [self-concept] that is for itself and therefore possesses *personality*—the practical, objective Notion determined in and for itself which, as person, is impenetrable atomic subjectivity—which nonetheless is not exclusive individuality, but explicitly *universality* and *cognition*, and in its other has *its own* objectivity for its object. All else is error, confusion, opinion, endeavor, caprice, and transitoriness; the absolute Idea is *being*, imperishable *life, self-knowing truth*, and is *all truth*.[31]

This passage is the most rhetorically inspired in the entire section on the absolute idea. Findlay called its phraseology pardonably gorgeous.[32] Yet most commentators mention the reference to "personality," and Hegel's metaphysical personalism, only in passing if at all.[33]

Very few commentators have appreciated the term's unmistakable function in situating the *Logic* in the context of the story of freedom of the philosophy of spirit. One such commentator is Giacomo Rinaldi, who points out how in the subjective logic of the self-concept Hegel leaves behind merely pure imageless thought to integrate self-conscious personality in the realm of the philosophy of spirit : "according to Hegel himself, the process of thought set forth in the *Science of Logic* is not merely 'ideal-objective' in character (as was on the contrary maintained, e.g., by B. Lakebrink)[34] but at the same time expresses the essential form of concrete human self-consciousness."[35]

The relations among the logical idea, nature, and absolute Spirit are articulated in three "syllogisms," only the third of which (spirit-logical idea-nature—see chapter 12 on this syllogism, which takes its departure from the most concrete sphere of spirit) is in the final resort "in and for itself" valid. This third syllogism explicitly asserts the self-conscious concreteness of the logical idea. This latter therefore cannot be distinguished from the category of absolute spirit.[36]

I only make explicit the contextual reference in the *Logic* to the French Revolution. In early nineteenth-century German philosophy no one could invoke a principle of personality without consciously referring to the Kantian notion of the person as a rational end in itself, and to the 1789 Declaration of the Rights of Man and of the Citizen. It is not in a side remark but in a key paragraph on the absolute idea that Hegel links the logic of pure imageless thought with world history. In so doing he does not take a break from pure logic, but he does use a term which, despite its pure logical content, has a precise historical locus and career at the climactic beginning of the end of history. To be sure, this is an extradialectical reflection within the logic—a reflection that is dialectically developed only in the philosophy of spirit.

The absolute includes more particularly each individual person. It includes all persons universally. Each person finds herself in all others. I only add that one finds oneself in all others as potential partners in truth-directed dialogue, potential partners whom one is practically committed to respect as a condition of the possibility of dialogue. The absolute is defined socially, by self-knowing universal intersubjectivity. As Hegel says in paragraphs 234–35 of the *Encyclopaedia*, the absolute idea is knowledge that the Kantian will to respect personality is no mere "ought" but on its way to institutional actualization. By theoretical reconstruction each person finds her historical self-construction in the entire objective world—including even construction of the person's astronomical and geological preconditions. And by moral striving, each person pursues not so much particular goals, but the further and more coherent construction of the world we know. The individual person finds self-knowledge in knowledge of the objective past, returning to the present with a renewed sense of identity with it and responsibility for its future. The concept of personality employed is Kantian: our identity as persons is grounded in our historical conscious of ourselves through time. Identifying with the objective past as the construction of ourselves, and with the future still under construction, a morally striving person is dedicated to manifesting the kingdom of ends, of personality, as the world's internal telos.

Practical reason is historical, emancipatory self-construction, while theoretical reason is reconstruction and hence further promotion of the same self-construction. Both theory and volition are included in personality. If personality defines the absolute, to pursue anything beyond personality is to pursue something outside the absolute, i.e., nothing.

Moral striving thus has a theological underpinning. It is based on the conviction that the ideal to which one devotes oneself by external goal-directed action is supported more than by one's own meager efforts. In its day in the sun, it is supported by the entire force, might, and substance of the universe. Nothing has barred the way to its present realization, however insecure. And even if the future way is barred, nothing can erase the unsurpassed cosmic achievement of personality thus far. Realization of the ideal of personality in the world is the world's internal self-realization of its own end—an achievement, however unconscious and unintended—which builds on all other astronomical, physical, chemical, and biological achievements.

The universal tragi-comedy of self-awareness founded on the *Logic* has a claim to being, to put it somewhat brazenly, the highest achievement of humanity, and through humanity of the absolute itself. Of course it is not humanity's only achievement, but it is arguably the highest. For it presupposes all other levels of achievement. It presupposes religious, artistic, political, economic, domestic, biological, and other achievements. The practice of philosophy understood at the end of the philosophy of absolute spirit is a concretely individual, historically situated activity—not the abstract activity it appears to be in the *Logic*. This practice presupposes religion, art, the state, civil society, the family, life, chemical process, and even purely mechanical cycles abstracted from nature.

The achievement of philosophy may not always remain actual. New dark ages are possible. Yet, because the temporal eclipse of infinite tragi-comic self-awareness cannot annul the fact that it once occurred, such self-awareness expresses an eternal possibility which always has been, and will remain, potential in the absolute. Infinite tragi-comic self-awareness after 1776 and 1789 revealed an actual revolutionary potentiality hidden in the absolute since time immemorial. As Lévi-Strauss notes, it may someday be forgotten.[37] Yet, it may also someday be recollected and again revealed—either with the romantic attraction of an ideal possibility, or the realistic attraction of a ideal wedded to material force in the world.

Our age is marked by the need for philosophy, Hegel wrote at the beginning of his 1801 *Differenzschrift* on Fichte and Schelling. But not everybody experiences this need subjectively. Some are satisfied by Biblically revealed truth.[38] Others flocked to Hegel's lectures on philosophical world history in the 1820s, and were satisfied. The science of logic is for those who are not satisfied by exoteric philosophy of history. Can it satisfy?

One question surrounding Hegel's vindication of human rights is that it may not convince persons of a nonreligious temperament. By such persons I mean those who entertain no definition of the absolute at all. There may be no such persons, though cases like Sartre, Camus, and Russell are worth investigating. Hegel holds that everyone has a definition of the absolute, of cosmically infinite power. Thus, for egotistic hedonists, the pursuit of private pleasure is vindicated by the implicit belief that pleasure is only in appearance a private and fleeting accident of the cosmos, but is backed up by cosmic force and might. Pleasure is the absolute itself, so that the pursuit of pleasure alone is self-actualization, a flight from nothingness. This interpretation of hedonism appears in Hegel's discussion of "pleasure and necessity" in the *Phenomenology*, which in the first sentence construes the hedonist as a metaphysical theologian:

"Self-Consciousness which, on the whole knows itself to be *reality*, has its object in its own self."[39] One pursues pleasure theoretically as a hedonist because one has implicitly absolutized it as all reality, and practically because one prefers self-realization to self-annihilation.

Holding that the absolute is the Kantian kingdom of moral ends while devoting one's life to the pursuit of private pleasure would be hedonism with a bad conscience, committing one to the pursuit of an illusion, a will-o'-the-wisp. The only rational project is to actualize outwardly what is inwardly coherent and thus potentially actual. The only rational objective is the manifest empowerment of what is already self-consistent and thus latently powerful. If this is true, the incoherence of mere private pleasure as a definition of the absolute is the incoherence of egotistic hedonism as a pursuit. To recognize the coherence of the absolute idea as the definition of the absolute is, by the same token, to recognize the unsurpassable rationality of the pursuit of respect for human rights—for the principle of "personality."[40] If personality defines the absolute, and if there is nothing outside the absolute, personality can fail to be actualized only because the universe is not yet mature or because persons are embroiled in conflict. If evolution has sufficiently matured the universe, actualization of the absolute's own internal end lies in our hands.

This issue leads to a critical perspective on the *Logic*. Can the *Science of Logic* satisfy us as the tragi-comic ideology of the modern world? Can the logic provide a rational ideological grounding for the world human rights revolution now over two hundred years old? A recent metaphysically skeptical, postmodernist movement suggests that even if the *Logic* succeeds as the self-comprehension of the modern world, this world has been superseded. But Enlightenment modernism received more than a short-term boost from the consequences of World War Two. Furthermore, the exotic adventures of romantic postmodernists depend on the protective shield provided to all by the official world of liberal human rights culture. If the logic is the successful self-comprehension of the modern world, then it succeeds as our own self-comprehension, too. It is largely the cliché of contemporary post-1848 continental or post-Auschwitz pessimism that blocks recognition of something close to Hegel's perennial philosophy (if not Hegelianism itself) as the dominant philosophy of our age. (Admittedly it is not the dominant philosophy of professional philosophers.) "In the twentieth century we are Hegelians no more. . . . Hegel's history of philosophy breathes an optimism—a confidence in reason and progress—that is out of touch with our age."[41] Without elaborating, it seems to me that rampant micropessimism—vocal criticism of abuses and atrocities that is probably more widespread than in any known age of the past—evidences an underlying macrooptimism, a revolution of rising moral expectations.

Yet, whether the *Logic* succeeds as ideology depends on more than the survival of the modern world. It depends on whether Hegel's theology of the absolute supports contemporary moral striving. The question is not whether everyone committed to individual human rights must grasp the science of logic, but whether comprehending acceptance of the *Logic* offers a coherent rational vindication of such rights. My own conclusion is that it does offer such a vindication, but not the only one, nor the most accessible one, nor perhaps the rhetorically most effective one.

Consider the rhetorical problem that would be faced by an argument for Newtonian physics based on the claim that such physics represents a victory of English over French physics. This would not be an argument well calculated to persuade the French. Similarly, an argument for human rights over against despotism based on the claim that human rights represent the triumph of the West over the East is poorly geared to persuade the East. Yet, this latter claim is implicit in the *Science of Logic,* and becomes explicit when the *Logic* is set in the context of a philosophy of spirit which includes the lectures on the philosophy of history with their notion that progress is Westward.

A rhetorically more effective argument would claim not that discovery of the rationality of the concept of individual personality is a Western triumph, but that it is a universal human triumph first articulated according to accidents of geography in the West. This is analogous to saying that it is preferable to argue for Newtonian physics on the ground that it is supported by universal scientific methodology rather than on the ground that it happens to be English.

Yet, if we are duly suspicious of the distinction between essence and accident, if we recognize that what seems marginal or peripheral or contextual can be the essence of the matter, we shall avoid ideologically stressing that the principle of personality arose even accidentally in the West. But the context of the *Logic* in the entire Hegelian system makes such avoidance difficult. For rhetorical purposes in universal cosmopolitan dialogue human rights should be placed on a non-Hegelian basis if "Hegelianism" is understood as the Hegelian text rather than a science of logic and system to which he was merely an outstanding contributor.

Hegelian contrasts in the text of the *Logic* between being, essence, and the self-concept are surrounded by invidious comparisons between the Far East, Hebraism, and the modern West. This becomes clear given our historical/contextual interpretation of the *Logic* and its vindication of personality in the present book. Though Hegel's references are, as we have admitted, illustrative for Western audiences, they cannot easily fulfill a useful ideological purpose in the global community.

The Hegelian dialectical justification of human rights threatens to interfere with the practice of human rights by giving comfort to a Western superiority complex which denies the Orient the basic human right of equal partnership in dialogue. Human rights are discovered along the road from Eastern substantiality to spirit in the West. The Hegelian dialectical justification of a universal right to dialogue casts Orientals in the role of junior partners. By relegating still living cultures to a dialectically superseded past, Hegel withholds the respect for certain non-Western cultures necessary for a full practice of human rights. The Hegelian speculative texts are not likely the exoteric spiritual Reformation needed, according to Hegel himself, to accompany the sociopolitical revolution begun in the United States and France. Yet, the speculative system expressed in those texts may still prove the heart of that Reformation. The most fundamental human right, the freedom of inquiry, is the vehicle by which knowledge, including absolute knowledge, installs itself in the modern world. "For it is the nature of humanity to press onward to agreement with others."[42]

The *Logic* has not proven an indispensable theoretical support of human rights in the world. Chaim Perelman and Jürgen Habermas, for example, point the way to a postmetaphysical vindication of human rights. For both, the basic human right is the right to be treated as a potential partner in dialogue with all other persons the pursuit of truth, without supposing that some participants in this dialogue suffer from ethnic or other handicaps. Neither philosopher makes theological use of the concept of personality. Persons are not respected because, in their cognitive identification with the internal end of the objective world, they act on behalf of the absolute. They are respected because they are necessarily valuable to all of us as potential critics in our quest for truth. As rational beings, what concerns us is fundamentally the uncovering of truth, and only therefore personality.

> I may ascribe a predicate to an object if and only if every other person who *could* enter into a dialogue with me *would* [exercising rights to material empowerment and freedom from coercion] ascribe the same predicate to the same object. In judging I make reference to the judgment of others—in fact to the judgment of all others with whom I could ever hold a dialogue (among whom I counterfactually include all the dialogue partners I could find if my life history were counterfactually coextensive with the history of mankind).[43]

However, criticisms of the *Logic* as the epic of human freedom—namely that it repeats Western cultural imperialism and is unnecessarily metaphysical—may be overcome.

1. In Germany Newtonian physics once *was* considered English physics by Goethe. Human rights may eventually be formulated more acceptably to the Orient as universal human obligations. Rights in the tradition of the French Revolution cause strife and litigation, since they are rights *against* others. Human obligations—most fundamentally the "obligation to dialogue"[44]—are rather *toward* all others. Hegel himself was critical of the one-sided atomistic individualism of the French Revolution.

2. It is also possible that rational personality—a theoretical awareness of the record of defining the absolute connected with a responsibility to general implementation of its true definition by personality—is the highest, most encompassing accomplishment of the universe. The *Logic* has of course never functioned publicly in the role of epic or ideological tragi-comedy. It is unlikely that Hegel ever intended that the *Logic* function publicly in this way. A philosophical masterpiece, it is probably destined to remain at most an esoteric tragi-comedy for a philosophical priesthood. Yet, this is consistent with an insistence on the role of the *Logic* as the theoretical foundation of the exoteric epic of human freedom.

Habermasian human pursuit of truth by universal discussion assigning rights to all is, from Hegel's metaphysical point of view, the absolute's pursuit of self-knowledge through human discussion protected by the same rights. Pursuit of victory by members of the team is, from another point of view, the team's pursuit of victory through its members. Yet, a team is not the infinite absolute. Habermas's postmetaphysical description of human rights can be supplemented by a metaphysical description calling attention to the infinite aggregate whole beyond any member. A "postmetaphysical" formulation redirects attention to the members of the aggregate without asking whether their whole is metaphysically absolute. If the members operate in an aggregate whole, human communication in East, West, North, and South is contained within the human spirit. An Hegelian dialectical justification of human rights as surmounting contradiction in the history of the world spirit is more effective than Habermasian procedural justification, which circularly justifies such rights only to those who already presuppose them in cosmopolitan discussion. Yet, this superiority is sacrificed when the justification is placed in the context of a Western story of the struggle for freedom against the East. The science of logic, however, is capable of correcting the *Science of Logic* in the latter's concrete context embracing the Western chauvinism of the *Lectures on the Philosophy of History.*

Recapitulation of the Logic

1. Basic Categories

This book has treated the science of logic in itself, but also in relation to history and the history of philosophy. We have only marginally treated it in relation to trends of philosophy today. Speculative philosophy as the definition of the absolute is not greatly in fashion in either continental or Anglo-American philosophy. Yet it represents an abiding reference point in the greater history of philosophy on which we continue to map ourselves.

In this chapter we take up the entire dialectic of the logic of defining the absolute in recapitulation. The present recapitulation distills a manageable twelve basic categories or definitions of the absolute—considerably fewer than the seventy-two categories cited by G.R.G. Mure,[1] or the some hundred and thirty-one listed by Johnston and Struthers.[2] A basic category is a paradigmatic definition of the absolute. The number of nonbasic categories and logical concepts in a broader sense greatly exceeds the number of basic categories.

Logical concepts without the status of basic categories include: nothing, becoming, quantum, the false mathematical infinite, finite measure, the false infinite of measure, difference, opposition, contradiction, consequent, necessity, the subjective concept, the objective concept. These and other concepts are often phases in the derivation of basic categories, forms of resistance to the emergence of a new basic category, or dependent aspects of such a category. They also include certain nonbasic categories developed within the scope of the indirect proof assumption of a basic category.

Becoming and quantity have not been treated as basic categorial definitions of the absolute. They are not indispensable to the progress of the dialectic. These nonbasic definitions arise in the *Logic*, we have argued, due to a lingering fixation of thinking on the basic categories, respectively, of pure being and the one. Nothing is a necessary concept in the development from the basic category of pure being to that of determinate being. It is the concept of pure being dialectically self-negated by its internal contradictoriness. But becoming expresses resistance to the advance from pure to determinate being through a return from nothing to pure being. The concept of pure quantity represents resistance to the basic category of the true infinite, the one's self-identification under qualitatively different descriptions. And so forth.

Whether the list of twelve basic categories is complete is a further question. Must the dialectic proceed in a single rationally motivated line of deduction from pure being to the self-concept?

Dialectically dispensable, nonbasic categories are parasitic on basic categories. Further, they each must be upheld somewhere in the history of philosophy, or have been institutionally assumed. Their number is not fixed. Still other nonbasic categories could be included if they were historically documented. For example, becoming is included as the Heraclitean alternation of pure being and its self-negation. But no category is made in the *Science of Logic* out of an alternation of positive and negative qualitative determination. Yet such a category might have been included if it had its Heraclitus.

But the question that is crucial to the completeness of the science of logic is whether basic categories are limited in number. The list of such categories to be reviewed in this chapter is:

1. being
2. determinate being
3. something in itself
4. something in itself and for another; i.e., something limited by another (dyad of two somethings)
5. finite aggregate of somethings
6. the true infinite or one
7. the appearance of many things
8. this world
9. the whole of empirically possible worlds
10. actuality
11. self-knowledge
12. the self-concept

The argument for the completeness of this list will be that each category in it has the paradigmatic place of a basic category in a complete cycle of dialectical phases, namely in an indirect proof assumption. Second, the cycles respectively identified with different basic categories form an ordered series from pure being to the self-concept. Every member of the series except the final member has one and only one successor. Successor categories to the self-concept, the last purely logical category which is developed but not superseded in the logic of the concept, focus on the empirical world of nature and spirit. That is why such successor categories are not primarily logical.

Even nonbasic categories or definitions of the absolute in the *Logic* are introduced as indirect proof assumptions. For example, the nonbasic quantitative and Pythagorean categories are introduced as subcategories under the stubborn refusal to relinquish the basic category of being-for-self or the one. But fixation on being-for-self in the dialectic of being is an arbitrary act. Without such stubborn fixation in defining the absolute, there would be no nonbasic categories in the scope of a primary category. And with more such fixations there than appear in the *Logic* we would expect more nonbasic categories. What prevents arbitrarily numerous indirect proof assumptions from being introduced as definitions of the absolute is that each definition in the series arises by reflection on the mediately discovered premise discovered in the breakdown of the prior basic category. Only logical analysis of Hegel's text can confirm that he implicitly designates twelve basic categories, or that he is correct in doing so.

In the logic of being the determination implicitly implied by being in general is general, though a general determination implies a particular determination to be discovered. In the logic of essence, basic categories explicitly but contradictorily include their determinate others. Each basic category except the first encompasses the prior basic category together with that category's "determinate other." But determinate others are implied only in general.

One thing noticeable in the present analysis is that the transition from book 1 to book 2 of the *Logic*, from the logic of being to that of essence, is not a transition between basic categories. It is presented as a transition from one nonbasic category to another, historically from Neoplatonism to Stoicism.

Since nonbasic categories are dialectically dispensable, oddly it appears that the entire transition from one book of the logic to the next is dispensable. The answer to this paradox consists in seeing that the deterministic Stoic ground of consequents is the last nonbasic definition of the absolute which presupposes the true qualitative infinite and the first such nonbasic definition to recognizes the determinate other of this infinite, to attempt to take account even if incompletely of the existing empirical world from which being-for-self detached itself at the end of the logic of quality. The infinite one (Anaximander), the one multiplied (atomism), the one equated with itself in is multiplication (theology of quantity), the one as the principle of underlying qualitative ratios (Pythagoras), and the one viewed as a point of return for many ones (Plotinus)—all such positions take a one to be absolute and unrelated to any other one. The atomist and Pythagorean ones redescribe the empirical world in terms of configurations of atoms or ratios, multiplying ones in the process. But the all-determining one of the Stoic holds promise of an explanation of the sensory world by one one, one ground, without falling back into the contradiction multiplication of ones. A body of facts about natural laws and the world state at a given time determines facts about future world states. And a divine Laplacean superscientist as the being-for-self of the explanatory ground holds promise of an explanation and prediction of world states. Yet the project fails. The determining ground is contradictorily absolute by itself, embracing its consequents deductively within itself, but also a relation to particular detached consequent facts about existing things that go beyond what is deducible from the one is revealing. The determining ground, since it is not all-determining, belongs to the logic of essence.

Should the list of twelve categories list prove satisfactory, the speculative tradition in philosophy which the logic reconstructs has a beginning, development, and conclusion. The present study can only touch upon philosophy since Hegel. It has been widely asserted—by thinkers such as Marx, Nietzsche, and Heidegger—that post-Hegelian philosophers are for the most part no longer in the speculative tradition of defining the absolute. Hegel, it has been supposed, brought this tradition to a conclusion. Competent critical thinkers have allegedly replaced the great speculative philosophers of the past.

Yet the existence of certain post-Hegelian philosophers in the Hegel tradition cannot be discounted. Two post-Hegelian philosophers —J. S. Mill and Whitehead—are used to exemplify categories of Hegel's logic in the recapitulation that concludes this chapter. If the list of twelve basic categories is complete, these post-Hegelians develop in a new way one of the twelve basic categories. They may illustrate resistance to one of these categories, or illustrate a phase in the development of one of them, or fix in thought one of their dependent aspects.

A common suspicion directed against Hegel's dialectical interpretation of philosophers is that it pigeonholes them in an ascending scale where the possibility of dialogue between themselves, and between them and us, is eclipsed by the monologue of our own dialectical reconstruction. There are three replies.

First, no philosopher's work is exhausted by a definition of the absolute. We do not propose reductionism. A definition of the absolute is universally determining in a philosopher's work, but is also essentially determinable and unpredictably variable in its particular determinations. No philosopher is reducible to a mere definition of the absolute. A historical philosopher espousing a false definition of the absolute may remain a real partner in dialogue with us on many other issues. He may win our assent in inquiry into something other than defining the absolute, and we may then integrate this contribution into our own definition of the absolute.

Second, in the tradition of defining the absolute, living truth is inseparable from reliving error and its correction. False historical definitions of the absolute must always be restored to life in a new context, and assumed true definitions must be put at risk in renewed dialogue, if the true definition is to remain vital, not a dogmatic assumption.

Third, in some cases positions in the dialectic of categories are ideal types that remain actualized only incompletely in any actual philosopher of pre-Hegelian history. The post-Hegelian phenomenalism of J. S. Mill is proposed below to construct a theological definition of the absolute as a whole of parts, even though Mill himself did not define "God" as the whole. We are not reducing the historical Mill according to the requirements of a logical category.

We are now ready to recapitulate the dialectic of definitions of the absolute examined in the previous chapters, with brief citations serving to anchor them in the history of philosophy. The dialectic of each definition adheres to the following now-familiar cycle:

1. Abstraction of x under predicate F.
2. Absolutization of term x apart from any relatum, or absolutization of F apart from any other predicate of x.
3. Theological absolutization of absolutized term x under absolutized predicate F.
4. Abstraction of a second term y to which x is related, or abstraction of x under a second predicate G.
5. Negation of y or G.
6. Self-negation of absolutization of absolutized x, or x under absolutized predicate F.
7. Negation of absolutized x's negation of y, or of negation of x's predicate G.
8. Negation of theological absolutization "3" . . .

The place of basic categories is "3" in the above paradigmatic dialectical cycle for a category of being, and "6" for a category in the logic of essence. Each new category or definition of the absolute amplifies the previous one only by adding no more than has just been justified in the previous dialectical cycle. Thus, since it is discovered that merely to be is to be determinate, the successor category to mere-being-without-determination is mere being-with-at-least-one-determination.

Nonbasic categories are dispensable to construction of a true definition of the absolute. They are necessary only to a full account of the history of philosophy, and to more or less unspoken theological fixations in civil society. I cite two examples: In the logic of being the multiplication of quantitative ones necessitating their Neoplatonic reduction to the one one appears as a logical diversion without any contribution to defining the absolute in the logic of essence and the self-concept. And, in the logic of essence, definition of the absolute as negating necessity (Fichte), instead of negating the absolutized but abstract self and its negation of necessity, is a contradictory escape from the embrace of necessity in the logic of the self-concept.

Logical concepts on which historical philosophers have fixed themselves sometimes presuppose unsurrendered prior definitions, as nothing and becoming presuppose the category of pure being. The concept of nothing in the *Logic* presupposes the nonsurrender of the absolute defined as pure being: nothing is self-negating pure being. Becoming presupposes the absolute as pure being, to which it always returns out of the self-negation such being. The theologically absolutized false infinite presupposes the absolutized finite. And appearance as the absolute presupposes theologically absolutized being-for-self which it negates.

2. Pantheistic Being-for-Self, Panextheistic Power, and Panentheistic Being-In-and-for-Itself

We now develop the above list of basic and nonbasic categories in outline form, with categories divided into three groups of definitions of the absolute. We shall designate these groups as, respectively, "pantheistic," "panextheistic," and "panentheistic." Basic categories are numbered, while nonbasic categories featured by Hegel are indented and identified by subletters. Finally, we allude to illustrative figures from the history of philosophy.

Pantheism grasps the absolute immediately as intuitively given. Panextheism grasps the absolute mediately, indirectly, as a purely inner essence reflected in external inessential accidents. Panextheism, unlike creationism, makes the essence contradictorily dependent on inessential accidents; the absolute is not self-sufficient apart from these external accidents which turn out to be essential. Thus, the accidents excluded from the essence are themselves the same essence in a correlative form.[3] Thus, to say that the absolute is essentially appearance is to say that it after all is the being-for-self essentially negated in the initial emergence of the logic of appearance: appearance becomes actuality which proves to be essentially for itself.

Panentheism grasps the absolute by self-mediation as an inner essence realized in all external manifestations, including finite human knowledge of it. Being-for-self, finding itself actualized in the phenomenal world, surrenders its abstraction and becomes the self-concept (*Begriff*).

The dialectic recapitulated below is one protracted argument of a speculative tradition in Western philosophy, proceeding from pantheistic categories, through panextheistic categories, to pantheistic categories. Pantheism has numerous variations. We mean by "pantheistic" definitions those which define the absolute in terms of what is directly given or intuited. The absolute is defined "in its immediacy"[4] as an object of contemplation, whether as pure being, something finite, being-for-self, a sum of atoms, a sum of ones, or the one one to which the many return out of contradiction.

What Hegel calls the "false infinite" is exemplified in his exposition of the logic of quality by the theistic creator God of the Old Testament, who according to the Psalms rises sublimely above everything finite in the finite world. The logic of quality in general is pantheistic. The false infinite—emerging in the logic of quality—essentially requires and yet contradictorily excludes something finite. But unlike the transcendent absolute of the logic of essence, which it otherwise resembles, it does not impose itself with dynamic power on the finite. It is a transcendent, quiescent, aesthetic false infinite: it is qualitatively given to intuition to those who join God in heaven, though not to us in the finite world. In the theistic logic of essence the false infinite of power is a continuing character of all basic categories of essence. It does not appear as a particular category of essence, but as the essence in general, as "universal and irresistible power" manifested outwardly by the submission of God's creatures.[5] Contradictorily, however, the very irresistibility of the absolute's power over creatures demonstrates the nonabsolute status of that power, dependent as it is on creaturely submission.

"Theistic" definitions contradictorily define the absolute by an essence mediated by external inessential accidents which nonetheless essentially reflect it. Theism is "panextheism" because a range of entities lies explicitly and contradictorily outside the aboslute. Sometimes everything throughout time and space is external to the absolute. The absolute is defined "in its reflection and mediation," as "the being-for-self [without being-in-itself] and show of the notion."[6] Consequent facts are facts about the existents that are external to (logically independent of) their ground; properties (in the form of elements) are external to the things that have them; primary matter is external to pure form; unstable appearances are external to their stable law; the dispersed worlds in their manifestation are external to the whole of empirically possible worlds; the inner/outer world of possible empirical appearances is external to the actual empirical world. Speculative thought thinking itself, surviving its demise in the logic of ground, is reborn from the heart of its phenomenalist opposition. Phenomenalism, equating the absolute with the sum of real or possible law-governed sense impressions, no longer views appearances in space and time as external to the absolute; rather, what lies outside space and time, thought thinking itself, is (awaiting actuality) for a time external to the absolute equated with the phenomenal world.

It is clear that the theism of the logic of essence is not limited to biblical creationism. Theistic positions in the logic exist at the level of pure thought, while creationism is articulated at the level of representation. In the science of logic, several positions are "theistic," which by the standard of "creationism" are not ordinarily viewed as such: for example: the Stoic deterministic theology of "the ground," which is deterministic rather than fatalistic because God operates by impersonal natural law rather than by intentions, and which projects spatiotemporal "consequents" upon events outside the explanatory ground of natural laws and initial conditions; or the theology (suggested by Mill) of the whole of empirically possible phenomenal worlds, which fall outside that absolute whole into apparently opposite empirical possible worlds or world states.

The Stoics and Mill were surely not "theists" in the creationist sense. At most we may say that Mill's phenomenalistic cosmology of what is in space-time lends itself to a theology of the whole whose parts are dispersed empirical world states. From Mill's perspective, such a whole qualifies as the absolute outside of which there is nothing, even if Mill personally preferred the cult of a finite god.

The basic pantheistic category of the self-concept defines the absolute as a self which is self-mediated, which is what it is by something that manifests its creative essence outwardly. The absolute exists "in its return into itself, . . . in and for itself."[7] Where a whole understood theistically excludes parts, a pantheistic whole includes them as moments of its self-creation. Everything throughout space and time is in the absolute.

3. Pathway of the Absolute's Self-Definition In Summary

Our recapitulation of the science of logic may now be presented. No attempt at formal or complete derivation is made here. The characteristic rhythm of each dialectical cycle will consist in: (1) the introduction of a definition of the absolute by indirect proof assumption; (2) an objection based on a mediately discovered premise implicit in the definition itself, introduced by "*But*"; and (3) a successor definition of the absolute. In the successor definition the first definition is expanded by deabsolutization of a term or predicate just enough to accommodate the objection. The new definition, technically a new indirect proof assumption allowed in all deduction, is not arbitrary: it preserves from the prior definition as much as accommodation to the objection allows. In its new definition, the absolute is limited to being no more than what its dialectic has so far proven it must be on the basis of the initial assumption together with the objection.

1. By the least developed assumption, the absolute is merely indeterminate being. "Only Being is; non-Being cannot be"[8] (Parmenides). *But* what is indeterminate being without further determination necessarily is nonbeing, nothing in particular.

    1a. By a still closer subassumption under the assumption that the absolute is merely indeterminate being, the absolute is pure indeterminate being without further determination, and thus is not being at all. It is contradictory, and hence nothing. "Nothing exists of the things that are"[9] (Gorgias). *But* if the absolute is nothing, there is nothing to define.

    1b. By a still closer subassumption under the assumption that the absolute is merely indeterminate being, the absolute is pure indeterminate being alternately affirmed and negated. "We are and we are not"[10] (Heraclitus). *But* if the absolute is alternately pure being and pure nonbeing, it is indefinable, eluding definition by either of these exhaustive and mutually exclusive alternatives.

2. By a still closer assumption, the absolute is merely positively determinate being. *But* if anything is positively determinate, necessarily it is also negatively determinate (Spinoza).

3. By a still closer assumption, the absolute is negatively as well as positively determinate, is merely something or other (*Etwas*). *But* if anything is something or other and thus is negatively determinate, there is something else which conceivably has positively the qualitative determination which the first being lacks, and which makes the first being limited or abstractly finite.

4. By a still closer assumption, the absolute is something self-limited through something else, which it expands to overreach. *But* given something internally self-limited by something else, there is always still something else again that limits it externally, so that the absolute is conceived contradictorily as limited or finite.

5. By a still closer assumption, the absolute is not finite or contradictory, but is qualitatively infinite beyond everything finite that is posited by judgments of the abstractive understanding. "Be exalted, O God, above the heavens!"—Psalms 108:5. *But* to be beyond the finite is another way of being finite.

6. By a still closer assumption, the absolute is the true qualitative infinite, which as a concretely thinking subject overreaches and includes the finite absolutized by stubborn fixations imposed by the abstractive understanding, thus revealing itself as a concretely thinking subject. "From what [infinite] source [finite] things arise, to that they return of necessity when they are destroyed; for they suffer punishment and make reparation to one another for their injustice according to the ordering of time"[11] (Anaximander). *But* an infinite thinking subject—self-limited by contradictory assumptions fixating the finite—also necessarily remains externally limited by the various objects to which it is contingently related.

6a. By a still closer subassumption under the assumption of an unrelinquished definition of the absolute as one true infinite thinking subject, the absolute is an aggregate of atomic thinking subjects. " . . . atoms and empty space; everything else is merely thought to exist."[12] *But* if there are different abstract atomic thinking subjects that vary only in that each excludes the others, they do not exclude one another but are qualitatively identical, differing only quantitatively.

6b. By a still closer subassumption under the assumption of an unrelinquished definition of the absolute as one true infinite thinking subject, the absolute is an aggregate of ones which are qualitatively identical but quantitatively distinct. *But* if the constant quality repeated in a quantitative series is a determinate quality, necessarily it is not the determinate quality of the units of some other series.

6c. By a still closer subassumption under the assumption of an unrelinquished definition of the absolute as one true infinite thinking subject, the absolute is a ratio of one quantitative series to another qualitatively distinct series. *But* every ratio is determinate through not being other ratios.

6d. By a still closer subassumption under the assumption of an unrelinquished definition of the absolute as one true infinite thinking subject, the absolute is a scale of ratios (e.g., graded chemical ratios such as the formulas for compounds). *But* one scale of ratios is qualitatively determinate only by not being a qualitatively distinct scale (e.g., continuous physical ratios such as force as ma).

6e. By a still closer subassumption under the assumption of an unrelinquished definition of the absolute as one true infinite thinking subject, the absolute is a master scale of scales. " . . . discerning in numbers the conditions and reasons of harmonies also—since, moreover, other things seemed to be like numbers in their entire nature, and numbers were the first of every nature—they [the Pythagoreans] assumed that the elements of numbers were the elements of all things, and that the whole heavens were harmony and number."[13] *But* if the quantitative ones in each term of a ratio are identical in some abstract quality, necessarily they are numerically identical, so that the numerical distinction of ones implied by ratios of ones and multiples of ones necessarily collapses.

6f. By a still closer subassumption under the assumption of an unrelinquished definition of the absolute as one true infinite thinking subject, the absolute is the indeterminate one one. "The One, as transcending Intellect, transcends knowing. The first is One, but undefined; a defined One would not be the One-Absolute: the absolute is prior to the definite. The One is in truth beyond all statement: Any affirmation is of a thing; but 'all-transcending, resting above even the most August divine mind'—this is the only true description, since it does not make it a thing among things"[14] (Plotinus). *But* if a thinking subject has at some time discovered its identity with the one one (which it has done, if we reflect on the above definition of the absolute in 6), necessarily that subject exists as a discernible description of the one one.

6g. By a still closer assumption under the assumption of an unrelinquished definition of the absolute as one true infinite thinking subject, the absolute is the determinate one, existing under a description that includes by implication a true definite description of every event or thing distinct from it (Stoicism). "God is Fate. . . . Fate is the . . . the logos of things according to which the things that have happened, have happened, the things that happen, happen, and the things that will happen, will happen."[15] A Laplacean superscientist would be the mind for whom such Fate would unfold. "Consider an intelligence which, at any instant, could have a knowledge of all forces controlling nature together with the momentary conditions of all the entities of which nature consists. If this intelligence were powerful enough to submit all this data to analysis it would be able to embrace in a single formula [the inner] the movements of the largest bodies in the universe and those of the lightest atoms [the outer]; for it nothing would be uncertain; the future and the past [the all-embracing outer] would be equally present to its [inner] eyes."[16] *But* if the one one satisfies an explanatory ("grounding") description implying a concretely existing event or thing distinct from it, necessarily that thing ex-ists multidimensionally under a further description not implied by the explanatory description.

7. By a still closer assumption, the absolute is the essential sum of interacting things incompletely grounded by one another. *But* if there is an essential sum of incompletely grounded existing things, necessarily each thing disappears into the sum of its properties understood as spatiotemporally coinciding portions of material elements (scattered particulars—Russell).[17]

8. By a still closer assumption, the absolute is the sum of logically independent material elements detached portions of which coincide, interpenetrate, and succeed one another in the things of this world. "Thus we remember to have seen that species of object we call *flame*, and to have felt that species of sensations we call *heat*. We likewise call to mind their constant conjunction in all past instances. Without further ceremony, we call the one the *cause* and the other the *effect*"[18] (Hume). *But* if there is a presently manifest world of lawfully coinciding, interpenetrating, or successive elements, necessarily it may be reversed by the appearance of the same possible world exhibiting opposite potentialities (e.g., winter opposed to summer), or by another empirically possible world manifesting contrary laws.

9. By a still closer assumption, the absolute is the sum total (whole) of phenomenal manifestations of this world with its laws, or conceivably of contrary empirically possible worlds each with different laws. "The first and most obvious distinction between Observation and Experiment is, that the latter is an immense extension of the former"[19] (Mill). A Marxian theory of laws manifest in present society yielding, by a revolutionary social experiment, to the manifestation of other laws in postcapitalist society illustrates such apocalyptic empiricism, which Mill called "experimentalism." So does the Sermon on the Mount. The totality of laws is not confirmed merely by phenomena observable in the immediately present world. *But* if there is a whole of contrary manifestations of this empirically possible world, or of different empirically possible worlds with contrary laws—where the sum of those contrary manifestations or laws exists essentially for thought without ever being phenomenally manifest all at once—necessarily that whole in itself disperses into independent phenomenal parts, i.e., into logically independent manifestations of the laws of this world or some other world.

9a. By a still closer subassumption under the assumption that the absolute is a sum whole of contrary manifestations of this empirically possible world, or of contrary possible worlds with different laws, the absolute is a whole of manifestations or empirically possible worlds which breaks apart into the diverse separate manifestations or worlds which express it. "Whatever can happen, happens"[20] (Herder). *But* the dispersion of a whole of manifestations or worlds—the expression, expansion, and division of the whole with internal force—is necessarily its dissipation, self-loss, and disappearance.

9b. By a still closer subassumption under the assumption that the absolute is a sum whole of contrary manifestations of this empirically possible world, or of contrary possible worlds with different laws, the absolute is the inner world of law in which contrary manifestations of this world or of different empirically possible external worlds are abstractly contemplated. "*Contingent possibles* can be known either separately or as all correlated in an infinity of entire possible worlds, each of which is perfectly known to God, though only one of them has been produced into existence"[21] (Leibniz). *But* given opposed abstractly contemplated empirically possible manifestations or worlds each defined by inner universal laws, these manifestations or worlds are self-actualized only in concretely occurring events.

10. By a still closer assumption, the absolute is the concrete self-actualization of the abstract potentiality for self-actualization contained in the laws of this world or conceivably of opposed empirically possible worlds. Present events actualize and particularize in outer expression the inner possibility offered by prior events, and contain the real inner possibility of future outer self-actualizations. "[Cosmic] process for its intelligibility involves the notion of creative activity belonging to the very essence of each occasion [*Sache*, event]. It is the process of eliciting into actual being factors in the universe which antecedently to that process exist only in the mode of unrealized potentialities [possibilities]. The process of self-creation is the transformation of the potential into the actual"[22] (Whitehead). *But* if an inner real empirical possibility actually manifests and actualizes itself outwardly, necessarily it does so for an observer.

11. By a still closer assumption, the absolute is the concrete self-actualization of potentially actual empirical possibility—a potentiality that manifests itself self-consciously to itself rather than any other. It observes itself. "The mind's intellectual love of God is the same divine love by which God loves himself"[23] (Spinoza). *But* if there is a power of self-conscious self-manifestation to oneself, necessarily such self-consciousness emerges over against consciousness of the independent force of necessity, the blind, dimly understood, relentless march of events in which the self is not immediately visible.

11a. By a closer subassumption under the assumption that the absolute attains self-awareness, the absolute is an endless striving for full self-consciousness through struggle against an external obstacle course in which it fails to achieve full self-consciousness. "[O]bjects are objects merely in so far and through this, that they do *not* exist through free activity; and this free activity must be checked and limited, if objects are to be. For free activity tends [forever] to cancel these objects" (Fichte).[24] *But* whoever grasps the self-construction of his or her self-concept in and through the external obstacle course of the necessary march of events is no longer limited by that external world.

12. By the closest logical assumption, the absolute is the thinking subject for whom the actualization of possibility exists, which finds itself in actuality but also finds itself in the necessary march of events as well. "The 'I' has neither to cling to itself in the *form* of self-consciousness as against the form of substantiality and objectivity, as if it were afraid of the externalization of itself" (Hegel).[25]

Clearly the order of philosophers illustrating the order of categories is not fully chronological. Whitehead does not predate Spinoza, and most scholars doubt that Parmenides preceded Heraclitus. The historical order follows at most in general the order of definitions of the absolute. The concluding chapter will investigate how it is possible for the rational order of the logic to diverge from the empirical order of philosophy's history without ceasing to be the rational order of this history.

Empirical versus Rational Order in the History of Philosophy

A consequence of viewing the *Logic* as a historical reconstruction is that Hegel philosophizes more on the basis of his work as a teacher of the philosophical tradition than on the basis of extraphilosophical work in a specialized field (e.g., biology, mathematics) outside philosophy. Our goal must be not to stop where the reading of Hegel has often stopped due to the difficulty of the text and subject matter, namely, at an attempt simply to understand the text. Rather, the goal is to understand something beyond Hegel through Hegel: to understand not merely Hegel but a progressive discovery of the absolute in history. This discovery brings Hegel to fruition by renouncing any positive intention of his own and intending only to be a vehicle for the intention of the text.

Hegel himself distinguished between original thinkers in the history of philosophy and philosophical teachers, and classed himself with the latter:

> I am a schoolmaster who has to teach philosophy, and that is why I also hold that philosophy must assume a regular structure as teachable as geometry. But knowledge of mathematics and of philosophy is one thing, while inventive and creative talent in mathematics as in philosophy is quite another. My sphere is to invent that scientific form, or to work towards its completion.[1]

Since he wrote these lines in 1810 as he was about to write the *Logic*, prima facie it is not plausible to interpret the *Logic* as an original discovery of Hegel's. The thinker enjoys the harvest of objective historical scholarship.

Original thinkers and teachers do not constitute mutually exclusive classes. Once this distinction is made, we may thus further define a class of *original thinkers of intraphilosophical historical inspiration*, whose thought strives to overcome some problem preoccupying the philosophical tradition. We find, in contrast to these philosophers, *original thinkers of extraphilosophical inspiration*, who generalize metaphysically an idea discovered in a nonphilosophical source (e.g., mathematics).

Though biographically Hegel started out in the 1790s under extraphilosophical influences from the study of theology and political history, he did his systematic work as an original intraphilosophical thinker. His original contribution in the philosophical history of defining the absolute, the concept of spirit, was initially abstracted from the revealed Christian theology in which he received his specialized training.[2] But that was the context of discovery. Passing to the context of justification, he was a teacher of history. His rhetorical genius led him to present the history of philosophy as teaching what Christianity has long since believed, that spirit is the solution to the problem of consistently defining the absolute. It is this history, and no partisan bias of Hegel's, that argues for Hegel's conclusion.

Thinkers of intraphilosophical inspiration justify an original definition of the absolute by showing how it logically arises from the internal self-criticism of prior definitions. Thinkers of extraphilosophical inspiration, like all who define the absolute, seek to reduce all things to manifestations of the absolute as they have defined it. But such philosophers do not justify this definition as arrived at by the internal self-criticism of previous definitions. Rather, it is arrived at by abstraction from the nonphilosophical world of institutions, science, art, and religion, and is justified only by its power in generating a universal account of phenomena.

Thus Pythagoras, who was first a creative mathematician, arguably abstracted the metaphysical category of number from arithmetic itself more than from hints as to the quantitative determination of quality in Anaximenes.[3] The definition of the absolute he established as an original philosopher of extraphilosophical inspiration is a hypothesis justified by its power in leading to the discovery of hidden numerical ratios in things other than music, his original concern.

But for some scholarly Pythagoreans who came after Pythagoras, the same definition of the absolute as number or ratio was justified by coopting historically prior definitions. Thus, Pythagoreans after Pythagoras could construct the Pythagorean definition of the absolute out of a critique of the post-Pythagorean pluralistic materialism of Empedocles. We may illustrate our general thesis about historical and rational order in the *Logic* by assuming for the sake of discussion certain insights of the historian John Burnet: "The view that the soul is a 'harmony,' or rather an attunement, is intimately connected with the theory of the four elements.

It cannot have belonged to the earliest form of Pythagoreanism; for, as shown in Plato's *Phaedo*, it is quite inconsistent with the idea that the soul can exist independently of the body."[4] These Pythagoreans did not repeat Empedocles. They did not say that the cosmos is an aggregate of elements (stirred by opposed forces), but rather that it was a harmony of them.

To come to our main concern, this helps explain why the reconstruction of the history of philosophy in the *Logic* corresponds only imperfectly to the succession of great original philosophers in empirical history. The first atomists came after Pythagoras. But the *Logic*, in treating the definition of the absolute as numerical ratio after its definition as an aggregate of atoms, invokes not so much the original Pythagoras but a later Pythagoreanism. This Pythagoreanism dialectically constructed the absolute as numerical ratio, not out of the four elements, but out of the incoherent atomist view of the absolute as essentially identical and yet mutually exclusive ones.[5]

The first atomist, Leucippus, held that atoms are in essence identical Parmenidean ones, implying that their differences of shape, position, and arrangement were accidental.[6] But being one of many is essential to being an atom as contrasted to Parmenidean being. Thus atoms are, contradictorily, both essentially and accidentally many, both essentially and accidentally distinguished by shape, position, and arrangement. If they are identical in essence and only accidentally distinct, the difference between Eleatic monism and atomism is itself accidental. The only way to secure atomism against a collapse back into the Eleatic position is to insist either that there are ungrounded contingent truths, or that atoms are essentially and not merely accidentally distinguished by different positions, arrangements, "figures," and "forms."[7]

Leucippus began with a view of atoms as Parmenides being multiplied: "all atoms are exactly alike in substance."[8] He thus defended himself against Zeno.[9] But the multiplication of descriptively identical ones is contradictory: numerical distinctness implies qualitative difference. Leucippus's final atomism thus can be interpreted as an internal self-critique of an atomism of identical ones: "the atoms are called 'forms' and 'figures,' a way of speaking which is clearly of Pythagorean origin."[10]

The atomist doctrine thus became a dialectical reconstruction of Pythagoras, but of a Pythagoras now immune to Zeno's criticism of the original Pythagorean "infinite divisibility" of the many. In a rational reversal of the empirical order of the great philosophers upheld in the *Logic*, what is more recent becomes a dialectical reconstruction of what is prior. We find here a small stretch of the *Logic* developed long before Hegel by ultimately Pythagorean atomists responding to the dilemma of multiplying Parmenidean ones. As a reconstruction of the history of philosophy, the *Logic* brings to fruition a dialectical impulse of the history of philosophy itself.

Generally, original philosophers of extraphilosophical inspiration change serial position as we pass from the empirical to the rational order in the history of philosophy. They come to assume the position held in rational history by their intraphilosophical vindicators. For example, identification of the absolute with the Holy Spirit was not original with Hegel.[11] It was present in the work of Joachim de Fiore (1132–1202) and his followers, who proclaimed that God was truly revealed neither as Father nor as Son but as Spirit. But Joachim was a philosopher of extraphilosophical (Biblical, historical) inspiration. The originality of Hegel was to have justified the identification of the absolute with spirit through the philosophical tradition, in particular through an internal self-criticism of Kantianism. In the rational order Joachim's place is Hegel's own at the very conclusion of the dialectic.

The most plausible way of accounting for discrepancies between the historical order and the logical order consistent with Hegel is, I think, somewhat as follows. Hegel asks us to believe that Pythagoras, like Joachim de Fiore, is objectively—but not necessarily in his own consciousness—a dialectically forward-leaping thinker. Joachim, drawing on mystical experience, held that God was truly revealed as Spirit. But his contemporaries were still in the age of the Father, concerned with proofs of God's existence as the Father or Creator.

Similarly, in defining the absolute as number Pythagoras used an extraphilosophical source to leap ahead of the contemporary dialectical development to a relatively more coherent category. Objectively, the Eleatic monists and atomists—historically posterior and yet dialectically prior to Pythagoras—were backward-looking thinkers. They articulated relatively more abstract categories necessary to the dialectical construction of a coherent Pythagoreanism—categories undeveloped by Pythagoras himself. Parmenides, who is not historically the first philosopher and who is in fact post-Pythagorean, is dialectically first because he defines the absolute as it must first be defined in a dialectical vindication of Pythagoreanism. In such a vindication, the Pythagorean definition is constructed as the self-correction of all more abstract definitions.

The *Logic* presents the history of philosophy as it would have transpired if the order of this history had not been perturbed by factors extraneous to philosophy, or by the genius of occasional great philosophers of extraphilosophical inspiration, like Pythagoras or Wittgenstein. Their intellectual power dispenses with dialectical erudition and derivation. The *Logic* presents the history of philosophy as if it had been solely the work of historically rooted dialectical thinkers immersed in the rational theological tradition, each pursuing definition of the absolute one step further by pondering the achievements and predicaments of predecessors. As if it had been a continuous progressive development, without anticipatory leaps of genius abstracting definitions of the absolute from extraphilosophical regions of culture.

I do not claim that a rational history of philosophy as attempted in the *Logic* diverges entirely from a presumed empirical order in history. On the contrary, we note a general correspondence between being, essence, and self-concept in the *Logic* and between pantheistic, theistic, and Christian panentheistic civilizations in world history as Hegel understood it. Yet—much as philosophy moves toward an understanding and acceptance of Christianity but not from it according to Hegel[12]—the science of logic moves toward an understanding and acceptance of world history in its main structure, not from such an understanding.

The parallel between logic and history—the essential rationality of history—can be vindicated empirically. Yet, this is possible only after the science of logic has been autonomously constructed by its own internal dialectic, without being guided by furtive side-glances at world history in general or at the history of philosophy in particular. Classical philosophers determined through their work the course of the empirical history of philosophy through a mixture of extraphilosophical personal willfulness and surrender to the self-movement reason. Yet, to defend a rational reconstruction of history by borrowing from the very history by which the reconstruction will be tested is a form of cheating. Precisely because the logic intends a rational reconstruction of the history of philosophy, methodologically its author must first feign ignorance of empirical history.

The self-determined character of the dialectic implies more than possible divergences between the rational and empirical orders of past philosophers. It also implies possible divergences between historical philosophers themselves and the rational reconstruction of those philosophers in the dialectic. The Parmenides of Hegel's dialectic, contrary to the Parmenides of history, knew nothing of Pythagoras. It is only the Parmenides of history who, on Hegelian grounds, can be presented as a "backward-leaping philosopher." The Spinoza of Hegel's logic of essence, we saw, is not exactly the Spinoza of history. The Spinoza of history did not view matter as a being-in-itself which develops itself as mind. And the atomists of history did not view the atom as thought thinking itself or being-for-self in condensed form. The different positions appearing in the dialectic of the logic are idealized models of historical philosophers. Yet, their deviation from historical philosophers is made possible only because, under descriptions rationalized for the purposes of the dialectic, they succeed nonetheless in referring to historical philosophers.

A purely dialectical history of philosophy would be by continuous historically informed correction of idealized predecessors. It would eliminate any need to uncover less coherent categories implicitly presupposed by a more coherent category parachuted in our midst, to provide a dialectical apology for a more adequate category revealed in an intuitive leap as if from nowhere. This history of philosophy as ideally as it perhaps might have been is, however anchored in empirical history, not the history which actually took place. Yet, the history which actually took place, in its attempted reconstructions of its own past, betrays a certain attraction exercised by that history which might have been.

The *Logic* is itself a rational reconstruction and regimentation of the empirical history of philosophy emerging within that history itself. Such reconstruction did not wait for Hegel; it has occurred throughout the empirical history of philosophy. Atomism constructs itself by reconstructing Parmenides, Aristotle constructs his theory of the four causes by reconstructing previous philosophy. Other thinkers offer no dialectical construction of their positions, and thus impose that task on Hegelian logicians. These logicians fill in missing links in a dialectical apology for a definition of the absolute which originally appeared nondialectically in the history of philosophy. Thus, certain fragments of the *Logic* may never before have been written in the history of philosophy.

Aristotle, as just noted, is an example of an original metaphysician who was incidentally a dialectical apologist of his own position. As a nondialectical original thinker he undertakes to explain everything by the hypothesis that the absolute is matter with a potentiality for receiving form. But in the first book of the *Metaphysics* he seeks to justify this hypothesis by a dialectical reconstruction of previous philosophy.

Hegel is also a dialectical apologist of a definition of the absolute which he, like Joachim, first discovered nondialectically. He borrows the concept of spirit from religion where "the truth has also long been present for itself in pious Christian faith."[13] But he is even more a dialectical apologist than Aristotle, since he uses no other justification than the dialectical method.

Hegel believed that world history in general develops toward a coherent, rational theological category as much as the history of philosophy in particular.[14] The history of philosophy is part of the history of the world. Its development reflects that of the whole, and from the idealistic perspective even exercises a determining influence on it. Hegel was not content to abstract the concept of spirit immediately from Christian piety as Pythagoras abstracted number from arithmetic, and the idea of cosmic harmony from music. In his mature system—in contrast to his own nondialectical method in his early writings reflecting on religious and political history[15]—he derived the definition of the absolute as spirit dialectically from prior philosophers.

Hegel and Aristotle construct their positions by an internal transcendence of historical philosophers, not just imagined ones. Whether Hegel has understood past philosophers is important to evaluating the *Logic*. Whether scholarship shows a historical realization of a logical dialectical order is also important. Yet, divergences between the chronological and the logical orders need not refute the thesis of the *Logic*. The logical order is a logical reconstruction of real history even if it diverges from the chronological order, so long as it is a rational reordering of historical philosophers. The construction resulting from speculative logic then matches a rational reconstruction of history independently achieved by the historian of philosophy. As Daniel Graham has written, the historian of philosophy must also be a philosopher who asks: "Is this [philosophical] position defensible given the historical context [of philosophical inquiry]? Should the philosopher have made this move? Such questions can be answered only in light of the concrete problem situations and actual alternatives open to a philosopher."[16]

Scholarship in corrective reconstruction of empirical history may help uncover a hidden correspondence between the *Logic* and real history. This discovery adds an important dimension to the *Logic*'s relevance to us. Perhaps the *Logic* might have been written by a creative individual as an original construction rather than as a reconstruction of the actual history of philosophy. It might have been written as a philosophical novel or fantasy. But in fact Hegel did not present himself as a philosophical novelist inventing and passionately fixing upon successive definitions of the absolute wholly in his imagination. Even though we have presented it as tragi-comedy, Hegel presents the *Logic* as a philosophical epic rather than as a novel.[17]

A novel is fiction, while epic is a celebration of history for those whom it has formed. The *Logic* is an epic celebration of the quest for a true definition of the absolute through history. It was Hegel's voyage of discovery only as an induction into and continuation of humanity's voyage.

The importance of the book as epic far exceeds what it would be as a novel. As a novel it would testify to the genius of its author, but the perspective it would propose would be only a provocative alternative to our own. As an epic the text offers an encounter with ourselves as we philosophically are, at the end of a historical reconstruction which at once confronts us with our present identity.

In conclusion, we have argued that the apparent lack of correspondence between the empirical history of philosophy and Hegel's *Logic* may be explained by the nondialectical position in empirical history of certain philosophers of extraphilosophical persuasion such as Pythagoras. However, a certain lack of correspondence remains unexplained by this hypothesis. It is striking that the logic of being, which is presented in book 1 of the *Logic*, and which reconstructs ancient philosophy from the Presocratics to Neoplatonism, contains no place for Aristotle or even the historical Plato. This remaining lack of correspondence is in part explained, as I already suggested at the end of my treatment of book 1, that the history of philosophy is a history of *movements*, not just of individual *philosophers*. Aristotle was, to be sure, an ancient philosopher, but the age in which the Aristotelian movement dominated was clearly the Middle Ages. In ancient philosophy Aristotle founded one school among many. In the Middle Ages he became, first among the Muslims and then among the Christians, the philosopher of reference. A similar story could be told of Plato. The Platonic movement dominated in the earlier Middle Ages in association with Church fathers such as Augustine.

Yet, there was a reason in their respective individual philosophies why Plato was embraced by the Church Fathers and Aristotle by later medievals. Both Plato and Aristotle were prototheistic thinkers who, in this respect, leaped out of their predominantly pantheistic age in ancient times. It is this forward-leaping genius in Plato and Aristotle that causes their movements to predominate in the Middle Ages in empirical history, and thus only in Hegel's broadly theistic logic of essence[18] (including matter and form) in the *Science of Logic*. The history of philosophy as a history of predominant movements indeed corresponds more closely to the dialectic than the chronology of individual philosophers. Thus, Pythagoras preceded Parmenides, but Pythagoreanism largely postdated it, and postdated the Eleatic movement in the *Logic*. But this explanation takes us back to the distinction borrowed from Hegel at the beginning of the chapter between individual philosophers as scholarly teachers like Hegel himself and as gifted precursors like Plato and Aristotle.

Notes

Introduction

German as well as English references are given for Hegel's *Science of Logic* as well as for other works, but not for his *Encyclopaedia of Philosophical Sciences*, because passages in the *Encyclopaedia* are referred to by paragraphs that remain constant in all editions, not by page numbers.

1. John Burbidge, *On Hegel's Logic* (Atlantic Highlands: Humanities Press, 1981), 4.

2. G. W. F. Hegel, *Science of Logic*, trans. A. V. Miller (London: Allen and Unwin, 1969), 70; *Die Wissenschaft der Logik*, vol. 1, ed. Georg Lasson (Hamburg: Meiner, 1969–74), 54. Hereafter abbreviated as *Logic*; *Logik*.

3. Ibid., 43; *Logik*, vol. 1, 23.

4. Ibid., 49; *Logik*, vol. 1, 30.

5. G. W. F. Hegel, *Phenomology of Spirit*, trans. A. V. Miller (Oxford: Oxford University Press, 1977), 445; *Die Phänomologie des Geistes*, ed. Wolfgang Bonsiepen and Reinhard Heede (Hamburg: Meiner, 1980), 393. George di Giovanni has objected to my characterization of absolute knowledge as "cosmic self-consciouness" in "Setting the Record Straight," *Owl of Minerva* 19, no. 2 (1988), 231. But I maintain my claim. I understand the "cosmos" in a neo-Pythagorean sense, where the cosmos is an intersubjective, embodied, and infinite world-soul, including us insofar as we know it, thus insofar as it knows itself in and through us. The "cosmos" understood as such is an undeveloped precursor to Hegel's concept of spirit.

6. G. W. F. Hegel, *Lectures on the History of Philosophy*, trans. E. S. Haldane and Frances Simson, 231–35; *Sämtliche Werke*, vol. 17, ed. Hermann Glockner (Stuttgart: Frommann, 1926), 284–89.

7. Errol Harris, *An Interpretation of Hegel's Logic* (Lanham: University Press of America, 1983), x.

8. Clark Butler, "Hegel and Indirect Proof," *The Monist* 75 (Fall 1991), 422–37.

9. Burbidge, *On Hegel's Logic*, 4.

10. G. W. F. Hegel, *The Encyclopaedia Logic, Part 1 of the Encyclopaedia of Philosophical Sciences*, trans. T. F. Garaets, W. A. Suchting, and H. S. Harris (Indianiapolis: Hackett, 1991), par. 86, add. 2.

11. G. W. F. Hegel, *Encyclopaedia of Philosophical Sciences*, 3d ed. (1830), trans. W. Wallace and A. V. Miller (Oxford: Oxford University Press, 1892–), pars. 576–77.

12. Ibid., 5.

13. André Doz, *La Logique de Hegel et les problèmes traditionnels de l'ontologie* (Paris: Vrin, 1987), 31.

14. Clark Butler, "Hermeneutic Hegelianism," *Idealistic Studies* 15, no. 2 (1985), 121–35.

15. John N. Findlay, *Hegel: A Re-examination* (London: Allen and Unwin, 1958), chap. 3, sec. 1.

16. Jean-Luc Nancy, *L'oubli de la philosophie* (Paris: Galilée, 1986), 15.

17. G. W. F. Hegel, *Lectures on the Philosophy of History,* trans. J. Sibree (New York: Dover, 1956), 56; *Sämtliche Werke,* vol. 11, ed. Hermann Glockner (Stuttgart: Frommann, 1926), 92.

18. Bertrand Russell, *Logic and Knowledge* (London: Macmillan, 1956), 270.

19. Hegel, *Logic,* 630; *Logik,* vol. 2, 272.

20. Clark Butler, "The Place of Process Cosmology in Absolute Idealism," *Owl of Minerva* 16, no. 2 (1985), 161–74.

21. Martin Heidegger, *An Introduction to Metaphysics,* trans. Ralph Mannheim (New York: Doubleday, 1961), 12.

22. In *"Erinnerung, Retrait,* Absolute Reflection: Hegel and Derrida," *Owl of Minerva,* 26, no. 2 (1995), Wendell Kisner argues that Hegel, for Derrida, fails to escape the reflective standpoint of opposition, which Derrida likewise fails to escape. I find myself agreeing with this Derridean view of Hegel. In principle, or as a method potentially proceeding to infinity, that negation of the negation surmounts all opposition to concrete being. But an infinity of reiterations of the method is in fact impossible. Hence, thought at any stage of absolutized concreteness always reflects residue of unthought concrete being. Yet, a distinction still remains between abstract reflective thought, which closes itself to negation, of the negation, and concrete reflective, which remains open to future reiterations of negation of the negation.

23. Hegel, *Logic,* 31–32; *Logik,* vol. 1, 9–10.

24. Jacques Derrida, *Writing and Difference,* trans. Alan Bass (Chicago: University of Chicago Press, 1978), 257, 263, 269.

25. G. W. F. Hegel, *The Letters,* trans. Clark Butler and Christiane Seiler, commtary by Clark Butler (Bloomington: Indiana University Press, 1984), Hoffmeister nos. 55, 278; *Die Briefe von und an Hegel,* ed. Johannes Hoffmeister (Hamburg: Meiner, 1952–54), nos. 55, 278.

26. Ibid., nos. 677–78.

27. Ibid. no. 603 (1829).

28. Hegel, Phenomology, 27; *Phänomologie,* 35.

29. Ibid., 23, *Phänomologie,* 31.

30. Ibid., 20; *Phänomologie,* 28.

31. Jacques Derrida, "On the University," interview by I. Salusinszky, *Southern Review* 19, no. 1 (1986), 3–12.

32. Deborah Chaffin, "Hegel, Derrida, and the Sign," in *Derrida and Deconstruction,* ed. Hugh Silverman (London: Routledge, 1989), 91.

33. Derrida, *Writing and Difference,* 252–53.

34. Jürgen Habermas, *Justification and Application: Remarks on Discourse Ethics*, trans. Ciaran Cronin (Cambridge: MIT Press, 1993), 165.

35. Ibid., 100.

36. Ibid., 136.

37. Hegel, *Logic*, 818–23; *Logik*, vol. 2, 477–83.

38. Jürgen Habermas, *Knowledge and Human Interests*, trans. Jeremy Shapiro (Boston: Beacon, 1971), 311, 211.

39. Hegel, *Phenomenology*, 8–9, 28–33; *Phänomenologie*, 16–17, 35–39.

40. G. W. F. Hegel, "Review of Göschel's *Aphorisms*," trans. Clark Butler, *Clio* 17, no. 4 (1988), 384; Hegel, *Sämtliche Werke*, vol. 20, 293–94.

41. Merold Westphal, *History and Truth in Hegel's Phenomenology* (Atlantic Highlands: Humanities Press, 1979), 4a.

42. Hegel, "Review of Göschel's *Aphorisms*," 384; *Sämtliche Werke*, vol. 20, 293–94.

43. G. R. G. Mure, *An Introduction to Hegel* (Oxford: Oxford University Press, 1940), 52–53.

44. G. W. F. Hegel, *Philosophical Propaedeutic*, trans. A. V. Miller, ed. Michael George and Andrew Vincent (London: Basil Blackwell, 1986). See my "Speculative Logic in the Gymnasium," 261–63, in Hegel, *The Letters*, chap. 10 ("The *Logic*") and pp. 171ff., esp. letter no. 122.

45. Hegel, *Science de la logique*, trans. Pierre-Jean Labarrière and Gwendoline Jarczyk (Paris: Aubier, 1972), book 1 (1812 edition).

46. G. W. F. Hegel, *Janaer Systementwürfe*, vol. 2, ed. Rolf-Peter Horstmann and Johann Heinrich Trede (Hamburg: Meiner, 1971), "*Logik*" and "*Metaphysik*" (1804–5), 1–178. See also H. S. Harris, *Hegel's Development: Night Thoughts (Jena: 1801–6)*, chap. 8.

47. Giacomo Rinaldi, *A History and Interpretation of the Logic of Hegel* (Lewiston: Edwin Mellen, 1992).

48. Hegel, *The Letters*, nos. 95, 109.

49. Ibid., no. 100.

50. Hegel, *Encyclopaedia Logic*, par. 131.

51. Hegel, *The Letters*, no. 54.

52. Philip Grier, "Abstract and Concrete in Hegel's Logic," in *Essays on Hegel's Logic* (Albany: State University of New York Press, 1990), 74.

53. J. Biard, et al., *Introduction à la lecture de la Science de la logique de Hegel* (Paris: Aubier, 1981–87), vol. 1, 9.

54. Hegel, *The Letters*, no. 254.

55. Stanley Rosen, *G. W. F. Hegel: An Introduction to the Science of Wisdom* (New Haven: Yale University Press, 1974), xii.

56. Friedrich Hogemann and Walter Jaeschke, "Die Wissenschaft der Logik," in *Hegel*, ed. Otto Pöggeler (Freiburg: Alber, 1977), 76.

57. Gabrielle Baptist, "Ways and Loci of Modality. The Chapter 'Actuality' in the *Science of Logic* between Its Absence in Jena and Its Disappearance in Berlin," in *Essays in Hegel's Logic*, ed. George di Giovannni (Albany: State University of New York Press, 1990), 127.

58. Hegel, *Logic*, 439; *Logik*, vol. 2, 58.

59. A. Sarlemijn, *Hegel's Dialectic* (Dordrecht: Reidel, 1975), 81.

60. Stanley Rosen, *G. W. F. Hegel*, 112.

61. Hegel, *Encyclopaedia Logic*, par. 119, add.

Chapter 1: Defining the Absolute in the Parmenidean Orbit

1. G. W. F. Hegel, *Science of Logic*, trans. A. V. Miller (London: Allen and Unwin, 1969), 82; *Wissenschaft der Logik*, vol. 1, ed. Georg Lasson (Hamburg: Meiner, 1969–74), 66. G. W. F. Hegel, *The Encyclopaedia Logic, Part 1 of the Encyclopaedia of Philosophical Sciences* (1830), trans. T. F. Garaets, W. A. Suchting, and H. S. Harris (Indianapolis: Hackett, 1991), par. 86.

2. G. W. F. Hegel, *The Letters*, trans. Clark Butler and Christiane Seiler, with commentary by Clark Butler (Bloomington: Indiana University Press), 265.

3. Hegel, *Logic*, chap. 1, rem. 1; *Logik*, vol. 1, chap. 1, *Anmerkung* 1.

4. Ibid., 113; *Logik*, vol. 1, 100.

5. *Selections from Early Greek Philosophy*, ed. Milton Nahm (New York: Appleton-Century-Crofts, 1964), Parmenides, "Way of Truth," frs. 3, 92.

6. G. W. F. Hegel, *Encyclopaedia Logic*, trans. T. F. Garaets, W. A. Suchting, and H. S. Harris (Indianapolis: Hackett, 1991), par. 86.

7. Hegel, *Logic*, 82; *Logik*, vol. 1, 66.

8. G. W. F. Hegel, *Die Wissenschaft der Logik* (1812–13), ed. Friedrich Hogemann and Walter Jaeschke (Hamburg: Meiner, 1978), 43.

9. Hegel, *The Letters*, Hoffmeister no. 628; *Die Briefe von und an Hegel*, 3 vols., ed. Johannes Hoffmeister (Hamburg: Felix Meiner, 1952–54), no. 628.

10. Hegel, *Logic*, 83; *Logik*, vol. 1, 68.

11. Hegel, *Lectures on the History of Philosophy*, vol. 1, trans. E. S. Haldane and Frances Simson (New York: Humanities Press, 1974), 378–84; *Sämtliche Werke*, vol. 18, ed. Hermann Glockner (Stuttgart: Frommann, 1926), 35–41.

12. Ibid., vol. 1, 380; *Werke*, vol. 18, 38.

13. Hegel, *Die Wissenschaft der Logik* (1812–13), 44.

14. Ludwig Feuerbach, *The Essence of Christianity*, trans. George Elliott (New York: Harper and Row, 1957), 14–15.

15. Willard van Orman Quine, *Methods of Logic*, 4th ed. (Cambridge: Harvard University Press, 1982), 103.

16. Hegel, *Logic*, 82–83, 105–08; *Logik*, vol. 1, 67, 92–95.

17. Hegel, *Lectures on the History of Philosophy*, vol. 1, 282; *Sämtliche Werke*, vol. 17, 348.

18. Hegel, *Logic*, 105–6; *Logik*, vol. 1, 92–93.

19. Ibid., 94–96; *Logik*, vol. 1, 80–82.

20. Hegel, *Encyclopaedia Logic*, par., 88, add.

21. Stephen Houlgate has argued that the dialectical method cannot be separated from its practice, and that its practice differs from section to section of the *Logic*; see *Freedom, Truth, and History: An Introduction to Hegel's Philosophy* (London: Routledge, 1991), chap. 2. We offer here a theory of the dialectic interpreted as a

reactment of historical dialectical practice. The practice admittedly differs from the logic of being, which is fixated on the absolutization of the finite, through the logic of essence, which is fixated on self-negation (negation of oneself by the negated other brought on by one's original negation of other), to the logic of the concept, which detaches itself from fixation on any stage of the dialectic, rendering its movement fluid.

22. Sigmund Freud, "Narcissism, An Introduction" (1914), trans. Cecil M. Baines, in *Freud: Genral Psychological Theory*, ed. Philip Rieff (New York: Cromwell-Collier, 1963), sec. 3, 74. See also Clark Butler, "Hegel and Freud: A Comparison," *Philosophy and Phenomenological Research* 36, no. 4 (1976), 506–522.

23. John McCumber finds the preceding seven-stage cycle, which in an earlier version I have translated into the first-order predicate calculus (Clark Butler, "On the Reducibility of Dialectical to Standard Logic," *The Personalist* 56 [1975], 414–31), to be "anachronistic" because predicate calculus had not yet been invented in Hegel's time (*The Company of Words: Hegel, Language, and Systematic Philosophy* [Evanston: Northwestern University Press, 1993], 124). But an English translation of Sophocles is not anachronistic because English was not invented in Sophocles' time. The only sort of anachronism that is vicious is anachronism of content, not linguistic form. McCumber makes the further objection that my strategy, and others like it, assumes that Hegel's system is a set of assertions, which is not credible because it supposes a fact other than any true statement, "while beginning with the *Science of Logic . . . all* otherness to thought has been overcome" so that "thinking can, in the system, purely in its own element" (ibid., 124–25). My reply is that the system must consist in assertions, since it is an inquiry into the true definition of the absolute, which is a true assertion arrived at after assertions dying numerous false definitional assertions. However, the otherness between thought and its object, which the *Logic* takes over from the *Phenomenology*, must not be interpreted as an identity of indifference. Thought is identical with the absolute by distinguished as being the highest agent and vehicle of its self-awareness.

J. N. Findlay has claimed to diverge from the account I still essentially maintain by holding that the dialectic progresses by "higher-level comment" or meta-level reflection, that the course of inference is not unilinear, that the dialectical method is (unlike formal deduction) a logic of discovery not fully guided by formal rules, that I had not thought the concept of identity and difference, and that the semantic shifts which emerge in the dialectic preclude its deductive formalization. He does grant that the dialectic advances by indirect proof, which is a technique of deductive formalization. And semantic shifts common to ordinary language may be artificially purged in formalization. Further, indirect proof provides for linguistic ascent, since reflection on the contradiction of an indirect proof assumption demotes it to an objective assertion no longer used. My considered opinion today is that deductive formalization is possible, that this possibility is an interesting theoretical point, but that formalization is not as useful or necessary in a clear narration of the dialectic as I thought in my 1974 paper at the Georgetown Hegel Society of America Conference (published as

"Hegel's Dialectic of the Organic Whole," in *Art and Logic in Hegel's Philosophy*, ed. Warren Steinkraus and Kenneth Schmitz [New Jersey: Humanities Press, 1980], 219–32, with "Comment" by J. N. Findlay, 233–37). As for identity in difference, I now formulate it in terms of identity under different descriptions.

24. Hegel, *Encyclopaedia Logic*, par. 89, rem.

25. *Selections from Early Greek Philosophy*, 71–72 (Heraclitus, frs. 44–46, 57, 59, 69, 78, 81).

26. Hegel, *Lectures on the History of Philosophy*, vol. 1, 279; *Sämtliche Werke*, vol. 17, 344–45.

27. G. S. Kirk and J. E. Raven, *The Pre-Socratic Philosophers* (Cambridge: Cambridge University Press, 1960), 182–83.

28. Hegel, *Lectures on the History of Philosophy*, vol. 1, 282–83; *Sämtliche Werke*, vol. 17, 348–49.

29. Aristotle, *Metaphysics*, trans. W. D. Ross, in *The Basic Works of Aristotle*, ed. Richard McKeon (New York: Random House, 1941), book 4, chap. 3.

30. *Selections from Early Greek Philosophy*, 72 (Heraclitus, fr. 81).

31. W. K. C. Guthrie, *A History of Greek Philosophy*, vol. 1 (Cambridge: Cambridge University Press, 1963), 451.

32. Andrew Reck, *Speculative Philosophy* (Albuquerque: University of New Mexico Press, 1972), 185.

33. Hegel, *Die Wissenschaft der Logik* (1812–13), 45.

34. Ibid., 44.

35. I fear John Burbidge risks leaving us with the same degree of puzzlement with which Hegel himself leaves us by equating the interpreter's intentions as a will to "to develop 'a plasticity and receptivity of understanding' so that we can appreciate the significance of what Hegel actually writes" ("The First Chapter of Hegel's Larger *Logic*," *Owl of Minerva* 21, no. 2 [1990], 178). Attempting to think through Hegelian claims that being and nothing are both the same and differt without highlighting a Fregean distinction between identity in sense and difference in reference between "being" and "nothing" (ibid., 180–82), he seems to pay a price in clarity for his fidelity to Hegel's linguistic forms. The reader must judge whether my "Fregean" reformulation distorts the substance of Hegel or expresses it more clearly, on the assumption that all inferentially successive definitions of the absolute differ in their ever more concrete sense but not in reference.

36. Hegel, *Encyclopaedia Logic*, par. 161, add.

Chapter 2: The Anonymous Theology of the Finite

1. F. H. Bradley, *Appearance and Reality* (Oxford: Oxford University Press, 1930), 123.

2. G. W. F. Hegel, *Lectures on the History of Philosophy*, vol. 1, ed. E. S. Haldane and Frances Simson (New York: Humanities Press, 1974), 279; *Sämtliche Werke*, vol. 17, ed. Hermann Glockner (Stuttgart: Frommann, 1926), 344.

3. G. W. F. Hegel, *Wissenschaft der Logik* (1812–13), ed. Friedrich Hogemann and Walter Jaeschke (Hamburg: Meiner, 1981), 59–60.

4. G. W. F. Hegel, *Science of Logic*, trans. A. V. Miller (London: Allen and Unwin, 1969), 114; *Die Wissenschaft der Logik*, vol. 1, ed. Georg Lasson (Hamburg: Meiner, 1969–74), 101.

5. W. E. Johnson, *Logic*, vol. 1 (Cambridge: Cambridge University Press, 1921), chap. 11.

6. G. W. F. Hegel, *The Encyclopaedia Logic, Part 1 of the Encyclopaedia of Philosophical Sciences* (1830), trans. T. F. Garaets, W. A. Suchting, and H. S. Harris (Indianapolis: Hackett, 1991), par. 119, add. 2.

7. Hegel, *Logic*, 121; *Logik*, vol. 1, 108.

8. Ibid., 108; *Logik*, vol. 1, 95.

9. Clark Butler, "Hermeneutic Hegelianism," *Idealistic Studies* 15, no. 2 (1985), 121–36.

10. Clark Butler, "Dialectic and Indirect Proof," *The Monist* 74, no. 3 (1991), 422–37.

11. Hegel, *Logic*, 111; *Logik*, vol. 1, 97–98.

12. Immanuel Kant, *The Critique of Pure Reason* (1787), book 2, chap. 1.

13. Hegel, *Logic*, 111; *Logik*, vol. 1, 97–98.

14. Ibid., 111–12; *Logik*, vol. 1, 98.

15. Gottfried Wilhelm Leibniz, *The Monadology* (1714), sec. 48. Hegel, *Logic*, 112; *Logik*, vol. 1, 99.

16. Leibniz, ibid., sec. 45.

17. Hegel, *Logic*, 155; *Logik*, vol. 1, 145.

18. Ibid., 120–21; *Logik*, vol. 1, 108.

19. Ibid., 155; *Logik*, vol. 1, 145.

20. Hegel, *Lectures on the History of Philosophy*, vol. 1, 177; *Sämtliche Werke*, vol. 17, 217.

21. Ibid., vol. 1, 179; *Sämtliche Werke*, vol. 17, 221.

22. Ibid., vol. 1, 174; *Sämtliche Werke*, vol. 17, 214.

23. Ibid., vol. 1, 179; *Sämtliche Werke*, vol. 17, 220.

24. Ibid., vol. 1, 173; *Sämtliche Werke*, vol. 17, 212–13. *Logic*, 88; *Logik*, vol. 1, 74.

25. Hegel, *Logic*, 113; *Logik*, vol. 1, 100.

26. Ibid., 114; *Logik*, vol. 1, 101.

27. Ibid., 117; *Logik*, vol. 1, 104.

28. Ibid., 115; *Logik*, vol. 1, 102.

29. Ibid., 119; *Logik*, vol. 1, 106.

30. Ibid., 120–21; *Logik*, vol. 1, 107–8.

31. Saul Kripke, *Naming and Necessity* (Cambridge: Harvard University, 1980), 44–45.

32. Hegel, *Encyclopaedia Logic*, par. 143, rem.

33. Ibid., par. 143, add.

34. Hegel, *Logic*, 122–29; *Logik*, vol. 1, 110–16.

35. Ibid., 136; *Logik*, vol. 1, 124.

36. Ibid.

37. Ibid., 126–27; *Logik*, vol. 1, 114.

38. Ibid., 131; *Logik*, vol. 1, 119.

39. Ibid., 124–25, 129; *Logik*, vol. 1, 111–12, 116.

40. Ibid., 136, *Logik*, vol. 1, 124.

41. Ibid., 132–35; *Logik*, vol. 1, 120–23.

42. Ibid., 125–29; *Logik*, vol. 1, 112–16.

43. Ibid., 131; *Logik*, vol. 1, 118–19.

44. Hegel, *Encyclopaedia Logic*, par. 119, add. 2.

45. Hegel, *Logic*, 440; *Logik*, vol. 2, 58.

46. Aristotle, *Metaphysics*, trans. W. D. Ross, in *The Basic Works of Aristotle*, ed. Richard McKeon (New York: Harper and Row, 1941), book 4, chap. 3.

47. G. W. F. Hegel, "Review of Göschel's *Aphorisms*," *Clio* 17, no. 4 (1988), 386–87; *Sämtliche Werke*, vol. 20, 297–98.

48. W. T. Stace, *The Philosophy of Hegel: A Systematic Exposition* (New York: Dover, 1955), 93.

Chapter 3: Anaximander and the Germination of the True Infinite

1. G. W. F. Hegel, *The Encyclopaedia Logic, Part 1 of the Encyclopaedia of Philosophical Sciences* (1830), trans. by T. F. Garaets, W. A. Suchting, and H. S. Harris (Indianapolis: Hackett, 1991), par. 112, add.

2. G. W. F. Hegel, *Science of Logic*, trans. A. V. Miller (London: Allen and Unwin, 1969), 137, 139–40; *Die Wissenschaft der Logik*, vol. 1, ed. Georg Lasson (Hamburg: Meiner, 1969–74), 125–26, 128.

3. Ibid., 129; *Logik*, vol. 1, 116.

4. Ibid., 439–42; *Logik*, vol. 1, 58–62.

5. Ibid., 131–32; Logik, vol. 1, 119–20.

6. H. S. Harris, *Hegel's Development: Toward the Sunlight, 1770–1801* (Oxford: Oxford University Press, 1972), 119–120, 122.

7. Michael Theunissen, *Hegels Lehre vom Absoluten Geist als theologisch-politischer Traktat* (Berlin: Walter de Gruyter, 1970), 347ff.

8. G. W. F. Hegel, "Neufassung des Anfangs" (1800), added to *Die Positivität der christlichen Religion* (1795–96), my translation from *Werke in Zwanzig Bände*, vol. 1, ed. Eva Moldenhauer and Karl Markus Michel (Frankfurt: Suhrkamp, 1971), 225–26.

9. G. W. F. Hegel, *Lectures on the Philosophy of Religion*, vol. 3, trans. E. B. Speirs and A. B. Sanderson (London: Routledge and Kegan Paul, 1968), 122; *Sämtliche Werke*, vol. 16, ed. Hermann Glockner (Stuttgart: Frommann, 1926), 329.

10. Rolf Ahlers, "The Overcoming of Critical Theory in the Hegelian Unity of Theory and Praxis," *Clio* 8, no. 1 (1978), 82–88.

11. Hegel, *Logic*, 142; *Logik*, vol. 1, 130–31.

12. Ahlers, "The Overcoming of Critical Theory," 86–87.

13. Hegel, *Logic*, 145–46; *Logik*, vol. 1, 134–35.

14. Keith Donnellan, "Reference and Definite Descriptions," *Philosophical Review* 75 (1966), 284–304.

15. Hegel, *Logic*, 185ff.; *Logik*, vol. 1, 177ff.

16. G. W. F. Hegel, *Lectures on Fine Arts*, vol.1, trans. T. M. Knox (Oxford: Oxford University Press), 339–40; *Sämtliche Werke*, vol. 12, 453–55.

17. Hegel, *Logic*, 134; *Logik*, vol. 1, 121.

18. Ibid., 139; *Logik*, vol. 1, 128.

19. Ibid., 142; *Logik*, vol. 1, 130–31.

20. Ibid., 138; *Logik*, vol. 1, 127.

21. Ibid., 141; *Logik*, vol. 1, 130.

22. Ibid., 148; *Logik*, vol. 1, 138.

23. John Burnet, *Early Greek Philosophy*, 4th ed. (Cleveland: Meridian, 1957), 52.

24. G. W. F. Hegel, *Lectures on the History of Philosophy*, vol. 1, trans. E. S. Haldane and Frances Simson (New York: Humanities Press, 1974), 186–87; *Sämtliche Werke*, vol. 17, 228.

25. Hegel, *The Letters*, trans. Clark Butler and Christiane Seiler, with commentary by Clark Butler (Bloomington: Indiana University Press, 1984), Hoffmeister no. 450; *Briefe von und an Hegel*, ed. Johannes Hoffmeister (Hamburg: Meiner, 1952–54), no. 450.

26. Hegel, *Logik*, 440; *Logik*, vol. 2, 59.

27. G. W. F. Hegel, *Encyclopaedia of Philosophical Sciences*, trans. W. Wallace and A. V. Miller (Oxford: Oxford University Press, 1892–1975), par. 523.

28. G. W. F. Hegel, *Phenomenology of Spirit*, trans. A. V. Miller (New York: Oxford University Press), 227–28; *Die Phänomenologie des Geistes*, ed. Wolfgang Bonsiepen and Reinhard Heede (Hamburg: Meiner, 1980), 207.

29. Hegel, *Lectures on the Philosophy of Religion*, vol. 3, 228; *Sämtliche Werke*, vol. 16, 426–27.

30. Hegel, *Logic*, 137–38; *Logik*, vol. 1, 126.

31. Hegel, *Phenomenology*, 11; *Phänomenologie*, 19.

32. Hegel, *Logic*, 137–38; *Logik*, vol. 1, 126.

33. G. S. Kirk and J. E. Raven, *The Pre-Socratic Philosophers* (Cambridge: Cambridge University Press, 1960), 105–6.

34. Hegel, *Logic*, 566; *Logik*, vol. 2, 198–99.

Chapter 4: Classical Atomism: Thought Thinking Itself Multiplied

1. G. W. F. Hegel, *The Encyclopaedia Logic*, trans. T. F. Garaets, W. A. Suchting, and H. S. Harris (Indianapolis: Hackett, 1991), par. 96, add.

2. G. W. F. Hegel, *Science of Logic*, trans. A. V. Miller (London: Allen and Unwin, 1969), 169–70; *Die Wissenschaft der Logik*, vol. 1, ed. Georg Lasson (Hamburg: Meiner, 1969–74), 160.

3. Ibid., 169; *Logik*, vol. 1, 160.

4. Ibid., 164; *Logik*, vol. 1, 154.

5. Giacomo Rinaldi, *A History and Interpretation of the Logic of Hegel* (Lewiston: Edwin Mellen, 1992), 309–10.

6. Hegel, *Logic*, 158; *Logik*, vol. 1, 148.

7. Ibid.

8. Ibid.

9. Ibid.

10. Ibid., 163; *Logik*, vol. 1, 154.

11. Ibid., 164; *Logik*, vol. 1, 154–55.

12. Aristotle, *Metaphysics*, trans. W. D. Ross, in *The Basic Works of Aristotle*, ed. Richard McKeon (New York: Harper and Row, 1941), book 1, chap. 5.

13. Ibid.

14. Hegel, *Logic*, 172; *Logik*, vol. 1, 163.

15. Ibid., 164; *Logik*, vol. 1, 154.

16. See G. W. F. Hegel, *Encyclopaedia Logic*, par. 24, on the Fall.

17. Ibid., par. 38.

18. Hegel, *Logic*, 169; *Logik*, vol. 1, 160.

19. Ibid.

20. Hegel, *Encyclopaedia Logic*, par. 97.

21. Hegel, *Logic*, 167–68; *Logik*, vol. 1, 157–58.

22. Ibid., 178; *Logik*, vol. 1, 170.

23. Ibid., 141–42; *Logik*, vol. 1, 130.

24. Ibid., 158; *Logik*, vol. 1, 148.

25. Ibid., 165–66; *Logik*, vol. 1, 156–57.

26. Ibid., 187; *Logik*, vol. 1, 179.

27. Ibid., 187; *Logik*, vol. 1, 179.

28. Hegel, *Encyclopaedia Logic*, par. 98, rem.

29. Hegel, *Logic*, 167–68; *Logik*, vol. 1, 157–59.

30. Ibid., 168; *Logik*, vol. 1, 158.

31. Hegel, *Encyclopaedia Logic*, par. 102.

32. Hegel, *Logic*, 185; *Logik*, vol. 1, 177.

33. Hegel, *Encyclopaedia Logic*, par. 117, add.

34. Hegel, *Logic*, 162; *Logik*, vol. 1, 152–53.

35. G. W. F. Hegel, *Encyclopaedia of Philosophical Sciences*, trans. W. Wallace and A. V. Miller (Oxford: Oxford University Press, 1892–1975), par. 117, add.

36. Aristotle, *Metaphysics*, book. 1, chap. 5.

37. Ibid.

38. Plato, *Phaedo*, 91D.

39. Parmenides, "Way of Truth," fr. 8.

40. Aristotle, *On Generation and Corruption*, trans. Harold Joachim, in *The Basic Works of Aristotle*, ed. Richard McKeon (New York: Random House, 1941), 498 (book 1, chap. 8).

41. Hegel, *Encyclopaedia Logic*, par. 98, add. 1.

42. G. W. F. Hegel, *Lectures on the History of Philosophy*, vol. 1, trans. E. S. Haldane and Frances Simson (New York: Humanities Press, 1974), 179; *Sämtliche Werke*, vol. 17, ed. Hermann Glockner (Stuttgart: Frommann, 1926), 219–20.

43. Ibid., vol. 1, 187; *Sämtliche Werke*, vol. 17, 228.

44. Ibid., vol. 1, 190; *Sämtliche Werke*, vol. 17, 231–32.

45. Hegel, *Logic*, 166; *Logik* vol. 1, 156.

46. Hegel, *Encyclopaedia Logic*, par. 98, rem.

47. Parmenides, "Way of Truth," fr. 8.

48. John Burnet, *Early Greek Philosophy* (New York: Meridian, 1957), 334.

49. Gottfried Wilhelm Leibniz, *The Monadology* (1714), pars. 1–14.

50. Hegel, *Logic*, 161–62; *Logik*, vol. 1, 152–53.

51. Ibid., 161, 165–66; *Logik*, vol. 1, 152, 156–57.

52. Ibid., 164; *Logik*, vol. 1, 154.

53. Ibid., 166; *Logik*, vol. 1, 156–57.

54. Hegel, *Encyclopaedia Logic*, pars. 95, rem.

55. Ibid., par. 96, add.

56. Ibid., par. 98, rem.

57. Ibid., par. 98, add. 1.

58. Hegel, *Logic*, 161–62; *Logik*, vol. 1, 152–53.

59. Gottfried Wilhelm von Leibniz, "Monadology," trans. Paul Schrecker and Ann Martin Schrecker, in *Monadology and Other Essays* (Indianapolis: Bobbs-Merrill, 1965), par. 20, 151.

Chapter 5: The Theology of Pure Quantity

1. Aristotle, *Physics*, trans. R. P. Hardie and R. K. Gaye, in *The Basic Works of Aristotle*, ed. Richard McKeon (New York: Random House, 1941), book 4, chap. 6.

2. G. W. F. Hegel, *The Encyclopaedia Logic, Part 1 of the Encyclopaedia of Philosophical Sciences* (1830), trans. T. F. Garaets, W. A. Suchting, and H. S. Harris (Indianapolis: Hackett, 1991), par. 106, add.

3. Terry Pinkard, *Hegel's Dialectic: The Explanation of Possibility* (Philadelphia: Temple University Press, 1988), 42.

4. Bertrand Russell, *An Introduction to Mathematics* (London: Allen and Unwin, 1919), 107.

5. Hegel, *Encyclopaedia Logic*, par. 98, add.

6. G. W. F. Hegel, *Science of Logic*, vol. 1, trans. A. V. Miller (London: Allen and Unwin, 1969), 163–64; *Die Wissenschaft der Logik*, vol. 1, ed. Georg Lasson (Hamburg: Meiner, 1969–74), 153–54.

7. Hegel, *Encyclopaedia Logic*, par. 104, add. 3.

8. Ibid.

9. Hegel, *Logic*, 214; *Logik*, vol. 1, 209.

10. Hegel, *Encyclopaedia Logic*, par. 96, add.

11. G. W. F. Hegel, *Phenomenology of Spirit*, trans. A. V. Miller (Oxford: Oxford University Press), 140; *Die Phänomenologie des Geistes*, ed. Wolfgang Bonsiepen and Reinhard Heede (Hamburg: Meiner, 1980), 131.

12. Hegel, *Encyclopaedia Logic*, par. 98.

13. Hegel, *Logic*, 86; *Logik*, vol. 1, 178.

14. Ibid., 423; *Logik*, vol. 2, 38.

15. Hegel, *Encyclopaedia Logic*, par. 117, rem. and add.

16. Hegel, *Logic*, 422–23; *Logik*, vol. 2, 38–39.

17. Ibid., 423; *Logik*, vol. 2, 39.

18. Hegel, *Encyclopaedia Logic*, par. 99, add.

19. Hegel, *Logic*, 375; *Logik*, vol. 1, 387–88.

20. Charles Taylor, *Hegel* (Cambridge: Cambridge University Press, 1975), 244.

21. Hegel, *Logic*, 216–17; *Logik*, vol. 1, 211–12.

22. F. W. J. Schelling, *Exposition of My System* (1801), preface.

23. B. Spinoza, *Ethics*, part 2, prop. 40, n. 2.

24. Hegel, *Logic*, 185, 201; *Logik*, vol. 1, 177, 195–96.

25. Ibid., 199–201; *Logik*, vol. 1, 193–94.

26. Hegel, *Encyclopaedia Logic*, pars. 105–6.

27. Hegel, *Logic*, 314; *Logik*, vol. 1, 322–23.

28. Ibid., 225; *Logik*, vol. 1, 222.

29. Ibid., 227–28, 238; *Logik*, vol. 1, 223–24, 236–37.

30. Ibid., 228; *Logik*, vol. 1, 225.

31. Ibid., 228; *Logik*, vol. 1, 225.

32. Hegel, *Encyclopaedia Logic*, par. 104, Rem.

33. Hegel, *Logic*, 314; *Logik*, vol. 1, 322.

34. Ibid., 229–30; *Logik*, vol. 1, 226–27.

35. Ibid., 239–40; *Logik*, vol. 1, 237–38.

Chapter 6: Pythagoras and the Logic of Measure

1. G. W. F. Hegel, *Science of Logic*, trans. A. V. Miller (London: Allen and Unwin, 1969), 315; *Die Wissenschaft der Logik*, vol. 1, ed. Georg Lasson (Hamburg: Meiner, 1969–74), 324.

2. G. W. F. Hegel, *The Encyclopaedia Logic, Part 1 of the Encyclopaedia of Philosophical Sciences* (1830), trans. T. F. Garaets, W. A. Suchting, and H. S. Harris (Indianapolis: Hackett, 1991), par. 99, rem.

3. Hegel, *Logic*, 240; *Logik*, vol. 1, 238–39.

4. Hegel, *Encyclopaedia Logic*, par. 107, add.

5. G. W. F. Hegel, *The Letters*, trans. Clark Butler and Christiane Seiler, with commentary by Clark Butler (Bloomington: Indiana University Press, 1984), Hoffmeister no. 145; *Briefe von und an Hegel*, ed. Johannes Hoffmeister (Hamburg: Meiner, 1952–54), no. 145.

6. Hegel, *Logic*, 334; *Logik*, vol. 1, 343–44.

7. Aristotle, *Metaphysics*, trans. W. D. Ross, in *The Basic Works of Aristotle*, ed. Richard McKeon (New York: Random House, 1941), book 1, chap. 5.

8. Hegel, *Logic*, 334; *Logik*, vol. 1, 343–44.

9. Ibid., 334, 337; *Logik*, vol. 1, 344, 347.

10. Ibid., 337; *Logik*, vol. 1, 346–47.

11. Ibid., 348; *Logik*, vol. 1, 358.

12. John Burnet, *Early Greek Philosophy*, 4th ed. (Cleveland: World Publishing Company, 1957), 335–47.

13. Hegel, *Logic*, 337; *Logik*, vol. 1, 347.

14. Ibid., 329; *Logik*, vol. 1, 339.

15. Hegel, *Encyclopaedia Logic*, par. 108.

16. Hegel, *Logic*, 367; *Logik*, vol. 1, 379–80.

17. Ibid., 331; *Logik*, vol. 1, 341.

18. Ibid., 332; *Logik*, vol. 1, 342.

19. Hegel, *Encyclopaedia Logic*, par. 109.

20. Ibid., par. 104.

21. Ibid., par. 107.

22. Ibid., par. 117, add.

23. Hegel, *Logic*, 375–76; *Logik*, vol. 1, 387–88.

24. Ibid., 375; *Logik*, vol. 1, 387–88.

25. Ibid., 383–84; *Logik*, vol. 1, 397.

26. Hegel, *Encyclopaedia Logic*, par. 96, add.

27. David Fideler, in *The Pythagorean Sourcebook and Library*, ed., trans. Kenneth Sylan Guthrie (Grand Rapids: Phanes Press, 1987), 41–42.

28. Hegel, *The Letters*, no. 514a.

Chapter 7: Neoplatonism and the Logic of Identity

1. G. W. F. Hegel, *The Encyclopaedia Logic, Part 1 of the Encyclopaedia of Philosophical Sciences* (1830), trans. by T. F. Garaets, W. A. Suchting, and H. S. Harris (Indianapolis: Hackett, 1991), par. 140, add.

2. G. W. F. Hegel, *Science of Logic*, trans. A. V. Miller (London: Allen and Unwin, 1969), 391; *Die Wissenschaft der Logik*, vol. 2, ed. Georg Lasson (Hamburg: meiner, 1969–74), 5–6.

3. Hegel, *Encyclopaedia*, par. 112.

4. Hegel, *Logik*, vol. 1, 397.

5. Ibid., 383–84; *Logik*, vol. 1, 397.

6. Hegel, *Encyclopaedia*, par. 112, add.

7. Ibid., par. 159.

8. Hegel, *Logic*, 605; *Logik*, vol. 2, 244–45.

9. Hegel, *Encyclopaedia*, par. 163, add.

10. Hegel, *Logic*, 550; *Logik*, vol. 2, 80.

11. Ibid., 389; *Logik*, vol. 2, 3.

12. Hegel, *Encyclopaedia*, par. 111.

13. Ibid., par. 113.

14. Ibid., par. 111, add.

15. Ibid., par. 111, add. 112.

16. Ibid., par. 112, add.

17. Ibid., par. 131.

18. Ibid., par. 136.

19. Gary Shapiro, "Notes on the Animal Kingdom of the Spirit," *Clio* 8, no. 3 (1979), 335, 337; Donald Verene, *Hegel's Recollection: A Study of Images in the "Phenomenology of Spirit"* (Albany: State University of New York Press, 1985), ix–x. Verene concedes that metaphor is less frequent in the *Logic*. We find it is still present in the *Logic*, though perhaps not irreducibly so.

20. Verene, *Hegel's Recollection*, 112.

21. Hegel, *Encyclopaedia Logic*, par. 112, add.

22. Hegel, *Logic*, 401; *Logik*, vol. 2, 15.

23. Ibid., 400; *Logik*, vol. 2, 14.

24. Ibid.

25. Ibid., 399; *Logik*, vol. 2, 13.

26. Ibid.

27. Hegel, *Encyclopaedia Logic*, par. 112, add.

28. Ibid., par. 112.

29. Hegel, *Logic*, 58; *Logik*, vol. 1, 40.

30. Ibid., 382–84; *Logik*, vol. 2, 396.

31. Ibid., 411; *Logik*, vol. 2, 26.

32. G. W. F. Hegel, *Lectures on the History of Philosophy*, vol. 2, trans. E. S. Haldane and Frances Simson (New York: Humanities Press, 1974), 114; *Sämtliche Werke*, vol. 19, ed. Hermann Glockner (Stuttgart: Frommann, 1926), 48–49.

33. Ibid., vol. 2, 413–14; *Sämtliche Werke*, vol. 19, 48–49.

34. Hegel, *Logic*, 413–15; *Logik*, vol. 2, 28–30.

35. Hegel, *Encyclopaedia Logic*, par. 117, add.

36. Ibid, par. 106, add.

37. Ibid., par. 19. Hegel, *Logic*, 424–27; *Logik*, vol. 2, 40–44.

38. Hegel, *Logic*, 431–32; *Logik*, vol. 2, 49–50.

39. Ibid., 440; *Logik*, vol. 2, 59.

40. Clark Butler, "Motion and Objective Contradiction," *American Philosophical Quarterly* 18, no. 2 (1981), 131–39.

41. Hegel, *Logic*, 440; *Logik*, vol. 2, 59.

42. Ibid., 440–41; *Logik*, vol. 2, 59–60.

43. Ibid., 440; *Logik*, vol. 2, 59.

44. Ibid., 435; *Logik*, vol. 2, 53.

45. Hegel, *Encyclopaedia Logic*, par. 122.

Chapter 8: The Deterministic Theology of the Explanatory Ground

1. G. W. F. Hegel, *The Encyclopaedia Logic, Part 1 of the Encyclopaedia of Philosophical Sciences* (1830), trans. T. F. Garaets, W. A. Suchting, and H. S. Harris (Indianapolis: Hackett, 1991), par. 115.

2. Ibid.

3. Ibid.

4. Ibid., par. 112.

5. G. W. F. Hegel, *Science of Logic*, trans. A. V. Miller (London: Allen and Unwin, 1969), 389–90; *Die Wissenschaft der Logik*, vol. 2, ed. Georg Lasson (Hamburg: Meiner, 1969–74), 3–4.

6. Ibid., 411–12; *Logik*, vol. 2, 26–27.

7. G. W. F. Hegel, *The Letters*, trans. Clark Butler and Christiane Seiler, with commentary by Clark Butler (Bloomington: Indiana University Press, 1984), 82.

8. Hegel, *Encyclopaedia Logic*, par. 115.

9. Hegel, *Logic*, 45; *Logik*, vol 1, 26.

10. Ibid., 172; *Logik*, vol. 1, 163.

11. Ibid., 391; *Logik*, vol. 2, 5.

12. Hegel, *Encyclopaedia Logic*, par. 115.

13. *Selections from Early Greek Philosophy*, ed. Milton Nahm (New York: Appleton-Century Crofts), 152–65.

14. Hegel, *Logic*, 50; *Logik*, vol. 1, 31.

15. Hegel, *Encyclopaedia Logic*, par. 112, add.

16. *Selections*, ed. Nahm, 161.

17. Ibid., 67–68.

18. Hegel, *Logic*, 458–61; *Logik*, vol. 1, 78–82.

19. Hegel, *Encyclopaedia Logic*, par. 120.

20. Hegel, *Logic*, 442–43; *Logik*, vol. 2, 62.

21. Hegel, *Encyclopaedia Logic*, par. 119, add.

22. Hegel, *Logic*, 442; *Logik*, vol. 2, 62.

23. Hegel, *Encyclopaedia Logic*, par. 121, add.

24. Ibid.

25. Hegel, *Logic*, 444; *Logik*, vol. 2, 63.

26. Ibid., 446; *Logik*, vol. 2, 65.

27. Ibid., 453–54; *Logik*, vol. 2, 73–74.

28. Ibid., 461; *Logik*, vol. 2, 82.

29. Ibid., 456; *Logik*, vol. 2, 76.

30. Ibid., 463; *Logik*, vol. 2, 84.

31. Ibid., 458; *Logik*, vol. 2, 78–79.

32. Willard van Orman Quine, *Methods of Logic*, 4th ed. (Cambridge: Harvard University Press, 1982), 194.

33. Hegel, *Logic*, 395; *Logik*, vol. 2, 8–9.

34. Quine, *Methods of Logic*, 194–95.

35. Hegel, *Logic*, 713–14; *Logik*, vol. 2, 366–67.

36. G. W. F. Hegel, *Phenomenology of Spirit*, trans. A.V. Miller (Oxford: Oxford University Press, 1977), 84; *Phänomenologie des Geistes*, ed. Wolfgang Bonsiepen and Reinhard Heede (Hamburg: Meiner, 1980), 85–86.

37. Hegel, *Logic*, 503; *Logik*, vol. 2, 127.

38. Ibid., 476–77; *Logik*, vol. 2, 98–99.

39. Ibid., 469; *Logik*, vol. 2, 90–91.

40. Ibid., 472; *Logik*, vol. 2, 94.

41. Ibid., 477; *Logik*, vol. 2, 99.

42. Ibid., 478, 481; *Logik*, vol. 2, 100, 102.

43. Ibid., 411–12; *Logik*, vol. 2, 26–27.

44. Ibid., 412–13; *Logik*, vol. 2, 26–29.

45. Hegel, *Encyclopaedia Logic*, par. 115.

46. Ibid., par. 112.

47. G. W. F. Hegel, *Lectures on the History of Philosophy*, vol. 2, trans. E. S. Haldane and Frances Simson (New York: Humanities Press, 1974), 414; *Sämtliche Werke*, vol. 19, ed. Hermann Glockner (Stuttgart: Frommann, 1926), 48–49.

48. Hegel, *Encyclopaedia Logic*, par. 120–21.

Chapter 9: The Phenomenalistic Definition of the Absolute

1. G. W. F. Hegel, *Science of Logic*, trans. A. V. Miller (London: Allen and Unwin, 1969), 474–84; *Die Wissenschaft der Logik*, vol. 2, ed. Georg Lasson (Hamburg: Meiner, 1969–74), 97–105.

2. Ibid., 488; *Logik*, vol. 2, 110.

3. Ibid., 488–89; *Logik*, vol. 2, 110–11.

4. Ibid., 478; *Logik*, vol. 2, 100.

5. Ibid., 487–88; *Logik*, vol. 2, 109–10.

6. Ibid., 491–92; *Logik*, vol. 2, 113–14.

7. G. W. F. Hegel, *The Encyclopaedia Logic, Part 1 of the Encyclopaedia of Philosophical Sciences* (1830), trans. T. F. Garaets, W. A. Suchting, and H. S. Harris (Indianapolis: Hackett, 1991), par. 126, add.

8. Hegel, *Logic*, 493–94; *Logik*, vol. 2, 115–17.

9. Ibid., 495–96; *Logik*, vol. 2, 118–19.

10. Ibid., 498; *Logik*, vol. 2, 121.

11. Hegel, *Encyclopaedia Logic*, par. 126.

12. Ibid., par. 126, add.

13. Ibid., par. 129.

14. Ibid., par. 128.

15. Ibid., par. 129.

16. Ibid., par. 130.

17. Hegel, *Logic*, 502–3; *Logik*, vol. 2, 126–27.

18. Ibid., 503; *Logik*, vol. 2, 127–28.

19. Ibid., 504; *Logik*, vol. 2, 128.

20. Ibid., 506–9; *Logik*, vol. 2, 130–34.

21. G. W. F. Hegel, *Phenomenology of Spirit*, trans. A. V. Miller (Oxford: Oxford University Press, 1977), 96–98; *Die Phänomenologie des Geistes*, ed. Wolfgang Bonsiepen and Reinhard Heede (Hamburg: Meiner, 1980), 96–99.

22. Hegel, *Logic*, 519; *Logik*, vol. 2, 145.

23. Hegel, *Phenomenology*, 90; *Phänomenologie*, 91. Hegel, *Encyclopaedia*, 136.

24. Hegel, *Logic*, 518; *Logik*, vol. 2, 144.

25. Ibid., 513; *Logik*, vol. 2, 138.

26. Ibid., 518–19; *Logik*, vol. 2, 144–45.

27. Hegel, *Encyclopaedia Logic*, par. 135.

28. Hegel, *Logic*, 518–19; *Logik*, vol. 2, 144–45.

29. Ibid., 523–24; *Logik*, vol. 2, 150.

30. Hegel, *Encyclopaedia Logic*, par. 140, add.

Chapter 10: Scientific Realism and Self-Manifesting Actual Reality

1. G. W. F. Hegel, *Science of Logic*, trans. A.V. Miller (London: Allen and Unwin, 1969), 550; *Die Wissenschaft der Logik*, vol. 2, ed. Georg Lasson (Hamburg: Meiner, 1969–74), 180. George di Giovanni ("The Category of Contingency in the Hegelian Dialectic," in *Art and Logic in Hegel's Philosophy* [New Jersey: Humanities Press, 1980], 196–97) recalls that this special concept of necessity—"the blind necessity of chance" in contrast to the general necessity of natural law—goes back to Aristotle's sea battle discussion (*De Interpretatione*, chap. 9).

2. G. W. F. Hegel, *The Encyclopaedia Logic, Part 1 of the Encyclopaedia of Philosophical Sciences* (1830), trans. T. F. Garaets, W. A. Suchting, and H. S. Harris (Indianapolis: Hackett, 1991), pars. 139–40.

3. David Hume, *A Treatise of Human Nature*, ed. L. A. Selby-Bigge (Oxford: Oxford University Press, 1967), 173–74.

4. Hegel, *Logic*, 505–9; *Logik*, vol. 2, 129–34.

5. Peter Forrest, "Why Most of Us Should Be Scientific Realists," *The Monist* 77, no. 1 (1994), 54.

6. Hegel, *Logic*, 529; *Logik*, vol. 2; 156.

7. Hegel, *Encyclopaedia Logic*, pars. 142, 149.

8. Clark Butler, "The Place of Process Cosmology in Absolute Idealism," *Owl of Minerva* 16, no. 2 (1985), 161–74.

9. Hegel, *Logic*, 106; *Logik*, vol. 2, 99.

10. Hegel, *Encyclopaedia Logic*, par. 148.

11. Hegel, *Logic*, 529; *Logik*, vol. 2, 156.

12. Hegel, *Encyclopaedia Logic*, par. 143.

13. Hegel, *Logic*, 546; *Logik*, vol. 2, 175–76.

14. Ibid., 545; *Logik*, vol. 2, 174.

15. Ibid., 546; *Logik*, vol. 2, 175–76.

16. Hegel, *Encyclopaedia Logic*, par. 6. Hegel comments on the famous preface to the *Philosophy of Right*.

17. G. W. F. Hegel, *Sämtliche Werke*, vol. 2, ed. Hermann Glockner (Stuttgart: Frommann, 1926), vol. 292.

18. Ibid.; G. W. F. Hegel, "Review of Göschel's *Aphorisms*," trans. Clark Butler, *Clio* 17, no. 4 (1988), 384.

19. Hegel, *Encyclopaedia Logic*, par. 131.

20. Ibid., pars. 150–51.

21. Hegel, *Logic*, 529; *Logik*, vol. 2, 156.

22. Hegel, *Encyclopaedia Logic*, par. 136.

23. Hegel, *Logic*, 530, 532, 536; *Logik*, vol. 2, 157, 160, 164.

24. Ibid., 556, 558, 567; *Logik*, vol. 2, 187, 189, 200. Hegel, *Encyclopaedia Logic*, par. 151.

25. B. Spinoza, *Ethics*, part 4, prop. 3.

26. Hegel, *Logic*, 559; *Logik*, vol. 2, 191.

27. Ibid., 390; *Logik*, vol. 2, 4.

28. Hegel, *Encyclopaedia Logic*, pars. 154–55; 158, add.

29. Hegel, *Logic*, 521; *Logik*, vol. 2, 147.

30. Ibid., 570–71; *Logik*, vol. 2, 203–4. Hegel, *Encyclopaedia Logic*, pars. 158–59.

31. G. W. F. Hegel, *The Letters*, trans. Clark Butler and Christiane Seiler, with commentary by Clark Butler (Bloomington: Indiana University Press, 1984), no. 123.

32. Hegel, *Logic*, 529; *Logik*, vol. 2, 156.

33. Ibid., 578; *Logik*, vol. 2, 214.

34. G. W. F. Hegel, *Encyclopaedia of Philosophical Sciences*, trans. W. Wallace and A. V. Miller (Oxford: Oxford University Press, 1892–1975), par. 377, add.

35. *Encyclopaedia Logic*, par. 123.

36. Ibid., par. 122; 123, add.

37. Ibid., pars. 158–59. Hegel, *Logic*, 577–83, 834; *Logik*, vol. 2, 213–21, 495.

38. Hegel, *Logic*, 571; *Logik*, vol. 2, 204–5.

39. Hegel, *Encyclopaedia Logic*, par. 147.

40. The idea of the necessity of contingency, as John Burbidge points out ("The Necessity of Contingency," in *Art and Logic in Hegel's Philosophy* [New Jersey: Humanities Press, 1980], 201), was revived by Dieter Henrich ("Hegel's Theorie über den Zufall," *Kantstudien* 50 [1958–59], 135). Contingency is indeed a logical necessity inherent in any realization of possibility. But it is consistent with Burbidge to likewise speak of the contingency of absolute necessity, of an all-embracing process circling between real possibility and actual determinate occurrence which might have been otherwise (Burbidge, 213).

41. Hegel, *Logic*, 550; *Logik*, vol. 2, 180.

42. Hegel, *Encyclopaedia Logic*, par. 143.

43. John Hoffmeyer, *The Advent of Freedom: The Presence of the Future in Hegel's Logic* (London: Associated University Presses, 1994).

44. Hegel, *Logic*, 533–39; *Logik*, vol. 2, 160–61. Hegel, *Encyclopaedia Logic*, par. 151.

45. Hegel, *Encyclopaedia Logic*, par. 151, add.

46. Hegel, *Logic*, 536–37; *Logik*, vol. 2, 164–65.

47. Ibid, 554; *Logik*, vol. 2, 184–85.

48. Ibid, 537; *Logik*, vol. 2, 165.

49. Spinoza, *Ethics*, part 1, def. 4.

50. Hegel, *Logic*, 536–37; *Logik*, vol. 2, 164–65.

51. Christian Hermann Weisse, in Hegel, *The Letters*, 539–40.

52. Hegel, *Logic*, 554; *Logik*, vol. 2, 184–85. Hegel, *Encyclopaedia Logic*, par. 151.

53. Hegel, *Encyclopaedia Logic*, par. 149.

54. Ibid., pars. 150–51.

55. Ibid., par. 150.

56. Ibid., par. 148c.

57. Hegel, *Logic*, 532, 536, 542; *Logik*, vol. 2, 160, 164, 170.

58. Ibid., 552; *Logik*, vol. 2, 183.

59. Ibid., 542–53; *Logik*, vol. 171–84.

60. Ibid., 552–53; *Logik*, vol. 2, 183–84.

61. Ibid., 553; *Logik*, vol. 2, 184.

62. Hegel, *Encyclopaedia Logic*, par. 159.

63. Hegel, *Logic*, 566; *Logik*, vol. 2, 198–99.

64. Ibid., 521; *Logik*, vol. 2, 147.

65. Ibid., 558, 567; *Logik*, vol. 2, 189, 199.

66. Ibid., 567–68; *Logik*, vol. 2, 199–200.

67. Ibid., 569–70; *Logik*, vol. 2, 202–3.

68. Ibid., 571; *Logik*, vol. 2, 204–5.

69. Spinoza, *Ethics*, part 5, prop. 36.

70. Hegel, *Logic*, 492; *Logik*, vol. 2, 119.

Chapter 11: The Subjective Self-Concept and Its Passage into Judgment

1. G. W. F. Hegel, *The Encyclopaedia Logic, Part 1 of the Encyclopaedia of Philosophical Sciences* (1830), trans. T. F. Garaets, W. A. Suchting, and H. S. Harris (Indianapolis: Hackett, 1991), par. 114.

2. Ibid., par. 124, add.

3. Ibid., par. 161.

4. G. W. F. Hegel, *Science of Logic*, trans. A.V. Miller (London: Allen and Unwin, 1969), 600; *Die Wissenschaft der Logik*, vol. 2, ed. Georg Lasson (Hamburg: Meiner, 1969–74), 239.

5. Ibid., 604–605; *Logik*, vol. 2, 243–45.

6. Ibid.

7. Ibid., 584; *Logik*, vol. 2, 221.

8. Ibid., 824; *Logik*, vol. 2, 484.

9. G. W. F. Hegel, "Review of Göschel's *Aphorisms*," trans. Clark Butler, *Clio* 17, no. 4 (1988), 382; *Sämtliche Werke*, vol. 20, ed. Hermann Glockner (Stuttgart: Frommann, 1926), 291.

10. Hegel, *Encyclopaedia Logic*, par. 161, add.

11. G. W. F. Hegel, *Phenomenology of Spirit*, trans. A.V. Miller (Oxford: Oxford University Press, 1977), 36–38; *Die Phänomenologie des Geistes*, ed. Wolfgang Bonsiepen and Reinhard Heede (Hamburg: Meiner, 1980), 42–44.

12. John N. Findlay, *Hegel: A Re-examination* (New York: Macmillan, 1958), 230–31.

13. Hegel, *Encyclopaedia Logic*, par. 169, add.

14. Hegel, *Logic*, 661–63; *Logik*, vol. 2, 306–8.

15. Ibid., 625; *Logik*, vol. 2, 266–67.

16. Donald Davidson, *Essays on Action and Events* (Oxford: Oxford University Press, 1980), 106–7.

17. Hegel, *Encyclopaedia Logic*, par. 166.

18. Errol Harris, *An Interpretation of Hegel's Logic* (Lanham: University Press of America), 228.

19. G. W. F. Hegel, *Encyclopaedia of Philosophical Sciences*, trans. W. Wallace and A. V. Miller (Oxford: Oxford University Press, 1892–1975), par. 246, add.

20. G. W. F. Hegel, *Lectures on the History of Philosophy*, trans. E. S. Haldane and Frances Simson (New York: Humanities Press, 1974), vol. 3, 217ff.; *Sämtliche Werke*, vol. 9, 328ff.

21. Hegel, *Logic*, 625; *Logik*, vol. 2, 266–67.

22. Hegel, *Lectures on the History of Philosophy*, vol. 3, 228–30; *Sämtliche Werke*, vol. 19, 339–41.

23. Ibid., vol. 3, 220, 251–52; *Sämtliche Werke*, vol. 19, 330, 367.

24. Ibid., vol. 3, 228; *Sämtliche Werke*, vol. 19, 339.

25. Ibid., vol. 3, 224, 240–41.

26. Davidson, *Essays*, 108.

27. Ibid.

28. Hegel, "Review of Göschel's *Aphorisms*," 391; *Sämtliche Werke*, vol. 20, 304.

29. Hegel, *Logic*, 57; *Logik*, vol. 1, 39–40.

30. Hegel, *Encyclopaedia Logic*, par. 171.

31. Hegel, *Logic*, 631; *Logik*, vol. 2, 273.

32. Ibid., 636; *Logik*, vol. 2, 278.

33. Ibid., 641; *Logik*, vol. 2, 284.

34. Ibid., 633; *Logik*, vol. 2, 275.

35. Ibid., 636; *Logik*, vol. 2, 278.

36. Ibid., 644; *Logik*, vol. 2, 287.

37. Ibid., 643; *Logik*, vol. 2, 286.

38. Ibid., 645; *Logik*, vol. 2, 288.

39. Ibid., 645–47; *Logik*, vol. 2, 288–90.

40. Ibid., 645; *Logik*, vol. 2, 288.

41. Ibid., 647–50; *Logik*, vol. 2, 290–92.

42. Ibid., 645; *Logik*, vol. 2, 288.

43. Hegel, *Encyclopaedia Logic*, par. 174.

44. Hegel, *Logic*, 645; *Logik*, vol. 2, 287–88.

45. Ibid., 649; *Logik*, vol. 2, 292–93.

46. Ibid., 650; *Logik*, vol. 2, 293–94.

47. Ibid., 654; *Logik*, vol. 2, 298.

48. Hegel, *Encyclopaedia Logic*, par. 178.

49. Hegel, *Logic*, 659; *Logik*, vol. 2, 303.

50. Ibid., 660; *Logik*, vol. 2, 303.

51. Ibid., 661; *Logik*, vol. 2, 306.

52. Ibid., 662; *Logik*, vol. 2, 306.

Chapter 12: Theology of the Rational Syllogism

1. G. W. F. Hegel, *The Encyclopaedia Logic, Part 1 of the Encyclopaedia of Philosophical Sciences* (1830), trans. T. F. Garaets, W. A. Suchting, and H. S. Harris (Indianapolis: Hackett, 1991), par. 114.

2. G. W. F. Hegel, *Science of Logic*, trans. A. V. Miller (London: Allen and

Unwin, 1969), 709; *Die Wissenschaft der Logik*, vol. 2, ed. Georg Lasson (Hamburg: Meiner, 1969–74), 358. Hegel, *Encyclopaedia Logic*, par. 193.

3. Hegel, *Logic*, 709–10; *Logik*, vol. 2, 358–59.

4. Ibid., 711; *Logik*, vol. 2, 359–60.

5. Ibid., 712; *Logik*, vol. 2, 361.

6. Ibid., 752–53; *Logik*, vol. 2, 404–5.

7. Ibid.

8. Ibid., 711; *Logik*, vol. 2, 360.

9. Ibid., 584ff., 709; *Logik*, vol. 2, 221ff., 358. G. W. F. Hegel, *Lectures on the History of Philosophy*, vol. 3, trans. E. S. Haldane and Frances Simson (New York: Humanities Press, 1974), 409–10, 515–16; *Sämtliche Werke*, vol. 19, ed. Hermann Glockner (Stuttgart: Frommann, 1926), 534–35, 650–52.

10. Hegel, *Logik*, 592; *Logik*, vol. 2, 230–31.

11. Hegel, *Encyclopaedia Logic*, par. 181.

12. Ibid., par. 192, add. 193.

13. Ibid., par. 182.

14. Hegel, *Logic*, 681, 686; *Logik*, vol. 2, 327–28, 333.

15. Ibid., 823; *Logik*, vol. 2, 483.

16. G. W. F. Hegel, *The Letters*, trans. Clark Butler and Christiane Seiler, with commentary by Clark Butler (Bloomington: Indiana University Press, 1984), Hoffmeister nos. 133, 175, 261, 263, 277, 279, 281–82, 285; *Briefe von und an Hegel*, ed. Johannes Hoffmeister (Hamburg: Meiner, 1952–54), nos. 133, 175, 261, 263, 277, 279, 281–82, 285.

17. Hegel, *Logic*, 667; *Logik*, vol. 2, 311.

18. Ibid., 674; *Logik*, vol. 2, 319–20.

19. Ibid., 681–82; *Logik*, vol. 2, 328.

20. G. W. F. Hegel, *Lectures on the Philosophy of Religion* (1827), trans. R. F. Brown, et al. (Berkeley: University of California Press, 1988), 415.

21. Ibid., 416–17.

22. Hegel, *Encyclopaedia Logic*, par. 181.

23. Hegel, *Logic*, 664; *Logik*, vol. 2, 308.

24. Hegel, *Encyclopaedia Logic*, par. 179.

25. Ibid., par. 181.

26. Ibid., par. 187, add.

27. Ibid., pars. 575–77.

28. Ibid., par. 182.

29. Ibid.

30. Ibid.

31. Ibid., par. 575.

32. Ibid., par. 576.

33. Ibid., par. 575.

34. Ibid., par. 576.

35. Ibid.

36. Hegel, *Logic*, 588; *Logik*, vol. 2, 226.

37. G. W. F. Hegel, *Phenomenology of Spirit*, trans. A.V. Miller (Oxford: Oxford University Press, 1977), 10; *Die Phänomenologie des Geistes*, ed. Wolfgang Bonsiepen and Reinhard Heede (Hamburg: Meiner, 1980), 18.

38. Ibid., 14; *Phänomenologie*, 22.

39. G. W. F. Hegel, *Encyclopaedia of Philosophical Sciences*, trans. W. Wallace and A. V. Miller (Oxford: Oxford University Press, 1892–1975), par. 577.

40. G. W. F. Hegel, "Review of Göschel's *Aphorisms*," trans. Clark Butler, *Clio* 17, no. 4 (1988), 391; *Sämtliche Werke*, vol. 20, 304.

41. Giacomo Rinaldi, *A History and Interpretation of the Logic of Hegel* (Lewiston: Edwin Mellen, 1992), 135–36, n. 20, 291–92; B. Lakebrink, *Kommentar zu Hegel's "Logik,"* vol. 1 (Freiburg: Alber, 1979), 98.

42. Hegel, *Logic*, 665; *Logik*, vol. 2, 309–10.

43. Ibid., 665–66; *Logik*, vol. 2, 310.

44. Ibid, 665; *Logik*, vol. 2, 310.

45. Ibid.

46. Hegel, *Encyclopaedia of Philosophical Sciences*, par. 246, add., 402, add. See also Clark Butler, "Hermeneutic Hegelianism," *Idealistic Studies* 15, no. 2 (1985), 124–28. I find myself (and Hegel) disagreeing with both Stephen Houlgate and Joseph Flay in *Owl of Minerva* 24, no. 22 (Spring 1993). Flay writes in "Hegel's Metaphysics" that this metaphysics arises not only from the way we must think being or think what is, from the way being or what-is is actually structured" (ibid., 152). Houlgate writes in reply that the "task of the *Phenomenology* is to undo the distinction upon which the idea of a relation between thought and being rests, and so to bring thought the recognition that it has the capacity to determine by itself the meaning of being (in the *Science of Logic*)" (ibid., 160). But, taking Hegel's conceptualism seriously, I cannot suppose that "the way being is actually structured" imposes itself on thought, nor that the distinction between being and thought is so dissolved that thought determines out of itself the meaning of being. Thought abstracts the conceptual meaning of being from preconceptualized being. The self-conceptualizing absolute includes both thought and a preconceptualized residue of being which is only in part explicitly conceptualized by the system. The system of spirit with its universal concepts only approximates spirit, though ever more closely as it develops the direction of spirit in its singularity, which includes this its own self-comprehension.

47. Hegel, Ibid., 685–86; *Logik*, vol. 2, 332.

48. Ibid., 703; *Logik*, vol. 2, 351.

49. Hegel, *Encyclopaedia Logic*, par. 188.

50. Hegel, *Logic*, 701; *Logic*, vol. 2, 349–50.

51. Hegel, *Encyclopaedia Logic*, par. 190.

52. Hegel, *Logic*, 696; *Logik*, vol. 2, 344.

53. Ibid., 701; *Logik*, vol. 2, 349.

54. Ibid., 666, 703–4; *Logik*, vol. 2, 310, 351–52.

55. Ibid., 669; *Logik*, vol. 2, 314.

Chapter 13: The Objective Self-Concept

1. G. W. F. Hegel, *Science of Logic*, trans. A.V. Miller (Allen and Unwin: 1969), 682; *Die Wissenschaft der Logik*, vol. 2, ed. Georg Lasson (Hamburg: Meiner, 1969–74), 328.

2. Ibid.

3. G. W. F. Hegel, *The Encyclopaedia Logic, Part 1 of the Encyclopaedia of Philosophical Sciences* (1830), trans. T. F. Garaets, W. A. Suchting, and H. S. Harris (Indianapolis: Hackett, 1991), par. 193.

4. Hegel, *Logic*, 665; *Logik*, vol. 2, 310.

5. Ibid.

6. Ibid.

7. Ibid., 128–29; *Logik*, vol. 1, 116.

8. Ibid., 665; *Logik*, vol. 2, 309.

9. Hegel, *Encyclopaedia Logic*, par. 114.

10. Hegel, *Logic*, 45; *Logik*, vol. 1, 26.

11. G. W. F. Hegel, *Encyclopaedia of Philosophical Sciences*, trans. W. Wallace and A. V. Miller (Oxford: Oxford University Press, 1892–1975), par. 467, add.

12. Hegel, *Logic*, 711; *Logik*, vol. 2, 360.

13. Diogenes Laertius, *Lives and Opinions of Those Who have Rendered Themselves Illustrious in Philosophy with a Summary Collection of the Doctrines of Each School*, published as *Lives of Eminent Philosophers*, 2 vols., trans. R. D. Hicks (Cambridge: Harvard University Press, 1925).

14. Wilhelm Gottlieb Tennemann, *Geschichte der Philosophie*, 11 vols. (Jena: 1798–1819).

15. G. W. F. Hegel, *Lectures on the History of Philosophy*, vol. 1, ed. E. S. Haldane and Frances Simson (Atlantic Highlands: Humanities Press, 1974), 11; *Sämtliche Werke*, vol. 17, ed. Hermann Glockner (Stuttgart: Frommann, 1926), 138–39.

16. Karl Rosenkranz, in *Hegel in Berichten seiner Zeitgenossen*, ed. Günther Nicolin (Hamburg: Meiner, 1970), 155.

17. Hegel, *Encyclopaedia Logic*, pars. 196, 197. Hegel, *Logic*, 21–23; *Logik*, vol. 2, 371–74.

18. Hegel, *Logic*, 714; *Logik*, vol. 2, 363.

19. Ibid., 711; *Logik*, vol. 2, 360.

20. Henri Bergson, *Le Rire* (Paris: 1900), chap. 1.

21. Hegel, *Logic*, 711; *Logik*, vol. 2, 360.

22. Hegel, *Lectures on the History of Philosophy*, vol. 3, 315; *Sämtliche Werke*, vol. 19, 440.

23. Hegel, *Logic*, 721–22; *Logik*, vol. 2, 371–72.

24. Hegel, *Encyclopaedia Logic*, par. 194.

25. Hegel, *Logic*, 714; *Logik*, vol. 2, 363.

26. Hegel, *Encyclopaedia Logic*, par. 194.

27. Ibid.

28. Ibid., *Logic*, pars. 98, 195, add.

29. Hegel, *Logic*, 713; *Logik*, vol. 2, 362.

30. Ibid., 727; *Logic*, vol. 2, 376.

31. Ibid.

32. Ibid.

33. Ibid., 728; *Logik*, vol. 2, 378.

34. Ibid., 729; *Logik*, vol. 2, 379.

35. Ibid.

36. Ibid., 728; *Logik*, vol. 2, 378.

37. Ibid., 734ff.; *Logik*, vol. 2, 383ff.

38. Ibid., 737; *Logik*, vol. 2, 387. Hegel, *Encyclopaedia Logic*, par. 204.

39. Hegel, *Logic*, 740–43; *Logik*, vol. 2, 391–93. Hegel, *Encyclopaedia*, pars. 205–7.

40. Hegel, *Encyclopaedia Logic*, par. 205.

41. Ibid., par. 143, add.

42. Ibid., par. 205.

43. Ibid.

44. See Ibid., par. 345 on "animal wants."

45. Hegel, *Logic*, 737; *Logik*, vol. 2, 387.

46. Ibid., 740–42; *Logic*, vol. 2, 391–93.

47. Ibid., 750–51; *Logik*, vol. 2, 401–3.

48. Ibid., 740; *Logic*, vol. 2, 391.

49. Hegel, *Encyclopaedia Logic*, par. 204. Hegel, *Logic*, 737; *Logik*, vol. 2, 387.

50. Hegel, *Encyclopaedia Logic*, par. 212, add.

51. Hegel, *Logic*, 743–44; *Logik*, vol. 2, 394–95. Hegel, *Encyclopaedia Logic*, pars. 207–9.

52. Hegel, *Logic*, 751; *Logik*, vol. 2, 403.

53. Ibid., 737; *Logik*, vol. 2, 387.

54. Hegel, *Encyclopaedia Logic*, par. 212.

55. Hegel, *Logic*, 741–42; *Logik*, vol. 2, 392–93.

56. Ibid., 753; *Logik*, vol. 2, 405–6.

57. Ibid., 702; *Logik*, vol. 2, 330.

58. Ibid., 701; *Logik*, vol. 2, 349.

59. Ibid.

60. Ibid., 711; *Logik*, vol. 2, 359–60.

61. Ibid., 709; *Logik*, vol. 2, 358.

62. Ibid., 739, 741, 743, 749; *Logik*, vol. 2, 390, 392, 394, 400. Hegel, *Encyclopaedia*, pars. 206–10.

63. Hegel, *Encyclopaedia Logic*, par. 204.

64. Ibid., par. 181.

65. Hegel, *Logic*, 706–8; *Logik*, vol. 2, 354–56.

66. Ibid., 707; *Logik*, vol. 2, 356.

67. Ibid., 709; *Logik*, vol. 2, 358. Hegel, *Encyclopaedia Logic*, par. 193.

68. Hegel, *Logic*, 708; *Logik*, vol. 2, 356–57.

69. Ibid., 709; *Logik*, vol. 2, 358.

70. Hegel, *Encyclopaedia Logic*, par. 24, add.

71. Hegel, *Logic*, 821, 823, 824, 830; *Logik*, vol. 2, 481, 483, 484, 491.

Chapter 14: The Absolute Idea: The Career of Freedom Grasping Itself in Pure Thought

1. G. W. F. Hegel, *Science of Logic*, trans. A.V. Miller (London: Allen and Unwin, 1969), 823; *Die Wissenschaft der Logik*, vol. 2, ed. Georg Lassson (Hamburg: Meiner, 1969–74), 483.

2. Ibid. *Logic*, 824; *Logik*, vol. 2, 483–84.

3. Ibid., 762; *Logik*, vol. 2, 414–15.

4. Ibid., 753–54; *Logik*, vol. 2, 405–6.

5. Ibid., 768; *Logik*, vol. 2, 421–22.

6. Ibid., 775; *Logik*, vol. 2, 429.

7. Ibid., 818; *Logik*, vol. 2, 477.

8. Ibid., 772; *Logik*, vol. 2, 426.

9. Ibid, 824; *Logik*, vol. 2, 483–44.

10. G. W. F. Hegel, *The Encyclopaedia Logic, Part 1 of the Encyclopaedia of Philosophical Sciences* (1830), trans. T. F. Garaets, W. A. Suchting, and H. S. Harris (Indianapolis: Hackett, 1991), par. 161, add.

11. Hegel, *Logic*, 823; *Logik*, vol. 2, 483.

12. Ibid., 711–54; *Logik*, vol. 2, 359–406.

13. Hegel, *Encyclopaedia Logic*, par. 212. Hegel, *Logic*, 753; *Logik*, vol. 2, 405.

14. Hegel, *Logic*, 775; *Logik*, vol. 2, 429.

15. Ibid., 785; *Logik*, vol. 2, 441.

16. Ibid., 800; *Logik*, vol. 2, 458.

17. G. W. F. Hegel, *Phenomenology of Spirit*, trans. A.V. Miller (Oxford: Oxford University Press, 1977), 149; *Die Phänomenologie des Geistes*, ed. Wolfgang Bonsiepen and Reinhard Heede (Hamburg: Meiner, 1980), 140.

18. Hegel, *Logic*, 806; *Logik*, vol. 2, 464.

19. Hegel, *Phenomenology*, 24; *Phänomenologie*, 31–34.

20. Hegel, *Logic*, 823; *Logik*, vol. 2, 483.

21. Ibid., 818; *Logik*, vol. 2, 477–78.

22. Ibid., 824; *Logik*, vol. 2, 483–84.

23. Hegel, *Encyclopaedia Logic*, par. 233, add.

24. J. N. Findlay, *Hegel: A Re-examination* (London: Macmillan, 1958), 287–88.

25. G. W. F. Hegel, *Encyclopaedia of Philosophical Sciences*, trans. W. Wallace and A. V. Miller (Oxford: Oxford University Press, 1892–1975), par. 376.

26. G. W. F. Hegel, *Lectures on Fine Arts*, trans. T. M. Knox (Oxford: Oxford University Press, 1975), 1064; *Sämtliche Werke*, vol. 14, ed. Hermann Glockner (Stuttgart: Frommann, 1926), 357–58.

27. G. W. F. Hegel, "Earliest System-Programme of German Idealism," in H. S. Harris, *Hegel's Development Toward the Sunlight* (Oxford: Oxford University Press, 1972), 511.

28. G. W. F. Hegel, *The Letters*, trans. Clark Butler and Christiane Seiler, with commentary by Clark Butler (Bloomington: Indiana University Press, 1984), Hoffmeister no. 29; *Briefe von und an Hegel*, ed. Johannes Hoffmeister (Hamburg: Meiner, 1952–54), no. 29.

29. Ibid., Hoffmeister no. 85. G. W. F. Hegel, *Lectures on the Philosophy of History*, trans. J. Sibree (New York: Dover, 1956), 453; *Sämtliche Werke*, vol. 11, 564.

30. Clark Butler, "Hegelian Panentheism as Joachimite Christianity," in *New Perspectives on Hegel's Philosophy of Religion*, ed. David Kolb (Albany: State University of New York Press, 1992), 140–41.

31. Hegel, *Logic,* 824; *Logik,* vol. 2, 483–84.

32. Findlay, *Hegel,* 267.

33. J. Biard, et al., *Introduction à la lectures de la science de la logique de Hegel,* vol. 3 (Paris: Aubier, 1981–87), 484; John Burbidge, *On Hegel's Logic* (Atlantic Highlands: Humanities Press, 1982), 220–21; Errol Harris, *An Interpretation of the Logic of Hegel* (Lanham: University Press of America, 1983), 287; John E. McTaggart, *A Commentary on Hegel's Logic* (Cambridge: Cambridge University Press, 1910), 309; G. R. G. Mure, *A Study of Hegel's Logic* (Oxford: Oxford University Press, 1950), 291.

34. B. Lakebrink, *Kommentar zur Hegels "Logik"* (Freiburg: Alber, 1979), 98.

35. Giacomo Rinaldi, *A History and Interpretation of the Logic of Hegel* (Lewiston: Edwin Mellen Press, 1992), 291.

36. Ibid., 333–34.

37. Claude Lévi-Strauss, *The Savage Mind* (Chicago: University of Chicago Press, 1966), 254.

38. Hegel, *The Letters,* Hoffmeister no. 422.

39. Hegel, *Phenomenology,* 217; *Phänomenologie,* 198.

40. Hegel, *Logic,* 824; *Logic,* vol. 2, 484.

41. Frederick Beiser, "Introduction," in Hegel, *Lectures on the History of Philosophy,* vol. 1 (Lincoln: University of Nebraska Press, 1995), xxix.

42. Hegel, *Phenomenology,* 43; *Phänomenologie,* 49.

43. Jürgen Habermas, "Wahrheitstheorien," in *Wirklichkeit und Reflexion: Festschrift für Walter Schulz* (Pfullingen: Neske, 1973), 219. See also Jürgen Habermas, *Remarks on Discourse Ethics,* trans. Ciaran Cronin (Cambridge: MIT Press, 1993).

44. Chaïm Perelman, "Can the Rights of Man be Founded?" in *The Philosophy of Human Rights: International Perspectives,* ed. Allen Rosenbaum (Westport: Greenwood Press, 1980), 50.

Chapter 15: Recapitulation of the Logic

1. G. R. G. Mure, *A Study of Hegel's Logic* (Oxford: Oxford University Press, 1950), 371–72.

2. Hegel, *Science of Logic,* trans. W. H. Johnston and L. G. Struthers (London: Allen and Unwin, 1929), 24–25.

3. G. W. F. Hegel, *The Encyclopaedia Logic: Part 1 of the Encyclopaedia of Philosophical Sciences* (1830), trans. T. F. Garaets, W. A. Suchting, and H. S. Harris (Indianapolis: Hackett, 1991), par. 112.

4. Ibid., par. 83.

5. Ibid., par. 122, add.

6. Ibid., par. 83.

7. Ibid.

8. Parmenides, fr. 3, excerpted in Robert Brumbaugh, *The Philosophers of Greece* (New York: Thomas Crowell, 1964), 51.

9. Socrates on Gorgias in *Orates et Epistolae*, 10, 3, excerpted in Milton Nahm, *Selections from Early Greek Philosophy* (New York: Appleton-Century-Crafts, 1964), 232.

10. Heraclitus, fr. 81, in John Burnet, *Early Greek Philosophy* (New York: Meridian, 1957), 139.

11. Anaximander, as cited by Simplicius in *Simplici in Aristotelis Physicorum Libros Quattor Priores*, in *Selections from Early Greek Philosophy*, 39–40.

12. Diogenes Laertius, trans. Gordon Clark and Isaac Husik, from *Lives and Opinions of Eminent Philosophers*, in *Selections from Early Greek Philosophy*, 155.

13. Aristotle, *Metaphysics*, trans. W. D. Ross, *The Basic Works of Aristotle*, ed. Richard McKeon, book 1, chap. 5.

14. Plotinus, *The Enneads*, trans. Stephen MacKenna, 3rd edition (London: Faber and Faber, 1956), Ennead 5, Sect. 3: 12–12, 395.

15. Strobaeus, in Giovannni Reale, *The Systems of the Hellenistic Age*, trans. John Caton (Albany: State University of New York Press, 1990), 251.

16. Pierre Simon Laplace, *An Essay on the Philosophy of Probabilities* (New York: Dover, 1951), 4.

17. See, e.g., Bertrand Russell, *My Philosophical Development* (New York: Simon and Schuster, 1959), 171.

18. David Hume, *Treatise on Human Nature*, ed. L. A. Selby-Bigge (Oxford: Oxford University Press, 1967), book 1, 87.

19. John Stuart Mill, *A System of Logic* (Toronto: University of Toronto Press, 1974), book 3, 382.

20. Johann Gottfried von Herder, *Reflections on the Philosophy of the History of Mankind*, ed. Frank Manuel (Chicago: University of Chicago Press, 1968), 116–17.

21. Gottfried Wilhelm von Leibniz, "A Vindication of God's Justice," trans. Paul Schrecker and Anne Martin Schrecker, in *Monadology and Other Philosophical Essays* (Indianapolis: Bobbs and Merrill, 1965), pars. 15–16, 116.

22. Alfred North Whitehead, *Process and Reality: An Essay in Cosmology* (New York: Macmillan, 1929), 206–7.

23. Spinoza, *Ethics*, part V, prop. 36.

24. Johann Gottlieb Fichte, *The Science of Rights*, trans. A. E. Kroeger (London: Trübner and Company, 1889), part 2, par. 1.

25. Hegel, *Phenomenology of Spirit*, trans. A. V. Miller (Oxford: Oxford University Press, 1977), 490; *Die Phänomenologie des Geistes*, ed. Wolfgang Bonsiepen and Reinhard Heede (Hamburg: Meiner, 1980), 431.

Chapter 16: Empirical versus Rational Order in the History of Philosophy

1. G. W. F. Hegel, *The Letters*, trans. Clark Butler and Christiane Seiler, with commentary by Clark Butler (Bloomington: Indiana University Press, 1984), Hoffmeister no. 288; *Briefe von und an Hegel*, 3 vols., ed. Johannes Hoffmeister (Hamburg: Meiner, 1952–54), no. 288.

2. G. W. F. Hegel, *Encyclopaedia of Philosophical Sciences*, trans. W. Wallace and A. V. Miller (Oxford: Oxford University Press, 1892–1975), par. 384.

3. Aristotle, *Metaphysics*, trans. W. D. Ross, in *The Basic Works of Aristotle*, ed. Richad McKeon (New York: Random House, 1941), book 1, sec. 5, 985b-986a.

4. John Burnet, *Early Greek Philosophy*, 4th ed. (New York: Meridian, 1957), 295.

5. G. W. F. Hegel, *Science of Logic*, trans. A. V. Miller (London: Allen and Unwin, 1969), 187; *Die Wissenschaft der Logik*, vol. 1, ed. Georg Lasson (Hamburg: Meiner, 1969–74), 177.

6. Burnet, *Early Greek Philosophy*, 333–36.

7. Ibid.

8. Ibid., 366.

9. Ibid., 335.

10. Ibid., 336.

11. Clark Butler, "Hegelian Panentheism as Joachimite Christianity," in *New Perspectives on Hegel's Philosophy of Religion*, ed. David Kolb (Albany: State University of New York Press, 1992), 131–42.

12. G. W. F. Hegel, "Review of Göschel's *Aphorisms*," trans. Clark Butler, *Clio* 17, no. 4 (1988), 382; *Sämtliche Werke*, vol. 20, ed. Hermann Glockner (Stuttgart: Frommann, 1926), 310.

13. Ibid., 373; *Sämtliche Werke*, vol. 20, 278.

14. G. W. F. Hegel, *Lectures on the Philosophy of History*, trans. J. Sibree (New York: Dover, 1956), 56; *Sämtliche Werke*, vol. 11, 92.

15. H. S. Harris, *Hegel's Development: Toward the Sunlight* (Oxford: Oxford University Press, 1972), 149, 361–62.

16. Daniel Graham, "The Structure of Explanation in the History of Philosophy," *Metaphilosophy* 19 (April 1988), 169.

17. G. W. F. Hegel, *The Encyclopaedia Logic, Part 1 of the Encyclopaedia of Philosophical Sciences* (1830), trans. T. F. Garaets, W. A. Suchting, and H. S. Harris (Indianapolis: Hackett, 1991), par. 86, add.

18. Ibid., par. 112.

Bibliography

Ahlers, Rolf. "The Overcoming of Critical Theory in the Hegelian Unity of Theory and Praxis." *Clio* 8, no. 1 (1978).

Aristotle. *The Basic Works of Aristotle.* Edited by Richard McKeon. New York: Random House, 1941.

Baptist, Gabrielle. "Ways and Loci of Modality: The Chapter 'Actuality' in the *Science of Logic* between Its Absence in Jena and Its Disappearance in Berlin." In *Essays in Hegel's Logic,* edited by George di Giovannni. Albany: State University of New York Press, 1990.

Beiser, Frederick. "Introduction." In G. W. F. Hegel, *Lectures on the History of Philosophy.* Vol. 1. Lincoln: University of Nebraska Press, 1995.

Bergson, Henri. *Le Rire.* Chap. 1. Paris, 1900.

Biard, J., et al. *Introduction à la lecture de la science de la logique de Hegel.* 3 vols. Paris: Aubier, 1981–87.

Bradley, F. H. *Appearance and Reality.* Oxford: Oxford University Press, 1930.

Brumbaugh, Robert. *The Philosophers of Greece.* New York: Thomas Crowell, 1964.

Burbidge, John. *On Hegel's Logic.* Atlantic Highlands: Humanities Press, 1981.

———— "The Necessity of Contingency." In *Art and Logic in Hegel's Philosophy,* 201–17. New Jersey: Humanities Press, 1980.

Burnet, John. *Early Greek Philosophy.* 4th ed. New York: Meridian, 1957.

Butler, Clark. *G. W. F. Hegel.* Boston: G. K. Hall, 1977.

————. "Hegel and Freud: A Comparison." *Philosophy and Phenomenological Research,* 36, no. 4 (1976), 506–22.

————. "Hegel and Indirect Proof." *The Monist* 74 (Fall 1991), 422–37.

————. "Hegelian Panentheism as Joachimite Christianity." In *New Perspectives on Hegel's Philosophy of Religion,* edited by David Kolb, 131–42. Albany: State University of New York Press, 1992.

————. "Hermeneutic Hegelianism." *Idealistic Studies* 15, no. 2 (1985), 121–35.

————. *History as the Story of Freedom.* Amsterdam: Editions Rodopi, 1996.

————. "Motion and Objective Contradiction." *American Philosophical Quarterly* 18, no. 2 (1981), 131–39.

————. "On the Reducibility of Dialectical to Standard Logic." *The Personalist* 56 (1975), 414–31.

————. "The Place of Process Cosmology in Absolute Idealism." *Owl of Minerva* 16, no. 2 (1985), 161–74.

Chaffin, Deborah. "Hegel, Derrida, and the Sign." In *Derrida and Deconstruction*, edited by Hugh Silverman. London: Routledge, 1989.

Derrida, Jacques. "On the University," interview by I. Salusinszky. *Southern Review* 19, no. 1 (1986), 3–12.

———— *Writing and Difference*. Translated by Alan Bass. Chicago: University of Chicago Press, 1978.

Donnellan, Keith. "Reference and Definite Descriptions." *Philosophical Review* 75 (1966), 284–304.

Davidson, Donald. *Essays on Action and Events*. Oxford: Oxford University Press, 1980.

Diogenes Laertius. *Lives and Opinions of Those Who Have Rendered Themselves Illustrious in Philosophy with a Summary Collection of the Doctrines of Each School*. Published as *Lives of Eminent Philosophers*. 2 vols. Translated by R. D. Hicks. Cambridge: Harvard University Press, 1925.

Doz, André. *La logique de Hegel et les problèmes traditionnels de l'ontologie*. Paris: Vrin, 1987.

Feuerbach, Ludwig. *The Essence of Christianity*. Translated by George Elliott. New York: Harper and Row, 1957.

Findlay, John N. "Comment" on "Hegel's Dialectic of the Organic Whole," by Clark Butler. In *Art and Logic in Hegel's Philosophy*, edited by Warren Steinkraus and Kenneth Schmitz, 233–37. New Jersey: Humanities Press, 1980.

————. *Hegel: A Re-examination*. London: Allen and Unwin, 1958.

Forrest, Peter. "Why Most of Us Should Be Scientific Realists." *The Monist* 77, no. 1 (1994), 47–70.

Freud, Sigmund. "Narcissism, An Introduction" (1914). Translated by Cecil M. Baines. In *Freud: General Psychological Theory*, edited by Philip Rieff. New York: Cromwell-Collier, 1963. Section 3, 74.

di Giovanni, George. "The Category of Contingency in the Hegelian Dialectic." In *Art and Logic in Hegel's Philosophy*, 179–200. New Jersey: Humanities Press, 1980.

Graham, Daniel. "The Structure of Explanation in the History of Philosophy." *Metaphilosophy* 19 (April 1988).

Grier, Philip. "Abstract and Concrete in Hegel's Logic." In *Essays on Hegel's Logic*. Albany: State University of New York Press, 1990.

Guthrie, Kenneth Sylan, ed., trans. *The Pythagorean Sourcebook and Library*. Grand Rapids: Phanes Press, 1987.

Guthrie, W. K. C. *A History of Greek Philosophy*. Vol. 1. Cambridge: Cambridge University Press, 1963.

Habermas, Jürgen. *Knowledge and Human Interests*. Translated by Jeremy Shapiro. Boston: Beacon, 1971.

————. *Justification and Application: Remarks on Discourse Ethics*. Translated by Ciaran Cronin. Cambridge: MIT Press, 1993.

————. "Wahrheitstheorien." In *Wirklichkeit und Reflexion: Festschrift für Walter Schulz*. Pfullingen: Neske, 1973.

Harris, Errol. *An Interpretation of Hegel's Logic.* Lanham: University Press of America, 1983.

Harris, H. S. *Hegel's Development: Toward the Sunlight, 1770–1801.* Oxford: Oxford University Press, 1972.

Hegel, G. W. F. "Earliest System-Programme of German Idealism." In H. S. Harris, *Hegel's Development Toward the Sunlight.*

———. *The Encyclopaedia Logic, Part 1 of the Encyclopaedia of Philosophical Sciences.* Translated by T. F. Garaets, W. A. Suchting, and H. S. Harris. Indianapolis: Hackett, 1991.

———. *Encylopaedia of Philosophical Sciences.* 3d edition (1830). Translated by W. Wallace and A. V. Miller. Oxford: Oxford University Press, 1892–1975.

———. *Lectures on Fine Arts.* Vol. 1. Translated by T. M. Knox. Oxford: Oxford University Press. In *Sämtliche Werke.* Vols. 12–14. Edited by Hermann Glockner. Stuttgart: Frommann, 1926.

———. *Lectures on the History of Philosophy.* Translated by E. S. Haldane and Frances Simson. New York: Humanities Press, 1974. In *Sämtliche Werke.* Vols. 17–19.

———. *Lectures on the Philosophy of History.* Translated by J. Sibree. New York: Dover, 1956. In *Sämtliche Werke.* Vol. 11.

———. *Lectures on the Philosophy of Religion.* 3 vols. Translation by E. B. Speirs and A. B. Sanderson. London: Routledge and Kegan Paul, 1968. In *Sämtliche Werke.* Vols. 15–16.

———. *The Letters.* Translated by Clark Butler and Christiane Seiler, with commentary by Clark Butler. Bloomington: Indiana University Press, 1984; *Die Briefe von und an Hegel.* Edited by Johannes Hoffmeister. Hamburg: Meiner, 1952–54.

———. "Neufassung des Anfangs" (1800), added *to Die Positivität der christlichen Religion* (1795–96). In *Werke in zwanzig Bände.* Vol. 1. Edited by Eva Moldenhauer and Karl Markus Michel, 225–26. Frankfurt: Suhrkamp, 1971.

———. *Phenomenology of Spirit.* Translated by A. V. Miller. Oxford: Oxford University Press, 1977; *Die Phänomenologie des Geistes.* Edited by Wolfgang Bonsiepen and Reinhard Heede. Hamburg: Meiner, 1980.

———. *Philosophical Propaedeutic.* Translated by A. V. Miller, edited by Michael George and Andrew Vincent. London: Basil Blackwell, 1986. In *Nürnberger und Heidelberger Schriften, 1808–1817.* Vol. 4 of *Werke in zwanzig Bände.* Edited by Eva Moldenhauer and Karl Markus Michel, part 1. Frankfurt: Suhrkamp, 1970.

——— "Review of Göschel's *Aphorisms.*" Translated by Clark Butler. *Clio* 17, no. 4 (1988) and vol. 18, no. 4 (1989). In *Sämtliche Werke.* Vol. 20.

——— *Science de la logique.* Book 1 (1812 edition). Translated by Pierre-Jean Labarrière and Gwendoline Jarczyk. Paris: Aubier, 1972.

——— *Science of Logic.* Translated by A. V. Miller. London: Allen and Unwin, 1969; *Die Wissenschaft der Logik.* 2 vols. Edited by Georg Lasson. Hamburg: Meiner, 1969–74.

————. *Die Wissenschaft der Logik.* Book 1 (1812–13). Edited by Friedrich Hogemann and Walter Jaeschke. Hamburg: Meiner, 1978.

Heidegger, Martin. *An Introduction to Metaphysics.* Translated by Ralph Mannheim. New York: Doubleday, 1961.

Herder, Johann Gottfried von. *Reflections on the Philosophy of the History of Mankind.* Edited by Frank Manuel. Chicago: University of Chicago Press, 1968.

Hogemann, Friedrich and Walter Jaeschke. "Die Wissenschaft der Logik." In *Hegel,* edited by Otto Pöggeler. Freiburg: Alber, 1977.

Houlgate, Stephen. *Freedom, Truth, and History: An Introduction to Hegel's Philosophy.* London: Routledge, 1991.

Hume, David. *A Treatise of Human Nature.* Edited by L. A. Selby-Bigge. Oxford: University of Oxford Press, 1967.

Johnson, W. C. *Logic.* Vol. 1. Cambridge: Cambridge University Press, 1921.

Kant, Immanuel. *The Critique of Pure Reason* (1787).

Kirk, G. S. and J. E. Raven. *The Pre-Socratic Philosophers.* Cambridge: Cambridge University Press, 1960.

Kisner, Wendell. "*Erinnerung, Retrait,* Absolute Reflection: Hegel and Derrida." *Owl of Minerva* 26, no. 2 (1995).

Kripke, Saul. *Naming and Necessity.* Cambridge: Harvard University, 1980.

Lakebrink, B. *Kommentar zur Hegels "Logik."* Freiburg: Alber, 1979.

Laplace, Pierre Simon. *An Essay on the Philosophy of Probabilities.* New York: Dover, 1951.

Leibniz, Gottfried Wilhelm. *The Monadology* (1714).

————. "A Vindication of God's Justice." Translated by Paul Schrecker and Anne Martin Schrecker. In *Monadology and Other Philosophical Essays.* Indianapolis: Bobbs and Merrill, 1965.

Lévi-Strauss, Claude. *The Savage Mind.* Chicago: University of Chicago Press, 1966.

McCumber, John. *The Company of Words: Hegel, Language, and Systematic Philosophy.* Evanston: Northwestern University Press, 1993.

Mill, John Stuart. *A System of Logic.* Books 1–3. Toronto: University of Toronto Press, 1974.

Mure, G. R. G. *An Introduction to Hegel.* Oxford: Oxford University Press, 1940.

Nahm, Milton, ed. *Selections from Early Greek Philosophy.* New York: Appleton-Century-Crofts, 1964.

Nancy, Jean-Luc. *L'oubli de la philosophie.* Paris: Galilée, 1986.

Nicolin, Günther, ed. *Hegel in Berichten seiner Zeitgenossen.* Hamburg: Meiner, 1970.

Perelman, Chaim. "Can the Rights of Man be Founded?" In *The Philosophy of Human Rights: International Perspectives,* edited by Allen Rosenbaum. Westport: Greenwood Press, 1980.

Pinkard, Terry. *Hegel's Dialectic: The Explanation of Possibility.* Philadelphia: Temple University Press, 1988.

Plotinus. *The Enneads.* 3d ed. Translated by Stephen MacKenna. London: Faber and Faber, 1956.

Plato. *The Phaedo.*

Quine, Willard van Orman. *Methods of Logic.* 4th ed. Cambridge: Harvard University Press, 1982.

Reale, Giovannni. *The Systems of the Hellenistic Age.* Translated by John Caton. Albany: State University of New York Press, 1990.

Reck, Andrew. *Speculative Philosophy.* Albuquerque: University of New Mexico Press, 1972.

Rinaldi, Giacomo. *A History and Interpretation of the Logic of Hegel.* Lewiston: Edwin Mellen, 1992.

Rosen, Stanley. *G. W. F. Hegel: An Introduction to the Science of Wisdom.* New Haven: Yale University Press, 1974.

Russell, Bertrand. *An Introduction to Mathematics.* London: Allen and Unwin, 1919.

———. *Logic and Knowledge.* London: Macmillan, 1956.

Sarlemijn, A. *Hegel's Dialecic.* Dordrecht: Reidel, 1975.

Schelling, F. W. J. *Exposition of My System* (1801).

Schopenhauer, Arthur. *The World as Will and Representation.* Book 1. Translated by E. F. J. Payne. New York: Dover, 1966.

Shapiro, Gary. "Notes on the Animal Kingdom of the Spirit." *Clio* 8, no. 3 (1979).

Spinoza, B. *Ethics* (1677).

Stace, W. T. *The Philosophy of Hegel: A Systematic Exposition.* New York: Dover, 1955.

Swami Prabhavananda and Frederick Manchester, trans. *The Upanishads.* New York: New American Library, 1957.

Taylor, Charles. *Hegel.* Cambridge: Cambridge University Press, 1975.

Tennemann, Wilhelm Gottlieb. *Geschichte der Philosophie.* Jena: 1798–1819. 11 vols.

Theunissen, Michael. *Hegels Lehre vom Absoluten Geist als theologisch-politischer Traktat.* Berlin: Walter de Gruyter, 1970.

Verene, Donald. *Hegel's Recollection: A Study of Images in the "Phenomenology of Spirit."* Albany: State University of New York Press, 1985.

Westphal, Merold. *History and Truth in Hegel's Phenomenology.* Atlantic Highlands: Humanities Press, 1979.

Whitehead, Alfred North. *Process and Reality: An Essay in Cosmology.* New York: Macmillan, 1929.

Index

Names

Hegel, whose name appears throughout the volume, has been omitted from this index. Since Pythagoras is not an historically recognized author, his name yields in this index to Pythagoreanism in the subject index.

Subjects